Business Drivers in Promoting Digital Detoxification

Simon Grima
Department of Insurance, Faculty of Economics, Management, and Accountancy, University of Malta, Malta & Faculty of Business, Management, and Economics, University of Latvia, Latvia

Shilpa Chaudhary
Lovely Professional University, India

Kiran Sood
Chitkara Business School, Chitkara University, India

Sanjeev Kumar
Lovely Professional University, India

A volume in the Advances in Marketing, Customer Relationship Management, and E-Services (AMCRMES) Book Series

Published in the United States of America by
>   IGI Global
>   Business Science Reference (an imprint of IGI Global)
>   701 E. Chocolate Avenue
>   Hershey PA, USA 17033
>   Tel: 717-533-8845
>   Fax: 717-533-8661
>   E-mail: cust@igi-global.com
>   Web site: http://www.igi-global.com

Library of Congress Cataloging-in-Publication Data

Names: Grima, Simon, editor.
Title: Business drivers in promoting digital detoxification / edited by
    Simon Grima, Shilpa Chaudhary, Kiran Sood, Sanjeev Kumar.
Description: Hershey, PA : Business Science Reference, [2024] | Includes
    bibliographical references and index. | Summary: "This book will show
    the current state of the art of business initiatives in the field of
    digital detox and will throw light on the limitless scope of innovative
    opportunities in the field of digital detoxification"-- Provided by
    publisher.
Identifiers: LCCN 2023049148 (print) | LCCN 2023049149 (ebook) | ISBN
    9798369311073 (hardcover) | ISBN 9798369311080 (ebook)
Subjects: LCSH: Information technology--Economic aspects. | Information
    technology--Social aspects. | Information technology--Health aspects.
Classification: LCC HC79.I55 B8568 2024 (print) | LCC HC79.I55 (ebook) |
    DDC 338.9/26--dc23/eng/20231102
LC record available at https://lccn.loc.gov/2023049148
LC ebook record available at https://lccn.loc.gov/2023049149

This book is published in the IGI Global book series Advances in Marketing, Customer Relationship Management, and E-Services (AMCRMES) (ISSN: 2327-5502; eISSN: 2327-5529)

British Cataloguing in Publication Data
A Cataloguing in Publication record for this book is available from the British Library.

All work contributed to this book is new, previously-unpublished material.
The views expressed in this book are those of the authors, but not necessarily of the publisher.

For electronic access to this publication, please contact: eresources@igi-global.com.

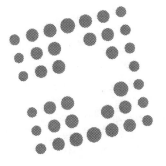

Advances in Marketing, Customer Relationship Management, and E-Services (AMCRMES) Book Series

ISSN:2327-5502
EISSN:2327-5529

Editor-in-Chief: Eldon Y. Li, National Chengchi University, Taiwan & California Polytechnic State University, USA

MISSION

Business processes, services, and communications are important factors in the management of good customer relationship, which is the foundation of any well organized business. Technology continues to play a vital role in the organization and automation of business processes for marketing, sales, and customer service. These features aid in the attraction of new clients and maintaining existing relationships.

The Advances in Marketing, Customer Relationship Management, and E-Services (AMCRMES) Book Series

addresses success factors for customer relationship management, marketing, and electronic services and its performance outcomes. This collection of reference source covers aspects of consumer behavior and marketing business strategies aiming towards researchers, scholars, and practitioners in the fields of marketing management.

COVERAGE

- Mobile Services
- CRM in financial services
- Cases on CRM Implementation
- Cases on Electronic Services
- Social Networking and Marketing
- Mobile CRM
- Telemarketing
- Data mining and marketing
- Customer Relationship Management
- Text Mining and Marketing

IGI Global is currently accepting manuscripts for publication within this series. To submit a proposal for a volume in this series, please contact our Acquisition Editors at Acquisitions@igi-global.com or visit: http://www.igi-global.com/publish/.

The Advances in Marketing, Customer Relationship Management, and E-Services (AMCRMES) Book Series (ISSN 2327-5502) is published by IGI Global, 701 E. Chocolate Avenue, Hershey, PA 17033-1240, USA, www.igi-global.com. This series is composed of titles available for purchase individually; each title is edited to be contextually exclusive from any other title within the series. For pricing and ordering information please visit http://www.igi-global.com/book-series/advances-marketing-customer-relationship-management/37150. Postmaster: Send all address changes to above address. Copyright © 2024 IGI Global. All rights, including translation in other languages reserved by the publisher. No part of this series may be reproduced or used in any form or by any means – graphics, electronic, or mechanical, including photocopying, recording, taping, or information and retrieval systems – without written permission from the publisher, except for non commercial, educational use, including classroom teaching purposes. The views expressed in this series are those of the authors, but not necessarily of IGI Global.

Titles in this Series

For a list of additional titles in this series, please visit:
http://www.igi-global.com/book-series/advances-marketing-customer-relationship-management/37150

Connecting With Consumers Through Effective Personalization and Programmatic Advertising
Jorge Remondes (Instituto Superior de Entre Douro e Vouga, Portugal & ISCAP, Instituto Politecnico do Porto, Portugal) Paulo Madeira (Instituto Superior de Entre Douro e Vouga, Portugal) and Carlos Alves (Instituto Superior de Entre Douro e Vouga, Portugal)
Business Science Reference • copyright 2024 • 320pp • H/C (ISBN: 9781668491461) • US $250.00 (our price)

Using Influencer Marketing as a Digital Business Strategy
Sandrina Teixeira (ISCAP, Polytechnic Institute of Porto, Portugal) Sara Teixeira (Polytechnic Institute of Porto) Zaila Oliveira (Unichristus, Brazil & Unifametro, Brazil) and Elnivan Souza (Christus University Center, Brazil)
Business Science Reference • copyright 2024 • 371pp • H/C (ISBN: 9798369305515) • US $265.00 (our price)

The Use of Artificial Intelligence in Digital Marketing Competitive Strategies and Tactics
Sandrina Teixeira (Centre for Organizational and Social Studies (CEOS), Porto Accounting and Business School, Polytechnic of Porto, Portugal) and Jorge Remondes (Centre for Organizational and Social Studies (CEOS), Porto Accounting and Business School, Polytechnic of Porto, Portugal)
Business Science Reference • copyright 2024 • 318pp • H/C (ISBN: 9781668493243) • US $250.00 (our price)

The Rise of Blockchain Applications in Customer Experience
Mohammed Majeed (Tamale Technical University, Ghana) Kwame Simpe Ofori (International University of Grand Bassam, Cote D'Ivoire) George Kofi Amoako (Ghana Communication Technology University, Ghana) Abdul-Raheed Alolo (Tamale Technical University, Ghana) and Gideon Awini (Business School, University of Ghana, Ghana)
Business Science Reference • copyright 2024 • 304pp • H/C (ISBN: 9781668476499) • US $250.00 (our price)

For an entire list of titles in this series, please visit:
http://www.igi-global.com/book-series/advances-marketing-customer-relationship-management/37150

701 East Chocolate Avenue, Hershey, PA 17033, USA
Tel: 717-533-8845 x100 • Fax: 717-533-8661
E-Mail: cust@igi-global.com • www.igi-global.com

Table of Contents

Detailed Table of Contents

Chapter 1
Rekha Mewafarosh, Indian Institute of Forest Management, India
Shivani Agarwal, Galgotias University, Greater Noida, India
Deeksha Dwivedi, Leslie's Pool Supply, USA

In the contemporary world, where everything is available in the blink of an eye, it can be appropriate to say that everything is available within a click. All the products and services are available in no time. But this facility of getting almost everything creates a feeling of missing out on the users which creates the further need for detoxification from the digital world. The study deals with the two major concepts of today's scenario which are fear of missing out (FOMO) and digital detoxification. In the study, the author will suggest the ways in which people can make a balance between FOMO and digital detoxification. The study will mention the challenges of dealing with FOMO and how to do digital detoxification for better functioning in the digital world.

Chapter 2
Rishi Prakash Shukla, Chandigarh University, India

In today's hyper-connected world, the constant use of digital devices and online platforms has become an integral part of daily life. While these technologies offer numerous advantages in terms of communication, productivity, and information access, they also bring about significant challenges, including digital addiction, burnout, and decreased well-being. The need for digital detoxification has emerged as a critical concern for both individuals and organizations. This chapter proposes to explore how businesses can play a pivotal role in promoting digital detoxification among their employees.

Chapter 3

Priya Makhija, Center for Management Studies, Jain University, India
Megha Kukreja, Center for Management Studies, Jain University, India
R. Thanga Kumar, Center for Management Studies, Jain University,
    India

As the global financial landscape continues to transform to technological improvements, the emergence of CBDCs represents a significant turning point in financial systems. The central bank of a country issues and controls CBDCs, which are digital representations of sovereign money. Fintech and CBDCs are closely related because of the building pieces of the CBDC operation, which include blockchain or distributed ledgers, digital currency wallets, and dependable payment gateways. The adoption of Central Bank Digital Currencies (CBDCs) has the potential to have a significant impact on the fintech industry and could, in some cases, result in a fintech boom. The goal of this study is to develop a comprehensive knowledge of CBDCs' integration with fintech, their wide-ranging effects on society, and the potential need for digital detoxification techniques to balance off the unwanted effects of growing digitalization which can lead to financial innovation and personal well-being in the digital era by looking at CBDCs from both a technology and human-centric standpoint.

Chapter 4

Balraj Verma, Chitkara University, India
Niti Chatterji, Chitkara University, India

This study examines the impact of digital detoxification on the psychological well-being of Generation Z in North India. Using structured questionnaires, data was collected from individuals aged 11 to 26. The measurement model's validity and reliability were confirmed using confirmatory factor analysis. Also, the mediation analysis was performed using the SPSS macro PROCESS by Hayes. The study confirms that digital detoxification positively influences well-being, mediated by reduced cognitive overload. Findings highlight the need for mindful technology use and periodic disconnection to enhance mental health. This research contributes insights into the complex interplay of digital detox, cognitive load, and well-being, offering implications for promoting healthier digital habits and improved psychological health.

Chapter 5

The literature has not extensively examined the dangers of digital-only financial inclusion. The purpose of this chapter is to highlight the dangers of digital-only financial inclusion (DOFI). Using the discourse analysis method, the study showed that digital-only financial inclusion may be difficult to achieve when there is uneven availability and uneven access to digital devices. It was also argued that digital-only financial inclusion could lead to high cost of internet broadband, and it places much emphasis on accelerating digital access rather than protecting users who use digital finance platforms. Furthermore, it pays little attention to risk mitigation, and produces digital ID schemes that enable government surveillance. It also prioritizes digital access rather than financial health; and makes it easier to perpetrate fraud using digital means. Finally, it can enable the endless pursuit of power, and it prioritizes a digital version of financial inclusion at any cost.

Chapter 6

Detox for Success: How Digital Detoxification Can Enhance Productivity and Well-Being 71

In the fast-digital age, the constant influx of information, relentless social media engagement, and an unending stream of push notifications have become an integral part of our lives. While these technological advancements have undoubtedly brought convenience and connectivity, they have also raised concerns about their impact on productivity, health, and overall well-being. Periodic digital detox not only restores focus and reduces stress but also rekindles the ability to concentrate on tasks, resulting in heightened productivity. The practice of digital detox holds the promise of balancing the scales in the digital age. This chapter highlights the pressing need to strike a balance between the advantages of digital technology and our fundamental need for digital well-being. This study offers how a person can respite from the constant digital barrage, leading to enhanced productivity, improved digital health, and a heightened sense of digital well-being.

Chapter 7

Mohammad Badruddoza Talukder, Daffodil Institute of IT, Bangladesh
Firoj Kabir, Daffodil Institute of IT, Bangladesh
Fahmida Kaiser, Daffodil Institute of IT, Bangladesh
Farhana Yeasmin Lina, Daffodil International University, Bangladesh

Although the widespread availability and convenience of digital gadgets have improved our quality of life, there is still a correlation between individuals and a wide range of health problems. As a result, many individuals put their phones and other technological gadgets aside for a while. Using the uses and gratifications theory as a guide, this chapter investigates what motivates people to take a tour without indulging in digital devices. This chapter identifies the definitions, theories, and drivers of digital detox. Adopting new information and communication technologies and our ongoing connection to them are given in contemporary society. People want to identify the trends in the tourism market and help create marketing plans that address consumer needs. This chapter discusses the latest developments in digital detox in the travel industry and how the tourism sectors will change with the new trends. By completing this chapter, we can learn how the digital world is growing fast. Also, how the rapid pace is also getting reverse attention can be understood.

Chapter 8

Anshul Garg, Taylor's University, Malaysia
Amrik Singh, Lovely Professional University, India
Jia Yanan, Taylor's University, Malaysia

Nowadays, smartphones are ubiquitous. People spend many hours daily on their smartphones or other digital gadgets. Unlike other electronic devices, smartphones enable such functions almost anytime and anywhere, with numerous consequences for our daily lives. Surfing social network sites or instant messaging can impair well-being and is related to clinical phenomena like depression. The proliferation of social networking platforms has resulted in a rise in usage frequency among young adults. Digital detox interventions have been suggested as a solution to reduce the negative impacts of smartphone use on outcomes like well-being or social relationships. Keeping in touch with their smartphones during lectures hinders students' learning experience. The primary objective of this study is to assess how digital detoxification affects student learning within higher education establishments. The research also delves into the prevalence of digital detoxification among university students, shedding light on their comprehension of social media detox and potential mental health consequences.

The adoption of digitalization and favorable regulatory initiatives resulted in the rapid growth of the Fintech sector in recent years. There are limitless opportunities for the person with the right vision and executor plan in the fintech sector from digital payments and peer-to-peer lending to wealth management and insurance. This chapter aims to explore the fintech sector and examines the remarkable new opportunities and significant challenges that fintech firms face as they strive for innovation and expansion. The research aims to provide valuable insights into the factors that contribute to the success or hindrance of fintech startups. The findings of the study show that there is a wide range of potential opportunities available for fintech firms globally, in sectors including lending, wealth management, and digital payments.

Chapter 10

Because of the urgency and high stakes involved in their trades, intraday traders are especially vulnerable to the perils of information overload in today's digital world. This chapter explores the potential benefits of digital detox programmes for intraday traders. The research uses the statistical programme SMart PLS to do a route analysis using primary data gathered via questionnaire. The results show that taking a break from technology may dramatically lower stress levels, which in turn boosts business efficiency. This correlation is moderated by traders' levels of expertise, however, indicating that newcomers to the market might gain the most from digital detox programmes. The last section of the study emphasises the chapter's central thesis, arguing for the inclusion of digital detox measures in training programmes and workplace rules in order to address the chapter's identified practical ramifications for traders, trading businesses, and regulatory agencies.

    *Nkholedzeni Sidney Netshakhuma, University of Cape Town, South
       Africa
    Itumeleng Khadambi, South Africa National Parks, South Africa*

This chapter aims to develop an information governance framework to achieve information hygiene. In this study, information hygiene is defined as a process to achieve proper information. Information hygiene is developed to prevent any form of fake news. Fake news in this context is defined as misrepresentation of information, created to harm the person. Fake information developed extensively during the spread of COVID-19 in 2019. This chapter will use literature to review the content of the study.

    *Pretty Bhalla, Lovely Professional University, India
    Jaskiran Kaur, Lovely Professional University, India
    Sayeed Zafar, College of Business Administration, University of
       Business and Technology, Jeddah, Saudi Arabia*

Digital transformation has long been prioritized by corporate companies, both big and small, in almost every sector, due to the urgency of market rivalry. Digital technology is present everywhere nowadays, and it plays a significant role in our daily lives. The fast development of inexpensive and widely available media technologies, together with almost universal internet connection, is profoundly changing how society functions. Digital technology is transforming how we obtain information and communicate with one another more quickly than before. The speed at which digital changes are occurring is having a significant impact on how we live, work, and interact. There seems to be a new cautionary tale about how digital technologies are ruining social life every day. Some of the discussion about the effects of digital technology in recent years has resembled a moral panic.

    *Neha Kamboj, IILM University, India
    Vinita Choudhary, K.R. Mangalam University, India
    Sonal Trivedi, VIT Bhopal University, India*

Due to growing environmental issues, including climate change, urban pollution, and the anticipated scarcity of fossil fuels, societal and political interest in electric mobility has surged recently. When switching from internal combustion engines to alternative drivetrain technologies, such as electric vehicles (EV), there is expected to be a decrease in the usage of fossil fuels and environmental effects. Several nations have already started initiatives to introduce electric vehicles to the market or set goals for the future share of these vehicles. For instance, the European Union wants to reduce the number of vehicles with internal combustion engines in half by 2030 and phase them out entirely in cities by 2050 and by 2030. China and Norway acting as the main drivers. The current chapter examines the LCA studies on electric vehicles and their corresponding batteries that have been published in the previous ten years. Also, the suitability of the employed assessment techniques for addressing the criticality of resources is confirmed.

Chapter 14

Sonal Trivedi, VIT Business School, VIT Bhopal University, India
Vinita Choudhary, K.R. Managalam University, India
Neha Kamboj, IILM University, India
Nirmaljeet Kaur Virk, K.R. Managalam University, India

This chapter delves into the evolving landscape of opportunities and challenges for start-ups, micro, small, and medium enterprises (MSMEs), as well as the Indian financial and insurance sectors. It explores the transformations driven by technological advancements, policy shifts, and market dynamics, shedding light on the current scenario of 2022-23. By examining the interplay between these sectors, the chapter aims to provide insights into their symbiotic relationship and prospects for growth.

Chapter 15

Jaskiran Kaur, Lovely Professional University, India
Amit Dutt, Lovely Professional University, India
Pretty Bhalla, Lovely Professional University, India
Vishal Kumar Poddar, Lovely Professional University, India
Varun Kumra, Lovely Professional University, India

Over the last few decades, it has become nearly impossible to imagine a workspace without highly integrated technology. Ever since cell phones entered the scene, co-workers have been able to collaborate on projects, no matter where in the world they are. Digital meeting spaces have allowed companies to stay connected across countries and even continents. Although these advancements have improved productivity and connectivity, it may be time for a step back. Since the global pandemic took over the world, working from home has been the norm. In a bid to keep operations moving and businesses flourishing, companies are doing everything in their captivity to make remote working as feasible as possible. Implementing digital detox strategies, such as setting boundaries on technology usage and promoting mindfulness practices, can empower entrepreneurs to maintain a healthier work-life balance and make more informed business decisions. This abstract explores meaning, importance, impact, and strategies of digital detoxification to mitigate the negative impacts of excessive digital engagement.

Chapter 16

Kanika Thapliyal, Graphic Era University (deemed), Dehradun, India
Chandan Gupta, Graphic Era University (deemed), Dehradun, India
Priya Jindal, Chitkara Business School, Chitkara University, India

An essential structural modification that is needed to halt the earth's rising temperature and advance ecological sound practices is through promoting green finance with increasing support of technological innovations. Technological innovations have the potential to accelerate green finance growth while balancing bank sustainability and profitability. Green finance as a financial tool can assure that both the economy and the environment can grow sustainably. Since its emergence, the presence of FinTech based on big data and artificial intelligence technology can be noticed in various fields. In light of the numerous advantages FinTech provides, it can be employed in blossoming green finance. Hence, the chapter aims to demonstrate the role of fintech in promoting green finance. This chapter also focuses on green finance, green finance's importance, projects that come under green finance, and the economic benefits green finance provides. Finally, this chapter explores the association between green finance, fintech, and environmental sustainability.

Chapter 17

Reepu, Chandigarh University, India
Pawan Kumar, Chandigarh University, India
Sanjay Taneja, Graphic Era University, India

Digital integration has become a ubiquitous feature of the workplace, leading to the blurring of work-life boundaries. This paper reviews the disconnective labor model, which outlines the key components and relationships to be studied in order to understand the impact of digital integration on work-life balance, well-being, and productivity. The model posits that digital integration is positively associated with work-life boundary blurring, and that engagement in disconnective labor is associated with improved individual and organizational outcomes. The model also suggests that coping mechanisms can mediate the relationship between digital integration, work-life boundary blurring, and disconnective labor, and that disconnective labor can mediate the relationship between work-life boundary blurring and individual and organizational outcomes. The findings of this review suggest that disconnective labor is an important concept for understanding the impact of digital integration on work-life balance, well-being, and productivity.

Preface

In this era of pervasive digital connectivity, the transformative impact of technology on both professional landscapes and personal lifestyles cannot be overstated. The evolution of digitalization from a mere efficiency tool to an integral driver of innovation, competitiveness, and global connectivity has ushered in unparalleled advancements. However, this exponential rise in technology adoption has also brought to light the critical need for balance and mindfulness in our engagement with digital devices.

The edited volume, *Business Drivers in Promoting Digital Detoxification*, spearheaded by Simon Grima, Shilpa Chaudhary, Kiran Sood, and Sanjeev Kumar, delves into the multifaceted landscape of digital detox. This compilation serves as a compass navigating the diverse initiatives across industries and underscores the expansive opportunities inherent in embracing digital detox practices.

Our exploration traverses the domains of tourism, health, e-commerce, technology, including Fintech, and beyond. The chapters within this volume illuminate the current trends and future trajectories in these sectors concerning digital detox. From the nuanced impact on entrepreneurial ventures to its profound influence on student learning and the organizational fabric, each facet unravels the intricate interplay between digital detoxification and diverse spheres of life.

We delve deep into the realms of public health, corporate social responsibility, sustainable livelihoods, agriculture, and consumer behavior, illuminating the profound implications of digital detox. Moreover, the volume unveils the burgeoning opportunities and challenges that emerge for start-ups, MSMEs, financial and insurance sectors amid this transformative shift.

Designed for academia, researchers, students, and industry professionals alike, this compendium serves as a reservoir of knowledge, illuminating the path towards a balanced and mindful coexistence with technology. It doesn't just dissect the phenomenon of digital detox; it amplifies the imperative need for balance in an increasingly digitized world.

The collection of chapters within this volume stands as a testament to the collaborative efforts of experts and enthusiasts alike, each contributing a unique perspective to this evolving discourse. As editors, we are privileged to present this culmination of insights and analyses, hoping it serves as a catalyst for informed discussions and proactive measures in embracing digital detoxification.

We invite you on a journey through these pages, where the convergence of business, technology, and human well-being unfolds in profound and enlightening ways.

ORGANIZATION OF THE BOOK

As editors of this comprehensive volume, we are pleased to present an overview encapsulating the diverse array of chapters that collectively explore the expansive landscape of digital detoxification across various sectors and domains. Each chapter contributes unique insights, shedding light on the multifaceted dimensions of balancing digital engagement and the imperative need for detoxification in today's hyper-connected world.

Chapter 1, authored by Rekha Mewarfarosh, Shivani Agarwal, and Deekhsha Dwivedi, delves into the contemporary challenge of balancing the Fear of Missing Out (FOMO) with the necessity for digital detoxification. The study explores strategies to achieve equilibrium between these concepts, addressing the challenges posed by FOMO and offering insights into effective digital detoxification techniques.

Rishi Shukla in Chapter 2 probes into the role of businesses in promoting digital detoxification. In an age where digital technologies are ubiquitous, the chapter examines how organizations can play a pivotal role in fostering detox practices among employees, highlighting the need for a mindful approach to digital engagement.

Chapter 3, penned by Dr. Priya Makhija, Megha Kukreja, and R. Thanga Kumar, explores the intersection of Central Bank Digital Currencies (CBDCs) and fintech innovations. This chapter assesses the socio-economic implications of CBDCs, emphasizing the potential need for digital detoxification techniques to mitigate the impact of escalating digitalization on financial innovation and personal well-being.

The impact of digital detoxification on psychological well-being is the focus of Chapter 4 by Balraj Verma and Niti Chatterji. Investigating the correlation between detoxification and reduced cognitive load, this study underscores the importance of mindful technology use in enhancing mental health.

Peterson Ozili, in Chapter 5, sheds light on the lesser-explored dangers of digital-only financial inclusion. This chapter critically examines the potential pitfalls of exclusive digital financial systems and their ramifications on users, raising concerns about access disparities and the risks of digital platforms.

Chapter 6, authored by Animesh Sharma and Rahul Sharma, advocates for periodic digital detox as a catalyst for heightened productivity and well-being. The chapter emphasizes the need for balance between technological advancements and digital well-being, offering strategies for improved digital health.

Mohammad Talukder, Firoj Kabir, Fahmida Kaiser, and Farhana Lina, in Chapter 7, delve into the digital detox movement in the tourism industry, exploring traveler perspectives and motivations for disconnecting from digital devices during travel. The chapter delineates the evolving trends in tourism shaped by the burgeoning digital detox movement.

Chapter 8, by Anshul Garg, Amrik Singh, and Jia Yanan, investigates the impact of digital detoxification on higher education students' learning experiences. It highlights the prevalence of digital detox among students and its potential influence on social media use and mental health within educational settings.

The potential opportunities and challenges for fintech startups are dissected in Chapter 9 by Anju Rohilla and Priya Jindal. This chapter provides valuable insights into the factors that contribute to the success or hindrance of fintech firms, uncovering a spectrum of possibilities in the sector.

Mukul Bhatnagar, Pawan Kumar, Sanjay Taneja, Kiran Sood, and Simon Grima, in Chapter 10, delve into the role of digital detox in enhancing intraday trading performance. The study underscores the correlation between technology breaks, stress reduction, and improved trading efficiency, shedding light on the relevance of detox measures in trading practices.

Chapter 11, authored by Nkholedzeni Sidney Netshakhuma and Itumeleng Khadambi, aims to construct an information governance framework to achieve information hygiene, addressing the challenges posed by fake news and misinformation.

The transition from Fear of Missing Out (FOMO) to Joy of Missing Out (JOMO) through digital detoxification is the focus of Chapter 12 by Pretty Bhalla, Jaskiran Kaur, and Sayeed Zafar. This chapter explores the transformative potential of digital detox in mitigating the adverse impacts of excessive digital engagement.

Neha Kamboj, Vinita Choudhary, and Sonal Trivedi, in Chapter 13, conduct a life cycle analysis of electric vehicles, assessing their environmental impact and contribution to sustainability within the transportation sector.

Chapter 14, authored by Dr. Sonal Trivedi, Dr. Vinita Choudhary, Dr. Neha Kamboj, and Nirmaljeet Virk, explores the evolving opportunities and challenges for start-ups, MSMEs, the Indian financial, and insurance sectors, illuminating the interplay between these domains.

The relationship between digital detoxification and entrepreneurial excellence is the crux of Chapter 15 by Jaskiran Kaur, Amit Dutt, Pretty Bhalla, Vishal Poddar, and Varun Kumra. This chapter highlights the significance of embracing detox strategies for fostering a healthier work-life balance and informed decision-making.

Kanika Thapliyal, Chandan Gupta, and Priya Jindal, in Chapter 16, delve into the role of fintech in advancing green financing, exploring the potential synergy between financial technology and environmentally sustainable practices.

Chapter 17, by Reepu, Pawan Kumar, and Sanjay Taneja, reviews the Disconnective Labor Model, elucidating the impact of digital integration on work-life balance, well-being, and productivity within contemporary workplaces.

These chapters collectively offer a comprehensive exploration of digital detoxification, addressing its implications across diverse sectors, ranging from finance and education to tourism and entrepreneurship. We invite readers to delve into these chapters, each a unique lens through which the complex interplay between digital engagement and detoxification is unraveled.

IN SUMMARY

As this compendium draws to a close, we reflect on the myriad insights and revelations unearthed within its pages. The journey through the realms of digital detoxification has been illuminating, unveiling the intricate tapestry of challenges, opportunities, and the imperative need for balance in our digital age.

From the examination of digital detox trends across industries to the profound impact on entrepreneurship, education, and societal constructs, each chapter has offered a unique vantage point. We've explored the depths of digital detox's influence on public health, corporate responsibility, sustainable livelihoods, and consumer behavior, unraveling a tapestry woven with possibilities and complexities.

The narrative woven by our contributors speaks not only of the challenges posed by excessive digital engagement but also of the vast opportunities that arise from a conscious, measured approach to technology. It resonates with the urgency for stakeholders across sectors to embrace a nuanced understanding of digital detoxification, leveraging its potential to foster healthier lifestyles, robust enterprises, and more connected communities.

Through these deliberations, it becomes evident that digital detox isn't merely about disengagement; it's about fostering a mindful relationship with technology. It's about striking the delicate balance between connectivity and disconnection, reaping the benefits of a digital world while safeguarding our well-being.

As editors, we extend our gratitude to the insightful contributions of our authors, whose expertise and passion have enriched this discourse. We hope this volume serves as a catalyst for ongoing conversations, spurring action and innovation in the realms of digital detoxification.

The journey towards a harmonious coexistence with technology is ongoing, and the insights encapsulated herein offer guiding lights for navigating this evolving landscape. May these discussions resonate, inspire, and pave the way for a future where technology enriches our lives without compromising our well-being.

With sincere appreciation for the collective endeavor that brought this volume to fruition, we invite you to carry forth the dialogue, fostering a world where digital engagement is mindful, purposeful, and conducive to a balanced and fulfilling existence.

Simon Grima
Department of Insurance, Faculty of Economics, Management, and Accountancy, University of Malta, Msida, Malta & Faculty of Business, Management, and Economics, University of Latvia, Riga, Latvia

Shilpa Chaudhary
Lovely Professional University, India

Kiran Sood
Chitkara Business School, Chitkara University, India & Research Fellow at the Women Researchers Council (WRC), Azerbaijan State University of Economics (UNEC)

Sanjeev Kumar
Lovely Professional University, India

Chapter 1
Balancing FOMO and Digital Detoxification

Rekha Mewafarosh
Indian Institute of Forest Management, India

Shivani Agarwal
ⓘ https://orcid.org/0000-0002-3205-552X
Galgotias University, Greater Noida, India

Deeksha Dwivedi
Leslie's Pool Supply, USA

ABSTRACT

In the contemporary world, where everything is available in the blink of an eye, it can be appropriate to say that everything is available within a click. All the products and services are available in no time. But this facility of getting almost everything creates a feeling of missing out on the users which creates the further need for detoxification from the digital world. The study deals with the two major concepts of today's scenario which are fear of missing out (FOMO) and digital detoxification. In the study, the author will suggest the ways in which people can make a balance between FOMO and digital detoxification. The study will mention the challenges of dealing with FOMO and how to do digital detoxification for better functioning in the digital world.

INTRODUCTION

The technology has paved the path for almost half of the world's people to use the internet through smartphones (Statista.com, 2021; We are Social, 2018). The rise

DOI: 10.4018/979-8-3693-1107-3.ch001

of technology has greatly connected the world and created a global community. However, this increased accessibility comes with its drawbacks, such as excessive usage by certain individuals. Researchers have started to examine this behavior in depth (Griffiths, 1996; Young, 1996). As a result, different terms like internet addiction (Young,1997), smartphone addiction, or social media addiction have been used to describe similar phenomenon leading to taxonomical issues. FOMO is term revolves around the constant need for connection with one's social network through frequent use of social networking sites and messaging services (Kwon et al., 2013; Andreassen, et.al., 2012). The scientific interest in FOMO aligns with the ongoing societal discussion on whether excessive "screen time" is detrimental for both children and adults.

LITERATURE REVIEW

Many psychopathological issues arise due to excessive use of internet results in suicidal attempt, stress, anxiety and, depression (Elhai, et.al., 2017; Demirci, et.al., 2015; Ryu, Choi, et.al., 2004). It leads to many habits which is detrimental to an individual like disturbance in sleep (Rod, Dissing, Clark, Gerds, & Lund, 2018), anxiety, depression, stress, and isolated feeling (Karsay, et.al., 2019; Weinstein et al., 2015), procrastination habit (Li, Griffiths, Mei, & Niu, 2020), disorders like, hostility and attention-deficit hyperactivity (Ko, et.al., 2012). Additionally, some individuals may feel nomophobia or the fear of being separated from mobile phones (King et al., 2014). Excessive use of the internet lead to strange behaviour, where individuals snub others using their smartphones, thereby damaging their relationships too (Al-Saggaf & O'Donnell, 2019). Moreover, prolonged internet use can cause various neurological issues among addictive users (Tripathi, 2017).

FOMO

The concept of FOMO emerged in the media during the early 2010s (Fake., 2020; Morford M.,2020). Notably, popular media characterized FOMO as a source of anxiety from its inception (Fake., 2020; Morford M.,2020). With the advancement and widespread availability of smartphones, accessing SNS became effortless, allowing individuals to easily become aware of potentially rewarding experiences they might be missing out on. This coincided with a significant rise in worldwide usage of social networking sites (Hitlin P.,2020; Poushter J.,2020). At the core of FoMo lies individuals' perceived necessity to continuously stay connected with their social network which often leads to frequent and sometimes excessive use of

2

social networking sites and messaging platforms. This heightened academic focus on FoMO coincides with ongoing societal discussions regarding whether excessive "screen time" poses harm to both children as well as to adults.

The phenomenon known as FOMO has been extensively studied in literature, where it is described as having two main aspects. The first aspect involves feeling anxious about missing out on satisfying experiences that others are having (Przybylski AK et.al.,2013). This component can be compared to the cognitive aspect of anxiety, involving worry and rumination. The second aspect of FOMO relates to a behavioral response aimed at alleviating this anxiety, much like how individuals with obsessive compulsive disorder engage in maladaptive behaviors to reduce their distress.

Currently, the most common behavioral response associated with FOMO is frequently checking social media in order to maintain social connections and avoid missing out on enjoyable experiences (Przybylski AK et.al.,2013). The phenomenon of FoMO is widely recognized in the context of the internet (Alt, 2015; Blackwell, et. al., 2017; Elhai, et. al., 2020; Przybylski, Murayama, DeHaan, & Gladwell, 2013; Van-Den-Eijnden, Doornwaard, & Ter Bogt, 2017; Wang, Wang, Yang, et al., 2019; Wolniewicz, Tiamiyu, Weeks, & Elhai, 2018).

Detrimental Effects of FOMO

In today's society, smartphones have become extremely prevalent, smartphones present numerous advantages like constant communication with friends, engaging leisure activities, use of vast amount of information through the internet, and positive effects on knowledge sharing (Omar et al., 2016; Lepp et al., 2013). Various literature have shown a correlation between smartphone use and higher rates of depression, anxiety, sleep difficulties, as well as musculoskeletal problems associated with excessive use (Lepp et al., 2014; Thomée, 2018)

Research indicates that the use of smartphones has a significant impact on health, well-being, performance, and social interactions. Past researchers have found only small negative effects of digital technology use on health and well-being (Dienlin & Johannes, 2020; Orben & Przybylski, 2019a; Orben & Przybylski, 2019b). Additionally, empirical evidence consistently demonstrates a negative relationship between smartphone use and academic performance which aligns with findings indicating reduced work productivity and engagement due to overuse of smartphones (e.g., Duke & Montag, 2017). For instance, there is evidence that smartphone users frequently express the need to take breaks from their devices through blog posts (Jorge, 2019; Kuntsman & Miyake, 2016). They also actively seek out strategies for managing their online time by using applications such as iOS Screen Time or Android Digital Well-Being. Additionally, organized groups have established an annual National Day of Unplugging which encourages people worldwide to disconnect from their devices for a day.

According to Markowetz, on average, we spend nearly three hours per day using our smartphones. Unlike other electronic devices, smartphones offer the flexibility of being able to utilize their functions at any time and in any location, which has a wide range of implications for our daily lives. The fear of missing out can lead to greater internet usage, while on the other hand, increased internet use may also contribute to higher levels of FoMO (Fernandez et al., 2020). Additionally, there are organized groups that hold annual National (and Global) Days of Unplugging with a substantial following. All the texts are reflecting on the growing concerns of usage of smartphone, it is offering guidance on restoring balance by limiting the smartphone usage in day to day life (Syvertsen, 2017). Similarly, travel agencies are promoting digital detox camps and "mobile free" vacation to rejuvenate from the growing trap digitalization. these types of vacations and events becoming increasingly popular in Asia Continent (Dickinson et al., 2016; Collier et al., 2009; Syvertsen, 2017).

The act of focusing on one's own smartphone while interacting ("phubbing") has increased. Past research affirms that it has negative affect and it diminishes the quality of social interactions (McDaniel & Radesky,2018; Nuñez-et-al.,2020), so addiction to smartphone can impair your overall the well-being, and this is become an area of concern to address to the researchers. Past studies have shown that smartphone users write blog posts advocating for taking breaks from their devices or actively seek out strategies to manage the screen time of using various digital applications to like Android Digital Well-Being, Moment, iOS Screen Time, Forest, Detox, OffTime etc (Kuntsman & Miyake, 2016; Jorge, 2019).

the mass media is overall supporting the fact that disconnecting from digital platform as a method for mitigating negative health effects caused by smartphone and all other kind of digital platforms. Various sources are available to self-help on different platforms like podcast, websites, books with titles like "24/6: The Power of Unplugging One Day a Week" (Syvertsen,2017; Price, 2018; Shlain, 2019). There is negative connection between the usage of digital technology and well-being and mental and physical health (Dienlin & Johannes, 2020; Orben & Przybylski, 2019a; Orben & Przybylski, 2019b;), the user of smartphone also express their concerns about their usage of different digital platform and screen time.

Digital Detoxification

Oxford Dictionaries has defined the digital detox as a temporary period during an individual's withholds the usage of digital devices to diminish stress or to encourage the focus on face-to-face social interaction (Oxford Dictionaries, 2019). The "digital detox" is used in to encompass all the different terms or platform used widely for screen time (e.g., Fioravanti et al., 2019; Brown & Kuss, 2020;). This term first emerged around 2012 (Felix & Dean, 2012). In order to address concerns about excessive digital usage and its detrimental effects on personal well-being, individuals have increasingly turned to the concept of "digital detox" as a potential solution (Gui and Büchi 2019). This widely-used term refers to periodic periods of disengagement from several digital platforms, strategies formulated to minimizing the digital involvement. One example is intentionally limiting the digital involvement in order to alleviate the information overload and reduce dependence on technology (Syvertsen and Enli 2019).

However, it is important to consider that undergoing a digital detox could hampers the social connectivity potentially resulting in feelings loneliness (Cho 2015). The aim of digital detox is not to completely eliminate the use of communication technology, but rather to promote awareness and provide strategies for using technology more intentionally (Syvertsen and Enli 2019). The shared characteristic among these terms is their description of a specific timeframe to restrict where the usage of digital applications with different devices like smartphones, tablets. It should be noted that this definition defines digital detox as a temporarily practice and does not involve permanent abstinence from illegitimate substances like under the effect of alcohol or drugs (Syvertsen & Enli, 2019). Particularly for those who are socially isolated, communication technology may serve as their primary means of maintaining social relationships. Therefore, further investigation is needed to understand how this decrease in social connectivity hampers individual well-being. When individuals engage in a digital detox, they may experience overall well-being as they perceive because of the reduced usage of digital devices (Syvertsen and Enli 2019; Gui and Büchi 2019).

Theoretical Background

The theory of compensatory internet use (CIUT; Kardefelt-Winther, 2014) presents the idea that people turn to the digital platforms as a replacement of something they require but do not have access to. As a consequence, individuals may turn to internet browsing as a means of alleviating negative emotions in response to stressful life events. This behavior can be seen as an attempt to cope with cognitive and emotional states by persistently engaging with technology. For instance, if someone craves social interaction, using a social media app might serve as a substitute for actual social connections. However, while this initial engagement may temporarily alleviate negative feelings, it can also trigger additional negativity when real-life issues remain unaddressed. From a theoretical standpoint, it could further contribute to the fear of missing out, as others may appear to have more enjoyable experiences than oneself (Kardefelt-Winther 2014a; 2014b; 2017).

This studies shed light on the complex nature of problematic internet usage and its potential underlying factors. In three separate studies by Kardefelt-Winther (2014a, 2014b, 2017), the author explores various aspects of excessive online gaming and internet addiction. The first study investigates the moderating role of psychosocial well-being on the relationship between escapism and excessive online gaming. The second study critically examines the conceptual and methodological approaches used in internet addiction research, proposing a model of compensatory internet use instead. Lastly, the third study delves into conceptualizing internet use disorders as either an addiction or coping process.

According to self-determination theory (SDT; Deci & Ryan, 1985), the psychological need for connectedness with others as an important factor in effectively self-regulating and psychological well-being of an individual (Deci & Ryan, 1985). Several studies evident that FoMO impacts the well-being and it affect an individual emotions (Baker et al., 2016, Milyavskaya et al., 2018). Higher level of FoMO in Adolescents leads to risk for excessive usage of social media (Franchina et al., 2018; Al-Menayes, 2016, Dhir et al., 2018; Blackwell et al., 2017). In order to compensate the psychological needs adolescents with high levels of FoMO are prone to excessive use of social media (Oberst, Wegmann, Stodt, Brand, & Chamarro, 2017).

Several studies affirms that the fear of missing out can have a detrimental impact on individuals' well-being, has negative affect and emotional disturbance (Baker et al., 2016, Milyavskaya et al., 2018). Adolescents high in FOMO has greater risk of emotional disturbance and they feel missing out on the important events shared by the others (Oberst et al., 2017), it also leads to fatigue due to excessive usage of social media (Dhir et al., 2018). The connect between the FoMO and emotional symptoms are largely unknown and poorly examined, or has been hypothesized only.

The phenomenon of FoMO can be connect with theory of self-determination (SDT; Deci & Ryan, 1985). Individuals with heightened levels of FoMO have higher risk of excessive use of digital platforms (Dhir et al., 2018; Franchina et al., 2018; Blackwell et al., 2017; Al-Menayes, 2016;). FoMO can be related to the psychological need for interpersonal and social connection for self-regulation and for the psychological well-being of an individual. This may be due to the heightened perception of not belonging and missing out on shared events and experiences on digital platforms and this leads to social fatigue (Oberst et al., 2017; Dhir et al., 2018).

Model to Create a Balance Between FOMO and Digital Detoxification

It is very significant to create a balance between FOMO and Digital Detoxification. On the basis of literature, author has framed one model which represent a good balance between FOMO and DD. In the contemporary epoch, it is very essential to create a balance between FOMO and DD for the better living of individuals. If the individuals are able to create this balance then they are able to maintain the good health, sharing good relationship, self-growth and Subjective well-being is shown below:

[A] **Health:** In today's addictive environment of social media. It is very much imperative to detox yourself from social media and try to relieve ourselves from FOMO. The consequence of the relieving from FOMO is that individuals would be able to maintain the health. For maintaining the balance between FOMO and DD, individuals need to exercise, yoga, relaxed their brains which helps them in feeling string inside out.

[B] **Sharing Good relationship:** Human being have social needs to maintain healthy relationship. With the involvement on social media, individuals are lacking healthy relationship. If they would be able to maintain a good balance between the above constructs then individuals would be able to devote more time with friends, more focussed towards family members and have ample amount of time for exploring new relationships.

[C] **Self Growth:** In the era of social media, people are fully engaged with online content which engrossed their brains and mostly people are involved in videos,

Figure 1.

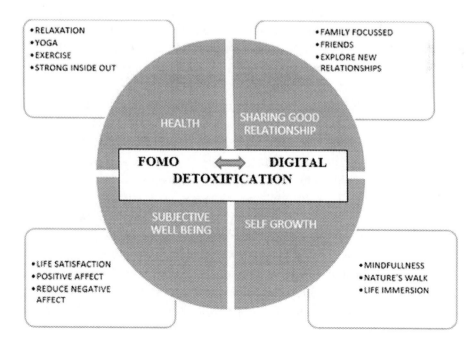

memes, articles etc. They are not able to find themselves and focussed on self-growth. To maintain the self-growth, individuals has to create a balance between the above constructs. Afterwards, individuals would be able to connect with nature, develop mindfulness and more immersed in life.

[D] **Subjective wellbeing:** After going through the content on digital media, the well being of individuals are missing. We are caught by the negative environment fully reason of which is everything is available within a click. So, it is mandatory to create a balance between the two. Consequently, it helps the individuals to maintain life satisfaction, positive affect and recuses the negative affect.

CONCLUSION

To conclude, it is very much evident from the literature that in the individuals of all the ages the usage of digital media has been increasing which is creating a feeling of "FOMO" in the individuals. So, it is the need of hour to refrain yourself from digital modes. Strategies has been suggested in the study to create a balance between FOMO and Digital detoxification which are as follows:

Strategies to balance between FOMO and Digital detoxification: There are several strategies which are the need of hour to save human race from FOMO along with digital detoxification which are as follows:

1) **Alert Yourself:** It is very much significant to remind yourself that individuals need to minimise the usage of digital media. As in the changing environment, it is not possible to remove it totally. But, individual need to train their brain that we should be alert while using digital media. Individuals need to give Intangible reminders constantly to themselves.

2) **Use Watch:** Instead of using mobile phones for knowing the time, for setting alarms, individuals need to increase the use of 'watch' for keep a watch on time and setting any sort of reminders for themselves. Make a diary/notepad for jotting down important things.

3) **Switch off Notifications:** It is very much apparent to switch off the pop up notifications on the mobile phones as every single app will pop up some notification and deviate the mind of individuals. Prepare yourself to check the mobile phones after every 2 hours as compare to every 2 minutes. Lately, you will realise and it will be in your habit to keep away from social media.

4) **Digital Free Meals:** Now a day, individuals have developed a habit of watching digital media while eating breakfast, lunch, evening snacks or dinner. But consciously, individuals need to drop this habit and have their meals with their loved ones talking about how they have spent their day, what they want to do

in their life, their future plans, just be with the family members whole heartily and spent quality time with them.

5) **Put on Airplane Mode:** People have developed a habit to sleep over phones which is not only harmful for their mental health but also for their physical health as well. In the longer run, pressure created via digital media will spoil the individual's life. So, it is suggested to put your cell phones in airplane mode, when phone is not in use.

REFERENCES

Al-Menayes, J. (2016). The fear of missing out scale: Validation of the Arabic version and correlation with social media addiction. *International Journal of Applied Psychology, 6*(2), 41–46.

Al-Saggaf, Y., & O'Donnell, S. B. (2019). Phubbing: Perceptions, reasons behind, predictors, and impacts. *Human Behavior and Emerging Technologies, 1*(2), 132–140. doi:10.1002/hbe2.137

Alt, D. (2015). College students' academic motivation, media engagement and fear of missing out. *Computers in Human Behavior, 49,* 111–119. https://doi.org/. 057. doi:10.1016/j.chb.2015.02

Amez, S., & Baert, S. (2020). Smartphone use and academic performance: A literature review. *International Journal of Educational Research, 103,* 101618. doi:10.1016/j.ijer.2020.101618

Andreassen, C. S., Torsheim, T., Brunborg, G. S., & Pallesen, S. (2012). Development of a Facebook addiction scale. *Psychological Reports, 110*(2), 501–517. doi:10.2466/02.09.18.PR0.110.2.501-517 PMID:22662404

Andreassen, C. S., Torsheim, T., Brunborg, G. S., & Pallesen, S. (2012). Development of a Facebook addiction scale. *Psychological Reports, 110*(2), 501–517. doi:10.2466/02.09.18.PR0.110.2.501-517 PMID:22662404

Baker, 2016

Blackwell, D., Leaman, C., Tramposch, R., Osborne, C., & Liss, M. (2017). Extraversion, neuroticism, attachment style and fear of missing out as predictors of social media use and addiction. *Personality and Individual Differences, 116,* 69–72. doi:10.1016/j.paid.2017.04.039

Brown, L., & Kuss, D. J. (2020). Fear of missing out, mental wellbeing, and social connectedness: A seven-day social media abstinence trial. *International Journal of Environmental Research and Public Health, 17*(12), 4566. doi:10.3390/ijerph17124566 PMID:32599962

Cho, J. (2015). Roles of Smartphone App Use in Improving Social Capital and Reducing Social Isolation. *Cyberpsychology, Behavior, and Social Networking, 18*(6), 350–355. (). doi:10.1089/cyber.2014.0657

Demirci, K., Akgönül, M., & Akpinar, A. (2015). Relationship of € smartphone use severity with sleep quality, depression, and anxiety in university students. *Journal of Behavioral Addictions, 4*(2), 85–92. doi:10.1556/2006.4.2015.010 PMID:26132913

Dhir, A., Yossatorn, Y., Kaur, P., & Chen, S. (2018). Online social media fatigue and psychological wellbeing—A study of compulsive use, fear of missing out, fatigue, anxiety and depression. *International Journal of Information Management, 40*, 141–152. doi:10.1016/j.ijinfomgt.2018.01.012

Dickinson, L. (1995). Autonomy and motivation a literature review. *System, 23*(2), 165–174. doi:10.1016/0346-251X(95)00005-5

Duke, É., & Montag, C. (2017). Smartphone addiction, daily interruptions and self-reported productivity. *Addictive Behaviors Reports, 6*, 90–95. doi:10.1016/j.abrep.2017.07.002 PMID:29450241

Elhai, J. D., Dvorak, R. D., Levine, J. C., & Hall, B. J. (2017). Problematic smartphone use: A conceptual overview and systematic review of relations with anxiety and depression psychopathology. *Journal of Affective Disorders, 207*, 251–259. doi:10.1016/j.jad.2016.08.030 PMID:27736736

Elhai, J. D., Gallinari, E. F., Rozgonjuk, D., & Yang, H. (2020). Depression, anxiety and fear of missing out as correlates of social, non-social and problematic smartphone use. *Addictive Behaviors, 105*, 106335. https://doi.org/. 106335. doi:10.1016/j.addbeh.2020

Elhai, J. D., Levine, J. C., Alghraibeh, A. M., Alafnan, A. A., Aldraiweesh, A. A., & Hall, B. J. (2018). Fear of missing out: Testing relationships with negative affectivity, online social engagement, and problematic smartphone use. *Computers in Human Behavior, 89*, 289–298. doi:10.1016/j.chb.2018.08.020

Elhai, J. D., Levine, J. C., Dvorak, R. D., & Hall, B. J. (2016). Fear of missing out, need for touch, anxiety and depression are related to problematic smartphone use. *Computers in Human Behavior, 63*, 509–516. doi:10.1016/j.chb.2016.05.079

Elhai, J. D., Yang, H., Fang, J., Bai, X., & Hall, B. J. (2020). Depression and anxiety symptoms are related to problematic smartphone use severity in Chinese young adults: Fear of missing out as a mediator. *Addictive Behaviors, 101*, 105962. doi:10.1016/j.addbeh.2019.04.020 PMID:31030950

Felix, L., & Dean, B. (2012). *Our story, 2 decades in the making.* Digital Detox. https://www.digitaldetox.com/our-story

Fioravanti, G., Prostamo, A., & Casale, S. (2019). Taking a short break from Instagram: The effects on subjective well-being. *Cyberpsychology, Behavior, and Social Networking.* doi:10.1089/cyber.2019.0400 PMID:31851833

Franchina, V., Vanden Abeele, M., Van Rooij, A. J., Lo Coco, G., & De Marez, L. (2018). Fear of missing out as a predictor of problematic social media use and phubbing behavior among Flemish adolescents. *International Journal of Environmental Research and Public Health, 15*(10), 2319. doi:10.3390/ijerph15102319 PMID:30360407

Gil, F., Chamarro, A., & Oberst, U. (2015). PO-14: Addiction to online social networks: A question of "fear of missing out"? *Journal of Behavioral Addictions, 4*(S1), 51–52.

Griffiths, M. D. (1996). Internet addiction: An issue for clinical psychology? *Clinical Psychology Forum, 97*(97), 32–36. doi:10.53841/bpscpf.1996.1.97.32

Griffiths, M. D. (1998). Internet addiction: Does it really exist? In J. Gackenbach (Ed.), *Psychology and the internet: Intrapersonal, interpersonal, and transpersonal implications.* Academic Press.

Gui, M., & Büchi, M. (2019). From Use to Overuse: Digital Inequality in the Age of Communication Abundance. *Social Science Computer Review*, 1–17. doi:10.1177/0894439319851163

Hitlin, P. (2018). Internet, social media use and device ownership in U.S. have plateaued after years of growth [Internet]. Pew Research. https://www.pewresearch.org/fact-tank/2018/09/28/internet-social-media-use-and-device-ownership-in-u-s-have-plateaued-after-years-of-growth/ » https://www.pewresearch.org/fact-tank/2018/09/28/internet-social-media-use-and-device-ownership-in-u-s-have-plateaued-after-years-of-growth/

İNal, E. E., Demİrcİ, İ., Çetİntürk, A. İ., Akgönül, M., & Savaş, S. İ. (2015). Effects of smartphone overuse on hand function, pinch strength, and the median nerve. *Muscle & Nerve, 52*(2), 183–188. doi:10.1002/mus.24695 PMID:25914119

Karsay, K., Schmuck, D., Matthes, J., & Stevic, A. (2019). Longitudinal effects of excessive smartphone use on stress and loneliness: The moderating role of self-disclosure. *Cyberpsychology, Behavior, and Social Networking, 22*(11), 706–713. doi:10.1089/cyber.2019.0255 PMID:31697600

King, A. L. S., Valença, A. M., Silva, A. C., Sancassiani, F., Machado, S., & Nardi, A. E. (2014). Nomophobia: Impact of cell phone use interfering with symptoms and emotions of individuals with panic disorder compared with A control group. *Clinical Practice and Epidemiology in Mental Health, 10*(1), 28–35. doi:10.2174/1745017901410010028 PMID:24669231

Ko, C. H., Yen, J. Y., Yen, C. F., Chen, C. S., & Chen, C. C. (2012). The association between internet addiction and psychiatric disorder: A review of the literature. *European Psychiatry, 27*(1), 1–8. doi:10.1016/j.eurpsy.2010.04.011 PMID:22153731

Kuss, D. J., & Griffiths, M. D. (2017). Social networking sites and addiction: Ten lessons learned. *International Journal of Environmental Research and Public Health, 14*(3), 311. doi:10.3390/ijerph14030311 PMID:28304359

Lepp, A., Barkley, J. E., & Karpinski, A. C. (2014). The relationship between cell phone use, academic performance, anxiety, and satisfaction with life in college students. *Computers in Human Behavior, 31*, 343–350. doi:10.1016/j.chb.2013.10.049

Lepp, A., Barkley, J. E., Sanders, G. J., Rebold, M., & Gates, P. (2013). The relationship between cell phone use, physical and sedentary activity, and cardiorespiratory fitness in a sample of U.S. college students. *The International Journal of Behavioral Nutrition and Physical Activity, 10*(1), 79. doi:10.1186/1479-5868-10-79 PMID:23800133

Li, L., Griffiths, M. D., Niu, Z., & Mei, S. (2020). The trait-state fear of missing out scale: Validity, reliability, and measurement invariance in a Chinese sample of university students. *Journal of Affective Disorders, 274*, 711–718. https://doi.org/. jad.2020.05.103. doi:10.1016/j

Markowetz, A. (2015). *Digitaler Burnout: warum unsere permanente Smartphone-Nutzung gefährlich ist*. Droemer eBook.

McDaniel, B. T., & Radesky, J. S. (2018). Technoference: Parent distraction with technology and associations with child behavior problems. *Child Development, 89*(1), 100–109. doi:10.1111/cdev.12822 PMID:28493400

Milyavskaya, M., Saffran, M., Hope, N., & Koestner, R. (2018). Fear of missing out: Prevalence, dynamics, and consequences of experiencing FOMO. *Motivation and Emotion, 42*(5), 725–737. doi:10.100711031-018-9683-5

Morford, M. (2010). Oh my God you are so missing out [Internet]. SF Gate. https://www.sfgate.com/entertainment/morford/article/Oh-my-God-you-are-so-missing-out-2536241.php

Nuñez, T. R., Radtke, T., & Eimler, S. (2020). Third-person perspective on phubbing: Observing smartphone-induced social exclusion generates negative affect, stress, and derogatory attitudes. *Cyberpsychology (Brno), 14*(3). doi:10.5817/CP2020-3-3

O'Connell, C. (2020). How FOMO (Fear of missing out), the smartphone, and social media may be affecting university students in the Middle East. *North American Journal of Psychology, 22*(1).

Oberst, U., Wegmann, E., Stodt, B., Brand, M., & Chamarro, A. (2017). Negative consequences from heavy social networking in adolescents: The mediating role of fear of missing out. *Journal of Adolescence, 55*(1), 51–60. doi:10.1016/j.adolescence.2016.12.008 PMID:28033503

Omar, M. K., Dahalan, N. A., & Yusoff, Y. H. M. (2016). Social media usage, perceived team-efficacy and knowledge sharing behaviour among employees of an oil and gas organisation in Malaysia. *Procedia Economics and Finance, 37*, 309–316. doi:10.1016/S2212-5671(16)30130-7

Oxford Dictionaries. (2019, January 30). Definition of *digital detox* in English. Oxford Press. http://www.oxforddictionaries.com/definition/english/digital-detox

Poushter, J., Bishop, C., & Chwe, H. (2018). *Social media use continues to rise in developing countries but plateaus across developed ones.* Pew Research. https://www.pewglobal.org/2018/06/19/social-media-use-continues-to-rise-in-developing-countries-but-plateaus-across-developed-ones/

Przybylski, A. K., Murayama, K., DeHaan, C. R., & Gladwell, V. (2013). Motivational, emotional, and behavioral correlates of fear of missing out. *Computers in Human Behavior, 29*(4), 1841–1848. doi:10.1016/j.chb.2013.02.014

Roberts, J. A., & David, M. E. (2020). The social media party: Fear of missing out (FOMO), social media intensity, connection, and well-being. *International Journal of Human-Computer Interaction, 36*(4), 386–392. doi:10.1080/10447318.2019.1646517

Rod, N. H., Dissing, A. S., Clark, A., Gerds, T. A., & Lund, R. (2018). Overnight smartphone use: A new public health challenge? A novel study design based on high-resolution smartphone data. *PLoS One, 13*(10), e0204811. doi:10.1371/journal.pone.0204811 PMID:30325929

Ryu, E. J., Choi, K. S., Seo, J. S., & Nam, B. W. (2004). The relationships of Internet addiction, depression, and suicidal ideation in adolescents. *Taehan Kanho Hakhoe Chi, 34*(1), 102–110. doi:10.4040/jkan.2004.34.1.102 PMID:15314344

Statista.com. (2021). *Number of smartphone users worldwide from 2016 to 2021 (in billions).* Statista. https://www.statista.com/statistics/330695/number-ofsmartpho neusers-worldwide/

Syvertsen, T., & Enli, G. (2019). Digital Detox: Media Resistance and the Promise of Authenticity. *Convergence (London),* 1–15. doi:10.1177/1354856519847325

Thomée, S. (2018). Mobile phone use and mental health: A review of the research that takes a psychological perspective on exposure. *International Journal of Environmental Research and Public Health, 15*(12), 2692. doi:10.3390/ ijerph15122692 PMID:30501032

Tripathi, A. (2017). Impact of internet addiction on mental health: An integrative therapy is needed. *Integrative Medicine International, 4*(3–4), 215–222.

Van-Den-Eijnden, R., Doornwaard, S., & Ter Bogt, T. (2017). OP117: Are smartphone dependence symptoms related to FOMO, craving and withdrawal symptoms during smartphone abstinence? Findings from a natural experiment. *Journal of Behavioral Addictions, 6*(S1), 56–57.

Wang, P., Wang, X., Nie, J., Zeng, P., Liu, K., Wang, J., Guo, J., & Lei, L. (2019). Envy and problematic smartphone use: The mediating role of FOMO and the moderating role of student-student relationship. *Personality and Individual Differences, 146,* 136–142. doi:10.1016/j.paid.2019.04.013

We are Social. (2018). *Digital in 2018 in western Asia.* Slideshare. https://www.slideshare.net/wearesocial/digital-in-2018-inwestern-asia-part-1- northwest86865983

Weinstein, A., Dorani, D., Elhadif, R., Bukovza, Y., Yarmulnik, A., & Dannon, P. (2015). Internet addiction is associated with social anxiety in young adults. *Annals of Clinical Psychiatry, 27*(1), 4–9. PMID:25696775

Wolniewicz, C. A., Rozgonjuk, D., & Elhai, J. D. (2020). Boredom proneness and fear of missing out mediate relations between depression and anxiety with problematic smartphone use. *Human Behavior and Emerging Technologies, 2*(1), 61–70. doi:10.1002/hbe2.159

Young, K. (1996). Psychology of computer use: XL. Addictive use of the internet: A case that breaks the stereotype. *Psychological Reports*, *79*(3), 899–902. doi:10.2466/pr0.1996.79.3.899 PMID:8969098

Young, K. S. (1997, August). What makes the internet addictive: Potential explanations for pathological Internet use. In *105th annual conference of the American Psychological Association* (*Vol. 15*, pp. 12–30). APA.

Chapter 2
Business Drivers in Promoting Digital Detoxification

Rishi Prakash Shukla

iD https://orcid.org/0000-0003-0854-7302
Chandigarh University, India

ABSTRACT

In today's hyper-connected world, the constant use of digital devices and online platforms has become an integral part of daily life. While these technologies offer numerous advantages in terms of communication, productivity, and information access, they also bring about significant challenges, including digital addiction, burnout, and decreased well-being. The need for digital detoxification has emerged as a critical concern for both individuals and organizations. This chapter proposes to explore how businesses can play a pivotal role in promoting digital detoxification among their employees.

INTRODUCTION

In an era dominated by the relentless hum of digital devices, the ceaseless torrent of notifications, and the unending expanse of online platforms, we stand at the precipice of an unparalleled digital revolution. The benefits are glaring: unmatched connectivity, heightened productivity, and an astonishingly expansive information landscape. However, amid this digital euphoria, we cannot afford to overlook the ominous clouds that loom over our digital landscape. The issues of digital addiction, the constant threat of burnout, and the gradual erosion of overall well-being cast shadows over this bold new world into which we plunge headfirst. As we grapple with the far-reaching effects of our digital entanglement, it becomes increasingly

DOI: 10.4018/979-8-3693-1107-3.ch002

clear that businesses are not mere participants in this unfolding story; they wield significant influence in shaping the contours of our digital reality. Beyond being contributors to the challenges, businesses possess the capacity to be instrumental in crafting solutions. This chapter endeavors to illuminate the path forward by delving into the myriad ways in which companies can serve as agents of change, redrawing the boundaries of our digital existence and aiding their employees in regaining a sense of equilibrium through the promotion of digital detoxification within their organizations.

The digital predicament, a conundrum at the nexus of progress and peril, lies at the heart of our contemporary digital odyssey. Enslaved to the siren song of screens by the digital platforms and technologies that have empowered us in unprecedented ways, we find ourselves ensnared in what can only be described as a predicament of the modern day. On one hand, we revel in the advantages of rapid communication, heightened efficiency, and boundless knowledge at our fingertips, creating a civilization unlike any other. Yet, on the other side of this digital coin, a more sinister story emerges. The pervasive threat of digital addiction, where obsessive behaviors bind us to our screens at the expense of genuine human connection, poses a formidable challenge in the face of the sheer prevalence of digital devices. In response to the challenges posed by our connected, ever-accelerating world, digital detoxification has risen to prominence, transcending individual preference to become a shared social problem. It entails purposeful and transient disengagement from digital gadgets and online activity, a deliberate effort to regain control over our digital lives. In a society that demands an unrelenting march forward, digital detoxification represents a return to the basics of what it means to be human. This chapter contends that businesses, often overlooked in the discourse surrounding digital detoxification, are crucial actors in this narrative. They possess the means not only to navigate the challenges presented by the digital age but also to actively shape the digital landscape within their organizations. Through the establishment of clearly defined policies and guidelines, education and training initiatives, the promotion of a salubrious workplace, encouragement of technological solutions, setting an example through leadership, and the creation of digital-free zones, businesses can spearhead a movement toward a healthier digital future.

Measuring the effectiveness of digital detoxification programs requires the implementation of key performance indicators (KPIs) such as productivity measurements, employee well-being surveys, and tracking the time spent unplugged. By actively seeking feedback and closely monitoring these measures, businesses can continuously refine their strategies, fostering a workplace environment that harmonizes the benefits of digital advancement with the imperative of employee well-being. As we struggle with the widespread effects of our digital entanglement, it becomes clear that businesses are essential to solving this problem. They are more than just participants in this story; they have a significant impact on how the digital world is shaped.

In conclusion, as we traverse the complex landscape of our digital journey, digital detoxification transcends being a fleeting trend; it emerges as a deliberate decision to reassess our digital lives and rediscover the joys of living free from the incessant hum of notifications. However, this transition is not a solo endeavor. Businesses, with their influential role in the digital realm, emerge as the linchpins of change, holding the keys to unlock a path toward a healthier, more balanced digital future. In an era defined by the relentless hum of digital devices, the ceaseless torrent of notifications, and the unending expanse of online platforms, we stand on the precipice of an unprecedented digital revolution. The benefits are obvious: unmatched connectivity, increased productivity, and an astonishingly expansive information landscape. However, we cannot overlook the ominous clouds that hang over this bold new world as we dive in headfirst: digital addiction, the constant threat of burnout, and the gradual degradation of our group's wellbeing. This chapter sets out to shed light on the future by examining the various ways in which companies might be the change agents. They may redraw the boundaries of our digital reality and assist their employees in regaining some form of balance by advocating for digital detoxification within their organisations. Digital detoxification has become essential in our connected, ever-accelerating world, surpassing individual preference. It is now a shared social problem rather than an issue of personal taste.

THE DIGITAL PREDICAMENT: OUR CONTEMPORARY JOURNEY

The conflict between progress and danger is the ancient conundrum at the centre of this ongoing digital odyssey. We are enslaved to the siren song of screens by the digital platforms and technologies(Day, 2011) that enable us in ways never before possible, creating what can only be called a predicament of the modern day.

We enjoy, on the one hand, the advantages of rapid communication, increased efficiency, and the seemingly endless sources of knowledge at our fingers. With a few swipes and clicks, we can now (Rust, 2020) seamlessly connect across continents and time zones, creating a civilization unlike any other. These are commendable achievements that have opened up a new era of potentially revolutionary possibilities.

Yet, a more sinister story is revealed on the opposite side of this digital coin. The threat of digital addiction, in (Cherry, 2009) which obsessive behaviours bind us to our screens, frequently at the price of real human connection, has emerged as a result of the sheer prevalence of digital devices.

The incessant demands of perpetual connectivity cause a blurring of the lines between work and personal life, which contributes to a mental health epidemic and epidemic of burnout. Our senses become overwhelmed by an overwhelming amount of data, leading to worry, anxiety, and a chronic feeling of being overwhelmed by digital information.

GETTING TO KNOW DIGITAL DETOXIFICATION: THE WAY BACK TO CONNECTION

Digital detoxification has become a crucial tool for people who want to reevaluate their connection with technology in light of this digital conundrum. To recover some semblance of control over our digital lives, it involves a purposeful and transient disengagement from digital(Zook & Graham, 2018) gadgets and online activity.

Setting up boundaries, controlling screen time, and practising mindfulness in our digital connections are all part of the process of digital detoxification. Reconnecting with ourselves, our inner selves and our physical environment is a meaningful act. In a society that frequently (Asih et al., 2019)demands an unrelenting march forward, it's a return to the basics of what it is to be human.

Businesses must assume leadership in digital well-being

The firms are the unsung heroes of the digital detox narrative. They have the power to change the digital environment (Balaji et al., 2016)within their organisations and, in doing so, foster a culture that puts the general welfare (Behera et al., 2023)

Creating Clearly Defined Policies and Guidelines: Organisations facilitate digital balance by developing and disseminating clear policies on the use of digital devices during working hours. Encouragement of employees to refrain from work-related contact beyond their assigned work hours (Xia et al., 2021)can be a means of recognising the significance of personal time and its correlation with overall well-being.

Educating and Training: It is a great tool to provide time management and digital literacy instruction. It gives workers the abilities they need to properly manage their digital life. Teaching employees the value of digital detoxification (Asih et al., 2019) for maintaining mental health is an investment that will benefit both their personal and professional lives.

Promoting a Salubrious Workplace: Nurturing the work environment is ingrained in firms' DNA. Employees are provided with the opportunity (Jadli et al., 2023)to refuel during the workday by means of regular breaks and downtime. Workplace cultures that actively support work-life balance and value individual time demonstrate a dedication to the overall health of their staff.

Encouraging Technological Solutions: It can be revolutionary to introduce technology that gives workers the ability to track and control (Heeks, 2008) their screen use. Businesses may help their employees become more adept at navigating the digital desert by giving them the tools and resources they need to prioritise and organise digital chores.

Setting an Example: The culture of an organisation is shaped by its leadership. Senior management can set an example of responsible (Verhoef et al., 2015)digital behaviours by unplugging during their own time. Acknowledging and praising staff members who effectively implement digital detoxing gives a strong signal of encouragement and support.

Establishing Digital-Free Zones: Setting aside particular sections of the office for the use of digital devices encourages genuine engagement and face-to-face conversation. It can serve as a haven where people can retreat from the constant din of technology.

MEASURING ACHIEVEMENT: AN INTROSPECTIVE JOURNEY

It is impossible to determine the effectiveness of digital detoxification programmes without a compass to guide one through the process. Companies can use key performance indicators (KPIs) to measure their development. A few of the guiding principles are productivity measurements, employee well-being surveys, and the amount of time spent unplugged(Stewart & Stanford, 2017). Businesses can continuously improve their activities by aggressively soliciting feedback and keeping a close eye on these measures.

We have learned that the advancement of technology has brought us both the benefits of progress and the dangers of overconsumption during our digital journey. We now live in a new kind of paradox brought about by the digital age, where limitless opportunities combine with the risk of (International Labour Organization, 2018) social unrest and personal upheaval.

Digital detoxification is becoming more and more necessary, not just a trend. It's a deliberate decision to take a step back, reassess our digital lives, and rediscover the pleasures of living a life free f(Khare et al., 2019)rom the incessant hum of notifications. It's an appeal to reconsider how we interact with technology and to strike a healthy balance between the virtual and real worlds.

But this is not a transition that people can handle on their own. Businesses emerge as the change-bearers in this endeavour. They possess the means, the clout, and the ability to spearhead the movement towards digital detoxification. Businesses can be the driving forces behind positive change through the implementation of legislation, provision of education, promotion of a healthy work environment, backing of technical solutions, setting an example, and establishment of digital-free zones.

CONCLUSION

Recommendations for Action: Opening the Path

As we wrap off this investigation, it's important to provide a list of recommended steps that companies can do to support digital detoxification:

Create Interdepartmental Task Forces: Assemble task forces with members drawn from different departments inside the company. These groups can work together to implement digital detox programmes and make sure they become part of the company's overall ethos.

Add Digital Detoxification to the Onboarding Process: Introduce new hires to the company's digital detox policies and initiatives as part of the onboarding process. This guarantees that the fundamentals of digital balance are ingrained from the start.

Encourage External Partnerships: To acquire knowledge and resources for successfully promoting digital detoxification, cooperate with institutions and authorities in the field of digital wellness.

Employee Feedback: Establish channels for staff members to offer regular input on how well digital detoxification programmes are working. Make necessary adjustments to your strategies based on this input.

Celebrate Success Stories: Highlight and recognise staff members who have effectively adopted digital detoxing on a regular basis, sharing their success stories to serve as an example to others.

Encourage Offline Team Building: Plan frequent team-building activities that foster in-person communication and assist staff in forging closer ties outside of the digital sphere.

Provide a Digital Wellness App: Construct a digital wellness platform or app that is unique to your business and helps staff members manage their digital life. Offer tools for tracking, resources, and reminders.

Encourage External Partnerships: Collaborate with organisations and authorities in the field of digital wellness to gain information and tools for effectively promoting digital detoxification.

Employee Feedback: Provide regular avenues for employees to provide feedback on the efficacy of digital detoxification initiatives. Based on this information, modify your methods as needed.

Celebrate Success Stories: To set an example for others, identify and honour staff members who have successfully implemented digital detoxification on a regular basis.

Promote Offline Team Building: Arrange regular team-building exercises that encourage face-to-face interactions and help employees develop stronger bonds away from the internet.

Offer a Digital Wellness App: Create a customised digital wellness platform or app for your company.

In the age dominated by the incessant hum of digital devices, the overwhelming deluge of notifications, and the expansive realm of online platforms, we find ourselves on the brink of an unparalleled digital revolution. While the benefits of this era are undeniable – unmatched connectivity, increased productivity, and an expansive information landscape – we cannot ignore the looming threats of digital addiction, the constant specter of burnout, and the gradual erosion of overall well-being. As we grapple with the pervasive effects of our digital entanglement, it becomes evident that businesses play a pivotal role in addressing this issue. They are not mere spectators in this narrative; rather, they exert a significant influence on shaping the digital world. This chapter aims to illuminate the path forward by exploring how companies can act as catalysts for change, redrawing the boundaries of our digital reality and assisting employees in reclaiming balance through the advocacy of digital detoxification within their organizations. The digital predicament, a clash between progress and peril, lies at the heart of our contemporary digital journey. While digital platforms and technologies have empowered us in unprecedented ways, they have also ensnared us in a predicament of the modern day. The advantages of rapid communication, increased efficiency, and boundless knowledge coexist with the darker side of digital addiction, where obsessive behaviors tether us to screens at the expense of genuine human connection. Digital detoxification emerges as a crucial tool in navigating the challenges of our connected, ever-accelerating world. Beyond individual preference, it has become a shared social problem, necessitating a purposeful and transient disengagement from digital gadgets and online activity to regain control over our digital lives. In a society that relentlessly propels forward, digital detoxification represents a return to the fundamentals of what it means to be human. Businesses, often unsung heroes in the digital detox narrative, wield the power to reshape the digital environment within their organizations. This involves the establishment of clearly defined policies and guidelines, education and training initiatives, promotion of a healthy workplace, encouragement of technological solutions, setting an example by leadership, and the creation of digital-free zones. Measuring the success of digital detoxification programs requires key performance indicators (KPIs) such as productivity measurements, employee well-being surveys, and tracking the time spent unplugged. Continuous improvement can be achieved by actively seeking feedback and closely monitoring these measures. In conclusion, as we navigate the complex terrain of our digital journey, digital detoxification transcends being a mere trend; it becomes a deliberate decision to reassess our digital lives and rediscover the joys of living free from the constant hum of notifications. This transition, however, is not one that individuals can undertake alone. Businesses emerge as the harbingers of change, possessing the means and influence to spearhead the movement toward digital detoxification. To facilitate this change, companies can take various actions, including the creation of interdepartmental task forces, integrating digital detoxification into the onboarding process, fostering external partnerships for knowledge and resources, actively seeking employee feedback, celebrating success stories, promoting offline team-building, and providing digital wellness apps tailored to their organizational needs. As we embark on this transformative journey, businesses hold the key to opening the path toward a healthier, more balanced digital future.

REFERENCES

Asih, S. N., Sucahyo, Y. G., Gandhi, A., & Ruldeviyani, Y. (2019). Inhibiting motivating factors on online gig economy client in Indonesia. *2019 International Conference on Advanced Computer Science and Information Systems, ICACSIS 2019*, (pp. 349–356). 10.1109/ICACSIS47736.2019.8979703

Balaji, D., Londhe, B. R., & Shukla, R. P. (2016). Successful Emotional Branding Campaigns on Television in India: An Exploration. *Indian Journal of Science and Technology, 9*(15). doi:10.1016/j.jclepro.2023.136605

Behera, R. K., Bala, P. K., & Rana, N. P. (2023). Creation of sustainable growth with explainable artificial intelligence: An empirical insight from consumer packaged goods retailers. Journal of Cleaner Production, 399, 136605. doi:10.1016/j.jclepro.2023.136605

Cherry, M. A. (2009). Working for (Virtually) Minimum Wage: Applying the Fair Labor Standards act in Cyberspace. *Alabama Law Review, 60*(5), 1077–1110.

Day, G. S. (2011). Closing the marketing capabilities gap. *Journal of Marketing, 75*(4), 183–195. doi:10.1509/jmkg.75.4.183

Heeks, R. (2008). Development Informatics. In *Development* (*Vol. 32*). University of Manchester. http://www.digitale-chancen.de/transfer/downloads/MD280.pdf

International Labour Organization. (2018). *The architecture of digital labour platforms: Policy recommendations on platform design for worker well-being*. ILO. www.ilo.org/publns

Jadli, A., Hain, M., & Hasbaoui, A. (2023). Artificial intelligence-based lead propensity prediction. *IAES International Journal of Artificial Intelligence, 12*(3), 1281–1290. doi:10.11591/ijai.v12.i3.pp1281-1290

Khare, A., Awasthi, G., & Shukla, R. P. (2019). Do mall events affect mall traffic and image? A qualitative study of Indian mall retailers. *Asia Pacific Journal of Marketing and Logistics, 32*(2), 343–365. doi:10.1108/APJML-01-2019-0021

Rust, R. T. (2020). The future of marketing. *International Journal of Research in Marketing, 37*(1), 15–26. doi:10.1016/j.ijresmar.2019.08.002

Stewart, A., & Stanford, J. (2017). Regulating work in the gig economy: What are the options? *Economic and Labour Relations Review, 28*(3), 420–437.

Verhoef, P. C., Kannan, P. K., & Inman, J. J. (2015). From Multi-Channel Retailing to Omni-Channel Retailing. Introduction to the Special Issue on Multi-Channel Retailing. *Journal of Retailing, 91*(2), 174–181. doi:10.1016/j.jretai.2015.02.005

Xia, M., Shao, H., Williams, D., Lu, S., Shu, L., & de Silva, C. W. (2021). Intelligent fault diagnosis of machinery using digital twin-assisted deep transfer learning. *Reliability Engineering and System Safety, 215*. doi:10.1016/j.ress.2021.107938

Zook, M., & Graham, M. (2018). Hacking code/space: Confounding the code of global capitalism. *Transactions of the Institute of British Geographers, 43*(3), 390–404. doi:10.1111/tran.12228

Chapter 3

CBDC's FinTech Innovations:
Socioeconomic Implications and the Need for Digital Detox

Priya Makhija
 https://orcid.org/0000-0002-7436-2798
Center for Management Studies, Jain University, India

Megha Kukreja
 https://orcid.org/0000-0003-2174-1249
Center for Management Studies, Jain University, India

R. Thanga Kumar
Center for Management Studies, Jain University, India

ABSTRACT

As the global financial landscape continues to transform to technological improvements, the emergence of CBDCs represents a significant turning point in financial systems. The central bank of a country issues and controls CBDCs, which are digital representations of sovereign money. Fintech and CBDCs are closely related because of the building pieces of the CBDC operation, which include blockchain or distributed ledgers, digital currency wallets, and dependable payment gateways. The adoption of Central Bank Digital Currencies (CBDCs) has the potential to have a significant impact on the fintech industry and could, in some cases, result in a fintech boom. The goal of this study is to develop a comprehensive knowledge of CBDCs' integration with fintech, their wide-ranging effects on society, and the potential need for digital detoxification techniques to balance off the unwanted effects of growing digitalization which can lead to financial innovation and personal well-being in the digital era by looking at CBDCs from both a technology and human-centric standpoint.

DOI: 10.4018/979-8-3693-1107-3.ch003

INTRODUCTION

FinTech, an acronym for financial technology, is an evolving buzzword that is supported by several cutting-edge, futuristic technologies. The financial market and supply of financial services have been significantly impacted by several new business models, technological advancements, goods, and services fueled by economic sharing, legislation, policy, and information technology (I. Lee & Shin, 2018). Due to its numerous benefits, including increased operational effectiveness, cost-effective operating cost reduction, disruption of the established industry structures, blurring of industry boundaries, facilitation of strategic disintermediation, the opening of new doors for entrepreneurship, and democratization of access to financial services, it has garnered a lot of attention (0Agarwal & Zhang, 2020; Li & Xu, 2021; Suryono et al., 2020; Wang et al., 2021). The development of fintech was fueled by improvements in e-finance and mobile technologies for financial institutions during the 2008 global financial crisis. e-finance inventiveness, digital technology, platforms for social networking, media platforms, neural networks, and big analytic data integration were all integrated into this development. The global fintech market was valued at $133.84 billion in 2022 and is projected to reach $556.58 billion by 2030. The global market is expected to grow, exhibiting a Compound Annual Growth Rate (CAGR) of 19.50% over the forecast period (Bzo, 2023).

Fintech is an example of new digital technology that offers consumers convenience and novel customer experiences, but it also creates technostress due to hazards associated with technological flaws and pressure to adapt to new technologies. While using financial services, consumers who constantly use different services and goods encounter technostress due to which the use of fintech services gets negatively influenced. Even young and knowledgeable consumers may find it challenging to consistently purchase new digital technology due to how quickly it evolves every day. Along with the pressure to buy new digital technology that is constantly updated, there are many other forms of technostress, such as issues with privacy invasion, shaky digital security, challenges using complicated digital devices, and pressure to replace new digital devices as a result of these updates. Therefore, the study conducted by (Ragu-Nathan et al., 2008; Tarafdar et al., 2014) revealed the intention to use fintech services is adversely correlated with four sub-dimensions of technostress: complexity, overload, invasion, and uncertainty.

Digital money that is issued by a central bank is known as central bank digital currency (CBDC). CBDCs are convertible into fiat money at a rate of one-to-one with cash or other forms of fiat money (Bolt et al., 2022; Bordo, 2021; Chaum et al., 2021). Although a CBDC would be guaranteed by central banks (as is the case for physical currency) and allow holders to store value and make payments online, other characteristics are still up for debate. Design considerations include whether the digital currency would be used for retail or wholesale transactions, the level of anonymity provided to users, whether it would pay interest, and whether the digital currency would be a digital representation of the current legal tender or a different parallel legal tender. A CBDC may be successful without the use of elements seen in private digital currencies, such as decentralized ledgers and blockchain. An existing system could be used to build a CBDC instead, but that would probably need a substantial investment in IT over several years. CBDCs could be mildly different from the current financial system, where banks hold value and make payments digitally from accounts kept at the Fed, depending on the proposals' treatment of key design elements. Proposals that permit nonbank firms or individuals to have digital access to funds directly from the Fed and, in some situations, open digital accounts at the Fed, differ fundamentally from the current system (Labonte et al., 2020).

According to the Bank of Canada, security and usability must be traded off throughout the creation of a CBDC. The risk of losing access to private keys or forgetting wallet passwords exists in the case of token-based CBDC since the currency is linked to these keys. When creating these systems, there must be thought-out decisions and concise rules (Kahn & Rivadeneyra, 2020). A secure and reliable third party is the inevitable result of a completely centralized system (Schilling, 2019). To safeguard user privacy and the network from targeted assaults, a CBDC will need to collect and handle user data with care. Overall, there appear to be too many hazards and security issues, but it is difficult to calculate the actual costs or risks. According to (Riksbank Sveriges, 2023), additional testing and study will be required for the pilot project in order to adequately evaluate security concerns because the function of conducting offline transactions will present some dangers.

DIGITAL INVESTMENT AND ITS GROWTH

In 2023, Digital Investment will be the largest market with an AUM of US$112,90 billion. In 2023, it is anticipated that the average AUM per user in the digital investment market will be USD 439.80. In 2024, the market for digital assets is anticipated to rise in terms of revenue by 33.6%. Users are anticipated to reach 5.48 billion in the digital payments market by 2027. The market for digital investments is expected to have a total AUM of $112.90 billion by 2023. The unique traits of KPIs in the FinTech industry make it impossible to combine and show them as a single number that represents the whole FinTech sector (*FinTech - Worldwide | Statista Market Forecast*, 2023). Peer-to-peer (P2P) lending over the Internet has a 2013 value of $3.5 billion and is anticipated to grow to $1 trillion by 2025 (*Value of Global P2P Loans 2012-2025*, 2015). According to the research 2022 Financial Services Global industry, the industry would increase at a compound yearly growth rate of 9.6% to

$37,343 billion in 2026 (*Financial Services Global Market Report 2023*, 2023). By 2030, it is predicted that the fintech sector, which presently accounts for about 2% of global financial services income, will generate $1.5 trillion in revenue annually, or over 25% of all global banking valuations. The greatest market is anticipated to be Asia-Pacific (APAC), particularly emerging Asia (China, India, and Southeast Asia), where fintech will assist in extending financial inclusion and account for 42% of all additional revenues (Marshall, 2023). In 2023, it is anticipated that the market for digital assets will generate US$56,420.00m, and by 2027, revenue is predicted to grow by 16.15% year (CAGR 2023–2027), reaching a total estimated value of US$102,700.00m. According to a global comparison, the United States will have the largest revenue in 2023 (US$27,410.00m). By 2027, it is anticipated that there will be 994.30 million users in the market for digital assets. In 2023, there will be 8.8% of users, and by 2027, 12.5% of users are anticipated (*Digital Assets Worldwide*, 2023). Blockchain is a decentralized digital ledger system that permits direct, direct, and secure transactions between two parties. The most well-known application of blockchain technology is cryptocurrency, which has drawn significant interest due to its differences from conventional money. Furthermore, a few banking institutions have begun experimenting with Central Bank Digital Currencies (CBDC) as a result of Web 3.0's growing popularity. Mass adoption has not yet occurred for notable examples like the Sand Dollar (by the Central Bank of The Bahamas) and the Digital Yuan (by the Central Bank of China) (Bzo, 2023).

The growing interest in digital assets that were privately produced suggests that central banks, which currently serve as the only source of money in sovereign countries, may face competition. A significant portion of people worldwide are active in trading, transacting, or holding digital assets, according to several recent sources, with rates in emerging nations being especially high. For instance, 10% of UK residents said they currently own or have ever owned a cryptocurrency (Fearn & Saunders, 2022). In six significant EU countries, the European Central Bank (ECB) reported that up to 10% of households possessed digital assets. (Cukierman, 2019)makes the case that, in order for central banks to maintain the efficiency of monetary policy in a world that is becoming more and more saturated with private digital currencies, central banks will need to issue their own digital currencies. (Bordo & Levin, 2017), look into how a CBDC may make monetary policy more transparent. They demonstrate that CBDC can only become a free medium of exchange, a safe haven for value, and a reliable unit of account if they are account-based and interest-bearing digital currencies issued by central banks. Although central banks want to issue a CBDC, (Boar et al., 2020) demonstrate that they will need to work together with other central banks to better assess the impact of private digital tokens for CBDC payments. The implementation of CBDC creates an unsolvable CBDC trilemma for central banks, which are the aims of efficiency, financial stability, and price stability, as demonstrated by (Fernández-Villaverde et al., 2020) . They contend that CBDC only permits the simultaneous achievement of two central bank objectives. Furthermore, according to (Bjerg, 2017), only two of the following three policy goals can be simultaneously pursued in a monetary system with two competing money creators—the central bank and the commercial banking industry—free convertibility between CBDC and bank money, parity between CBDC and bank money, and central bank monetary sovereignty. According to (Ozili, 2022), while most central banks are researching CBDC, very few are currently using them as pilot projects. Even fewer central banks consider the creation of a CBDC as a short- or medium-term objective.

(D. K. C. Lee et al., 2021) Central banks that adopt CBDCs will have to decide between using distributed ledger technology or the current central bank infrastructure as the CBDC's foundation. It is further demonstrated that the countries with a competitive advantage will be those with greater knowledge of distributed ledger technology. If a CBDC were to become an official method of payment, as (Bossu et al., 2020) speculate, then existing laws would need to be continuously reviewed in order to support them and updated anytime global dynamics changed the CBDC environment. Further analysis reveals that account-based and token-based CBDC are two distinct categories of currency and that the legal status of each will rely on the particular features of its design (Auer et al., 2020). CBDC is a central bank liability that has been disguised as a digital token and distributed to consumers. According to research, more central banks are offering retail CBDC structures where the CBDC is a direct cash-like claim on the central bank. (Engert & Fung, 2017)claim that the effect of central bank digital currency (CBDC) issuance on the contestability of retail payments is dependent on the CBDC's special features and may not be a very strong rationale.

DIGITAL DETOX

The expanding use of information technology (IT) has a significant impact on all aspects of society, including the nature and boundaries of the workplace. The majority of working hours are spent on digital devices by individual professionals, and knowledge workers in particular, and a record number of people spend their free time using applications for digital entertainment and persuasively designed social media (Orlikowski et al., 2016).

As per (Lohmeier, 2023) 33.1 million Germans use the Internet "multiple times a day," and 11 million of them even claim to use it "constantly, almost the entire time". In the past ten years, there has been an increase in the number of internet users in Germany. We have counted almost 67 million people in 2022 so far. This is

29

a big change from 49 million in 2010. Research unmistakably shows that excessive screen time might have negative effects on a person's wellness (Pflügner et al., 2021). The COVID-19 pandemic has exacerbated changes in work-life boundaries, making technostress a major social concern (Thomas et al., 2020). The inability to turn off gadgets beyond regular working hours has a negative impact on employee well-being, according to 86 percent of participants in a 2019 study (Stewart, 2021) . As a result, people experience a sense of being overloaded by communication content and interpersonal interactions online, which has a negative impact on both their personal and professional lives (Gui & Büchi, 2021).

Social media are interactive technologies that enable the creation and sharing of information, ideas, hobbies, and other kinds of expression throughout digital environments (Obar & Wildman, 2015). Having developed digital devices, especially the iPhone and other similar gadgets with large screens, social media has given rise to a new way of studying, working, interacting, and socializing (Ahmed et al., 2019). The number of smartphone owners has increased significantly since 2016, when there were only 3.668 billion users, accounting for 49.40 percent of the population at the time. Following the number of smartphone owners, 4.48 billion people are currently using social media, with an average time spent on social media of around 2 hours and 24 minutes per day (Dixon, 2021). Global mobile user numbers were 7.1 billion in 2021, and predictions indicate that this number will likely increase to 7.26 billion by 2022. Global mobile usage is anticipated to reach 7.49 billion people in 2025 (*Number of Global Mobile Users since 2010*, 2023). In 2023, Statista estimates that there will be 6.92 billion smartphone users worldwide, which means that 85.95% of people will be smartphone owners. This number is significantly more than it was in 2016 when there were just 3.668 billion users or 49.40% of the world's population (*HOW MANY SMARTPHONES ARE IN THE WORLD?*, 2023).

The idea of "digital detox" has lately entered popular culture and Information Systems (IS) studies as a strategy to combat technostress and its detrimental effects on personal welfare and productivity (Mirbabaie et al., 2022). According to (Syvertsen & Enli, 2019),"digital detox" refers to tactics that assist users in engaging with technology less frequently as well as occasional disconnections from it.

A purposeful and brief hiatus from using digital gadgets and online platforms is called a "digital detox." To lessen how detrimental technology is to our mental and physical health, it includes cutting ourselves apart from screens, social media, and digital communication channels. There are several reasons to engage in digital detox, including: reducing screen time, mental health, productivity, etc. However, spending time outside, reading actual books, having in-person discussions, and practicing mindfulness are all examples of things that can be included in a digital detox. It gives people back control over their digital behaviors and helps them strike a better balance between the virtual and real worlds. A "period during which a person refrains from using their electronic devices, such as smartphones, considered to be an opportunity to reduce stress or focus on social interaction in the physical world" is referred to as a "digital detox." (*Oxford Reference*, 2013).

Digital detox interventions exert some promising effects on usage itself and depression symptoms. However, the inconsistent findings regarding other outcomes across all scented studies prevent making a recommendation as to whether to promote or discard digital detox interventions, as positive and counterproductive consequences need to be examined more clearly. Thus, it is recommended that more investment in empirical high-quality research be implemented to understand under which circumstances digital detox is helpful and for whom. Thus, potential moderating and mediating variables need to be examined in the future – including the duration of the digital detox period, the level of smartphone addiction, or the level of technology-related stress – before the utility of digital detox interventions can be determined adequately (Radtke et al., 2022).

CONCLUSION

CBDCs are a potentially substantial source of financial innovation that could alter the socioeconomic landscape by lowering transaction costs and streamlining payment systems. The industry's dedication to using technology for better financial services is demonstrated by the incorporation of distributed ledger and blockchain technologies in CBDC development. Additionally, it can make it easier for marginalized communities to obtain financial services, speed up international trade, and increase the openness of monetary policy. They do, however, also bring up issues like data privacy, the digital gap, and the potential for further surveillance. The necessity of a digital detox is a key topic of conversation. There is a chance that people will become even more digitally dependent as CBDCs are integrated more deeply into our daily lives. For mental health, it's critical to strike a balance between the advantages of CBDCs and the necessity of occasionally unplugging from technology. Strong legal frameworks and security safeguards are needed for the creation and execution of CBDCs. Central banks and governments must prioritize ensuring the security of digital currency transactions, safeguarding user data, and avoiding cyberattacks. The financial environment may change as a result of CBDCs. They have the potential to undermine the hegemony of conventional currencies, alter the function of global financial institutions, and affect geopolitical dynamics. The management of this shift requires synchronized actions and international coordination. Therefore, their implementation should be handled carefully, taking privacy, security, and digital reliance into account.

REFERENCES

Agarwal, S., & Zhang, J. (2020). FinTech, Lending and Payment Innovation: A Review. *Asia-Pacific Journal of Financial Studies*, *49*(3), 353–367. doi:10.1111/ajfs.12294

Ahmed, Y. A., Ahmad, M. N., Ahmad, N., & Zakaria, N. H. (2019). Social media for knowledge-sharing: A systematic literature review. *Telematics and Informatics*, *37*, 72–112. doi:10.1016/j.tele.2018.01.015

Auer, R., Cornelli, G., & Frost, J. (2020). *Rise of the central bank digital currencies: drivers, approaches and technologies* (880). BIS. https://www.bis.org/publ/work880.pdf

Bjerg, O. (2017). Designing New Money - The Policy Trilemma of Central Bank Digital Currency. SSRN *Electronic Journal*. https://doi.org/ doi:10.2139/SSRN.2985381

Boar, C., Holden, H., & Wadsworth, A. (2020). Impending arrival – a sequel to the survey on central bank digital currency. *BIS Papers*. www.bis.org

Bolt, W., Lubbersen, V., & Wierts, P. (2022). *GETTING THE BALANCE RIGHT: Crypto, stablecoin and CBDC* (736). https://www.dnb.nl/media/jo3h1dlu/working_paper_no-_736.pdf

Bordo, M. D. (2021). *Central Bank Digital Currency In Historical Perspective: Another Crossroad In Monetary History* (29171). NBER. https://www.nber.org/system/files/working_papers/w29171/w29171.pdf

Bordo, M. D., & Levin, A. T. (2017). Central Bank Digital Currency and the Future of Monetary Policy. In *National Bureau of Economic Research Working Paper Series* (23711). NBER. doi:10.3386/w23711

Bossu, W., Itatani, M., Margulis, C., Rossi, A., Weenink, H., & Yoshinaga, A. (2020). Legal Aspects of Central Bank Digital Currency: Central Bank and Monetary Law Considerations. SSRN *Electronic Journal*. https://papers.ssrn.com/sol3/papers.cfm?abstract_id=3758088 doi:10.5089/9781513561622.001

Bzo, I. (2023). *Fintech trends worth following in 2023 and beyond*. Fintech Nexus. https://www.fintechnexus.com/fintech-trends-worth-following-in-2023-and-beyond/

Chaum, D., Grothoff, C., & Moser, T. (2021). How to Issue a Central Bank Digital Currency. *Ideas*. https://ideas.repec.org/p/arx/papers/2103.00254.html

Cukierman, A. (2019). Welfare and Political Economy Aspects of a Central Bank Digital Currency. *Federal Reserve Bank of Dallas, Globalization Institute Working Papers, 2019*(355). Reserve Bank of Dallas. doi:10.24149/gwp355

Digital Assets Worldwide. (2023). Statista. https://www.statista.com/outlook/dmo/fintech/digital-assets/worldwide#revenue

Dixon, S. J. (2021). *Number of worldwide social network users 2027*. Statista. https://www.statista.com/statistics/278414/number-of-worldwide-social-network-users/

EngertW.FungB. S. C. (2017). *Central Bank Digital Currency: Motivations and Implications*. Bank of Canada. doi:10.34989/SDP-2017-16

Fearn, A., & Saunders, C. (2022). *Individuals holding cryptoassets: uptake and understanding*. Skadden. https://www.skadden.com/-/media/files/publications/2022/09/cryptoasset-seizures-and-forfeitures/individuals_holding_cryptoassets_uptake_and_understanding.pdf

Fernández-Villaverde, J., Schilling, L., & Uhlig, H. (2020). Central Bank Digital Currency: When Price and Bank Stability Collide. SSRN *Electronic Journal*. https://papers.ssrn.com/sol3/papers.cfm?abstract_id=3753955 doi:10.2139/ssrn.3606226

Financial Services Global Market Report 2023. (2023). Report Linker. https://www.reportlinker.com/p06277918/Financial-Services-Global-Market-Report.html?utm_source=GNW

FinTech – Worldwide, Statista Market Forecast. (2023). Statista. https://www.statista.com/outlook/dmo/fintech/worldwide

Gui, M., & Büchi, M. (2021). From Use to Overuse: Digital Inequality in the Age of Communication Abundance. *Social Science Computer Review*, *39*(1), 3–19. doi:10.1177/0894439319851163

HOW MANY SMARTPHONES ARE IN THE WORLD? (2023). Bank My Cell.Com. https://www.bankmycell.com/blog/how-many-phones-are-in-the-world#:~:text=How

Kahn, C., & Rivadeneyra, F. (2020). *Security and convenience of a central bank digital currency*. Publications. https://publications.gc.ca/collections/collection_2020/banque-bank-canada/FB3-7-2020-21-eng.pdf

Labonte, M., Nelson, R. M., & Perkins, D. W. (2020). *Financial Innovation: Central Bank Digital Currencies*. Every CRS Report. https://www.everycrsreport.com/files/2020-03-20_IF11471_deb83c3c9793651d65de8303485538b6f979962e.pdf

Lee, D. K. C., Yan, L., & Wang, Y. (2021). A global perspective on central bank digital currency. *China Economic Journal, 14*(1), 52–66. doi:10.1080/17538963. 2020.1870279

Lee, I., & Shin, Y. J. (2018). Fintech: Ecosystem, business models, investment decisions, and challenges. *Business Horizons, 61*(1), 35–46. doi:10.1016/j. bushor.2017.09.003

Li, B., & Xu, Z. (2021). Insights into financial technology (FinTech): A bibliometric and visual study. *Financial Innovation, 7*(1), 1–28. doi:10.118640854-021-00285-7 PMID:35024290

Lohmeier, L. (2023). *Statistics on internet usage in Germany.* Statista. https:// de.statista.com/themen/2033/internetnutzung-in-deutschland/#topicOverview

Marshall, A. (2023). *Global Fintech 2023: Reimagining the Future of Finance.* QED Investors. https://www.qedinvestors.com/blog/global-fintech-2023-reimagining-the-future-of-finance

Mirbabaie, M., Stieglitz, S., & Marx, J. (2022). Digital Detox. *Business & Information Systems Engineering, 64*(2), 239–246. doi:10.100712599-022-00747-x

Number of global mobile users since 2010. (2023). Statista. https://www.statista.com/ statistics/218984/number-of-global-mobile-users-since-2010/#statisticContainer

Obar, J. A., & Wildman, S. (2015). Social media definition and the governance challenge: An introduction to the special issue. *Telecommunications Policy, 39*(9), 745–750. doi:10.1016/j.telpol.2015.07.014

Orlikowski, W. J., Scott, S. V., & Elgar, E. (2016). MIT Open Access Articles Digital Work: A Research Agenda DIGITAL WORK: A RESEARCH AGENDA. *A Research Agenda for Management and Organization Studies,* 88–96. https://dspace. mit.edu/bitstream/handle/1721.1/108411/Digital

Ozili, P. K. (2022). Central bank digital currency research around the world: a review of literature. *Journal of Money Laundering Control.* https://doi.org/https:// doi.org/10.1108/JMLC-11-2021-0126

Pflügner, K., Maier, C., Mattke, J., & Weitzel, T. (2021). Personality Profiles that Put Users at Risk of Perceiving Technostress: A Qualitative Comparative Analysis with the Big Five Personality Traits. *Business & Information Systems Engineering, 63*(4), 389–402. doi:10.100712599-020-00668-7

Radtke, T., Apel, T., Schenkel, K., Keller, J., & Von Lindern, E. (2022). Digital detox: An effective solution in the smartphone era? A systematic literature review. *Mobile Media & Communication, 10*(2), 190–215. doi:10.1177/20501579211028647

Ragu-Nathan, T. S., Tarafdar, M., Ragu-Nathan, B. S., & Tu, Q. (2008). The Consequences of Technostress for End Users in Organizations: Conceptual Development and Empirical Validation. *Information Systems Research, 19*(4), 417–433. doi:10.1287/isre.1070.0165

Riksbank Sveriges. (2023). *E-krona report E-krona pilot, phase 3*. Risbank. https://www.riksbank.se/globalassets/media/rapporter/e-krona/2023/e-krona-pilot-phase-3.pdf

Schilling, L. (2019). Risks Involved with CBDCs: On Cash, Privacy, and Information Centralization. SSRN *Electronic Journal*. doi:10.2139/ssrn.3479035

Stewart, C. (2021). *Negative effect of tech on employee's well-being in the UK 2019 | Statista*. Statista. https://www.statista.com/statistics/1134262/negative-effect-of-tech-on-employee-s-well-being-in-the-uk/

Suryono, R. R., Budi, I., & Purwandari, B. (2020). Challenges and Trends of Financial Technology (Fintech): A Systematic Literature Review. *Information, 11*(12), 590. doi:10.3390/info11120590

Syvertsen, T., & Enli, G. (2019). Digital detox: Media resistance and the promise of authenticity. *Convergence (London), 26*(5–6), 1269–1283. doi:10.1177/1354856519847325

Tarafdar, M., Tu, Q., Ragu-Nathan, B. S., & Ragu-Nathan, T. S. (2014). The Impact of Technostress on Role Stress and Productivity. *Journal of Management Information Systems, 24*(1), 301–328. doi:10.2753/MIS0742-1222240109

Thomas, O., Hagen, S., Frank, U., Recker, J., Wessel, L., Kammler, F., Zarvic, N., & Timm, I. (2020). Global Crises and the Role of BISE. *Business & Information Systems Engineering, 62*(4), 385–396. doi:10.100712599-020-00657-w

Value of global P2P loans 2012-2025. (2015). Statista. https://www.statista.com/statistics/325902/global-p2p-lending/

Wang, Y., Xiuping, S., & Zhang, Q. (2021). Can fintech improve the efficiency of commercial banks?—An analysis based on big data. *Research in International Business and Finance, 55*, 101338. doi:10.1016/j.ribaf.2020.101338

Chapter 4

Cognitive Unburdening:
Investigating the Mediated Pathway From Digital Detox to Psychological Well Being Through Reduced Cognitive Load

Balraj Verma
Chitkara University, India

Niti Chatterji
Chitkara University, India

ABSTRACT

This study examines the impact of digital detoxification on the psychological well-being of Generation Z in North India. Using structured questionnaires, data was collected from individuals aged 11 to 26. The measurement model's validity and reliability were confirmed using confirmatory factor analysis. Also, the mediation analysis was performed using the SPSS macro PROCESS by Hayes. The study confirms that digital detoxification positively influences well-being, mediated by reduced cognitive overload. Findings highlight the need for mindful technology use and periodic disconnection to enhance mental health. This research contributes insights into the complex interplay of digital detox, cognitive load, and well-being, offering implications for promoting healthier digital habits and improved psychological health.

INTRODUCTION

The world has become more connected than ever. People across the globe are increasingly using digital tools, not just at their workplace but also in general whether

DOI: 10.4018/979-8-3693-1107-3.ch004

it is home or any other place. This has been further accentuated by the digital shift created by the COVID-19 pandemic. The event has been a black swan event that has disrupted people's lives in more than many ways one can think of. Due to the constraints imposed by the lockdowns and social distancing work from home has become the new normal and people are relying more and more on digital tools, online platforms, and other text-based communication tools. These are becoming increasing substitutes for face-to-face and personal interactions. The general conversation is becoming more focused on overuse as a negative consequence of digital communication. The idea of consumers' perceived digital overuse (PDO), which is a pervasive social phenomenon sensitive to current inequities is increasingly being spoken about (Gui & Buchi, 2021). The construct of perceived digital overuse was investigated in this study. From a representative sample of Italian internet users, the results revealed that digital communication use and the level of social pressure to function digitally are positively related to perceived digital overuse. Authors also believe that use of digital technologies, on one hand, has led to increased flexibility in terms of time, place, and device (Shepherd-Banigan et al.,2015) while on the other, this is also resulting in increased stress and overload due to the exacerbated bombardment of information and heightened use of digital tools to manage work (Karr-Wisniewski & Lu, 2010). As a result, people are beginning to realize that more and more use of digital tools is leading to a dip in productivity instead of enhancing it. Similar thoughts were expressed in many other studies (Bawden & Robinson, 2009; Becker et al., 2013) where media multitasking was brought out as a unique predictor of anxiety and depression. People who work remotely and have few leisure activities to choose from when they're feeling lonely are more likely to abuse technology. Its effects can include everything from problems with technology addiction to mental health impairment. "Digital detoxing," a technique that advocates purposefully limiting technology use to lower digital participation and physiological stress, has gained popularity thanks to a conforming countermovement (Mirbabaie et al.,2020).

A highly significant assessment regarding the state of global health and healthcare, as well as an analysis of the current state of play in the industry, was released in January 2023. Widening global health disparities, digital innovation, artificial intelligence, and connectivity, worsening mental health and well-being of carers, carer shortages, and carer burnout were identified as burning trends/issues in global healthcare, according to the report (Global Health and Healthcare Strategic Outlook: Shaping the Future of Health and Healthcare, World Economic Forum, 2023). It was revealed that COVID-19 came with severe challenges that people already faced—such as burnout and issues with mental health and wellbeing—even more severe. There is still a risk even with initiatives to enhance working conditions in the healthcare industry, such as the WHO and ILO guidance on developing and implementing better occupational health programmes for health professionals.

As a result of burnout and other health-related issues, this may cause professional attrition and reduced recruiting. But this phenomenon does not only confine itself to a particular industry. People in general are also victims of digital bombardment.

Because of the reasons mentioned above, concepts like digital detoxification and digital minimalism are being studied extensively by researchers (Newport, 2019; Syvertsen & Enli, 2019). A major chunk of the workday of an average employee is consumed by interruptions due to the use of technology. Ironically, while companies continue to invest heavily in technology-based processes, business intelligence, and decision support systems, employees are resorting to low-tech methods and ways to regain their lost productivity. This clearly indicates that enhanced usage of digital and technology-based tools may not serve the purpose of increasing productivity; rather it can be counterproductive (Karr-Wisniewski & Lu, 2010). In social science and psychological research, this phenomenon has been termed as cognitive load or cognitive overload (Jiang et al., 2020; Sweller, 1994). Researchers have termed this concept as technology overload.

The domain of technology overload stemmed from the concept of the "Productivity ParPWBx" which was first talked about in the decades of 1980s (Dendrick et al., 2003) when no significant relationship was found between investment in technology infrastructure and productivity. The concept was specifically applicable to white-collar employees and knowledge workers who are mostly engaged in generating, processing, and distributing information. Based on the law of diminishing marginal returns, it was expected that once the use of technology exceeds the optimum levels, it can actually incur negative outcomes. The concept of technology overload can be further related to the phenomena of cognitive overload which posits that productivity may be hurt by system feature overload when a certain technology is unnecessarily complicated for a given job (Sweller, 1988). This means that adding features to technology gives returns in the form of enhanced productivity only up to a certain optimum level (Hsi & Potts, 2000).

The present paper tried to study the impact of digital detoxification on the psychological well-being of Generation Z who is the worst affected demographic group as far as technology and cognitive overload are concerned. The study proposes that reduced cognitive overload acts as a mediator in the relationship between digital detoxification and psychological well-being.

THEORETICAL BACKGROUND AND REVIEW OF LITERATURE

Digital Detoxification

Though a new concept, the usage of the term digital detox has increased rapidly. In 2013 the term was included in the Oxford dictionary (Syvertsen & Enli, 2019).

Drawing on the analysis of several texts propagating digital detoxification like memoirs, literature on self-help and company websites, the research discusses how the problems with digital media are defined and also recommends strategies to cope up with those problems. While it is impossible for people to eliminate the conditions that create cognitive overload, there can certainly be some strategies that can help them cope with the pressures created by cognitive overload and its negative repercussions. Moreover, it is important to indulge in such methods of detoxification because the absence of this can have severe consequences for employees and organizations (De Jonge et al., 2012). As mentioned in the earlier section, in order to deal with the negative outcomes of cognitive overload, digital minimalism and digital detoxification concepts are receiving a lot of attention from researchers (Radtke et al., 2021). It has been explained as a periodic disconnection from digital and online tools with the objective of reducing one's involvement with them. Digital detox is a phenomenon that promises authenticity since it offers ways to counter the inauthenticity that comes with online interaction, digital communication, and artificial intelligence-based processes (Karlsen & Syvertsen, 2016; Syvertsen & Enli, 2019).

The idea is to take a break from digital media, tools, and devices and have a positive effect on outcomes like social relationships and well-being by focusing on the real physical world. Researchers have pointed to the fact that switching off notifications, turning off smart devices after a point of time in the evening, and answering e-mails at a certain predetermined time during the day improves the quality of sleep and productivity for the next day (Lanaj et al., 2014; Schmuck,2020) while there are thoughts that are on a different line (Przybylski et al., 2021). But a strong line of research regarding digital detox comes on the premise that online and digital communication is less true as compared to offline communication and co-presence in physical space is immensely important for a genuine conversation to happen. It also suggests that online communication portrays a less-than-healthy body image. Hence research recommends a reduction in the extent of social media and online communication and rather engaging in physical, in-person, and trustworthy communication with people around (Abeele et al.,2022; Baumer et al., 2013; Portwood-Stacer, 2012; Tandon et al., 2022; Woodstock, 2013). This supports the concept of digital detox tourism that celebrates temporary disconnection from the virtual world to experience an authentic world (Staheli & Stoltenberg, 2022). Further, authors (Mirbabaie et al.,2020) tried to take cognizance of the effects of digital overuse and provide empirical evidence by taking a middle path between digital overuse and perceived social connectedness. The study proposed that completely obliterating the use of digital media was not possible in today's times but there can be a sweet spot between digital overuse and perceived social connectedness. Hence, authors proposed a mixed-method design to investigate the influence of digital detox measures with the hope that the results of the study would help to understand better how the effects of digital overuse can be mitigated by remote employees and how can organizations contribute to this process. These researchers further extended their work and proposed that the interdependencies of knowledge work arrangements and the technostress that comes along with such work make a strong ground for research exploring the concept of digital detox (Mirbabaie et al.,2022). The authors also concluded that additional theorizing is important to understand, predict, and explain behavior related to digital detoxification at workplaces. This gives further support to the present study.

Reduced Cognitive Overload

From a psychological context, the state of being overloaded in which input in the form of information exceeds one's processing capabilities is called cognitive overload (Eppler & Mengis, 2004). While many researchers have addressed this phenomenon as information overload (Edmunds & Morris, 2000; Grise & Gallupe, 1999; Nelson, 1994), in psychological and social science research the terminology of cognitive overload or cognitive load has been popularly used (Jiang et al.,2020; Sweller,1994; Vollmann, 1991). An important study (Kirsh, 2000) was conducted to address questions like what causes cognitive overload at workplaces, how to understand how employees interact with their work environment and how can environments be restructured to reduce the cognitive burden on employees. As far as the first question was concerned, it was found that information bombardment, constant interruption, multitasking, and inadequate infrastructure at the workplace to help reduce the need for processing too much information are some of the major factors that contribute to cognitive overload among employees. Many times learners can get overwhelmed by the quantity of information that is required to be processed and the psychological repercussions of being confronted with such humungous information can lead to something called a cognitive overload. Research has shown that the factors that determine cognitive overload are individual, and technological/situational (Eppler & Mengis, 2004; Schmitt et al., 2017; Tarafdar et al., 2010). Individual factors include cognitions, frustrations, and technical skills while technological/situational factors comprise timeline, technical support, and task difficulty. An important study on cognitive overload and its impact on psychological well-being concluded that social and information overload indirectly impacts the psychological well-being of employees through social network service addiction (Choi & Lim, 2016). The present study builds on this study and tries to explore the impact of digital detoxification on psychological well-being where cognitive overload acts as the mediator. Unlike the above-mentioned study, the present study targets Generation Z since members of this demographic group are much more technology-dependent and technology savvy, and spend the maximum chunk of their day glued to digital devices and tools.

The present study takes the social and technological factors of cognitive overload as was also suggested by Choi and Lim (2016). By including both elements the study covers both social overload and technology overload as part of cognitive overload.

Psychological Well Being

Well being due to technostress has been investigated in case of white collar workers (Pflugner et al., 2020) and brought out the significance of practising mindfulness at workplaces. Applying the transactional model of stress and the model of mindfulness, it was found that mindfulness reduces the perception of techno-stressors and helps mitigate the impact of techno stress on job burnout. Too much information to handle exaggerated by multiple channels available for communication has resulted in the concept of information overload. Other consequences that researchers have brought out have been termed infobesity, information avoidance, and information anxiety (Bawden & Robinson, 2009). The outcome of all these processes tends to manifest itself in the psychological well-being, emotional stability, and overall mental health of people. In psychology, well-being refers to the concept of optimal experience. It can be referred to an individual's full functionality (Choi & Lim, 2016). It can be said to be a pursuit of perfection that reflects the true potential of an individual. It focusses on a positive relation with people around, meaningfulness in life and personal growth. But feeling bombarded by the use of digital tools can lead to inefficient processing of information, confusion, control loss and impact the overall psychological well being of an individual. This may even extend to increased depressive symptoms. Studies have shown that cognitive overload due to overwhelming digital involvement contributes negatively towards job productivity (Eppler & Mengis, 2004; Schmuck, 2020). An important study demonstrated how being digitally literate in the age of social media requires a trade-off between retrieving and processing information and coping up with the overload, uncertainty, and invasion (Bucher et al.,2013). Authors, through the study, tried to bring out the stress potential of social media thus supporting the conclusions of the other studies mentioned above. The present study takes forward the study by exploring the impact of digital detoxification on an individual's psychological well-being. Based on the aforementioned material, the following hypothesis has been made:

H_1: Digital detoxification has a positive effect on psychological well-being.

H_2: The effect of Digital detoxification on psychological well-being is mediated by reduced cognitive overload.

Figure 1. Conceptual framework

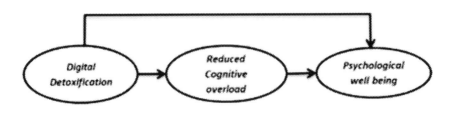

METHODOLOGY

Research Design

This research adopted a quantitative approach, focusing on the Gen-Z demographic in North India. The unit of analysis comprised individuals aged between 11 and 26 years, and data collection was facilitated through structured questionnaires based on a pre-established measurement scale. Utilizing a cross-sectional methodology, this study explored the impact of digital detoxification on the psychological well-being of Gen-Z. Additionally, it sought to discern the potential influence of reduced cognitive overload on the psychological well-being of this demographic.

Data Collection

Structured questionnaires were employed as the primary data collection method. In particular, the study embraced purposive sampling methods to meticulously select participants who met specific conditions relevant to the research subject or the characteristics of the population under investigation (Bryman, 2016, p. 251). The researcher applied a convenience sampling technique for data collection, utilizing Google Forms as the medium for questionnaire delivery.

A total of 426 individuals responded to the questionnaire; after meticulous validation to rectify missing or incomplete entries, 389 completed questionnaires emerged as eligible for analysis. Notably, 37 surveys were excluded due to incompleteness, rendering them unsuitable for further investigation. Before dissemination, the questionnaires underwent thorough scrutiny by professionals and academicians, whose constructive feedback was thoughtfully addressed, thereby fortifying the validity of the study instruments. Notably, these experts were provided with comprehensive insight into the study's objectives and scope before their evaluation.

The questionnaires employed in this study are bifurcated into two sections. The initial segment, Section 1, encompasses demographic factors such as age and education, while Section 2 delves into items instrumental for constructing the study's framework.

Variable's Measurement

The variables in this study were derived from an existing and previously established scale. To ensure the robustness of our measures, a pilot test was conducted using questionnaires to assess validity, reliability, and accuracy. Each item was evaluated on a 5-point Likert scale, where "strongly agree" was assigned a value of 1 and "strongly disagree" was assigned a value of 5. Further elaboration on the measurements of the variables is provided below.

Digital Detoxification

For the measurement of Digital detoxification, we used standardized scale adapted from (SARITEPECİ, 2021).

Reduced Cognitive Overload

Our study used scales for the measurement of leader's reduced cognitive overload, which was adapted from (Ouwehand, et al., 2021)

Psychological Well-Being

The Psychological well-being is measured through adapted from (Czyżowska & Gurba, 2022).

Quality Checks

Several preliminary checks were conducted before the final analysis. To examine non-response bias, a comparison was made between early respondents (n=50) and late respondents (n=50) for mean differences. The results revealed no significant difference between the two groups, indicating the absence of such bias. Subsequently, the final sample size of 389 participants was employed for in-depth investigation.

Moreover, concerns regarding Common Method Bias (CMB) were addressed. The variance attributed to a single factor of CMB was merely 22.64%, falling below the established threshold. This finding definitively rules out the potential influence of CMB on the outcomes.

DATA ANALYSIS

Sample Statistics

Table 1 presents an overview of the survey participants' demographics. Male respondents accounted for 61.95% of the sample, while female participants constituted 38.05%. The age bracket most prominently represented was 16 to 20 years, encompassing 38.3% of the respondents. Additionally, the average daily mobile phone usage hours among Gen-Z individuals are provided in both percentage and frequency distributions. Notably, the data reveal that 36.50% of respondents dedicate 3 to 4 hours to mobile phone usage, while 24.68% of respondents allocate 7 to 10 hours for the same purpose.

Measurement Model

The measurement model yielded a range of goodness-of-fit values across various indices: chi-square (399) = 1124.99, $p < 0.05$, $\chi2/df = 2.82$, CFI = 0.923, IFI = 0.936, TLI = 0.929, and RMSEA = 0.059. In accordance with Kline's (2005) recommendations, we assessed convergent validity, which revealed that all item loadings for sub-constructs exceeded the suggested threshold of 0.60, spanning from 0.611 to 0.975. Moreover, each scale item exhibited critical ratios surpassing 1.96, further confirming convergent validity. The composite reliabilities (CRs) of the constructs, ranging from 0.793 to 0.906, underscore strong internal consistency.

Table 1. Sample statistics

Demographic Variable	Categories	Frequency	Percentage
Gender	Boy	241	61.95
	Girl	148	38.05
Age (in Years)	11-15	130	33.42
	16-20	149	38.3
	21-26	110	28.28
Avg. no. of hours Gen-Z spend using their Mobile phone each day	Less than1 Hour	16	4.11
	1 - 2 Hours	85	21.85
	3 - 4 Hours	142	36.50
	7 - 10 Hours	96	24.68
	11 - 15 Hours	29	7.46
	16 and more	21	5.40

Source: Authors' Computation

Table 2. Measurement model

		Estimate	S.E.	C.R.	p-value
CPB1	Digital detoxification (Compulsive Behavior)	0.973			
CPB2	Digital detoxification (Compulsive Behavior)	0.872	0.027	38.919	***
CPB3	Digital detoxification (Compulsive Behavior)	0.655	0.04	19.629	***
CPB4	Digital detoxification (Compulsive Behavior)	0.92	0.018	48.913	***
CPB5	Digital detoxification (Compulsive Behavior)	0.648	0.058	12.186	***
CPB6	Digital detoxification (Compulsive Behavior)	0.972	0.055	26.272	***
CPB7	Digital detoxification (Compulsive Behavior)	0.611	0.046	12.996	***
CPB8	Digital detoxification (Compulsive Behavior)	0.963	0.017	43.854	***
EST1	Digital detoxification (Excessive Screen Time)	0.847			
EST2	Digital detoxification (Excessive Screen Time)	0.956	0.058	18.401	***
EST3	Digital detoxification (Excessive Screen Time)	0.869	0.02	42.137	***
EST4	Digital detoxification (Excessive Screen Time)	0.846	0.047	16.509	***
LOC1	Digital detoxification (Loss of Control)	0.917			
LOC2	Digital detoxification (Loss of Control)	0.974	0.015	57.252	***
LOC3	Digital detoxification (Loss of Control)	0.975	0.015	57.626	***
RCL1	Reduced cognitive overload	0.957			
RCL2	Reduced cognitive overload	0.918	0.014	58.12	***
RCL3	Reduced cognitive overload	0.957	0.012	69.872	***
RCL4	Reduced cognitive overload	0.954	0.012	67.746	***
RCL5	Reduced cognitive overload	0.706	0.026	21.585	***
RCL6	Reduced cognitive overload	0.966	0.02	45.236	***
RCL7	Reduced cognitive overload	0.718	0.026	22.234	***
PWB1	Psychological well-being	0.812			
PWB2	Psychological well-being	0.798	0.046	20.64	***
PWB3	Psychological well-being	0.792	0.041	21.259	***
PWB4	Psychological well-being	0.726	0.045	18.084	***
PWB5	Psychological well-being	0.748	0.071	14.586	***
PWB6	Psychological well-being	0.745	0.073	14.554	***

Source: Authors' Calculations

The square root of the Average Variance Extracted (AVE) values, as displayed in Table 3, span from 0.822 to 0.939. Notably, these values surpass the inter-item correlation coefficients, indicating that the constructs do not exhibit high levels of correlation, thus aligning with the principles outlined by Fornell and Larcker

Table 3. Measures' discriminant validity

	CPB	**EST**	**LOC**	**RCL**	**PWB**
CPB	*0.931*				
EST	0.280	*0.939*			
LOC	0.386	0.264	*0.925*		
RCL	0.399	0.207	0.419	*0.822*	
PWB	0.186	0.244	0.333	0.218	*0.854*

Source: Authors' Calculations (Values in bold are the square root of the AVE.)

(1981) as well as Hair et al. (2010) for discriminant validity. Consequently, all prerequisites for establishing discriminant validity have been successfully fulfilled. The measurement model demonstrates robust reliability and validity across its entirety, thereby rendering it well-prepared for subsequent structural testing.

Mediation Test

Unlike the typically employed multistep approach for mediation assessment, this study adopts a more streamlined approach. Specifically, the SPSS macro PROCESS developed by Hayes (2013) is employed, focusing on simple mediation (Model 4). Within this study's framework, the PROCESS macro by Hayes (2013) serves as the analytical tool to unravel the mediation role of the leader's reduced cognitive overload in the intricate interplay between Digital Detoxification and Psychological Well-Being. Mediation has been used in previous studies to study the relationships between service innovations, company reputation, and word of mouth (Manohar et al.,2020).

Simple Mediation Analysis

Employing a straightforward mediation analysis, we delved into the hypothesis that the journey from Digital Detoxification to Psychological Well-Being is facilitated through the intermediary of Leader's Reduced Cognitive Overload. To execute this analysis, we harnessed Hayes' (2013) PROCESS tool, specifically utilizing Model 4.

Table 4 reveals mediation analysis outcomes for hypotheses 1 and 2. DDT significantly influences RCL ($\beta = 0.273$, $p < 0.001$) and PWB ($\beta = 0.221$, $p < 0.001$). RCL significantly affects PWB ($\beta = 0.239$, $p < 0.001$), and DDT maintains its impact on PWB even in the presence of RCL ($\beta = 0.334$, $p < 0.001$). RCL partially mediates DDT's effect on PWB, confirmed by non-zero confidence intervals. Table 5's Sobel test reaffirms mediation with an effect size > 0 and significant p-value,

Table 4. Regression results from simple mediation

Model	Coeff.	se	t	p	LLCI	ULCI	Outcome
constant	2.605	0.27	15.828	0	2.459	3.091	RCL
DDT	0.273	0.147	9.492	0	0.369	0.517	RCL
constant	1.694	0.354	7.355	0	1.382	2.345	PWB
DDT	0.221	0.158	6.27	0	0.295	0.487	PWB
RCL	0.239	0.167	5.654	0	0.296	0.522	PWB
constant	2.549	0.306	13.483	0	2.333	3.105	PWB
DDT	0.334	0.155	9.096	0	0.413	0.594	PWB

Source: Authors' Calculations

Table 5. Sobel test

Effect	se	Z-value	P-value (2-tailed)	Lower bound	Upper bound
0.113	0.021	5.234	0.000	0.046	0.216

Source: Authors' Calculations

solidifying RCL's role as mediator. Hence, H1 and H2 are supported, revealing the intertwined role of digital detox and cognitive load in enhancing well-being.

DISCUSSION AND CONCLUSION

This study has unveiled profound insights into the intricate interplay among digital detoxification, psychological well-being, and the mediating role of cognitive overload. The results compellingly establish the affirmative impact of digital detoxification on psychological well-being. Moreover, these affirmative effects are discernibly linked to the alleviation of cognitive overload, illuminating a potential underlying mechanism that explicates how digital detoxification contributes to the augmentation of mental health.

H1: Digital detoxification has a positive effect on psychological well-being.

The observed salutary influence of digital detoxification on psychological well-being harmonizes seamlessly with the burgeoning body of research that underscores the detrimental effects of excessive digital device usage and online engagement on mental health. Our findings substantively extend this discourse by empirically substantiating that purposeful reduction or temporary disconnection from digital platforms engenders noteworthy enhancements in psychological well-being. The implications of this discovery resonate profoundly, particularly in the context of the ubiquity of digital technology in contemporary society. The capacity to fortify psychological well-being through conscientious digital detoxification underscores the significance of cultivating a mindful relationship with technology, advocating for periodic respites from the digital milieu to reap potential benefits.

H2: The effect of Digital detoxification on psychological well-being is mediated by reduced cognitive overload.

Of particular intrigue in our findings is the pivotal role played by diminished cognitive overload in mediating the association between digital detoxification and psychological well-being. Cognitive overload, typified by an inundation of information and tasks that strain cognitive resources, has been intricately tied to diminished cognitive functioning and heightened stress levels. Our results illuminate that digital detoxification acts as a mechanism that alleviates cognitive overload, thus contributing to the enhancement of psychological well-being.

The nexus between digital detoxification, attenuated cognitive overload, and heightened psychological well-being proffers a compelling rationale for the observed effects. By momentarily distancing oneself from digital devices and online platforms, individuals can potentially curtail the ceaseless deluge of information and notifications. This mitigation of cognitive demands may culminate in enhanced attentional mastery, refined cognitive processing, and reduced stress, ultimately fostering improved emotional regulation, uplifted mood, and an overarching sense of well-being.

Implications and Future Directions

The implications stemming from this study hold relevance for both research pursuits and pragmatic interventions targeted at nurturing psychological well-being within the digital epoch. From a research standpoint, our study accentuates the imperative of delving deeper into the intricate mechanisms underpinning the interplay between digital detoxification, cognitive overload, and psychological well-being. Prospective investigations could delve into the temporal dynamics of these effects, as well as the potential moderators that could sway the potency of these interrelationships.

On a practical note, our findings advocate for individuals aspiring to enrich their psychological well-being to integrate periodic digital detoxification practices into their routines. Educational initiatives and awareness campaigns could be artfully designed to promote conscientious technology utilization and advocate for phases of digital disengagement. In addition, workplaces and academic institutions might contemplate instating policies that endorse respite from digital devices, thereby mitigating cognitive overload and bolstering the mental health of employees and students alike.

In summation, this study extends the frontiers of comprehension surrounding the intricate interplay of digital detoxification, cognitive overload, and psychological well-being. The results lend empirical credence to the notion that intentional disconnection from digital platforms can potentiate augmented mental well-being, facilitated through the mitigation of cognitive overload. As society navigates the ever-evolving digital landscape, these insights possess the potential to shape strategies that engender a more harmonious and balanced rapport with technology, ultimately redounding to the advancement of individual psychological health and overall quality of life.

REFERENCE

Abeele, M. M. V., Halfmann, A., & Lee, E. W. (2022). Drug, demon, or donut? Theorizing the relationship between social media use, digital well-being and digital disconnection. *Current Opinion in Psychology*, *45*, 101295. doi:10.1016/j. copsyc.2021.12.007 PMID:35123383

Baumer, E. P., Adams, P., Khovanskaya, V. D., Liao, T. C., Smith, M. E., Schwanda Sosik, V., & Williams, K. (2013, April). Limiting, leaving, and (re) lapsing: an exploration of facebook non-use practices and experiences. In *Proceedings of the SIGCHI conference on human factors in computing systems* (pp. 3257-3266). ACM. 10.1145/2470654.2466446

Bawden, D., & Robinson, L. (2009). The dark side of information: Overload, anxiety and other paradoxes and pathologies. *Journal of Information Science*, *35*(2), 180–191. doi:10.1177/0165551508095781

Becker, M. W., Alzahabi, R., & Hopwood, C. J. (2013). Media multitasking is associated with symptoms of depression and social anxiety. *Cyberpsychology, Behavior, and Social Networking*, *16*(2), 132–135. doi:10.1089/cyber.2012.0291 PMID:23126438

Bryman, A. (2016). *Social research methods* (5th ed.). Oxford University Press.

Bucher, E., Fieseler, C., & Suphan, A. (2013). The stress potential of social media in the workplace. *Information Communication and Society*, *16*(10), 1639–1667. do i:10.1080/1369118X.2012.710245

Choi, S. B., & Lim, M. S. (2016). Effects of social and technology overload on psychological well-being in young South Korean adults: The mediatory role of social network service addiction. *Computers in Human Behavior*, *61*, 245–254. doi:10.1016/j.chb.2016.03.032

Czyżowska, N., & Gurba, E. (2022). Enhancing meaning in life and psychological well-being among a european cohort of young adults via a gratitude intervention. *Frontiers in Psychology*, *12*, 751081. doi:10.3389/fpsyg.2021.751081 PMID:35058837

De Jonge, J., Spoor, E., Sonnentag, S., Dormann, C., & van den Tooren, M. (2012). "Take a break?!" Off-job recovery, job demands, and job resources as predictors of health, active learning, and creativity. *European Journal of Work and Organizational Psychology*, *21*(3), 321–348. doi:10.1080/1359432X.2011.576009

Dedrick, J., Gurbaxani, V., & Kraemer, K. L. (2003). Information technology and economic performance: A critical review of the empirical evidence. *ACM Computing Surveys*, *35*(1), 1–28. doi:10.1145/641865.641866

Edmunds, A., & Morris, A. (2000). The problem of information overload in business organisations: A review of the literature. *International Journal of Information Management*, *20*(1), 17–28. doi:10.1016/S0268-4012(99)00051-1

Eppler, M. J., & Mengis, J. (2008). The Concept of Information Overload-A Review of Literature from Organization Science, Accounting, Marketing, MIS, and Related Disciplines (2004). *The Information Society: An International Journal*, *20*(5), 271–305.

Fornell, C., & Larcker, D. F. (1981). Evaluating structural equation models with unobservable variables and measurement error. *JMR, Journal of Marketing Research*, *18*(1), 39–50. doi:10.1177/002224378101800104

Grisé, M. L., & Gallupe, R. B. (1999). Information overload: Addressing the productivity paradox in face-to-face electronic meetings. *Journal of Management Information Systems*, *16*(3), 157–185. doi:10.1080/07421222.1999.11518260

Gui, M., & Buchi, M. (2021). From Use to Overuse: Digital Inequality in the Age of Communication Abundance. *Social Science Computer Review*, *39*(1), 3–19. doi:10.1177/0894439319851163

Hair, J. F., Black, W. C., Babin, B. J., Anderson, R. E., & Tatham, R. L. (2010). *Multivariate data analysis* (7th ed.). Prentice Hall.

Hayes, A. F. (2013). *Introduction to mediation, moderation, and conditional process analysis: A regression-based approach*. Guilford Press.

Hsi & Potts. (2000, October). Studying the evolution and enhancement of software features. In *Proceedings 2000 International Conference on Software Maintenance* (pp. 143-151). IEEE.

Jiang, D., Kalyuga, S., & Sweller, J. (2021). Comparing face-to-face and computer-mediated collaboration when teaching EFL writing skills. *Educational Psychology, 41*(1), 5–24. doi:10.1080/01443410.2020.1785399

Karlsen, F., & Syvertsen, T. (2016). You can't smell roses online: Intruding Media and Reverse Domestication. *Nordicom Review, 37*(1), 25–39. doi:10.1515/nor-2016-0021

Karr-Wisniewski, P., & Lu, Y. (2010). When more is too much: Operationalizing technology overload and exploring its impact on knowledge worker productivity. *Computers in Human Behavior, 26*(5), 1061–1072. doi:10.1016/j.chb.2010.03.008

Kirsh, D. (2000). A Few Thoughts on Cognitive Overload. *Intellectica, 30*(1), 19–51. doi:10.3406/intel.2000.1592

Kline, R. B. (2005). *Principles and practice of structural equation modeling* (2nd ed.). The Guilford Press.

Lanaj, K., Johnson, R. E., & Barnes, C. M. (2014). Beginning the workday yet already depleted? Consequences of late-night smartphone use and sleep. *Organizational Behavior and Human Decision Processes, 124*(1), 11–23. doi:10.1016/j.obhdp.2014.01.001

Manohar, S., Mittal, A., & Marwah, S. (2020). Service innovation, corporate reputation and word-of-mouth in the banking sector: A test on multigroup-moderated mediation effect. *Benchmarking, 27*(1), 406–429. doi:10.1108/BIJ-05-2019-0217

Mirbabaie, M., Marx, J., Braun, L. M., & Stieglitz, S. (2020). Digital Detox—Mitigating Digital Overuse in Times of Remote Work and Social Isolation. *arXiv preprint arXiv:2012.09535.*

Mirbabaie, M., Stieglitz, S., & Marx, J. (2022). Digital Detox. *Business & Information Systems Engineering, 64*(2), 239–246. doi:10.100712599-022-00747-x

Nelson, M. R. (1994). We have the information you want, but getting it will cost you! held hostage by information overload. *XRDS: Crossroads. The ACM Magazine for Students, 1*(1), 11–15.

Ouwehand, K., Kroef, A. V. D., Wong, J., & Paas, F. (2021, September). Measuring cognitive load: Are there more valid alternatives to Likert rating scales? []. Frontiers Media SA.]. *Frontiers in Education, 6,* 702616. doi:10.3389/feduc.2021.702616

Pflugner, K., Maier, C., & Weitzel, T. (2020). The direct and indirect influence of mindfulness on techno-stressors and job burnout: A quantitative study of white-collar workers. *Computers in Human Behavior*, 106566.

Portwood-Stacer, L. (2013). Media refusal and conspicuous non-consumption: The performative and political dimensions of Facebook abstention. *New Media & Society*, *15*(7), 1041–1057. doi:10.1177/1461444812465139

Przybylski, A. K., Nguyen, T. V. T., Law, W., & Weinstein, N. (2021). Does taking a short break from social media have a positive effect on well-being? Evidence from three preregistered field experiments. *Journal of Technology in Behavioral Science*, *6*(3), 507–514. doi:10.100741347-020-00189-w

Radtke, T., Apel, T., & Lindern, E. (2022). Digital detox: An effective solution in the smartphone era? A systematic literature review. *Mobile Media & Communication*, *10*(2), 190–215. doi:10.1177/20501579211028647

Saritepeci, M. (2021). Multiple screen addiction scale: Validity and reliability study. *Instructional Technology and Lifelong Learning*, *2*(1), 1–17.

Schmitt, J. B., Breuer, J., & Wulf, T. (2021). From cognitive overload to digital detox: Psychological implications of telework during the COVID-19 pandemic. *Computers in Human Behavior*, *124*, 124. doi:10.1016/j.chb.2021.106899 PMID:34566255

Schmuck, D. (2020). Does digital detox work? Exploring the role of digital detox applications for problematic smartphone use and well-being of young adults using multigroup analysis. *Cyberpsychology, Behavior, and Social Networking*, *23*(8), 526–532. doi:10.1089/cyber.2019.0578 PMID:32354288

Shepherd-Banigan, M., Bell, J. F., Basu, A., Booth-LaForce, C., & Harris, J. R. (2015). Workplace Stress and Home Influence Depressive Symptoms Among Employed Women with Young Children. *International Journal of Behavioral Medicine*, *23*(1), 102–111. doi:10.100712529-015-9482-2 PMID:25894581

Sood, K., Kaur, B., & Grima, S. (2022). Revamping Indian non-life insurance industry with a trusted network: Blockchain technology. In *Big Data: A game changer for insurance industry* (pp. 213–228). Emerald Publishing Limited. doi:10.1108/978-1-80262-605-620221014

Stäheli, U., & Stoltenberg, L. (2022). Digital detox tourism: Practices of analogization. *New Media & Society*. doi:10.1177/14614448211072808

Sweller, J. (1994). Cognitive load theory, learning difficulty, and instructional design. *Learning and Instruction*, *4*(4), 295–312. doi:10.1016/0959-4752(94)90003-5

Syvertsen, T., & Enli, G. (2020). Digital detox: Media resistance and the promise of authenticity. *Convergence (London)*, *26*(5-6), 1269–1283. doi:10.1177/1354856519847325

Tandon, U., Jhamb, B., & Chand, P. (2022). Hedonic Pleasure, Cyber-Dating, Live-In Relationship, and Social Acceptance Amongst IT Professionals. *International Journal of Human Capital and Information Technology Professionals*, *13*(1), 1–18. doi:10.4018/IJHCITP.300311

Tarafdar, M., Tu, Q., & Ragu-Nathan, T. S. (2010). Impact of technostress on end-user satisfaction and performance. *Journal of Management Information Systems*, *27*(3), 303–334. doi:10.2753/MIS0742-1222270311

Vollmann, T. E. (1991). Cutting the Gordian knot of misguided performance measurement. *Industrial Management & Data Systems*, *91*(1), 24–26. doi:10.1108/02635579110138126

Woodstock, L. (2014). The news-democracy narrative and the unexpected benefits of limited news consumption: The case of news resisters. *Journalism*, *15*(7), 834–849. doi:10.1177/1464884913504260

Chapter 5
Dangers of Digital–Only Financial Inclusion

Peterson K. Ozili

 https://orcid.org/0000-0001-6292-1161
Central Bank of Nigeria, Nigeria

ABSTRACT

The literature has not extensively examined the dangers of digital-only financial inclusion. The purpose of this chapter is to highlight the dangers of digital-only financial inclusion (DOFI). Using the discourse analysis method, the study showed that digital-only financial inclusion may be difficult to achieve when there is uneven availability and uneven access to digital devices. It was also argued that digital-only financial inclusion could lead to high cost of internet broadband, and it places much emphasis on accelerating digital access rather than protecting users who use digital finance platforms. Furthermore, it pays little attention to risk mitigation, and produces digital ID schemes that enable government surveillance. It also prioritizes digital access rather than financial health; and makes it easier to perpetrate fraud using digital means. Finally, it can enable the endless pursuit of power, and it prioritizes a digital version of financial inclusion at any cost.

1. INTRODUCTION

The term 'financial inclusion' is commonly defined as access and use of affordable formal financial services (Ozili, 2021a). Digital-only financial inclusion (DoFI) is the use digital technology to promote financial inclusion (Gallego-Losada et al, 2023). It involves using innovative digital technology to accelerate access and use of formal financial services (Ozili, 2022). An avid observer of the global trends

DOI: 10.4018/979-8-3693-1107-3.ch005

in financial inclusion in the last five to ten years will admit that there is much emphasis on digital-only financial inclusion today. The evidence for this can be found everywhere you turn to. You will see buzzwords such as "digital financial inclusion", "digital financial services", and "fintech". How did we get to this point?

Recall that in 2017 the World Bank estimated that 2 billion people do not have a formal bank account which they can use to access available financial services (Ozili, 2021a), meaning that these people are financially excluded. This statistic led many experts to think of strategies to accelerate financial inclusion, by reducing the number of adults without a bank account (Dev, 2006; Atkinson and Messy, 2013; Peric, 2015). As a result, private sector actors, development organizations and government agencies reached a consensus that digital technology is the most effective way to accelerate financial inclusion in the 21st century. Therefore, promoters of financial inclusion began to place great emphasis on achieving financial inclusion using digital means, with little consideration for non-digital strategies for financial inclusion.

Existing research show overwhelming evidence that technology-enabled digital innovations, such as mobile phones, fintech and central bank digital currencies (CBDCs), can accelerate financial inclusion much quicker if the right conditions and incentives are in place (Ouma et al, 2017; Sahay et al, 2020; Ozili, 2023a). However, there is little academic and policy discourse about the associated dangers or risks of digital-only financial inclusion (DOFI). In fact, the critical literature has shown that the benefits of DOFI are either overstated or the conclusions are formed based on incomplete information (Ozili, 2020). Proponents of digital-only financial inclusion seem to forget that digital technology is only a tool, and that is all it will be – both now and in the future. This should make the reader think deeply about what digital-only financial inclusion has to offer, bearing in mind that digital technology is only a tool to accelerate financial inclusion, meanwhile, financial inclusion itself entails much more than providing digital access to formal financial services.

This chapter identifies the dangers of digital-only financial inclusion (DOFI). The discussion in this chapter adds to the existing literature that explores the harmful consequences of technology in society (e.g., Feenberg, 2010; Healy, 2012; Biggi and Giuliani, 2021). The discussion presented in this chapter also adds to the financial inclusion literature that identifies some benefits of digital-only financial inclusion (e.g., Ozili, 2018; Daud, 2023; Shaikh et al, 2023; Obiora and Ozili, 2023; Peng and Mao, 2023; Ozili, 2023b), but which have not extensively identified the associated risks of digital-only financial inclusion. The analysis in this chapter further adds to the development literature that explore the benefits and challenges of technology-enabled development (see. Gorman, 2002; Vinuesa et al, 2020; and Mubarak and Petraite, 2020).

The remaining sections of this chapter are classified as follows. The related literature is discussed in section 2, while some dangers of digital-only financial inclusion are highlighted in section 3. A discussion on technology risk is presented in section 4. The concluding remarks are presented in section 5 while some recommendations are presented in section 6.

2. RELATED LITERATURE

Existing studies document some benefits of digital-only financial inclusion but offer very little insight into the dangers of DOFI. For instance, Tay et al (2022) conducted a review of the existing literature based on analyses of different countries and found that Asian countries adopt DOFI because it helps in their poverty reduction efforts. They also observed that there is a wide gap in DOFI among the different gender, the wealthy, the poor, and among people in urban and rural areas. The authors concluded their review by proposing that Asian countries should improve their digital infrastructure, simplify banking procedures, prioritize financial education, and enable DOFI. Obiora and Ozili (2023) showed that benefits of digital-only financial inclusion include convenience, ensuring digital access to financial services, reaching the poorest in remote areas, and increasing digital literacy.

Naumenkova et al (2019) examined DOFI in Ukraine. They were interested in investigating the hindrances to DOFI in Ukraine in comparison to other countries. They found that digital financial inclusion can strengthen the financial system. Ahmad et al. (2021), focused on China, and showed that the recent adoption of DOFI in China significantly improved access, and made financial services become more affordable. They also showed that DOFI and human capital significantly contribute to economic growth. Aziz and Naima (2021) argued that although digital technology has made it much easier to access financial services for many people, the benefits of digital technology is limited by poor internet connection, high financial illiteracy and lack of awareness.

Liu et al (2021) examined whether DOFI can promote economic growth. The authors analysed 2011 to 2019 data from several provinces in China. They found that DOFI development can contribute to economic growth. However, they noted that small and medium-sized enterprise entrepreneurship and residents' consumption are the two important channels through which DOFI development might affect economic growth. Khera, Ng, Ogawa and Sahay, (2022) assessed whether adopting DOFI increased financial inclusion in 52 countries. They showed that adopting DOFI had positive benefits in the countries that adopted it, and the benefits varied across countries and regions, and the greatest benefits were found in Africa and Asia.

Ozturk and Ullah (2022) focused on the impact of DOFI on economic growth, and its possible impact on environmental sustainability in 42 countries between 2007 to 2019. Interestingly, the authors found that DOFI can increase economic growth;

but it leads to a decrease in environmental quality via increase in CO2 emissions. Koh, Phoon and Ha (2018) surveyed the current state of financial inclusion in Southeast Asian (SEA) nations from 2011 to 2014 and found a large variation in bank account penetration, stage of bank infrastructure development, and use of financial technology in Southeast Asian countries. Shen, Hu and Hueng (2021) also investigated the effect of DOFI on economic growth in 105 countries. They found that DOFI had a beneficial impact on economic growth, and there were spillover benefits on neighbouring countries.

Lee et al (2022) showed that DOFI reduced carbon intensity by accelerating per capita disposable income and digitization, while DOFI increased carbon sequestration via green space and green technology. Huang, Mbanyele, Fan and Zhao (2022) examined the relationship between digital financial inclusion and energy-environment performance for 282 prefecture-level cities in China from 2011 to 2019. They found that DOFI has a non-linear effect on energy-environment performance, implying that DOFI increased energy-environment performance up to a threshold and up to a point where further increases in DOFI decreased energy-environment performance.

Lee, Lou and Wang (2023) argued that digital financial inclusion may curtail poverty in China. They examined the role of digital financial services in alleviating poverty. They found that DOFI contributes to poverty alleviation, and that DOFI has a different impact on users with differing levels of poverty. They also found that the level of income play an important role in alleviating poverty. Kofman and Payne (2021) showed that DOFI has advantages for women. They argued that DOFI allows more women to enjoy a wide array of financial products and services. They also pointed out that the risks of DOFI must be mitigated for women to achieve meaningful financial inclusion. They conclude that policymakers, for-profit organisations, and nonprofit organisations should actively assist in removing the barriers that prevent women financial inclusion.

Kelikume (2021) examined the case of African countries and found that mobile phone penetration and the use of the Internet reduced poverty in African countries. Shaikh et al (2023) showed that mobile money is effective in increasing financial inclusion. Ji, Wang, Xu and Li (2021) examined the impact of DOFI on the urban-rural income gap in China from 2014 to 2018. They found that DOFI reduced the gap. They also found that the breadth of coverage of DOFI reduced the gap, while DOFI alleviates the gap through residents' entrepreneurship.

Niu et al (2022) examined the association between DOFI and broadband infrastructure in rural China and found that broadband infrastructure helps to increase DOFI in a significant way, and the impact of broadband infrastructure on DOFI is stronger in areas with higher bank branches and higher human and social capital. Lu et al (2023) examined the effect of DOFI on diversified investments in China. They found that DOFI has a positive effect on diversified investments because it reduced transaction cost for investors. They also found that DOFI was more useful among investors that are less sophisticated, less financially literate, below 45 years old, less experienced and females. Peng and Mao (2023) examined the impact of DOFI on the rate of poverty on households in urban China and found that DOFI reduced the risk that households would fall into poverty. They also observed that DOFI encouraged entrepreneurship and enabled households to participate in the financial market, thereby giving them an opportunity to generate wealth and avoid falling into poverty.

Meanwhile, only few studies showed the dangers of DOFI. For instance, Ozili (2020) argued that the risks of DOFI is too high for the poor, and that DOFI could reinforce inequalities, expose poor people to risks, and worsen the welfare of poor people.

3. DANGERS OF DIGITAL-ONLY FINANCIAL INCLUSION (DOFI)

Digital financial inclusion comes with some challenges. A few of the challenges are harmful to users of digital financial services. This section identifies some dangers of DOFI.

3.1. DOFI is Difficult to Achieve When There is Uneven Availability and Uneven Access to Digital Devices

Achieving digital-only financial inclusion requires using digital devices, e.g., mobile phones, a bank app or fintech software, to access affordable formal financial services. However, digital-only financial inclusion may be difficult to achieve if there is uneven availability and access to digital devices. Digital devices may be in short supply relative to the size of the population (Andrianaivo and Kpodar, 2012; 2018). Also, some banked adults live in rural areas where there is limited supply of digital devices compared to urban areas (Aker and Mbiti, 2010; Bhavnani, Chiu, Janakiram, Silarszky and Bhatia, 2008), and when some digital devices become available in rural areas, they are not cheap to purchase (Scott, Batchelor, Ridley and Jorgensen, 2004). As a result, poor banked adults, and people with low income, are unable to purchase digital devices which limits their ability to access financial services.

3.2. High Cost of Internet Broadband

Achieving financial inclusion through digital solutions require internet connectivity. In most cases, the cost of internet broadband is not cheap. Since the emergence of DOFI, the cost of internet broadband has remained high in many poor and developing countries (Friedline et al, 2020 Niu et al, 2022). The implication is that DOFI will likely increase the cost of internet broadband, rather than reduce it. High cost of internet broadband is not good for financial inclusion because the poor won't be able to afford it and won't be able to use internet-enabled digital devices to access affordable financial services. Therefore, any discussion about promoting digital-only financial inclusion must include deliberations about reducing the cost of internet broadband.

3.3. Digital-Only Financial Inclusion Places Much Emphasis on Accelerating Digital Access Rather Than Protecting Users Who Use Digital Finance Platforms

Since the emergence of DOFI, there has been much emphasis on "accelerating digital access" (Shen et al, 2020), with little attention paid to other important aspects of financial inclusion like protecting the users of digital finance platforms (Ozili, 2020). As a result, the people who are being targeted for financial inclusion could be negatively impacted when they use digital platforms or digital tools that have very little safeguards to protect them (Malladi et al, 2021). Providers of digital financial services must ensure that they give equal emphasis and priority to protecting users of digital finance platforms while accelerating digital access (Chou, 2019; Mahalle, Yong and Tao, 2019; Akanfe, Valecha and Rao, 2020).

3.4. Digital-Only Financial Inclusion Pays Little Attention to Risk Mitigation

Oftentimes, the promoters of digital-only financial inclusion pay inadequate attention to risk mitigation when designing digital financial services that serve the purpose of financial inclusion. The implication is that, while users may enjoy the benefits that come with using digital financial services, such benefits are easily eroded when adverse risk or loss events occur such as digital fraud and theft arising from unauthorized access to bank accounts (Ozili, 2021b; Ediagbonya and Tioluwani, 2023). Providers of digital financial services should pay more attention to risk mitigation when designing digital financial services. This will help to mitigate risk or loss events that wipe out the benefits that users stand to gain from using digital financial services (Ozili, 2022).

3.5. Digital-Only Financial Inclusion Produces Digital ID Schemes That Enable Government Surveillance

Attempts by government to increase DOFI has led to the development of national digital identification (ID) schemes or programs that use biometric information to authenticate individuals' financial activity on digital platforms. Under such schemes or programs, users will be mandated to authenticate their digital ID to access digital financial services. In some cases, having a digital ID is a requirement to vote or to make cross-border transactions. For many countries, the emergence of digital ID schemes or programs is a result of the government's effort to increase digital-only financial inclusion. The governments will strive to make ID schemes legal and argue that the ID schemes can help to build a modern database of citizens, improve cybersecurity, and assist financial institutions in their know-your-customers (KYC) functions. However, there are strong concerns that national ID schemes or programs, which are a result of digital-only financial inclusion, can enable unnecessary government surveillance of private citizens' financial activity, and could shift the government's focus from financial inclusion to State surveillance (Lim, Cho, Sanchez, 2009; Lips, Taylor and Organ, 2009; Whitley, 2013).

3.6. Digital-Only Financial Inclusion Prioritizes Digital Access Rather Than Financial Health

Digital-only financial inclusion appears to prioritize digital access rather than financial health. This is evident in the performance metrics used by digital finance platforms such as the number of onboarded individuals on digital platforms, volume of transactions and number of registered accounts, among others. These metrics are mostly access-based performance metrics. They do not measure the financial health of users, such as a user's personal savings to debt ratio on a digital banking platform. It would be much better for digital-only financial inclusion to promote good financial health which would better serve the needs of consumers rather than aiming for digital access only. Focusing on financial health rather than digital access is the first step towards designing products that deliver a lasting positive impact on users of digital financial services.

3.7. Digital-Only Financial Inclusion Makes it Easier to Perpetrate Fraud Using Digital Means

Digital-only financial inclusion could make it easier to perpetrate digital fraud because fraudsters could exploit poor data protections, and those weak points may be exploited to steal users' personal information or steal users' money. This can erode public trust in digital finance products and erode trust in government or private sector digital identity initiatives (Oehler and Wendt, 2018; Müller and Kerényi, 2019).

3.8. Digital-Only Financial Inclusion Can Enable the Endless Pursuit of Power

Digital-only financial inclusion can be a conduit for exploitation by those seeking power and more power. Powerful financial institutions are hurriedly scaling their digitization programs, using the cover of financial inclusion, to increase profit significantly and to acquire new market power or to retain their existing market power (Feghali, Mora and Nassif, 2021). The pursuit of DOFI has also enabled politicians to increase their power by using mobile surveillance to influence users of digital financial services to vote for them in elections (Jain and Gabor, 2020), enabling them to pry into users' privacy, which leads to digital authoritarianism.

3.9. Digital-Only Financial Inclusion Prioritizes a Digital Version of Financial Inclusion at Any Cost

There are concerns that digital-only financial inclusion prioritizes a digital version of financial inclusion at any cost. It increases the potential for exploitation and misuse by individuals, financial sector agents, and public institutions who might use the cover of DOFI to pursue goals that are contrary to the goals of financial inclusion, e.g., the financialization of poverty, profiteering, amplifying state power and surveillance, while ignoring real outcomes of financial inclusion.

4. DIGITAL TECHNOLOGY RISK

It would seem unfair to criticize digital-only financial inclusion without also criticizing 'digital technology' for bearing inherent risks which are transferred to financial inclusion programs. The digital technologies used to accelerate financial inclusion are varied such as the Internet of Things (IoT), blockchain, distributed ledger technology, financial technology (Fintech), machine learning and artificial Intelligence (AI). These technologies, no matter how beneficial they are for financial inclusion, bear risks that could hinder financial inclusion efforts (Hoang, Nguyen and Le, 2022; Nguyen, Sermpinis and Stasinakis, 2023). Some of these risks include cybersecurity risk, third-party risk, automation risk, data privacy risk and social engineering risk. Cybersecurity risk is the risk that a malicious actor will damage or destroy the digital platforms, software applications, or systems that are used to accelerate digital financial inclusion in order to gain unauthorized access to users' sensitive information and then use the information maliciously to extort or disrupt an existing service (Florackis et al, 2023; Katsumata, Hemenway and Gavins, 2010). Cybersecurity risk may take the form of malware attacks and distributed denial of services (DDoS) attacks that prevent users from accessing basic financial services (Wangen, Shalaginov and Hallstensen, 2016). Cybersecurity risk may be avoided by detecting cybersecurity vulnerabilities early and closing the vulnerabilities (Jaramillo, 2018; Katsumata, Hemenway and Gavins, 2010).

Another important risk is third-party risk. Third-party risk is the risk that arises from financial service providers relying on outside parties to ensure that digital finance platforms and applications are working effectively (Ale and Piers, 2000; Vitunskaite et al, 2019). Third-party risk is a big risk because financial service providers often rely on a supplier, vendor, or digital service provider to ensure that their digital finance platforms are working well. However, trusting third parties to fulfill their commitment may be difficult, and it creates vulnerabilities that could adversely affect users of digital financial services and become a setback for digital financial inclusion. To avoid third-party risk, financial service providers should develop a third-party risk management framework to mitigate third-party risks on time, and the framework should carefully spell out the procedures, processes, and policies for dealing with third-party risks when they arise (Ale and Piers, 2000; Vitunskaite et al, 2019). There may be a need to regularly audit vendors and ensure that they have appropriate cybersecurity measures in place to mitigate risks that emanate from their own end.

Automation risk is another digital technology risk that affect digital-only financial inclusion. While automation is often considered to be the future of risk management, automation poses some risk for digital-only financial inclusion (Arntz, Gregory, and Zierahn, 2017; Davis, Kumiega and Van Vliet, 2013; Pandita, Xiao, Yang, Enck and Xie, 2013). Automation risk is the risk that arises when digital platforms or applications are automated in a way that limit choice of digital financial services for users. In addition to limiting users' choice, automation can unintentionally introduce redundant operational complexity or software incompatibility issues once software is updated. However, some measures to reduce automation risks include troubleshooting digital platforms to detect early any vulnerabilities.

Another risk is data privacy risk which arises from unauthorized access to users' personal information such as users' name, email address, password, physical address, date of birth and transaction details of users (Theoharidou, Papanikolaou, Pearson, and Gritzalis, 2013; Wagner and Boiten, 2018). Malicious persons can gain unauthorized access to this information with the intention to cause harm to users (Onik et al, 2019). To avoid data privacy risks, there is a need to implement strong cybersecurity measures, adopt multi-factor authentication protocols, and adopt a dynamic password policy.

Another risks to consider is social engineering risk. This risk arises when malicious actors launch phishing attacks using social media, emails, and text messages, with the intent to trick the user to disclose their username, login password, social security number, credit card information, bank account information and any other sensitive information which malicious actors can use to gain unauthorized access to users' account (Abraham and Chengalur-Smith, 2010). To avoid social engineering risk, there is a need to implement cybersecurity awareness training for users of digital finance platforms and educate them on how to recognize and avoid phishing attacks (Salahdine and Kaabouch, 2019).

5. CONCLUSION

This chapter has identified the dangers of digital-only financial inclusion. It was argued that digital-only financial inclusion may be difficult to achieve when there is uneven availability and uneven access to digital devices. It was also argued that digital-only financial inclusion could lead to high cost of internet broadband, and it places much emphasis on accelerating digital access rather than protecting users who use digital finance platforms. Furthermore, it pays little attention to risk mitigation, and produces digital ID schemes that enable government surveillance. It also prioritizes digital access rather than financial health; and makes it easier to perpetrate fraud using digital means. Finally, it can enable the endless pursuit of power, and it prioritizes a digital version of financial inclusion at any cost.

In summary, it was argued that financial inclusion can achieve a lot more for people if there is a wholistic approach to financial inclusion, not just a digital approach. Indeed, it is fair to concede that people need access to basic financial services, and that digital tools can facilitate access to basic financial services to a great extent. For instance, digital-only financial inclusion can increase convenience for financially included people, and lead to cost savings for providers of financial services. But enforcing a model of financial inclusion that is only digital is risky. Advancing digital-only financial inclusion plays down cyber risk, digital illiteracy risk and other risks, while placing much emphasis on accelerating digital access above all else. As much as possible, the strategies used to advance financial inclusion should not be too dependent on digital technologies because they only offer digital access and more access, but may not, on their own, improve financial health in a significant way.

6. RECOMMENDATIONS

It is recommended that policymakers should consider designing a non-digital approach to financial inclusion that can co-exist with existing digital approach to financial inclusion. And, where possible, they should strive to adopt both a digital and non-digital approach to financial inclusion. This would broaden financial inclusion and meet the needs of the excluded population who are not digitally-savvy.

It is also recommended that policymakers who are adopting a digital-only approach to financial inclusion should consider how digital financial inclusion programs can be designed to enhance users' wellbeing, not just giving them access to digital finance tools. There is a need for policymakers to develop policies that ensure that digital-only financial inclusion programs improve users' wellbeing, and legislation should be introduced to prevent digital-only financial inclusion from being captured as a tool for monopoly power by powerful corporations for profiteering or as a tool for State surveillance. Regulation should also be used to control unbridled capitalism, while more legislation can be introduced to address consumer protection and data protection issues.

It is also recommended that policymakers should place more emphasis on promoting a digital-first approach to financial inclusion rather than a digital-only approach to financial inclusion. A digital-first approach to financial inclusion is an approach to financial inclusion that use digital tools to expand financial services to unbanked and underserved people, and use non-digital means to reach and serve those who cannot be reached or served by digital means. A digital-first approach to financial inclusion will be very useful in developing countries where people in urban and sub-urban cities can be served digitally while people in very remote areas can be best served using non-digital means or using human agents.

REFERENCE

Ahmad, M., Majeed, A., Khan, M. A., Sohaib, M., & Shehzad, K. (2021). Digital financial inclusion and economic growth: Provincial data analysis of China. *China Economic Journal*, *14*(3), 291–310. doi:10.1080/17538963.2021.1882064

Akanfe, O., Valecha, R., & Rao, H. R. (2020). Design of an inclusive financial privacy index (INF-PIE): A financial privacy and digital financial inclusion perspective. [TMIS]. *ACM Transactions on Management Information Systems*, *12*(1), 1–21. doi:10.1145/3403949

Aker, J. C., & Mbiti, I. M. (2010). Mobile phones and economic development in Africa. *The Journal of Economic Perspectives*, *24*(3), 207–232. doi:10.1257/jep.24.3.207

Ale, B. J. M., & Piers, M. (2000). The assessment and management of third party risk around a major airport. *Journal of Hazardous Materials, 71*(1-3), 1–16. doi:10.1016/ S0304-3894(99)00069-2 PMID:10677651

Andrianaivo, M., & Kpodar, K. (2012). Mobile phones, financial inclusion, and growth. *Revista de Economia Institucional, 3*(2), 30.

Arntz, M., Gregory, T., & Zierahn, U. (2017). Revisiting the risk of automation. *Economics Letters, 159*, Aziz, A., & Naima, U. (2021). Rethinking digital financial inclusion: Evidence from Bangladesh. *Technology in Society, 64*, 101509.

Atkinson, A., & Messy, F. A. (2013). *Promoting financial inclusion through financial education: OECD/INFE evidence, policies and practice*. OECD.

Bhavnani, A., Chiu, R. W. W., Janakiram, S., Silarszky, P., & Bhatia, D. (2008). *The role of mobile phones in sustainable rural poverty reduction*.

Biggi, G., & Giuliani, E. (2021). The noxious consequences of innovation: What do we know? *Industry and Innovation, 28*(1), 19–41. doi:10.1080/13662716.202 0.1726729

Chou, A. (2019). What's in the Black Box: Balancing Financial Inclusion and Privacy in Digital Consumer Lending. *Duke Law Journal, 69*, 1183.

Daud, S. N. M., & Ahmad, A. H. (2023). Financial inclusion, economic growth and the role of digital technology. *Finance Research Letters, 53*(103602), 157–160. doi:10.1016/j.frl.2022.103602

Davis, M., Kumiega, A., & Van Vliet, B. (2013). Ethics, finance, and automation: A preliminary survey of problems in high frequency trading. *Science and Engineering Ethics, 19*(3), 851–874. doi:10.100711948-012-9412-5 PMID:23138232

Demirgüç-Kunt, A., Klapper, L. F., Singer, D., & Van Oudheusden, P. (2015). The global findex database 2014: Measuring financial inclusion around the world. *World Bank Policy Research Working Paper*, No. 7255.

Dev, S. M. (2006). Financial inclusion: Issues and challenges. *Economic and Political Weekly*, 4310–4313.

Ediagbonya, V., & Tioluwani, C. (2023). The role of fintech in driving financial inclusion in developing and emerging markets: Issues, challenges and prospects. *Technological Sustainability, 2*(1), 100–119. doi:10.1108/TECHS-10-2021-0017

Feenberg, A. (2010). Ten Paradoxes of Technology. *Techné: Research in Philosophy and Technology, 14*(1).

Feghali, K., Mora, N., & Nassif, P. (2021). Financial inclusion, bank market structure, and financial stability: International evidence. *The Quarterly Review of Economics and Finance, 80*, 236–257. doi:10.1016/j.qref.2021.01.007

Florackis, C., Louca, C., Michaely, R., & Weber, M. (2023). Cybersecurity risk. *Review of Financial Studies, 36*(1), 351–407. doi:10.1093/rfs/hhac024

Friedline, T., Naraharisetti, S., & Weaver, A. (2020). Digital redlining: Poor rural communities' access to fintech and implications for financial inclusion. *Journal of Poverty, 24*(5-6), 517–541. doi:10.1080/10875549.2019.1695162

Gallego-Losada, M. J., Montero-Navarro, A., García-Abajo, E., & Gallego-Losada, R. (2023). Digital financial inclusion. Visualizing the academic literature. *Research in International Business and Finance, 64*, 101862. doi:10.1016/j.ribaf.2022.101862

Gorman, M. E. (2002). Types of knowledge and their roles in technology transfer. *The Journal of Technology Transfer, 27*(3), 219–231. doi:10.1023/A:1015672119590

Healy, T. (2012). The unanticipated consequences of technology. *Nanotechnology: ethical and social Implications*, 155-173.

Hoang, T. G., Nguyen, G. N. T., & Le, D. A. (2022). Developments in financial technologies for achieving the Sustainable Development Goals (SDGs): FinTech and SDGs. In *Disruptive technologies and eco-innovation for sustainable development* (pp. 1–19). IGI Global. doi:10.4018/978-1-7998-8900-7.ch001

Huang, H., Mbanyele, W., Fan, S., & Zhao, X. (2022). Digital financial inclusion and energy-environment performance: What can learn from China. *Structural Change and Economic Dynamics, 63*, 342–366. doi:10.1016/j.strueco.2022.10.007

Jaramillo, L. E. S. (2018). Malware detection and mitigation techniques: Lessons learned from Mirai DDOS attack. *Journal of Information Systems Engineering & Management, 3*(3), 19. doi:10.20897/jisem/2655

Ji, X., Wang, K., Xu, H., & Li, M. (2021). Has digital financial inclusion narrowed the urban-rural income gap: The role of entrepreneurship in China. *Sustainability (Basel), 13*(15), 8292. doi:10.3390u13158292

Katsumata, P., Hemenway, J., & Gavins, W. (2010, October). Cybersecurity risk management. In *2010-MILCOM 2010 Military Communications Conference* (pp. 890-895). IEEE.

Kelikume, I. (2021). Digital financial inclusion, informal economy and poverty reduction in Africa. *Journal of Enterprising Communities: People and Places in the Global Economy, 15*(4), 626–640. doi:10.1108/JEC-06-2020-0124

Khera, P., Ng, S., Ogawa, S., & Sahay, R. (2022). Measuring digital financial inclusion in emerging market and developing economies: A new index. *Asian Economic Policy Review*, *17*(2), 213–230. doi:10.1111/aepr.12377

Kofman, P., & Payne, C. (2021). Digital financial inclusion of women: An ethical appraisal. *Handbook on ethics in finance*, 133-157.

Koh, F., Phoon, K. F., & Ha, C. D. (2018). Digital financial inclusion in Southeast Asia. In Handbook of Blockchain, Digital Finance, and Inclusion, Volume 2 (pp. 387-403). Academic Press.

Lee, C. C., Lou, R., & Wang, F. (2023). Digital financial inclusion and poverty alleviation: Evidence from the sustainable development of China. *Economic Analysis and Policy*, *77*, 418–434. doi:10.1016/j.eap.2022.12.004

Lee, C. C., Wang, F., & Lou, R. (2022). Digital financial inclusion and carbon neutrality: Evidence from non-linear analysis. *Resources Policy*, *79*, 102974. doi:10.1016/j.resourpol.2022.102974

Lim, S. S., Cho, H., & Sanchez, M. R. (2009). Online privacy, government surveillance and national ID cards. *Communications of the ACM*, *52*(12), 116–120. doi:10.1145/1610252.1610283

Lips, A. M. B., Taylor, J. A., & Organ, J. (2009). Managing citizen identity information in E-government service relationships in the UK: The emergence of a surveillance state or a service state? *Public Management Review*, *11*(6), 833–856. doi:10.1080/14719030903318988

Liu, Y., Luan, L., Wu, W., Zhang, Z., & Hsu, Y. (2021). Can digital financial inclusion promote China's economic growth? *International Review of Financial Analysis*, *78*, 101889. doi:10.1016/j.irfa.2021.101889

Lu, X., Lai, Y., & Zhang, Y. (2023). Digital financial inclusion and investment diversification: Evidence from China. *Accounting and Finance*, *63*(S2), 2781–2799. doi:10.1111/acfi.13043

Mahalle, A., Yong, J., & Tao, X. (2019, October). Protecting privacy in digital era on cloud architecture for banking and financial services industry. In *2019 6th International Conference on Behavioral, Economic and Socio-Cultural Computing (BESC)* (pp. 1-6). IEEE. 10.1109/BESC48373.2019.8963459

Malladi, C. M., Soni, R. K., & Srinivasan, S. (2021). Digital financial inclusion: Next frontiers—Challenges and opportunities. *CSI Transactions on ICT*, *9*(2), 127–134. doi:10.100740012-021-00328-5

Mubarak, M. F., & Petraite, M. (2020). Industry 4.0 technologies, digital trust and technological orientation: What matters in open innovation? *Technological Forecasting and Social Change, 161*, 120332. doi:10.1016/j.techfore.2020.120332

Müller, J., & Kerényi, Á. (2019). The Need for Trust and Ethics in the Digital Age–Sunshine and Shadows in the FinTech World. *Financial and Economic Review, 18*(4), 5–34. doi:10.33893/FER.18.4.534

Naumenkova, S., Mishchenko, S., & Dorofeiev, D. (2019). Digital financial inclusion: Evidence from Ukraine. *Investment Management & Financial Innovations, 16*(3), 194–205. doi:10.21511/imfi.16(3).2019.18

Nguyen, D. K., Sermpinis, G., & Stasinakis, C. (2023). Big data, artificial intelligence and machine learning: A transformative symbiosis in favour of financial technology. *European Financial Management, 29*(2), 517–548. doi:10.1111/eufm.12365

Niu, G., Jin, X., Wang, Q., & Zhou, Y. (2022). Broadband infrastructure and digital financial inclusion in rural China. *China Economic Review, 76*, 101853. doi:10.1016/j.chieco.2022.101853

Obiora, K., & Ozili, P. K. (2023). Benefits of digital-only financial inclusion. In *The Impact of AI Innovation on Financial Sectors in the Era of Industry 5.0* (pp. 261–269). IGI Global.

Oehler, A., & Wendt, S. (2018). Trust and financial services: The impact of increasing digitalisation and the financial crisis. In *The Return of Trust? Institutions and the Public after the Icelandic Financial Crisis* (pp. 195–211). Emerald Publishing Limited. doi:10.1108/978-1-78743-347-220181014

Onik, M. M. H., Chul-Soo, K. I. M., & Jinhong, Y. A. N. G. (2019, February). Personal data privacy challenges of the fourth industrial revolution. In *2019 21st International Conference on Advanced Communication Technology (ICACT)* (pp. 635-638). IEEE. 10.23919/ICACT.2019.8701932

Ouma, S. A., Odongo, T. M., & Were, M. (2017). Mobile financial services and financial inclusion: Is it a boon for savings mobilization? *Review of development finance, 7*(1), 29-35.

Ozili, P. K. (2020). Contesting digital finance for the poor. *Digital Policy. Regulation & Governance, 22*(2), 135–151. doi:10.1108/DPRG-12-2019-0104

Ozili, P. K. (2021a). Financial inclusion research around the world: A review. *The Forum for Social Economics, 50*(4), 457–479. doi:10.1080/07360932.2020.1715238

Ozili, P. K. (2021b). Financial inclusion-exclusion paradox: How banked adults become unbanked again. *Financial Internet Quarterly, 17*(2), 44–50. doi:10.2478/fiqf-2021-0012

Ozili, P. K. (2022). Digital financial inclusion. In *Big Data: A game changer for insurance industry* (pp. 229–238). Emerald Publishing Limited. doi:10.1108/978-1-80262-605-620221015

Ozili, P. K. (2023a). CBDC, Fintech and cryptocurrency for financial inclusion and financial stability. *Digital Policy. Regulation & Governance, 25*(1), 40–57. doi:10.1108/DPRG-04-2022-0033

Ozili, P. K., & Mhlanga, D. (2023b). Why is financial inclusion so popular? An analysis of development buzzwords. *Journal of International Development*, jid.3812. doi:10.1002/jid.3812

Ozturk, I., & Ullah, S. (2022). Does digital financial inclusion matter for economic growth and environmental sustainability in OBRI economies? An empirical analysis. *Resources, Conservation and Recycling, 185*, 106489. doi:10.1016/j.resconrec.2022.106489

Pandita, R., Xiao, X., Yang, W., Enck, W., & Xie, T. (2013). {WHYPER}: Towards automating risk assessment of mobile applications. In *22nd USENIX Security Symposium (USENIX Security 13)* (pp. 527-542).

Peng, P., & Mao, H. (2023). The effect of digital financial inclusion on relative poverty among urban households: A case study on China. *Social Indicators Research, 165*(2), 377–407. doi:10.100711205-022-03019-z

Peric, K. (2015). Digital financial inclusion. *Journal of Payments Strategy & Systems, 9*(3), 212–214.

Sahay, M. R., von Allmen, M. U. E., Lahreche, M. A., Khera, P., Ogawa, M. S., Bazarbash, M., & Beaton, M. K. (2020). *The promise of fintech: Financial inclusion in the post COVID-19 era*. International Monetary Fund.

Scott, N., Batchelor, S., Ridley, J., & Jorgensen, B. (2004). The impact of mobile phones in Africa. *Commission for africa, 19*(04).

Shaikh, A. A., Glavee-Geo, R., Karjaluoto, H., & Hinson, R. E. (2023). Mobile money as a driver of digital financial inclusion. *Technological Forecasting and Social Change, 186*, 122158. doi:10.1016/j.techfore.2022.122158

Shen, Y., Hu, W., & Hueng, C. J. (2021). Digital financial inclusion and economic growth: A cross-country study. *Procedia Computer Science*, *187*, 218–223. doi:10.1016/j.procs.2021.04.054

Shen, Y., Hueng, C. J., & Hu, W. (2020). Using digital technology to improve financial inclusion in China. *Applied Economics Letters*, *27*(1), 30–34. doi:10.108 0/13504851.2019.1606401

Tay, L. Y., Tai, H. T., & Tan, G. S. (2022). Digital financial inclusion: A gateway to sustainable development. *Heliyon*, *8*(6), e09766. doi:10.1016/j.heliyon.2022. e09766 PMID:35785228

Theoharidou, M., Papanikolaou, N., Pearson, S., & Gritzalis, D. (2013, December). Privacy risk, security, accountability in the cloud. In *2013 IEEE 5th International Conference on Cloud Computing Technology and Science* (Vol. 1, pp. 177-184). IEEE. 10.1109/CloudCom.2013.31

Vinuesa, R., Azizpour, H., Leite, I., Balaam, M., Dignum, V., Domisch, S., Felländer, A., Langhans, S. D., Tegmark, M., & Fuso Nerini, F. (2020). The role of artificial intelligence in achieving the Sustainable Development Goals. *Nature Communications*, *11*(1), 1–10. doi:10.103841467-019-14108-y PMID:31932590

Vitunskaite, M., He, Y., Brandstetter, T., & Janicke, H. (2019). Smart cities and cyber security: Are we there yet? A comparative study on the role of standards, third party risk management and security ownership. *Computers & Security*, *83*, 313–331. doi:10.1016/j.cose.2019.02.009

Wagner, I., & Boiten, E. (2018). Privacy risk assessment: from art to science, by metrics. In *Data Privacy Management, Cryptocurrencies and Blockchain Technology: ESORICS 2018 International Workshops* Springer..

Wangen, G., Shalaginov, A., & Hallstensen, C. (2016). Cyber security risk assessment of a ddos attack. In Information Security: 19th International Conference. Springer.

Whitley, E. A. (2013). Perceptions of government technology, surveillance and privacy: the UK identity cards scheme. In *New directions in surveillance and privacy* (pp. 133–156). Willan.

Chapter 6
Detox for Success:
How Digital Detoxification Can Enhance Productivity and Well–Being

Animesh Kumar Sharma
ⓘ https://orcid.org/0000-0002-6673-319X
Lovely Professional University, India

Rahul Sharma
Lovely Professional University, India

ABSTRACT

In the fast-digital age, the constant influx of information, relentless social media engagement, and an unending stream of push notifications have become an integral part of our lives. While these technological advancements have undoubtedly brought convenience and connectivity, they have also raised concerns about their impact on productivity, health, and overall well-being. Periodic digital detox not only restores focus and reduces stress but also rekindles the ability to concentrate on tasks, resulting in heightened productivity. The practice of digital detox holds the promise of balancing the scales in the digital age. This chapter highlights the pressing need to strike a balance between the advantages of digital technology and our fundamental need for digital well-being. This study offers how a person can respite from the constant digital barrage, leading to enhanced productivity, improved digital health, and a heightened sense of digital well-being.

INTRODUCTION

Smartphones, social media, the internet, and other digital technologies have grown at an exponential rate in the modern period (Milicevic, 2015). While these advancements

DOI: 10.4018/979-8-3693-1107-3.ch006

have provided countless benefits, they have also introduced new issues, such as information overload, constant distractions, shorter attention spans, and increased stress and anxiety (Wilcockson et al., 2019). Digital detoxification tries to address these concerns by giving people back control over their technology habits and establishing healthy relationships with their devices (Miksch and Schulz, 2018). Taking a break from technology and media is not a novel idea (Anrijs et al., 2018). Concerns about internet addiction and its detrimental impacts on personal life and productivity began to arise in the late 1990s and early 2000s, as the internet became more widely available to the general public (Schmitt et al., 2021). People's reliance on digital gadgets was growing, raising awareness of the need to create a balance between technology and real-life experiences. The term "digital detox" became popular in the mid-2000s as smartphones and social media platforms proliferated (Radtke et al., 2022).

Digitization is transforming society in many ways, including the workplace and people's personal lives (Cijan et al., 2019). As a result, professionals are confronted with technology not just in the context of their employment, but also during their working hours. Communication technology has altered how people organize and carry out their social activities (Madianou et al., 2015). It mediates how people communicate with one another as well as how relationships are formed and sustained (Cascio et al., 2016). As a result, communication technology is frequently considered a tool that individuals utilize to satisfy their need for belonging and relatedness to feel socially connected. Individuals are at risk of social isolation as remote work arrangements become more prevalent because of a shift in working styles across industries and unforeseeable emergencies such as the COVID-19 epidemic (Sharma et al., 2019). In times of social isolation, adopting communication technologies may assist individuals in remaining socially connected (Chen and Schulz, 2016). However, because of the continual permeation of digitally mediated communication in public, professional, and private activities, this socio-technical circuit results in increased screen time and unprecedented effects (Syvertsen and Enli, 2020). As a result, perceived digital overuse can be identified as a new social concern and is characterised as a common, but less pathological, sense of being overwhelmed by communication content and connections (Gui et al., 2017). Affected persons may suffer unfavourable effects on both a personal and professional level, as well as have their general well-being compromised (Gui and Büchi, 2020). Eventually, perceived digital usage can develop into IT addiction, which is a psychological condition of maladaptive dependency on IT use manifested through obsessive-compulsive habits (Pontes et al., 2015). The constant connectivity and notifications from these devices began to influence people's attention spans, sleep patterns, and overall well-being (Kuss and Griffiths, 2017). At this point, the concept of intentionally stepping away from technology for a period to recharge and reconnect with the offline world had become a prominent topic in self-help books, wellness blogs, and media discussions (Kwon et al., 2016). The phrase "digital detox" gained even more traction with the growth of the digital wellness movement, which encourages the thoughtful and aware use of technology (Wilcockson et al., 2019). To combat burnout and digital weariness, businesses and organisations began to offer programmes, courses, and retreats focused on disconnecting from technology (Schmuck, 2020).

As technology continues to permeate every aspect of our lives, the idea of a digital detox has developed (Ugur and Koc, 2015). The phrase has become more inclusive, encompassing not only taking breaks from computers and cellphones but also intentionally limiting the amount of time spent on social media, establishing guidelines for work-related communications after hours, and generally using technology more purposefully (Nguyen, 2022). A digital detox is a period when a person purposefully cuts back on or gives up using technology and digital devices to reclaim their feeling of balance and well-being and to escape a never-ending state of connectedness (Mirbabaie et al., 2022). The word "detox" is taken from the field of addiction and substance abuse, where it refers to the withdrawal process from drugs or alcohol to purify the body and mind (Kent, 2020). Regarding technology, it entails unplugging for a while from tablets, laptops, smartphones, social media, and other online accounts (Kour, 2016). Our growing dependence on technology in our daily lives is the reason behind the necessity for a digital detox (Abeele et al., 2022). People frequently find themselves spending excessive amounts of time on screens, checking emails and social media notifications continuously, and becoming involved in various online activities as technology gets more and more prevalent (Alrobai et al., 2016). The term "digital detox" describes a time when a person chooses to abstain from using digital gadgets and technology, including computers, tablets, smartphones, and social media sites (Nguyen, 2022). A digital detox aims to limit screen time, break free from an unhealthy dependence on technology, and establish a more harmonious balance between the virtual and physical worlds (Scheppe and Seiffen, 2022). It enables people to switch off from the cacophony of digital devices, unwind mentally, and get back into offline pursuits like hobbies, time spent with loved ones, and time in the great outdoors. Overuse can have detrimental effects such as poor mental health, disturbed sleep, decreased productivity, social isolation, etc. (Nguyen et al., 2022). Making conscious efforts to establish a more positive balance between online and offline life is known as digital detoxing (Syvertsen, 2023).

Depending on personal tastes and requirements, a digital detox's duration can change. It could last a few hours, a few days, or even a few weeks (Sutton, 2017). The idea is to improve people's relationships with technology and make more deliberate use of it to improve their general well-being (Agha and Obinna, 2023). In a technologically driven world, digital detoxification offers the chance to take back control over one's time, focus, and mental health (Vialle et al., 2023).

People can achieve a more meaningful and full existence by adopting frequent detox practices that help them achieve a healthier balance between their digital and real-world experiences. To regain equilibrium and well-being in the digital age, digital detoxification is the deliberate disconnection or reduction of one's use of digital devices and technology for a predetermined amount of time (Dutt, 2023). In a world where technology permeates every part of our existence, it is now crucial for maintaining good mental, emotional, and even physical health to take periodic breaks from screen time and online interaction (Robertson, 2023).

REVIEW OF LITERATURE

A detailed review of the literature is performed and the literary work is division into the below sections;

Social Media Usage

Communication technologies and other IT systems are ingrained in people's personal and professional lives (Abeele, 2018). Social relationships integrated digitally are made possible by those platforms. persons can connect locally, with persons in close vicinity, over long distances, or without being dependent on time or location. Engaging in solely virtual social interactions can also elicit emotions of cosiness, acceptance, and enthusiasm (Purohit et al., 2020). That way, loneliness can be minimised and a person's need for social interaction can be met. In this context, a brief feeling of relatedness and belonging might be used to characterise social connectivity (El-Khoury et al., 2021). It may be elicited by relationship salience and quantitative and qualitative social judgements. When one thinks of others, the latter manifests and can evoke the sense of being together even when there is no physical touch. Individual and societal levels are the two domains in which social connectivity is present (Schmuck, 2020). People experience social connections with their entire social network on an aggregate level, but they only experience social connections with a single person on an individual basis. To this, social isolation is the opposite. It is characterized as a social discomfort that indicates a person's relationships with others are deteriorating or have entirely broken, and experiencing it is akin to feeling alone. People's drive to preserve and mend the relationships with others that are essential to their mental health and overall well-being is fueled by their fear of social isolation (Apostolopoulos et al., 2016).

According to research, social isolation raises the risk of depression, increased negativity, and lower general cognitive performance (Vishwakarma, 2022). Reducing social isolation and increasing social connectedness can be achieved through purposeful smartphone use for communication. However, using technology can also hurt one's well-being. When utilising technology excessively, for example, unintentional repercussions could arise (Boguszewicz et al., 2021).

Digital Mobile Usage

When discussing problematic, obsessive, or excessive Internet use, including pathologic consumption, research so far has mostly concentrated on Internet addiction (Curran et al., 2017). On the other hand, generalised digital overuse perception is a new societal problem that is considerably more widespread but less destructive (Bol et al., 2018). A new social norm has emerged as a result of the widespread use of social media and the Internet: continuous availability. While they frequently disrupt other ongoing operations, features like push alerts enable access anytime and anywhere. But people could be seen as socially irresponsible if they don't reply when it's acceptable. Despite their overwhelming feelings, people desire to always be connected because of the so-called fear of missing out (FOMO). FOMO is the acronym for the fear of missing out on social interactions or vital information that happens all the time online (Alutaybi et al., 2020). Consequently, FOMO causes people to use technology more frequently.

Perceived digital overuse can be defined as the experience of feeling overwhelmed and intellectually overburdened (Montag and Walla, 2016). Digital overuse is an individual's problematic experience of using technology too much, not a normative top-down perspective about what is "excessive" or "too much" (Prasad and Quinones, 2020)." A widespread and hidden problem known as "digital overuse" arises when a person's regular Internet usage exceeds a personal benchmark or imprecise notion of their optimal level (Mutsvairo et al., 2022). Affected individuals looked for ways to reduce perceived digital overuse because it is associated with feelings of stress and overwhelm. Reducing screen time on various devices (computers, tablets, and smartphones) has become popular as a way for individuals to focus on the real world and reduce stress (Monge Roffarello and De Russis, 2019).

Digital Detox

The term "digital detox" has gained a lot of traction despite being a relatively new idea. Detox generally refers to a procedure wherein a person abstains from harmful substances (Logacheva et al., 2022). A period during which a person refrains from using electronic devices, such as smartphones or computers, regarded as an opportunity to reduce stress or focus on social interaction in the physical world is how the Oxford Dictionary defined "digital detox" in 2013. As of this writing, however, there isn't a recognised and well-defined concept in academic literature.

The same problem is referred to by several names, such as "digital diet" or "media diet" (Roberts et al., 2017). Nevertheless, the phrase "digital detox" has gained traction and is currently the most used one. It is defined as "efforts to restrict the use of smartphones and digital tools, as well as take a longer or shorter break from online or digital media."Many inspirations and motivations impact the practice of digital detoxification (Syvertsen and Enli, 2020). Self-optimization is one of the driving forces behind digital detoxification. By doing so, people make better use of software and technology, while minimising digital distraction (Rosen and Samuel, 2015). Mindfulness and concepts of balance are further motivations. The ultimate goal of a digital detox is to lessen stress induced by excessive use of technology by avoiding distractions that come with being always connected (Wood and Muñoz, 2015).

Vialle et al. (2023) investigated whether a smartphone digital detox efficiently reduces stress in the short term when people feel a perceived misuse of technology. This was done to see if doing a digital detox had the desired impact of lowering stress. The writers observed the subjects for two weeks to achieve that goal. The participants were free to use their smartphones as usual during the first week (Syvertsen, 2023). The participants engaged in digital detoxification during the second week. The authors created a screen-time tracking program to regulate smartphone usage (Radtke et al., 2022). Their findings demonstrated a decrease in physiological stress. Therefore, previous research suggests that digital detoxification could be a useful coping strategy for individuals who feel stressed out due to excessive usage of digital devices (Ugur and Koc, 2015).

However, technology can be both a cause of stress and a means of relieving it when one is feeling socially or lonely (Sutton, 2017). When used, it can contribute to a social Consequently, the question of whether digital detoxification during periods of social isolation a good idea is still or if it exacerbates stress and injury due to a diminished sense of social connectivity emerges (Anrijs et al., 2018).

Research Gap

Despite the increasing amount of research on the connection between technology usage, productivity, and well-being, there is still a distinct lack of investigation into the specific mechanisms and consequences of digital detoxification in improving both individual and organizational success. Existing studies often focus on the negative impact of excessive digital engagement, but there is a limited understanding of the potential benefits and strategies associated with intentional and structured digital detox programs. There is a dearth of empirical evidence on the long-term effects of digital detoxification on workplace productivity, employee satisfaction, and overall well-being. Moreover, the intersectionality of digital detoxification with diverse demographic factors, job roles, and industries has not been comprehensively examined. Addressing these gaps in the literature is crucial for developing evidence-based recommendations for individuals and organizations seeking to implement effective digital detox strategies to improve both productivity and well-being in the digital age. It is crucial to develop evidence-based insights that can guide individuals, employers, and policymakers in fostering a healthy and productive balance between digital technology use and well-being. Consequently, a comprehensive investigation into the efficacy, sustainability, and contextual factors influencing the outcomes of digital detox interventions is essential for advancing our understanding of the role of technology in contemporary work environments.

Research Objectives

Accordingly, this research study aims to the research objectives as below,

RQ1: How does implementing digital detoxification strategies impact individuals' productivity and well-being in a digitalized work environment?

RQ2: What are the key factors that contribute to the success of such detox programs?

RQ3: How do different digital detox strategies, such as intermittent technology breaks, unplugging during non-working hours, and mindfulness practices, influence the psychological well-being and stress levels of individuals striving for success in their careers?

RESEARCH METHODOLOGY

This research paper is based on secondary data, encompassing scholarly journals, electronic books, periodical publications, weblogs, and comprehensive reports. The study explores the efficacy of digital detoxification in enhancing success and well-being, employing a predominantly qualitative, pragmatic research approach. In this research study, a qualitative research methodology is employed, utilizing content analysis within the framework of the netnography approach. Content analysis is chosen as the primary method for examining and interpreting textual, visual, or audio-visual data to identify patterns, themes, and underlying meanings. This method allows for a systematic and objective analysis of the content, providing insights into the context and the nuanced aspects of the data under investigation. Netnography, on the other hand, involves the observation and analysis of online communities and interactions. By adopting a netnographic approach, the study leverages the unique context of online platforms, such as social media forums or discussion groups, to explore the behaviours, opinions, and experiences of participants within a specific virtual community. This combined qualitative approach enables a comprehensive understanding of the complex social phenomena under investigation, contributing to a rich and contextualized exploration of the research questions at hand.

DISCUSSIONS

Today's fast-paced, technologically evolved culture depends largely on digital devices for work, leisure, information, and communication. The frequent and excessive use of these technologies might lead to many issues, despite their great convenience and usefulness. In an increasingly technologically driven society, digital detoxification offers a chance to take back control over one's time, focus, and mental health. A more meaningful and full existence can result from adopting frequent detox practices that help people achieve a better balance between their digital and real-world experiences. To regain equilibrium and well-being in the digital era, doing a "digital detox" involves purposefully cutting back on or disconnecting from digital gadgets and technology for a predetermined amount of time. In a society where technology permeates every part of our lives, it is now crucial for maintaining good mental, emotional, and even physical health to take breaks from excessive screen time and online interaction. The usage of cell phones, social media, the internet, and other digital technology has increased dramatically in the modern period. While there are many advantages to these advancements, there are drawbacks as well, including information overload, continual diversions, shorter attention spans, and elevated tension and anxiety. By giving people back control over their computer habits and fostering healthy relationships with digital gadgets, digital detoxification seeks to solve these problems. In the research study, a digital detoxification framework is identified.

Take the following actions to carry out a digital detox:

Set goals and boundaries: Establish explicit guidelines for the duration and extent of the digital detox, as well as defined goals for it. One day or a longer period, like a weekend or vacation, could be dedicated to avoiding screens. Establish clear time slots during the day—during meals, right before bed, or during family time—when you will not use digital devices. Decide how long and how much anyone wants to spend detoxing online. It might extend for many hours, a day, a weekend, or even longer. Establish explicit guidelines for the duration and extent of the digital detox, as well as defined goals for it. One day or a longer period, like a weekend or vacation, could be dedicated to avoiding screens.

Digital well-being tools: The concept of digital detoxification gained traction among productivity specialists, mental health specialists, and wellness advocates to prioritize self-care and develop a better relationship with technology. The idea was

Figure 1. Digital detoxification framework

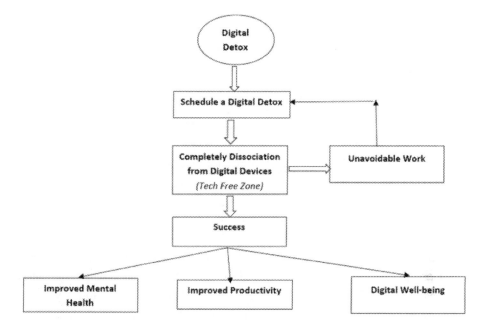

publicized by several media sites, which helped it become more widely accepted. With the help of digital detox features and apps, users can now monitor how much time they spend on screens, establish usage restrictions, and get alerts when it's time to put down their phones. Share your digital detox plan with friends, family, and coworkers so they know why you might not be as accessible during that period. Store your gadgets away, disable notifications, and think about utilizing features or apps that restrict access to particular websites or apps while you're detoxing. To moderate expectations and lessen any anxiety brought on by unresponsiveness, let friends, family, and coworkers know about your plans for a digital detox. To minimize interruptions and limit exposure to notifications, switch smartphone to Aeroplan mode.

Digital detox apps: Oddly enough, certain applications were developed to assist users in controlling their screen time and minimizing their reliance on gadgets. These apps have features like break notifications, screen time tracking, and incentives for not using a screen. Individuals may get driven to continually check their devices, which can result in addictive behaviors that disrupt daily life and interpersonal interactions. To reduce distractions and recover time, remove pointless apps from the gadgets. removing all digital devices use for a predetermined amount of time, such as a day or weekend, during which one unplug all electronics. Computers, tablets, cell phones, and other devices fall under this category.

Designate tech-free zones: Make zones—like the bedroom—where using digital devices is prohibited in the house or place of business. In the house or place of business, identify certain zones that are off-limits to digital gadgets. As a result, temptation may be lessened. Better attention and interpersonal communication can be achieved by establishing designated places in house or place of employment where using digital gadgets is prohibited. A digital sabbatical is a term used to describe prolonged intervals of time (days, weeks, or even months) in which people completely cut off from using digital devices. The goal of this detox fad was to reestablish a person's connection with technology and live a life free from continual digital distractions. Digital decluttering entailed organizing and minimizing digital files, emails, and apps, just like decluttering physical environments. The goals of this movement were to enhance gadget performance, lessen digital noise, and make it simpler to locate crucial information. Disconnecting from all digital devices and online platforms for a predetermined amount of time—a day, a weekend, a week, or longer—is known as a "digital sabbatical." People spend this time doing something other than staring at devices, like going outside, reading, or doing hobbies. Designating particular locations or periods where using digital devices is not allowed at home, work, or social events. Making areas free from technology encouraged deeper conversations with people face-to-face and lessened the urge to constantly check devices. The practice of designating areas in public or at home where technology is not allowed is gaining traction. Encouraging in-person interactions and minimizing distractions from screen time, some spaces have been marked as device-free zones. Families have begun to observe screen-free days or hours to spend valuable time together without being distracted by technology. This practice enhanced communication and bonded families together.

Engage in offline activities: Cut down on how much time is spent on social media, or think about going cold turkey on them. Consider imposing stringent time limitations on social media use if total digital abstinence is not possible. Reconnect with hobbies, exercise, read books, or spend time in nature without relying on digital devices. Reconnect with offline hobbies, interests, and activities that the person enjoy but may have neglected due to excessive screen time. Choose in-person interactions over text or email correspondence wherever possible. Revisiting pastimes or pastimes that are done away from screens, including reading books on paper, playing sports outside, creating art, or spending time with loved ones. To detach from screens and find relaxation, people began rediscovering analogue hobbies like knitting, drawing, journaling, reading physical books, and going outside to do things. To counterbalance their digital lifestyles, many people took up analogue pastimes and interests. Some examples include reading books in print, keeping a pen and paper journal, knitting, drawing, playing board games, and spending more time outside. Adopting analogue hobbies, including knitting, drawing, journaling, or board games, encourages creativity and relaxation while offering a respite from digital pursuits. The term began to emerge more regularly in popular culture as it gained popularity, including conversations on social media, books, articles, and even commercials. Instead of relying on digital interactions, people scouted out more offline social events, hiking groups, and board game nights to build deep friendships.

Practice mindfulness: To help anyone relax and centre himself, try mindfulness exercises like yoga, meditation, or just spending time in nature. Evaluate how the digital detox affected life both during and after. Think back on the newfound knowledge and contemplate long-term adjustments to the online routine. Regularly being surrounded by digital information might shorten attention spans and make it harder to concentrate on activities that call for more in-depth thought. Numerous smartphone features and applications can assist in monitoring and restricting screen time while prompting to take breaks. Ironically, as real face-to-face encounters decline, over-connectivity on digital platforms can exacerbate feelings of loneliness. As guided practises to help users unwind, de-stress, and become more present without relying on social media or other digital distractions were made available, mindfulness and meditation apps witnessed a rise in popularity. Intriguingly, some people adopted digital tools to lower stress and cultivate awareness. To encourage meditation, relaxation, and mental health, there were numerous mindfulness apps and technological resources available.

Going on tech-free retreats: vacationing somewhere that forbids or highly discourages the use of digital gadgets. Because of this, people can fully engage with the present and their surroundings without being interrupted by digital distractions. These are vacations or retreats that are intended to help people unplug from technology and spend time in nature or practising mindfulness. To have a distraction-free experience, participants are urged to put their electronics away. It became common to create areas devoid of technology in homes, offices, and public areas. These spaces were set aside for in-person conversations or just some alone time away from screens. Digital detox retreats provide an organised setting where attendees can unplug from electronics and partake in a range of health-promoting activities. These retreats frequently incorporate mindfulness- and digital-balance-promoting workshops, outdoor activities, and meditation sessions.

Social media detox: People started clearing out their digital lives, motivated by the minimalist movement. File purging, unsubscribing from pointless emails, and digital space organisation were all included in this. To get away from the never-ending comparison and information overload and to be more present in the real world, many people have chosen to take short-term or long-term hiatuses from social media. A lot of people are stepping away from social media in order to free themselves from the stress of comparison, lower their anxiety levels, and get more time back. Setting stringent time limitations for app usage and temporarily removing or deactivating accounts were common practices associated with social media detoxes. Some people are choosing to use social media mindfully as an alternative to completely giving it up. This entails imposing time constraints, selecting more uplifting and educational content for them to read, and unfollowing accounts that make them feel stressed out or depressed.

Unplugged vacations: The unplugged vacation trend urged people to entirely disconnect from their gadgets while they were away from work or other obligations, as opposed to using vacation time to catch up on emails or keep connected. They were therefore able to enjoy the trip and the companionship of loved ones to the fullest extent possible. Digital minimalism is a way of living in which people purposefully use fewer digital tools and platforms only retaining those that are useful in their daily lives. The goal of this movement is to get rid of distractions and digital clutter. A practice known as "dopamine fasting" is briefly giving up all pleasurable activities, including spending too much time in front of a screen. The goal is to lessen addiction-like behaviors linked to digital devices and social media by resetting the brain's reward system. The practice of putting away electronic gadgets and spending quality time with one another without interruptions—known as "screen-free evenings"—is becoming increasingly popular among people and families. Enhancing ties and communication Realizing the value of work-life balance, some businesses and organizations implemented rules encouraging workers to unplug after work to prevent burnout and boost output. The term "no-tech travel" describes travels or holidays where people consciously decide not to use their digital devices for work or play. Instead of continuously shooting photos for social media, they immerse themselves in the trip, concentrating on the location and their friends.

Healthy lifestyle: Bedroom tech-free has become popular as a way to encourage better sleep and lessen screen dependency. Individuals would avoid utilising screens right before bed and charge their gadgets outside of the bedroom. Some are switching to tech-free sleep schedules to improve the quality of their sleep. This entails avoiding using screens right before bed, which can interfere with sleep patterns, by keeping cell phones, tablets, and other electronic gadgets out of the bedroom. The body's natural sleep-wake cycle may be disturbed by the blue light emitted by displays, which can result in poorer sleep quality and difficulty falling asleep. For better sleep and general health, avoid using screens at least an hour before bed. Adopting habits and making deliberate decisions that support mental, emotional, and physical health are components of a healthy lifestyle. It covers a range of facets of living, including social interactions, physical activity, sleep, stress reduction, and diet.

Key Components of a Healthy Lifestyle and Digital Well-Being

Keeping up a healthy lifestyle requires an all-encompassing strategy that includes some crucial elements. A balanced diet is the first and most important thing that the body needs to get its necessary nutrients from. Incorporating a variety of nutrient-dense foods, including fruits, vegetables, whole grains, lean meats, and healthy fats, is part of this. To maintain cardiovascular health, muscular strength, and flexibility, frequent exercise is essential in addition to a balanced diet. To maintain general health and optimal cognitive function, getting seven to nine hours of good sleep every night is equally important. By lowering stress levels, stress management practises like deep breathing and meditation improve both mental and physical health. Since they might harm health, it is imperative to abstain from dangerous substances including alcohol, tobacco, and recreational drugs. Emotional health and cognitive vigour are further enhanced by fostering social relationships and partaking in mentally stimulating activities like reading, solving puzzles, or acquiring new skills. To track health and identify possible problems early on, making frequent health checkups a priority can eventually ensure a better and healthier life.

Benefits of a Healthy Lifestyle

There are several advantages to adopting a healthy lifestyle including improved mental and physical health. It greatly enhances physical health first and foremost by lowering the risk of chronic illnesses like obesity, diabetes, and heart disease. This proactive strategy leads to a better quality of life as well as an increased lifespan. A healthy lifestyle also improves cognitive performance and reduces the risk of anxiety and depression, which has a good impact on mental health. Health-conscious people have more energy and can accomplish daily tasks with more strength and endurance. An additional benefit is improved weight management, as a healthy weight may be maintained with a balanced diet and frequent exercise. A healthy lifestyle ultimately leads to a longer, more satisfying existence where people not only live longer but also live better.

IMPLICATIONS

Implications of this study are discussed in the below sections i.e. i) Theoretical ii) practical implications;

Theoretical Implications

As technology continues to evolve rapidly, embracing digital detox can open new doors of opportunities and present unique challenges for start-ups, MSMEs (Micro, Small, and Medium Enterprises), the Indian financial sector, and the insurance sector. Start-ups and MSMEs can capitalize on the rising demand for products and services that support digital detox. These can include apps, gadgets, or wellness programs aimed at helping individuals manage their screen time Start-ups can collaborate with wellness and mental health-focused businesses to create comprehensive solutions that combine digital detox practices with mindfulness, stress reduction, and overall well-being. Businesses can create opportunities for people to connect in person and experience real-world interactions through events, workshops, or retreats. Start-ups can organize gatherings that promote face-to-face networking and socializing, appealing to those looking for meaningful connections beyond the digital realm.

Practical Implications

Digital detoxification refers to the intentional and temporary disconnection from digital devices and online platforms to restore balance, reduce stress, and improve overall well-being. This practice has had a profound impact on individuals and society as a whole. As the consequences of excessive digital use become more evident, public health policies may be shaped to address these issues. This might include campaigns promoting digital well-being, guidelines for screen time limits in educational settings, and measures to protect vulnerable populations from the negative effects of digital technology. This study would help in public health initiatives to encourage constructive modifications in online digital conduct. Effective work habits, a focus on work-life balance, and regular integration of digital detox periods into daily routines are the main areas of focus for public health campaigns.

CONCLUSION

Digital detoxification involves taking a break from digital devices to find a healthier balance in life. It is essential to maintain ethical practices during this period, including respecting intellectual property rights and avoiding plagiarism in any creative endeavours pursued during the detox. The benefits of digital detoxification include improved Mental Well-being, enhanced productivity and focus, better interpersonal relationships, increased creativity and physical health improvement. Digital detox is the practice of intentionally reducing or completely eliminating the use of digital devices and technologies, such as smartphones, computers, tablets, and social media platforms, in order to disconnect from the digital world and alleviate the negative effects of constant digital engagement. The goal of a digital detox is to create a healthier balance between the online and offline aspects of life and to restore a sense of mindfulness, focus, and well-being. digital detoxification can profoundly influence various aspects of an individual's life, leading to improved mental health, enhanced productivity, stronger relationships, better sleep quality, increased physical activity, heightened creativity, and greater digital awareness. Incorporating regular digital detoxes into one's routine can pave the way for a healthier and more balanced relationship with technology, ultimately contributing to a happier and more fulfilling life.

LIMITATIONS AND SCOPE OF FUTURE RESEARCH

This research study is primarily rooted in short-term or cross-sectional investigations, offering a snapshot of the immediate outcomes of digital detox interventions. Nevertheless, there exists a compelling necessity for more comprehensive and longitudinal research endeavours to comprehensively appraise the enduring ramifications of digital detox and to ascertain whether the advantages it purports to offer are sustained over protracted periods. The present study, while shedding light on the initial impacts, may fall short of sufficiently acknowledging the nuanced interplay of individual disparities in technology consumption patterns, psychological variables, and idiosyncratic preferences. Future research initiatives should, therefore, delve into the intricate interrelationship of these elements to gain deeper insights into how they influence the efficacy of various digital detox strategies in enhancing well-being and success outcomes.

REFERENCES

Abeele, M. M. V., Halfmann, A., & Lee, E. W. (2022). Drug, demon, or donut? Theorizing the relationship between social media use, digital well-being and digital disconnection. *Current Opinion in Psychology*, *45*, 101295. doi:10.1016/j.copsyc.2021.12.007 PMID:35123383

Abeele, M. V., De Wolf, R., & Ling, R. (2018). Mobile media and social space: How anytime, anyplace connectivity structures everyday life. *Media and Communication*, *6*(2), 5–14. doi:10.17645/mac.v6i2.1399

Agha, C. J., & Obinna, A. H. (2023). TECH-FREE ZONES ESTABLISHMENT AND DUMB-PHONE UTILIZATION AS DIGITAL DETOXIFICATION PREDICTORS OF STUDENTS' ACADEMIC IMPROVEMENTS IN UNIVERSITIES IN RIVERS STATE. [IJMR]. *EPRA International Journal of Multidisciplinary Research*, *9*(2), 149–155.

Alrobai, A., McAlaney, J., Phalp, K., & Ali, R. (2016). Online peer groups as a persuasive tool to combat digital addiction. In *Persuasive Technology: 11th International Conference*. Springer.

Alutaybi, A., Al-Thani, D., McAlaney, J., & Ali, R. (2020). Combating fear of missing out (FoMO) on social media: The FoMO-R method. *International Journal of Environmental Research and Public Health*, *17*(17), 6128. doi:10.3390/ijerph17176128 PMID:32842553

Anrijs, S., Bombeke, K., Durnez, W., Van Damme, K., Vanhaelewyn, B., Conradie, P., & De Marez, L. (2018). MobileDNA: Relating physiological stress measurements to smartphone usage to assess the effect of a digital detox. In *HCI International 2018–Posters' Extended Abstracts: 20th International Conference, HCI International 2018*.

Anrijs, S., Bombeke, K., Durnez, W., Van Damme, K., Vanhaelewyn, B., Conradie, P., & De Marez, L. (2018). MobileDNA: Relating physiological stress measurements to smartphone usage to assess the effect of a digital detox. In *HCI International 2018–Posters' Extended Abstracts: 20th International Conference, HCI International 2018, Las Vegas, NV, USA, July 15-20, 2018* [Springer International Publishing.]. *Proceedings*, *20*(Part II), 356–363.

Apostolopoulos, Y., Sönmez, S., Hege, A., & Lemke, M. (2016). Work strain, social isolation and mental health of long-haul truckers. *Occupational Therapy in Mental Health*, *32*(1), 50–69. doi:10.1080/0164212X.2015.1093995

Boguszewicz, C., Boguszewicz, M., Iqbal, Z., Khan, S., Gaba, G. S., Suresh, A., & Pervaiz, B. (2021). The fourth industrial revolution-cyberspace mental wellbeing: Harnessing science & technology for humanity. *Global foundation for cyber studies and research*.

Bol, N., Helberger, N., & Weert, J. C. (2018). Differences in mobile health app use: A source of new digital inequalities? *The Information Society*, *34*(3), 183–193. doi:10.1080/01972243.2018.1438550

Cascio, W. F., & Montealegre, R. (2016). How technology is changing work and organizations. *Annual Review of Organizational Psychology and Organizational Behavior*, *3*(1), 349–375. doi:10.1146/annurev-orgpsych-041015-062352

Chen, Y. R. R., & Schulz, P. J. (2016). The effect of information communication technology interventions on reducing social isolation in the elderly: A systematic review. *Journal of Medical Internet Research*, *18*(1), e4596. doi:10.2196/jmir.4596 PMID:26822073

Cijan, A., Jenič, L., Lamovšek, A., & Stemberger, J. (2019). How digitalization changes the workplace. *Dynamic relationships management journal, 8*(1), 3-12.

Curran, V., Matthews, L., Fleet, L., Simmons, K., Gustafson, D. L., & Wetsch, L. (2017). A review of digital, social, and mobile technologies in health professional education. *The Journal of Continuing Education in the Health Professions*, *37*(3), 195–206. doi:10.1097/CEH.0000000000000168 PMID:28834849

Dutt, B. (2023). Wellbeing Amid Digital Risks: Implications of Digital Risks, Threats, and Scams on Users' Wellbeing. *Media and Communication, 11*(2), 355–366. doi:10.17645/mac.v11i2.6480

El-Khoury, J., Haidar, R., Kanj, R. R., Ali, L. B., & Majari, G. (2021). Characteristics of social media 'detoxification' in university students. *The Libyan Journal of Medicine*, *16*(1), 1846861. doi:10.1080/19932820.2020.1846861 PMID:33250011

Gui, M., & Büchi, M. (2021). From use to overuse: Digital inequality in the age of communication abundance. *Social Science Computer Review*, *39*(1), 3–19. doi:10.1177/0894439319851163

Gui, M., Fasoli, M., & Carradore, R. (2017). Digital well-being. Developing a new theoretical tool for media literacy research. *Italian Journal of Sociology of Education*, *9*(1), 155–173.

Kent, R. (2020). Self-tracking health over time: From the use of Instagram to perform optimal health to the protective shield of the digital detox. *Social Media + Society*, *6*(3), 2056305120940694. doi:10.1177/2056305120940694

Kour, G. (2016). Digital Detoxification: A content analysis of user generated videos uploaded on Youtube by Facebook Quitters. *Media Watch*, *7*(1), 75–83.

Kuss, D. J., & Griffiths, M. D. (2017). Social networking sites and addiction: Ten lessons learned. *International Journal of Environmental Research and Public Health*, *14*(3), 311. doi:10.3390/ijerph14030311 PMID:28304359

Kwon, H. E., So, H., Han, S. P., & Oh, W. (2016). Excessive dependence on mobile social apps: A rational addiction perspective. *Information Systems Research*, *27*(4), 919–939. doi:10.1287/isre.2016.0658

Logacheva, V., Dementieva, D., Ustyantsev, S., Moskovskiy, D., Dale, D., Krotova, I., & Panchenko, A. (2022, May). Paradetox: Detoxification with parallel data. In *Proceedings of the 60th Annual Meeting of the Association for Computational Linguistics (*Volume 1*: Long Papers)* (pp. 6804-6818).

Madianou, M. M., Longboan, L., & Ong, J. C. (2015). *Finding a voice through 'humanitarian technologies'?* Communication technologies and participation in disaster recovery.

Miksch, L., & Schulz, C. (2018). Disconnect to reconnect: The phenomenon of digital detox as a reaction to technology overload.

Milicevic, M. (2015). Contemporary education and digital technologies. *International Journal of Social Science and Humanity*, *5*(7), 656–659. doi:10.7763/IJSSH.2015.V5.535

Mirbabaie, M., Stieglitz, S., & Marx, J. (2022). Digital detox. *Business & Information Systems Engineering*, *64*(2), 239–246. doi:10.100712599-022-00747-x

Monge Roffarello, A., & De Russis, L. (2019, May). The race towards digital wellbeing: Issues and opportunities. In *Proceedings of the 2019 CHI conference on human factors in computing systems* (pp. 1-14). ACM. 10.1145/3290605.3300616

Montag, C., & Walla, P. (2016). Carpe diem instead of losing your social mind: Beyond digital addiction and why we all suffer from digital overuse. *Cogent Psychology*, *3*(1), 1157281. doi:10.1080/23311908.2016.1157281

Mutsvairo, B., Ragnedda, M., & Mabvundwi, K. (2022). 'Our old pastor thinks the mobile phone is a source of evil.' Capturing contested and conflicting insights on digital wellbeing and digital detoxing in an age of rapid mobile connectivity. *Media International Australia*, 1329878X221090992.

Nguyen, M. H., Büchi, M., & Geber, S. (2022). Everyday disconnection experiences: Exploring people's understanding of digital well-being and management of digital media use. *new media & society*, 14614448221105428.

Nguyen, V. T. (2022). The perceptions of social media users of digital detox apps considering personality traits. *Education and Information Technologies*, *27*(7), 9293–9316. doi:10.100710639-022-11022-7 PMID:35370441

Pontes, H. M., Szabo, A., & Griffiths, M. D. (2015). The impact of Internet-based specific activities on the perceptions of Internet addiction, quality of life, and excessive usage: A cross-sectional study. *Addictive Behaviors Reports*, *1*, 19–25. doi:10.1016/j.abrep.2015.03.002 PMID:29531976

Prasad, A., & Quinones, A. (2020). Digital overload warnings-"the right amount of shame"? In *Human-Computer Interaction. Human Values and Quality of Life: Thematic Area*. Springer.

Purohit, A. K., Barclay, L., & Holzer, A. (2020, April). Designing for digital detox: Making social media less addictive with digital nudges. In *Extended Abstracts of the 2020 CHI Conference on Human Factors in Computing Systems* (pp. 1-9).

Radtke, T., Apel, T., Schenkel, K., Keller, J., & von Lindern, E. (2022). Digital detox: An effective solution in the smartphone era? A systematic literature review. *Mobile Media & Communication*, *10*(2), 190–215. doi:10.1177/20501579211028647

Roberts, A. L., Fisher, A., Smith, L., Heinrich, M., & Potts, H. W. (2017). Digital health behaviour change interventions targeting physical activity and diet in cancer survivors: A systematic review and meta-analysis. *Journal of Cancer Survivorship: Research and Practice*, *11*(6), 704–719. doi:10.100711764-017-0632-1 PMID:28779220

Robertson, D. J., Malin, J., Martin, S., Butler, S. H., John, B., Graff, M., & Jones, B. C. (2023). Social media use: attitudes, 'detox', and craving in typical and frequent users.

Rosen, L., & Samuel, A. (2015). Conquering digital distraction. *Harvard Business Review*, *93*(6), 110–113.

Scheppe, M. M., & Seiffen, A. L. (2022). Is it time for a Social Media Detox? *Understanding the journey of intermittent discontinuance of Instagram among Gen Y*.

Schmitt, J. B., Breuer, J., & Wulf, T. (2021). From cognitive overload to digital detox: Psychological implications of telework during the COVID-19 pandemic. *Computers in Human Behavior*, *124*, 106899. doi:10.1016/j.chb.2021.106899 PMID:34566255

Schmuck, D. (2020). Does digital detox work? Exploring the role of digital detox applications for problematic smartphone use and well-being of young adults using multigroup analysis. *Cyberpsychology, Behavior, and Social Networking*, *23*(8), 526–532. doi:10.1089/cyber.2019.0578 PMID:32354288

Sharma, M. K., Anand, N., Ahuja, S., Thakur, P. C., Mondal, I., Singh, P., Kohli, T., & Venkateshan, S. (2020). Digital burnout: COVID-19 lockdown mediates excessive technology use stress. *World Social Psychiatry*, *2*(2), 171–172. doi:10.4103/WSP.WSP_21_20

Sutton, T. (2017). Disconnect to reconnect: The food/technology metaphor in digital detoxing. *First Monday*, *22*(6). doi:10.5210/fm.v22i6.7561

Syvertsen, T. (2023). Framing digital disconnection: Problem definitions, values, and actions among digital detox organisers. *Convergence (London)*, *29*(3), 658–674. doi:10.1177/13548565221122910

Syvertsen, T., & Enli, G. (2020). Digital detox: Media resistance and the promise of authenticity. *Convergence (London)*, *26*(5-6), 1269–1283. doi:10.1177/1354856519847325

Ugur, N. G., & Koc, T. (2015). Time for digital detox: Misuse of mobile technology and phubbing. *Procedia: Social and Behavioral Sciences*, *195*, 1022–1031. doi:10.1016/j.sbspro.2015.06.491

Vialle, S. J., Machin, T., & Abel, S. (2023). Better than scrolling: Digital detox in the search for the ideal self. *Psychology of Popular Media*.

Vishwakarma, M. (2022). Social media: An addiction in disguise. *Peer Reviewed and UGC-CARE Listed Bilingual Journal of Rajasthan Sociological Association*, 85.

Wilcockson, T. D., Osborne, A. M., & Ellis, D. A. (2019). Digital detox: The effect of smartphone abstinence on mood, anxiety, and craving. *Addictive Behaviors*, *99*, 106013. doi:10.1016/j.addbeh.2019.06.002 PMID:31430621

Wood, N. T., & Muñoz, C. (2021). Unplugged: Digital detox enhances student learning. *Marketing Education Review*, *31*(1), 14–25. doi:10.1080/10528008.2020.1836973

Chapter 7
Digital Detox Movement in the Tourism Industry:
Traveler Perspective

Mohammad Badruddoza Talukder
ⓘ https://orcid.org/0000-0001-7788-2732
Daffodil Institute of IT, Bangladesh

Fahmida Kaiser
ⓘ https://orcid.org/0009-0002-4113-207X
Daffodil Institute of IT, Bangladesh

Firoj Kabir
ⓘ https://orcid.org/0009-0001-3014-3163
Daffodil Institute of IT, Bangladesh

Farhana Yeasmin Lina
ⓘ https://orcid.org/0009-0006-8308-5549
Daffodil International University, Bangladesh

ABSTRACT

Although the widespread availability and convenience of digital gadgets have improved our quality of life, there is still a correlation between individuals and a wide range of health problems. As a result, many individuals put their phones and other technological gadgets aside for a while. Using the uses and gratifications theory as a guide, this chapter investigates what motivates people to take a tour without indulging in digital devices. This chapter identifies the definitions, theories, and drivers of digital detox. Adopting new information and communication technologies and our ongoing connection to them are given in contemporary society. People want to identify the trends in the tourism market and help create marketing plans that address consumer needs. This chapter discusses the latest developments in digital detox in the travel industry and how the tourism sectors will change with the new trends. By completing this chapter, we can learn how the digital world is growing fast. Also, how the rapid pace is also getting reverse attention can be understood.

DOI: 10.4018/979-8-3693-1107-3.ch007

1. INTRODUCTION

The expanding use of information technology (IT) significantly impacts all aspects of society, including the nature and boundaries of the workplace (Al-Fudail & Mellar, 2008). Professionals and knowledge workers, in particular, spend most people's working hours around digital gadgets. Additionally, a record number of people spend their free time using applications for digital entertainment and persuasively designed social media. According to a recent study, 11 million Germans claim to use the Internet "constantly, almost the entire time," and 33.1 million claim to use it "multiple times a day" (Adam et al., 2017). It is abundantly evident from research that excessive screen time can have adverse effects on people's wellness. Technostress, described as "any negative impact on attitudes, thoughts, behaviors, or body physiology that is caused either directly or indirectly by technology," can result from utilizing IT (Syvertsen, 2023). Because of the COVID-19 pandemic's impact on the blurring of work and home life, technological stress has emerged as a significant societal issue (Al-Fudail & Mellar, 2008). Eighty-six percent of respondents to a 2019 survey reported that they could not switch off their devices when they left the office. This leads to stress about keeping up with one's online social and communication obligations, which spills over into one's personal life and professional responsibilities (Syvertsen, 2023).

However, the conceptualization and empirical study of "Digital Detox" have remained hazy (Jiang & Balaji, 2022). Early research has shown contradictory findings regarding the ability of digital detox to enhance personal well-being. Despite some ambiguity, the literature frequently emphasizes the necessity of taking specific breaks from IT and urges further study in this area (Rodriguez-Ruiz et al., 2019). There will be a growing desire for digital detox before, during, and most likely after the COVID-19 epidemic, fundamentally challenging how people utilize IT (Talukder et al., 2023). People are finding themselves wishing for time away from the constant presence of IT more and more, which, in our opinion, is a sign of a significant issue—the negative impacts of IT use on health and job satisfaction (Ayyagari et al., 2011).

2. THE IDEA BEHIND DIGITAL DETOX

According to its etymology, the word "detox" refers to a procedure to reduce the levels of dangerous drugs (Ayyagari et al., 2011). Although it has been around for more than ten years, the Oxford Dictionary first listed digital detox in 2013, defining it as "A period during which a person refrains from using electronic devices such as smartphones or computers, regarded as an opportunity to reduce stress or focus on social interaction in the physical world" (Oxford Dictionary, 2013). On the other hand, in contrast to abstinence, which is recommended to recover from drug misuse, a digital detox is a temporary "cleaning." A situation in which a person stops or suspends the use of digital tools for social interactions and activities, as defined by the Technology Dictionary, is referred to as a digital detox (Syvertsen, 2023). Because of this, the individual can alleviate the stress and worry brought on by excessive use of ICTs. Detoxification from technology occurs when an individual stops using all digital devices (Al-Fudail & Mellar, 2008). The current usage of information and communication technologies is assumed to be risky and harmful under these standards. Oxford (2013) and the Technology Dictionary define a digital detox as an opportunity to improve mental well-being by minimizing dependency or fixation with information and communication technologies (ICTs) and appreciating the real world. Because of this, the word is included in an extensive collection of metaphors about health that media critics utilize. To complete a digital detox, it is necessary to power off all forms of information and communication technology (ICT), including mobile devices, telephones, tablets, and laptops (Brown & Kuss, 2020). A detox from digital technology entails cutting out all other forms of media consumption, such as watching television or using work-related computer tools and programming, as well as cutting out all forms of online media and gaming (Brown & Kuss, 2020).

The concept of digital detox capitalizes on the promise of authenticity by providing strategies to counteract the effects of virtual experiences in conjunction with faceless online communication, artificial intelligence, and online interactions. The concept of digital detox capitalizes on the promise of authenticity by providing strategies to counteract the effects of virtual experiences in conjunction with faceless online communication, artificial intelligence, and online interactions (Braukmann et al., 2018). The concept of personal accountability serves as the foundation for this authenticity. The resistance to the potentially adverse effects of information and communication technologies is the basis for a digital detox (Jiang & Balaji, 2022). The term "digital detox" refers to various attempts to take a vacation from online or digital media for a longer or shorter period, as well as other limits on mobile phones and digital devices. Taking a break from technology, sometimes known as "digital detox," may be as short as putting down your phone for an hour or two or taking a trip that lasts several weeks (Talukder et al., 2022). The concept of "digital detox" is becoming increasingly common and is being discussed in several publications. One method to improve self-awareness and stress management capacity is to take periodic breaks from using technology (Brynjolfsson et al., 2020). The primary goals of the awareness and balance approach are regulating information and communications technology and creating an understanding of the right balance of time spent in the physical and digital worlds. This helps maintain a healthy equilibrium between engaging in everyday activities and utilizing technology. Because excessive use of information and communications technology (ICT) can lead to several health problems that need people to undergo a digital detox, its necessity may be directly tied to the rate at which ICT is consumed (Brown & Kuss, 2020). The key reasons digital transformation is essential for tourism service providers, and travelers are the search for alternative information, establishing brand reputations, and improving visitors' experiences at destinations (Kumar et al., 2023). However, social media and digital technologies harm travelers' mental and general well-being. To illustrate the lousy life experiences of tourists, such as superficiality, meaninglessness, letting go of social conventions, and self-isolation during vacations, the idea of "e-lineation" has been developed. The negative emotions and dark characteristics associated with using these technologies, such as disconnection from social and physical surroundings, slowed recovery. An imbalance in wellness during the holidays motivates travelers to disconnect from social media and digital technology (Kumar et al., 2023).

2.1 Digital Detox Vacation

Digital detox is a growing trend that solves information overload and the negative consequences of new media and digital devices. It is a new type of disconnected or unplugged travel (Talukder & Hossain, 2021). According to this topic's tourism research, putting more emphasis on the physical world than the virtual one can help mitigate the detrimental effects of ICTs on the vacation experience. Digital detox vacations are described by several researchers as a type of unplugged tourism, a term currently used in many travel firms' product listings (Rodriguez-Ruiz et al., 2019). Because people share a similar mindset, travel websites frequently employ the terms "digital detox holidays" alongside "digital detox retreat," "well-being," and "tech-free tourism." Companies increasingly provide offline activities like boot camps or vacation packages centered on nature in places where people may shun ICTs and the Internet (Andersen et al., 2016). These businesses cater to consumers looking to unwind by stepping away from technology. Considering these developments, tourism research has concentrated on digital detox vacations over the past decade. These kinds of trips have been referred to in various ways, including digital-free, digital-free travel, digital-free holidays, unplugged tourism, disconnected tourism, and the dead zone in tourism (Syvertsen, 2023). People get uncomfortable due to their increased use of information and communication technologies (ICT), which in turn prompts them to attempt to flee the situation. Pearce and Gretzel (2020) were the ones who carried out the preliminary research on dead zones in disconnected tourism in the year 2012.

People argued that "technology dead zones," which people described as "locations with little to no internet technology access," could be advantageous for tourists (Bozan & Treré, 2023). Similarly, Li et al. (2018) proposed "digital-free tourism (DFT)," which people characterized as "tourism spaces where internet and mobile signals are either absent or where the use of digital technology is controlled. The rise in popularity of travel and lodging goods such as DFT, digital-free cafés and restaurants, digital dead zones, disconnected holidays, and digital detox camps has led to a surge in academic interest in disconnected tourism, particularly digital detox (Bagozzi & Yi, 1988). Articles by Cai et al. (2020), Paris et al. (2015), Pawowska-Legwand and Matoga (2020), and Pearce and Gretzel (2020) are among the most influential on the topic of disconnected tourism and, more specifically, digital detox. According to Li et al. (2018), there have been three stages of media discourse surrounding digital-free tourism: the first occurred between 2009 and 2013, the second between 2014 and 2015, and the third between 2016 and 2017. Digital detox vacations are very similar to digital-free tourism. "Taking a break from technology" and "the essence of life" were people's definitions of the final stage (Karadas et al., 2023). People described digital detox as "a period during which a person refrains from using electronic devices such as smartphones or computers, regarded as an opportunity to reduce stress or focus on social interaction in the physical world" (Bagozzi & Yi, 1988) and DFT as "nature-based, remote, rural and consciously designed: retreat, wellness, and mindfulness." It was described as "switching-off for a specific period" by Neuhofer and Ladkin (2017) and as "a person who uses the internet to a limited extent to connect with people's home while traveling" (Andersen et al., 2016). Based on these, digital detox holidays can be defined as a form of tourism where people who want to disconnect from ICTs because of the adverse social, physical, or mental effects engage in activities like outdoor, experiential, well-being, and health activities in locations with unlimited connectivity (like digital detox hotels, campsites, rural areas, small towns, or woodlands), and stay disconnected for the duration of people's vacation except for emergency communications (Karadas et al., 2023). Significant digital detox efforts have been organized by the hospitality industry, the food and beverage industry, and even some religious organizations (Al-Fudail & Mellar, 2008). For instance, since the middle of 2012, the Eva Restaurant in Los Angeles has given discounts to patrons who turn in people's intelligent gadgets to the staff (Mutsvairo et al., 2022). What started as a movement has subsequently evolved into digital detox holidays. Before spreading to the USA in 2013 and Europe in 2015, people originally appeared in Saint Vincent and Grenadine in the Caribbean. Hotels that provide digital detox services are frequently located near scenic areas and historic buildings (Mutsvairo et al., 2022). Due to people's natural surroundings, historic and remote structures (such as monasteries) or camping grounds are the preferred lodging options for digital detox vacations. Although most hospitality facilities offer cutting-edge ICT, the number of digital detox hospitality facilities is also growing. For instance, the Four Seasons hotel chain has not adopted the trend towards increased use of technology in travel. As of 2018, it has provided digital detox to visitors at its Desroches Island hotel in the Seychelles, devoid of a mobile phone base station. Instead, wireless internet access is restricted to the building. Tourism professionals have been working to position digital detox travel as one of the newest travel trends. The market for digital detox tourism has previously been experimentally investigated across the prisms of intention, experiences, and motivation. To gain a deeper comprehension of digital detox tourism, it illustrates how technologies have proliferated to the point where they infiltrate almost every area of human lives, including travel and leisure (Talukder et al., 2023).

Both providers and consumers are changing as a result of digitalization. Websites, applications, and social media are affordable ways to advertise travel locations and draw tourists. Travelers continue to follow message-checking habits, utilize digital maps, and post about their experiences on social media. However, research indicates that multitasking and digital distractions can lead to conflicts within families and groups and negatively impact travel experiences (González-Padilla, 2022). Ever since the advent of smartphones, ever-evolving electronic devices have significantly changed our lives and society. Almost two-thirds of the world's population now own a mobile phone, and three-quarters own a smartphone (Mutsvairo et al., 2022). On the positive side, these technological advances allow to connect with friends and loved ones anytime, anywhere, expand our horizons through a large amount of online information, and participate in leisure activities online (Jiang & Balaji, 2022).

At the same time, excessive use of smartphones can be life-threatening. Psychologists have shown that the adverse effects of excessive smartphone use include decreased self-control. Other adverse effects of smartphone use include technology anxiety, depression, loneliness, and sleep (Rathebe & Mosoeu, 2023). It was also found that college students who use smartphones excessively feel that their leisure time is more limited. Excessive use of smartphones has not only attracted the attention of psychologists. Ethicists are concerned about a diminished capacity for empathic engagement, saying electronic devices can distract people from face-to-face interactions and make them oblivious to other people's emotional states (Rodriguez-Ruiz et al., 2019). Fortunately, both the public and academia are taking steps to counter the adverse effects of smartphones. For example, the term "digital detox" refers to a period during which people consciously or voluntarily give up the use of digital devices (such as smartphones, tablets, and computers) and electronic media (such as social media and messaging apps). Digital detox is an opportunity to reduce stress and prioritize social interaction in the physical world, as well as self-motivation to reduce the potential negative impact of digital technologies on health and well-being. Researchers believe that this is an effective intervention strategy. Media studies, on the other hand, evaluate digital detox from social and cultural perspectives. Pinto et al. (2022) argue that while digital detox is advocated offline, it is also actively introduced online as a trending buzzword and a symbol of self-expression and identity. Therefore, digital detox has undoubtedly influenced the creation of new business opportunities. In the tourism context, tourism products have rebranded their offline status as digital detox vacations and digital detox camps on vacation. Digital detox promises the desired results through a break in communication with potential customers. Tourism was therefore conveyed as an expectation of a 'fantasy world' where tourists could escape from everyday life.

This has become a growing marketing trend that promises to provide tourists with rich sensory, emotional, cognitive, and relational experiences through digital-free activities in digital-free environments. Digital detox tourism products aim to enable a digital disconnect from nature, authenticity, and connection with oneself and others. On travel websites, digital detox tourism is often associated with images of yoga, retreats, spas, and natural sites (Dryglas & Klimkiewicz, 2023).

Camp Grounded, America's most famous digital detox camp, offers analog camping where travelers can relax and immerse themselves in nature with various activities, including yoga, meditation, campfires, archery, and more. Time to Log Off, a digital detox company founded in the UK offers seven-day rural digital detox holidays. Additionally, digital shutdowns were integrated into marketing communications in the Austrian and Swiss Alpine regions (Irimiás, 2023).

3. CAUSES TO DIGITAL DETOX

3.1 To Reacquaint People With Their Surroundings

People will be amazed at what a beautiful place it can be when they look up from their phones, take off their headphones, and experience all the sights and sounds surrounding them. This is especially true when taking a digital detox retreat abroad (Ayyagari et al., 2011).

3.2 To Reestablish Connections With Other People

While many people use digital devices to stay in touch with one another, doing so frequently keeps them from interacting with people in other people's immediate environment (Syvertsen, 2023). People will be astonished at how much more involved people will feel when they put their devices aside and permit themselves to appreciate the company of those around them.

3.3 To Find New Pastimes

A surprising amount of time is spent using our digital gadgets, time that could be spent learning a new digitalized game or resuming an old one (Brynjolfsson et al., 2020). Use that time to practice yoga, read, sketch, or anything else, and people will undoubtedly feel much more content.

3.4 To Get More Rest

Numerous studies have demonstrated that using digital devices before night, especially in the hour before bed, can interfere with our ability to fall asleep. People can get a better night's sleep and avoid being awakened in the middle of the night by something that could wait until morning if people turn off their devices (Braukmann et al., 2018).

3.5 To Give Oneself Some Alone Time

Sometimes people need to unplug themselves from technology to enjoy the moments of solitude and get the opportunity to reconnect with themselves. People can unwind fully and turn off their minds; electronics users are not instantly reachable (Mutsvairo et al., 2022).

Many behaviors, like checking people's phones or other devices, have developed into unconscious habits that perform without realizing it. However, it is a habit people do not need, especially if it causes people to feel the urge to check people's phones at every opportunity or circumstance. While breaking the cycle can be challenging, a digital detox provides the ideal setting for ultimately kicking this terrible habit.

3.6 To Increase Concentration

Continuing from the preceding point, a digital detox will help people eliminate their technology devices, which can be an unwelcome distraction (Ayyagari et al., 2011). A digital detox will help people stop this from happening. Whether people are working, hanging out with friends, or just relaxing, lighting up people's phone screens is enough to instantly divert people's focus from what people are doing and make people far less effective.

3.7 To Enhance People's Well-Being

It has been established that frequent usage of digital devices affects people's health. A digital detox will assist in changing the behaviors that contribute to these issues, making people happier and healthier (Pinto et al., 2022).

3.8 To Improve Communication With Technology

A digital detox can help people improve their relationship with technology rather than requiring them to give it up completely. People will learn to use their electronics just when people are beneficial and not when they become a problem after the detox helps people stop being so reliant on them and highlights when people genuinely improve their lives (Coca-Stefaniak, 2021).

3.9 To Live More Fully

When people add up all these justifications, the solution is to go on a digital detox to enhance people's enjoyment of life (Bagozzi & Yi, 1988). Being present, feeling connected to the people and environment around people, being happier and healthier, and having more time to do the things people enjoy are essential.

4. DIGITAL DETOX TRENDS IN TRAVEL

Smartphones, tablets, and PDAs are just a few examples of digital detox technologies that have advanced incredibly quickly to become indispensable tools for daily living. While ICT is a driving force in the modern tourism industry, some travel agencies and hotels have recently discovered a niche market for those looking to "escape" from the digital life by offering "digital detox travel packages" or trips to far-flung locations with little access to ICTs. While has investigated how tourists react to being forced to disconnect, it has not yet sufficiently examined why visitors might decide to go on a digital detox vacation. Therefore, this chapter aims to understand why travelers take digital detox vacations and their outcomes for leading healthy and relaxed lifestyles.

5. REASONS FOR A DIGITAL DETOX VACATION

5.1. Aspects of Physical Health

According to research, smartphone screens emit blue light, which has been shown to affect the circadian system, the body's internal clock that controls sleep requirements. According to the Swedish National Survey of Public Health from 2010, men's and women's sleep problems have been prospectively linked to intensive computer and mobile phone use (intense: more than 2 hours without pauses) (Bozan & Treré, 2023).

5.2. Psychiatric Variables

Addiction to digital devices is frequently linked to psychological problems. Internet addiction is one of the most prevalent types of digital addiction in modern culture. There are two common psychological factors, according to the World Health Organization: "withdrawal," which refers to "feelings of anger, tension, anxiety, and depression when the internet and computers are inaccessible," and "negative repercussions" or "conflict," which refers to "self-imposed social isolation and disintegration, lying, arguing, poor academic and occupational achievement, and fatigue." However, a lack of access to ICTs can also trigger suicidal thoughts. According to (Mutsvairo et al., 2022), there is a connection between adolescent sadness, Internet addiction, and suicidal ideation.

5.3. Social Science Factors

The sociological aspects are described as "the facts and experiences that influence individuals' personality, attitudes, and lifestyle." This definition includes factors that impact people's behavior in social settings. Problems in relationships are one widespread sociological issue brought on by digital addiction, according to the most recent study (Rodriguez-Ruiz et al., 2019).

5.4. Technical Aspects

ICT innovation is widely established throughout Europe. Boredom and worries about online privacy are also linked to social media weariness, which frequently affects early adopters. As a result, people of all ages may develop a dislike of technology for a variety of reasons. As a result of the numerous studies emphasizing the detrimental impacts of ICTs on people's lives over the past ten years, several businesses have begun to adjust how people's employees use ICTs both within and outside the workplace (Brynjolfsson et al., 2020).

5.5. Geographic and Economic Variables

Geographical and economic factors are two elements that could be viewed as limitations. Even while economic and geographic variables may not directly relate to digital detoxing, people must be considered when evaluating reasons for a digital detox vacation (Braukmann et al., 2018). The cost is one of the most significant economic elements influencing the choice of a vacation place.

6. DIGITAL DETOX TRENDS IN TOURISM

6.1. Digital Detox Will Not Go Away

People can unwind psychologically and physically when imagining being free of all digital influences. However, being in touch with people self and their surroundings is another benefit of digital detoxification that should not be overlooked. Time is spent on things like drawing with a pencil and paper, playing board games with family, or starting on a walk without technology (Karadas et al., 2023).

6.2. Travelling Slowly the Entire Route

Flygskam, or "flight shame," is a notion popularized by Swedish adolescent environmentalist Greta Thunberg that makes responsible travelers reevaluate how frequently and where people fly. With people's new 'Fly Responsibly' campaign, airlines like the Dutch KLM are urging people to pass less. As a result, many individuals choose to take trains this decade instead of flying. The European railway operator TGV Lyria is already counting on more robust demand by increasing the volume of transport services from Paris to various locations in Switzerland by 30% (Coca-Stefaniak, 2021).

6.3. Exploring Local Cultures Through Homestays

It is understandable why hybrid home-tells are becoming popular, as Airbnb lists hotels on its site more frequently, and hotels work to design homes with a more local feel. In today's luxury hotels, visitors do not want to feel removed from the locations they are visiting (Karadas et al., 2023).

6.4. Workday the Ideal Situation

'Bleisure' has been a well-known idea for many years. It combines travel for business with leisure and tourism. Tourism for peace has many different forms. Some folks choose to go on a vacation while on a business trip. In other instances, businesses plan excursions as a reward in between hectic workdays.

6.5. The Growth of the Internet of Things (IoT) and AI

Hotelier AI is arguably the most fascinating trend in tourism. Following the Hilton Hotel chain's introduction of Connie, the robot concierge, several hotels adopted the interactive robot trend by placing them to do specific welcome tasks or even deliver food and drinks to visitors (Juncal et al., 2022).

6.6. Unplugged Accommodations

To take advantage of people's "unplugged" or "digital detox" packages, hotels, resorts, and lodges started asking visitors to give up their electronic devices when people checked in. These places frequently offered non-technological alternatives to entertainment through amenities and activities.

6.7. Here Are Some Ways Hotels May Help People's Visitors Have a Digital Detox Experience

- **Limited Wi-Fi Access**: Hotels can provide limited or no Wi-Fi in public spaces and guest rooms (Hoang et al., 2023).
- **No TV or Fewer Channels**: Some hotels might not provide televisions in the guest rooms. In contrast, others might restrict the number of channels.
- **Unplugged Zones**: These are designated locations within the hotel where electronic devices are not permitted, such as comfort lounges, meditation spaces, or particular spa facilities.
- **Technology-Free Activities**: To keep visitors interested, hotels can plan various technology-free activities and services (Hoang et al., 2023).
- **Promoting Outdoor Exploration**: Highlight the natural beauty of the hotel's surroundings and nudge customers to spend less time indoors and more time outdoors.
- **Offer Offline Resources**: Provide hardcopy guides, maps, and brochures about points of interest and activities in the area so that visitors will not rely solely on digital devices to organize people's day (Harmon & Duffy, 2023).
- **Establish a Relaxing Ambiance**: Include aspects in the hotel's design and furnishings that promote calmness and repose, such as calming color palettes, inviting seating places, and nature-inspired accents.
- **Offer awards or Discounts for Guests**: Give guests an extra incentive to disconnect by offering prizes or discounts for those who choose to participate in the digital detox activities.
- **Educational Resources**: Inform visitors about the advantages of a digital detox and how cutting back on screen time may enhance well-being (Bozan & Treré, 2023).

6.8. Nature Retreats and Eco-Tourism

Tourists looked for locations where people could get close to nature and engage in outdoor activities without being constantly connected. For individuals seeking to disconnect from technology, eco-lodges and wilderness vacations have become attractive options (Al-Fudail & Mellar, 2008).

6.9. The Following Are Some Probable Developments and Trends in Digital Detox in Eco-Tourism

- **Technology-free zones**: A few eco-lodges, resorts, and travel agencies have begun establishing technology-free zones on people's property
- **Off-the-grid experiences**: Eco-tourism locations that provide off-the-grid experiences, where cellular and internet connectivity is constrained or nonexistent, have grown in appeal with tourists looking to entirely unplug from the digital world (Dryglas & Klimkiewicz, 2023).
- **Wellness and mindfulness initiatives**: Eco-tourism companies include wellness and mindfulness exercises in people's itineraries.
- **Digital detox retreats**: To meet the needs of tourists seeking to disconnect from the constant connectedness of modern life, specialized digital detox retreats with a focus on eco-tourism and sustainable practices have arisen (Dryglas & Klimkiewicz, 2023).
- **Nature-focused activities**: Digital detox in eco-tourism sometimes entails participating in outdoor activities like hiking, wildlife observation, bird watching, and stargazing.
- **Environmental education**: Eco-tourism providers may use digital detox experiences to inform visitors about the local ecosystem, wildlife, and conservation initiatives, creating a greater appreciation for nature.
- **Personalized travel experiences**: A few eco-tourism providers provide itineraries that may be customized to a traveler's specific needs by letting them choose how much connectivity they want while away from home (Talukder, 2021).
- **Social media mindfulness**: A purposeful attempt to reduce social media sharing and encourage more thoughtful and responsible online behavior may result from this knowledge (Ayyagari et al., 2011).

6.10. Technology-Free Tours

Tour operators started offering technology-free tours, on which visitors were asked not to use electronic devices so people could fully take in the beauty and culture of the area (Adam et al., 2017).

6.11. Traveler's Encouragement

Travelers are encouraged to be present, interact with the local community, and leave as little digital trace as possible to the growing popularity of mindful travel practices.

6.12. Travelling "Off-Season"

Some travelers visit places during the off-peak season to avoid crowds and lessen the desire to capture every moment on camera.

6.13. Detoxing From Digital Media

Digital detox aims to lessen the detrimental impacts of technology on physical and mental health, including eye strain, disturbed sleep, and social media addiction. Travelers may reconnect with the world around them, partake in more fulfilling activities, and enhance general well-being by taking a vacation from screens (Andersen et al., 2016).

6.14. Think About Using Apps for Mindfulness

More mindfulness apps that support people in developing mindfulness practices in people's daily lives are anticipated this year. These apps will feature breathing exercises, daily affirmations, and guided meditations (Brown & Kuss, 2020).

6.15. Screen Time Monitoring

Everything can be done using phones, from paying bills to supermarket shopping. However, people are not alone if they spend too much time in front of a screen. Fortunately, several apps can assist people in taking control of their digital lives and finding a sense of balance.

6.16. Purchasing a Standing Desk

Everybody has experienced the discomfort of spending hours at a computer stooped over while typing. If people have ever been in this uncomfortable situation, people thought about the advantages of standing while people work. The use of treadmill workstations and standing desks has grown in favor in recent years to reduce the harmful consequences of extended sitting (Díaz-Meneses & Estupinán-Ojeda, 2022).

6.17. Establishing a Tech-Free Zone

Avoid having people's home offices in people's bedrooms as much as possible. However, suppose people must unplug and switch off any electronics before retiring for the evening. In that case, travelers can create a calm, distraction-free environment that encourages sound sleep and permits concentrated work (Karadas et al., 2023).

6.18. Electronics Must Be Unplugged While Not in Use

Numerous appliances, computers, and televisions emit a huge number of EMF radiation. For minimizing the negative effects of EMF radiation, People can disconnect the appliances when they are not using those.

6.19. Putting People's Phones on Airplane Mode or Off

Tce EMF-emitting technologies in people's homes should be turned off whenever people sleep. Even though leaving these gadgets on may be more practical, doing so adds a few extra minutes to people's day. It spares people hours of needless EMF exposure (Mutsvairo et al., 2022).

7. CONCEPTUAL MODEL

Figure 1. Digital detox in tourism (self-developed)

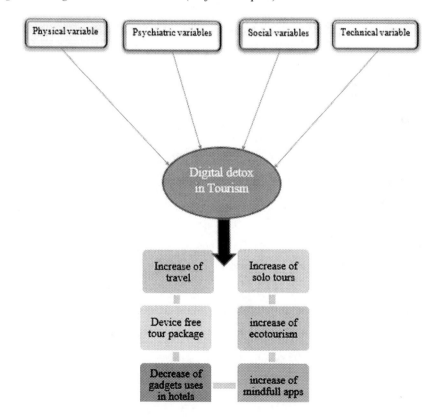

8. CONCLUSION

Digital detox is increasing with the development of technology. There will be a significant effect of digital detox on every sector of the world. However, tourism is the most progressive industry that will be affected. Some emerging trends are highlighted, and these trends will change the tourism industry in the future as technology is becoming the boss of the end along with tourism. The tourism industry has significant importance on the economy and, up until 2023, generated substantial cash flows. In the last few years, we have witnessed a massive implementation of technological solutions in tourism. Despite the fantastic importance of digitalization in tourism, which can be partially viewed as a boosting engine, the practice of overuse is disturbing and getting our attention. Since the COVID-19 pandemic necessitates the accelerated use of digital tools, numerous studies highlighted the psychological challenges of digitalization and its associated overload. A digital detox can help eliminate all the exceeding stress and improve wellness and well-being. The concept of digital detox is incredibly the burgeoning trend to the world as a potential wellness destination, so this chapter has the intention to explore in depth the concepts of digital detox and its effect on users, to present the negative aspects of digitalization, to examine the current state of digitalization in the world and to try to position the country as a digital detox destination.

REFERENCES

Adam, M. T. P., Gimpel, H., Maedche, A., & Riedl, R. (2017). Design Blueprint for Stress-Sensitive Adaptive Enterprise Systems. *Business & Information Systems Engineering*, 59(4), 277–291. doi:10.100712599-016-0451-3

Al-Fudail, M., & Mellar, H. (2008). Investigating teacher stress when using technology. *Computers & Education*, 51(3), 1103–1110. doi:10.1016/j.compedu.2007.11.004

Andersen, K. H., De Vreese, C., & Albæk, E. (2016). Measuring Media Diet in a High-Choice Environment—Testing the List-Frequency Technique. *Communication Methods and Measures*, 10(2–3), 81–98. doi:10.1080/19312458.2016.1150973

Ayyagari, G., Grover, & Purvis. (2011). Technostress: Technological Antecedents and Implications. *Management Information Systems Quarterly*, 35(4), 831. doi:10.2307/41409963

Bagozzi, R. P., & Yi, Y. (1988). On the evaluation of structural equation models. *Journal of the Academy of Marketing Science*, 16(1), 74–94. doi:10.1007/BF02723327

Bozan, V., & Treré, E. (2023). When digital inequalities meet digital disconnection: Studying the material conditions of disconnection in rural Turkey. *Convergence (London)*, *135485652311745*. Advance online publication. doi:10.1177/13548565231174596

Braukmann, J., Schmitt, A., Ďuranová, L., & Ohly, S. (2018). Identifying ICT-Related Affective Events Across Life Domains and Examining their Unique Relationships with Employee Recovery. *Journal of Business and Psychology*, *33*(4), 529–544. doi:10.100710869-017-9508-7

Brown, L., & Kuss, D. J. (2020). Fear of Missing Out, Mental Wellbeing, and Social Connectedness: A Seven-Day Social Media Abstinence Trial. *International Journal of Environmental Research and Public Health*, *17*(12), 4566. doi:10.3390/ijerph17124566 PMID:32599962

Brynjolfsson, E., Horton, J., Ozimek, A., Rock, D., Sharma, G., & Tu Ye, H.-Y. (2020). *COVID-19 and Remote Work: An Early Look at US Data* (w27344; p. w27344). National Bureau of Economic Research. doi:10.3386/w27344

Coca-Stefaniak, J. A. (2021). Beyond smart tourism cities – towards a new generation of "wise" tourism destinations. *Journal of Tourism Futures*, *7*(2), 251–258. doi:10.1108/JTF-11-2019-0130

Díaz-Meneses, G., & Estupinán-Ojeda, M. (2022). The Outbreak of Digital Detox Motives and Their Public Health Implications for Holiday Destinations. *International Journal of Environmental Research and Public Health*, *19*(3), 1548. doi:10.3390/ijerph19031548 PMID:35162570

Dryglas, D., & Klimkiewicz, K. (2023). Emerging trends in employee competencies in Polish therapeutic tourism enterprises. *International Journal of Spa and Wellness*, *6*(1), 157–175. doi:10.1080/24721735.2022.2152849

González-Padilla P. (2022). *Tourist behavior and demand for digital disconnection: A review*. doi:10.34623/TP23-A945

Harmon, J., & Duffy, L. (2023). Turn off to tune in: Digital disconnection, digital consciousness, and meaningful leisure. *Journal of Leisure Research*, 1–21. doi:10.1080/00222216.2023.2246042

Hoang, Q., Cronin, J., & Skandalis, A. (2023). Futureless vicissitudes: Gestural anti-consumption and the reflexively impotent (anti-)consumer. *Marketing Theory*, *147059312311531*(4), 585–606. Advance online publication. doi:10.1177/14705931231153193

Irimiás, A. (2023). The Young Tourist and Social Media. In A. Irimiás, The Youth Tourist: Motives, Experiences and Travel Behaviour (pp. 63–81). Emerald Publishing Limited. doi:10.1108/978-1-80455-147-920231005

Jiang, Y., & Balaji, M. S. (2022). Getting unwired: What drives travellers to take a digital detox holiday? *Tourism Recreation Research*, *47*(5–6), 453–469. doi:10.10 80/02508281.2021.1889801

Juncal, B., Vides, G., Matos, P., & Sousa, B. B. (2022). Digital Detox, Trends, and Segmentation in Tourism. In C. M. Q. Ramos, S. Quinteiro, & A. R. Gonçalves (Eds.), (pp. 155–169). Advances in Business Strategy and Competitive Advantage. IGI Global. doi:10.4018/978-1-7998-8165-0.ch010

Karadas, T., Dilci, T., & Sagbas, N. Ö. (2023). Life in the Digital World. In R. Sine Nazlı & G. Sari (Eds.), (pp. 192–216). Advances in Human and Social Aspects of Technology. IGI Global. doi:10.4018/978-1-6684-8397-8.ch013

Kumar, S., Talukder, M. B., Kabir, F., & Kaiser, F. (2023). Challenges and Sustainability of Green Finance in the Tourism Industry: Evidence from Bangladesh. In S. Taneja, P. Kumar, S. Grima, E. Ozen, & K. Sood (Eds.), (pp. 97–111). Advances in Finance, Accounting, and Economics. IGI Global. doi:10.4018/979-8-3693-1388-6.ch006

Mohammad, B. T., & Mokarram Hossain, M. (2021). Prospects of future tourism in Bangladesh: An evaluative study. *I-Manager's. Journal of Management*, *15*(4), 31. doi:10.26634/jmgt.15.4.17495

Mutsvairo, B., Ragnedda, M., & Mabvundwi, K. (2022). 'Our old pastor thinks the mobile phone is a source of evil.' Capturing contested and conflicting insights on digital wellbeing and digital detoxing in an age of rapid mobile connectivity. *Media International Australia*, 1329878X2210909. doi:10.1177/1329878X221090992

Pinto, A., Cardinale, Y., Dongo, I., & Ticona-Herrera, R. (2022). An Ontology for Modeling Cultural Heritage Knowledge in Urban Tourism. *IEEE Access : Practical Innovations, Open Solutions*, *10*, 61820–61842. doi:10.1109/ACCESS.2022.3179664

Rathebe, P. C., & Mosoeu, L. G. (2023). Fruits and vegetables contaminated with particles of heavy metals: A narrative review to explore the use of electromagnetic fields as an alternative treatment method. *Cogent Food & Agriculture*, *9*(1), 2231686. doi:10.1080/23311932.2023.2231686

Rodriguez-Ruiz, A., Lång, K., Gubern-Merida, A., Broeders, M., Gennaro, G., Clauser, P., Helbich, T. H., Chevalier, M., Tan, T., Mertelmeier, T., Wallis, M. G., Andersson, I., Zackrisson, S., Mann, R. M., & Sechopoulos, I. (2019). Stand-Alone Artificial Intelligence for Breast Cancer Detection in Mammography: Comparison With 101 Radiologists. *Journal of the National Cancer Institute, 111*(9), 916–922. doi:10.1093/jnci/djy222 PMID:30834436

Syvertsen, T. (2023). Framing digital disconnection: Problem definitions, values, and actions among digital detox organisers. *Convergence (London), 29*(3), 658–674. doi:10.1177/13548565221122910

Talukder, M., Shakhawat Hossain, M., & Kumar, S. (2022). Blue Ocean Strategies in Hotel Industry in Bangladesh: A Review of Present Literatures' Gap and Suggestions for Further Study. SSRN *Electronic Journal*. doi:10.2139/ssrn.4160709

Talukder, M. B. (2020). The Future of Culinary Tourism: An Emerging Dimension for the Tourism Industry of Bangladesh. I-Manager's. *Journal of Management, 15*(1), 27. doi:10.26634/jmgt.15.1.17181

Talukder, M. B. (2021). An assessment of the roles of the social network in the development of the Tourism Industry in Bangladesh. *International Journal of Business, Law, and Education, 2*(3), 85–93. doi:10.56442/ijble.v2i3.21

Talukder, M. B., Kumar, S., Sood, K., & Grima, S. (2023). Information Technology, Food Service Quality and Restaurant Revisit Intention. *International Journal of Sustainable Development and Planning, 18*(1), 295–303. doi:10.18280/ijsdp.180131

Vos, S. R., Clark-Ginsberg, A., Puente-Duran, S., Salas-Wright, C. P., Duque, M. C., Herrera, I. C., Maldonado-Molina, M. M., Castillo, M. N., Lee, T. K., Garcia, M. F., Fernandez, C. A., Hanson, M., Scaramutti, C., & Schwartz, S. J. (2021). The family crisis migration stress framework: A framework to understand the mental health effects of crisis migration on children and families caused by disasters. *New Directions for Child and Adolescent Development, 2021*(176), 41–59. doi:10.1002/cad.20397 PMID:33634569

Wang, Y., & Li, M. (2021). Family identity bundles and holiday decision making. *Journal of Travel Research, 60*(3), 486–502. doi:10.1177/0047287520930091

Yu, X., Anaya, G. J., Miao, L., Lehto, X., & Wong, I. A. (2018). The impact of smartphones on the family vacation experience. *Journal of Travel Research, 57*(5), 579–596. doi:10.1177/0047287517706263

Zhao, Z., Shi, D., Qi, X., Shan, Y., & Liu, X. (2023). Family travel among people with autism: Challenges and support needs. *International Journal of Contemporary Hospitality Management*, *35*(11), 3743–3763. doi:10.1108/IJCHM-10-2022-1229

Chapter 8

Exploring the Impact of Digital Detoxification on Higher Education Students' Learning

Anshul Garg

(iD) https://orcid.org/0000-0001-8297-9256
Taylor's University, Malaysia

Amrik Singh

(iD) https://orcid.org/0000-0003-3598-8787
Lovely Professional University, India

Jia Yanan
Taylor's University, Malaysia

ABSTRACT

Nowadays, smartphones are ubiquitous. People spend many hours daily on their smartphones or other digital gadgets. Unlike other electronic devices, smartphones enable such functions almost anytime and anywhere, with numerous consequences for our daily lives. Surfing social network sites or instant messaging can impair well-being and is related to clinical phenomena like depression. The proliferation of social networking platforms has resulted in a rise in usage frequency among young adults. Digital detox interventions have been suggested as a solution to reduce the negative impacts of smartphone use on outcomes like well-being or social relationships. Keeping in touch with their smartphones during lectures hinders students' learning experience. The primary objective of this study is to assess how digital detoxification affects student learning within higher education establishments. The research also delves into the prevalence of digital detoxification among university students, shedding light on their comprehension of social media detox and potential mental health consequences.

DOI: 10.4018/979-8-3693-1107-3.ch008

INTRODUCTION

Technology and new digital tools can improve student learning. But the opposite may also be true. The explosion of technology and digital media can help students understand how these technologies influence consumer behaviour and how marketers use them. Digital detox is a widely used term for a situation where a person "takes a step back" from all electronic and digital devices (e.g., smartphones, tablets, computers). The goal is to alleviate the stress, anxiety, and depression that often result from too much exposure to the digital world and to focus on real relationships and connections to real-world events. One of the best ways to digitally detox is to get into a green environment. However, a period of digital detox can help you better understand the importance of technology in today's life and learn how to manage its role in society. It is a beneficial addition to our daily life. Young people, in particular, need a deep understanding of how technology can help them in education and other areas of life. However, you must be careful not to engage with the technology and make it not worth your time. To achieve this goal, teachers and educators can play an important role in helping students develop mindfulness through digital detox sessions. These three tips will help you: A digital detox should allow a person to relax. It is, therefore, important to help students and children choose successful goals and avoid the risk of disappointment if the task is unsuccessful. It's a good idea to start by setting small limits each day. For example, students can be invited to slowly eliminate the presence of their technological devices from some parts of their day. This kind of "gradual detoxing" helps to eliminate digital dependencies incrementally. Students feel more in control and can focus on thinking about the usefulness of their devices and how they interact with them instead of focusing on the bad sensation of feeling "empty" because of withdrawal symptoms created by a total sharp interruption. The Covid-19 pandemic gave rise to e-Learning and EdTech like never before. Education can no longer be associated within the four walls. By exploring technological solutions and prioritising education, various institutions and individuals have invested time and effort in giving the best e-learning experiences to students. But in the era of e-learning, eliminating digital clutter has become essential as students spend more time on screens throughout the day for learning or entertainment. Research from Guilford Journals suggests limiting social media use to 30 minutes daily can improve mental health and well-being. Others said you should limit screen time to at least three weeks to see noticeable changes. Constant use of technology can cause mental and physical stress for students and teachers. Using a smartphone or tablet for long periods can be tiring and harmful. Often, parents don't know how to encourage their students to spend more time using digital devices because these devices fail to meet their children's needs when they need them most. Some work and strategies may be needed to help students break free from digital media. Overuse of technology – whether it is time spent on smartphones, social media or other digital screens – can lead to unexpected consequences and create its effects. The rise of the Internet and digital devices has somewhat changed people's lives. However, excessive use of this technology can lead to physical and mental fatigue, affecting not only one's health but also the relationship quality of students and parents. To prevent this, parents must demonstrate the same behaviour. Sometimes, parents may not be aware of the inappropriate content and online harassment their children are being exposed to. While it is important to incorporate digital detox programs into students' daily lives, parents should also be aware of the problems that arise from excessive use of digital devices. A digital detox is nothing more than limiting the use of electronic devices for a certain period. There are many fun detox challenges/guides created by various authors that can be helpful to students. This includes taking regular breaks, spending time outdoors, and posting school times. Parents can help their wards create a schedule that balances screen time and outdoor time. Taking a digital detox, or at least embracing new, mindful technology practices, can be a healthy development. We must remember that breaking digital habits can be challenging because we do things against our habits. Some mindful steps students can follow include taking short breaks from screens. Ophthalmologists also recommend following the 20:20:20 rule. That means spending 20 minutes on the screen. We must look at or focus on an object 20 feet away for 20 seconds. Another step you can take is to spend time outdoors after learning online. Physical activity always makes more sense and is a great way to distract yourself from other thoughts. Automatic reminders that help people stop checking their phones. Parents can prevent their children from waking up and looking at their phones after bedtime. Counselling and teaching students how to regulate their emotions (FOMO – Fear of Missing Out) can also be very effective. It turns out that time away from electronic devices can also benefit our brains.

LITERATURE REVIEW

The Role of Digital Devices in Modern Higher Education

Since the 20th century, with the development and popularisation of computers and the Internet, the relationship between digital devices and students receiving higher education has become increasingly closer (Händel et al., 2022). Digital devices appear in the teaching process as learning tools and widely participate in students' daily lives (Haleem et al., 2022). As learning tools, digital devices can help students improve learning engagement and efficiency through reasonable application, stimulate students' attention, and become a powerful tool to enhance students' learning initiate (Tripathi et al., 2023). The effectiveness of digital device-assisted learning can ultimately be reflected in improving students' daily tests and performance points (Haleem et al., 2022; Hover & Wise, 2022). In an ideal situation, digital devices can also become assistants in students' daily lives and maintain health. For example, social media can make communication between classmates and between classmates and teachers more timely, immediately and smoothly, improving communication efficiency and saving time (Maqableh & Alia, 2021).Oztosun et al. (2023) pointed out that digital devices effectively alleviate students' psychological problems during particular periods, such as COVID-19.

Before COVID-19, people's attitudes towards e-learning tools showed a negative trend (Zawacki-Richter, 2021). The outbreak of the pandemic has promoted the popularity of electronic learning tools, and many universities have chosen to teach online and use social media to communicate to avoid cross-infection between students and faculty (Selvaraj et al., 2021; Williamson, 2021). Some scholars have a positive attitude towards this phenomenon, believing that the pandemic has promoted digital innovation in higher education and will positively impact people's attitudes (Williamson, 2021; Zawacki-Richter, 2021). However, everything has two sides. Some scholars are concerned about this phenomenon. They believe many factors are not conducive to student learning in a teaching environment that relies too much on electronic devices. For example, online education using digital devices reduces interaction between teachers and students, and genuine interaction is crucial to learning effectiveness (Selvaraj et al., 2021).

There are a variety of digital devices in the higher educational environment, and their different functions make them play different roles in the education process (Al Rawashdeh et al., 2021). For example, bullet screen provides opportunities to increase classroom interaction (Yang et al., 2021), and virtual reality technology can reproduce teaching material content more vividly and provide virtual scientific experiment scenes (Williams, 2022). With the development of portable electronic devices and the enrichment of smartphone applications, smartphones play a crucial role that cannot be ignored in the modern education environment. While it affects and changes education methods, it also affects students' learning, life, and physical and mental health (Webster & Paquette, 2023).

The Impact of Smartphones on the Learning of Higher Education Students

As the world continues to develop towards intelligence and digitisation, smartphones have become one of the essential learning tools for contemporary young people (Webster & Paquette, 2023). A survey as early as 2015 showed that almost all college students have mobile phones and carry them at all times, even in class (Ugur & Koc,

2015). Mobile phones are popular in universities because smartphones are becoming more portable and intelligent, but also because they are influenced by education policies and universities which hope to use smartphones to provide students with a personalised and efficient learning environment (Zdravkova, 2023). Therefore, using smartphones to change students' learning methods, learning efficiency, and learning effects is not only a concern for many students and teachers but also attracts the attention of researchers in education. To explore the impact of smartphones on students in the higher education environment, scholars have studied the beneficial and adverse effects of smartphones on student learning.

Smartphones' interactive functions, personalised functions, and portability provide students with more learning opportunities and improve their proactive and initiative in learning. First, smartphones offer students and teachers with more interactive learning opportunities. For example, knowledge can be discussed and shared between students or between students and teachers through social media, which can improve student engagement and learning performance (Alismaiel et al., 2022). The personalisation of applications is one of the critical reasons for smartphones to play an essential role in learning environments. This feature allows smartphones to improve students' learning abilities without strict restrictions, making it a powerful learning tool for different subject backgrounds (Firmansyah et al., 2020). Personalised learning procedures help students develop learning independence and improve their enthusiasm for learning (Kacetl & Klímová, 2019). Its portability is also an important factor conducive to student learning. Portable smartphones break the restrictions on teaching locations in the original education scene, allowing students more freedom in choosing their learning time and place (Lin et al., 2022; Rekha Asmara, 2020).

Compared with the positive effects of smartphones, their adverse effects have attracted more attention from scholars. Scholars have analysed the phenomenon and reasons why smartphones are not conducive to learning from multiple perspectives, such as distracting attention, information overload, and being detrimental to time management. The distraction of attention will not only reduce students' learning efficiency but will also cause serious consequences by affecting the accuracy of students' practical behaviours(Mahsud et al., 2021; Troll et al., 2021). Taking nursing students as an example, distraction caused by smartphones will cause severe mistakes in their internship positions, which will, in turn, threaten patient safety (Zarandona et al., 2019). Smartphones can provide students with vibrant learning resources, but they also bring specific negative impacts to students. The amount of information in smartphones far exceeds students' information processing capabilities, which increases the technological pressure they feel and ultimately harms academic performance (Yao & Wang, 2023).

Student's reliance on smartphones will lead to the formation of addictive behaviours, and they will excessively use mobile phones for entertainment activities unrelated to study, eventually taking up study time (Lei et al., 2020; Mahsud et al., 2021). Some studies have also confirmed that addictive behaviour is one of the essential reasons why students cannot concentrate when studying (Mahsud et al., 2021). This substance addiction behaviour will also threaten students' physical and mental health and indirectly affect students' learning results (Mustafaoglu et al., 2021).

The Impact of Smartphones on the Health and Life of Higher Education Students

Good health and living habits are important factors that affect students' learning efficiency and effectiveness (Tadese et al., 2022). For young people, smartphones are not only their learning tools but also play the role of life assistants and have profoundly affected their living habits and even their physical and mental health (Csibi et al., 2021; Wacks & Weinstein, 2021). Therefore, while analysing the direct impact of smartphones on students' learning, the indirect effect of affecting students' health and living habits should also be considered.

Smartphones are essential for improving life efficiency (Csibi et al., 2021; Lei et al., 2020). First, it can shorten the resources consumed by daily activities. For example, compared with going out for shopping, people can save more time and money by shopping online through smartphones (Allah Pitchay et al., 2022; Meher Neger & Burhan Uddin, 2020). In addition, smartphones provide students with a more convenient way to maintain social connections. Students can communicate with family or friends through social media to strengthen emotional ties without time and location limitations (David & Roberts, 2021). In addition to helping students in daily life, smartphones can also be a helper in improving and maintaining health if used properly. Some smartphones can provide health detection functions, which can help students better understand and manage their health status by tracking and recording their health data (Kajitani et al., 2020).

However, for researchers in the field of education, the negative impact of smartphones is of more significant concern than the positive effect. With the development of smartphones, its rich functions attract young people to spend a lot of time using mobile phones daily (Maurya et al., 2022). Although smartphones can help young people improve their quality of life if used wisely, the fact is that young people often cannot control their usage behaviour well when using smartphones. Some surveys show that compared with people of other age groups, young people are more likely to experience excessive use when using smartphones, which is a symptom of substance addiction (Csibi et al., 2021). Substance addiction will cause many adverse effects on the mental health of addicted individuals, such as a positive correlation between mobile phone addiction and the incidence of depression (Lei et al., 2020). In addition to the impact on mental health, excessive smartphone use can also negatively affect physical health. For example, staring at the mobile phone screen for a long time will reduce students' visual function, sleep quality and cause musculoskeletal pain (Maurya et al., 2022; Mustafaoglu et al., 2021; Wang et al., 2020; Wang et al., 2019).

The Concept and Methods of Digital Detoxification-Digital Detoxification

As digital devices become increasingly popular, people's dependence on electronic products has become increasingly prominent (Desai &Vidyapee, 2019). Although digital devices can bring many noticeable beneficial effects to people's studies, life and work, the negative impact on people's lives is also becoming more and more prominent (Abi-Jaoude et al., 2020; Alotaibi et al., 2022; Bucci et al., 2019; Maurya et al., 2022). Some scholars have found that sometimes the negative impacts of digital devices are far greater than the benefits they bring to people, especially when people misuse electronic products(Abi-Jaoude et al., 2020; Csibi et al., 2021). Therefore, although the development of society and the improvement of living conditions have made people pay more attention to the quality of life and health (Zhang & Ma, 2020), the negative impact caused by the side effects of digital devices will cause significant obstacles to improving the quality of life and health (Alotaibi et al., 2022).

The above phenomena have made people gradually realise the importance of rational use of digital devices and restraining addictive behaviours of electronic products (Csibi et al., 2021), which led to the birth of the concept of digital detoxification. Digital detox is "when a person does not use digital devices such as smartphones or computers, especially to reduce stress and relax" (Oxford Dictionaries, 2023). It is worth noting that this definition is somewhat different from the definition provided by Oxford Dictionaries recorded in previous literature (Radtke et al., 2022). The latest definition corrects the purpose of digital detoxification. The original definition emphasises that digital detoxification aims to reduce stress or maintain real-life social activities(Radtke et al., 2022). The new definition removes the purpose of maintaining social activities and replaces it with the word relax, which makes the purpose more focused on improving personal status.

Smartphones are one of the most popular electronic devices and one of the most addictive. According to the survey by Alotaibi et al. (2022), people who own smartphones will spend an average of 6-8 hours a day using smartphones. Socialising and entertainment are the primary purposes of using smartphones among those surveyed, and more than half of them have digital addiction behaviours(Alotaibi et al., 2022). The prominence of this phenomenon of smartphone addictive behaviour has contributed to the richness of digital detoxification-related research. Researchers have explored detoxification methods for smartphone users and compared and analysed the effects and differences of various practices (Schmuck, 2020; Wang et al., 2019).

Improving people's dependence on smartphones can be approached from multiple angles. First, individual addictive behaviours can be directly changed through psychological and behavioural support. Previous research has confirmed that interpersonal help, such as interpersonal support, behavioural guidance, and stress management, are effective ways for digital detoxification (Wang et al., 2019). Secondly, the contact between the individual and the smart device can be cut off or controlled. Unplugged tourism is one of the most popular methods of this type, in which individuals reduce or do not use digital devices by interacting with the real world during travel (Egger et al., 2020). Changing mobile phone devices that are less likely to lead to addiction or conducting digital detoxification through auxiliary software or facilities are also feasible measures. For example, some software can prompt or force-lock the phone when the preset usage time is reached, allowing users to reduce usage time passively(Nguyen, 2022).

The Effectiveness and Sustainability of Digital Detoxification's Impact on College Students-Digital Detoxification

The negative impact of digital devices, especially smartphones, on students receiving higher education, has received widespread attention from society. As an effective means to reduce this negative impact, digital detoxification has begun to be promoted in higher education settings, subsequently triggering a series of related research. Scholars discuss the need for digital detoxification of students. Although a series of evidence indicates that electronic products have the function of improving learning efficiency (Alismaiel et al., 2022; Kacetl & Klímová, 2019), it turns out that digital devices, especially smartphones, have a more negative impact on students' learning than positive effect (Troll et al., 2021; Ugur & Koc, 2015; Wood & Muñoz, 2021). Overuse of smartphones is detrimental to students' learning and can even harm their health (Mahsud et al., 2021; Maurya et al., 2022; Troll et al., 2021). Therefore, it is essential to carry out digital detoxification for students in higher education environments.

As a young group, students should take digital detoxification measures promptly. First of all, this is because students are not only the group most prone to excessive use of smartphones (Csibi et al., 2021). Secondly, as people age, their bodies and minds respond more strongly to digital detoxification, and they will experience stronger negative emotions and various physical withdrawal symptoms (Csibi et al., 2021; Wood & Muñoz, 2021). Last but not least, reasonable digital detoxification can improve the negative physical and mental state caused by addictive behaviours in many aspects. For example, providing students with smartphone addiction with interpersonal support, behavioural guidance, and stress management can help improve their bad sleeping habits caused by overuse of smartphones (Wang et al., 2019). In short, although digital detoxification will cause students to have withdrawal reactions in the short term, it is generally beneficial to students in a long time.

However, since digital devices have penetrated the higher education environment, it is not easy to detoxify digitally by prohibiting students from using them directly (Wood & Muñoz, 2021). Therefore, digital detoxification for students can be implemented in two ways: interpersonal help and software assistance. Universities can provide a variety of activities to provide interpersonal support to students who need digital detoxification, such as providing sports activities, behavioural guidance or carrying out psychological assistance therapy (Wang et al., 2019). Digital detoxification software is a semi-passive self-management method. First, it requires students to actively obtain relevant software and enable permissions for the software to work. Detoxification software can effectively alleviate the negative relationship between electronic device use and students' well-being (Schmuck, 2020). No matter which method is used, it requires the active cooperation of the students themselves. Although electronic detoxification activities have been started in some areas, the time range is limited and is only performed at night (Green et al., 2022). Developing larger-scale and more effective electronic detoxification activities requires support from all aspects. Therefore, increasing the attention paid by students and teachers to digital addiction is still necessary to effectively carry out digital detoxification activities in higher education environments.

IMPLICATIONS

Theoretical Implications

This study explores and analyses the development and changes in the role of digital devices in higher education environments in the context of rapid technological development and emphasises the importance of digital detoxification. It points out that if used appropriately, digital devices can become a tool for students to improve efficiency and effectiveness in learning (Maqableh & Alia, 2021). This provides researchers in education with a more comprehensive research perspective and reference direction. This study also emphasises that although digital devices can positively impact the learning and life of higher education students, their negative impact cannot be ignored (Arokiyaraj et al., 2021), especially on students' concentration. The negative impact of force is particularly worthy of continued attention from scholars.

In addition to this, this study has theoretical value in the field of psychology, especially on the topic of digital addiction. This study points out that related research on digital detoxification and digital addiction should not be limited to the general group but should be more focused on topics related to digital addiction and digital detoxification among people in similar backgrounds (Csibi et al., 2021) because the environment and individual characteristics are important factors that contribute to the occurrence of digital addiction behaviours. People with similar unique characteristics in the same environment will have more consistent performance in digital addiction behaviours. For example, this study emphasises the higher education environment as a fixed area. The groups in this environment are similar regarding the educational environment and age characteristics, so that the study results will be more accurate.

Finally, this study also has specific implications for the intersection of education and psychology because this article emphasises the multiple impacts of smartphones on students' psychological states and learning effects in higher education environments. This inspires future research on related issues, such as digital device-based learning strategies in higher education contexts.

Practical Implications

This study provides practical reference opinions for those involved in the higher education environment from three perspectives. First of all, from the perspective of educational policymakers, they should not only pay attention to the negative impacts of digital education environments but also consider formulating reasonable digital detoxification measures and strategies. Reasonably composing the layout and application areas of digital devices in the educational environment is one of the essential steps for effective digital detoxification (Wang et al., 2019). This study analyses the current application status of digital devices, especially smartphones, in higher education environments from multiple perspectives and serves as a reference for educational decision-makers to formulate reasonable plans.

Secondly, under the guidance of education policies, university administrators should implement personalised educational policies related to digital devices based on the specific conditions of the university and the differences between various disciplines and student groups. This can effectively improve student learning effects while reducing the burden on classroom teachers (Garad et al., 2021; Maatuk et al., 2021). The management of the living environment in universities is also an issue that university administrators should focus on. Unlike other types of education, college students will spend more time on campus. Therefore, besides integrating digital devices into the teaching environment, administrators should rationally arrange digital devices in university living facilities. This can improve students' quality of life and efficiency and indirectly benefit students' learning.

Last but not least, this study also provides sound advice on digital detoxification for students, who play the most crucial role in educational settings. Learning knowledge is one of the main tasks they must complete in college. Facing digital devices with rich functions, the students' reasonable use will bring a series of benefits to their learning ability and learning effect. Digital devices have been highly integrated into their daily lives and are a vital tool to improve the convenience of their lives (Haleem et al., 2022). Although students can recognise the impact of digital addiction on themselves, they lack the awareness and methods to help them control and improve this addictive behaviour. This study helps raise students' awareness of their digital addiction behaviours and points to multiple ways to implement digital detoxification.

DISCUSSION

In short, this study provides a theoretical reference for scholars in education, psychology, and the intersection of educational psychology. This study identifies the opportunities and challenges digital devices face in higher education settings from a student perspective. Researchers in related fields can further explore the various impacts of other types of digital device addiction behaviours on students in higher education settings based on this study. They can also continue to have a more in-depth discussion on the impact of smartphones on the higher education environment from multiple perspectives, such as teachers, managers, and educational policymakers in higher education. Secondly, with the diversification of digital devices, exploring the application of other digital devices in higher education environments will also be an important research direction. Finally, researchers could also explore the impact of digital addiction in different settings and among other groups, especially those in occupations requiring extensive smartphone use.

REFERENCES

Abi-Jaoude, E., Naylor, K. T., & Pignatiello, A. (2020). Smartphones, social media use and youth mental health. *Canadian Medical Association Journal*, *192*(6), E136–E141. doi:10.1503/cmaj.190434 PMID:32041697

Al Rawashdeh, A. Z., Mohammed, E. Y., Al Arab, A. R., Alara, M., Al-Rawashdeh, B., & Al-Rawashdeh, B. (2021). Advantages and Disadvantages of Using e-Learning in University Education: Analysing Students' Perspectives. *Electronic Journal of e-Learning*, *19*(3), 107–117. doi:10.34190/ejel.19.3.2168

Alismaiel, O. A., Cifuentes-Faura, J., & Al-Rahmi, W. M. (2022). Online Learning, Mobile Learning, and Social Media Technologies: An Empirical Study on Constructivism Theory during the COVID-19 Pandemic. *Sustainability (Basel)*, *14*(18), 11134. doi:10.3390u141811134

Allah Pitchay, A., Ganesan, Y., Zulkifli, N. S., & Khaliq, A. (2022). Determinants of customers' intention to use online food delivery application through smartphone in Malaysia. *British Food Journal*, *124*(3), 732–753. doi:10.1108/BFJ-01-2021-0075

Alotaibi, M., Fox, M., Coman, R., Ratan, Z., & Hosseinzadeh, H. (2022). Smartphone Addiction Prevalence and Its Association on Academic Performance, Physical Health, and Mental Well-Being among University Students in Umm Al-Qura University (UQU), Saudi Arabia. *International Journal of Environmental Research and Public Health*, *19*(6), 3710. doi:10.3390/ijerph19063710 PMID:35329397

Arokiyaraj, S., Radhin, V., Ka, N., Benson, N., & Mathew, A. J. (2021). Effect of pandemic based online education on teaching and learning system. *International Journal of Educational Development*, *85*, 102444. doi:10.1016/j.ijedudev.2021.102444 PMID:34518732

Asmara, R. (2020). Teaching English in a virtual classroom using WhatsApp during COVID-19 pandemic. *Language and Education Journal*, *5*(1), 16–27. doi:10.52237/lej.v5i1.152

Bucci, S., Schwannauer, M., & Berry, N. (2019). The digital revolution and its impact on mental health care. *Psychology and Psychotherapy: Theory, Research and Practice*, *92*(2), 277–297. doi:10.1111/papt.12222 PMID:30924316

Csibi, S., Griffiths, M. D., Demetrovics, Z., & Szabo, A. (2021). Analysis of Problematic Smartphone Use Across Different Age Groups within the 'Components Model of Addiction'. *International Journal of Mental Health and Addiction*, *19*(3), 616–631. doi:10.100711469-019-00095-0

David, M. E., & Roberts, J. A. (2021). Smartphone Use during the COVID-19 Pandemic: Social Versus Physical Distancing. *International Journal of Environmental Research and Public Health*, *18*(3), 1034. doi:10.3390/ijerph18031034 PMID:33503907

Desai, V., & Vidyapee, B. (2019). Digital Marketing: A Review. *International Journal of Trend in Scientific Research and Development, Special Issue*(Special Issue-FIIIIPM2019), 196–200. doi:10.31142/ijtsrd23100

Dictionaries, O. (2023, September 16). *Definition of digital detox noun from the Oxford Advanced Learner's Dictionary.* Oxford Press. https://www.oxfordlearnersdictionaries.com/definition/english/digital-detox

Egger, I., Lei, S. I., & Wassler, P. (2020). Digital free tourism – An exploratory study of tourist motivations. *Tourism Management, 79,* 104098. doi:10.1016/j.tourman.2020.104098

Firmansyah, R. O., Hamdani, R. A., & Kuswardhana, D. (2020). The use of smartphone on learning activities: Systematic review. *IOP Conference Series. Materials Science and Engineering, 850*(1), 012006. doi:10.1088/1757-899X/850/1/012006

Garad, A., Al-Ansi, A. M., & Qamari, I. N. (2021). THE ROLE OF E-LEARNING INFRASTRUCTURE AND COGNITIVE COMPETENCE IN DISTANCE LEARNING EFFECTIVENESS DURING THE COVID-19 PANDEMIC. *Cakrawala Pendidikan: Jurnal Ilmiah Pendidikan, 40*(1), 81–91. doi:10.21831/cp.v40i1.33474

Haleem, A., Javaid, M., Qadri, M. A., & Suman, R. (2022). Understanding the role of digital technologies in education: A review. *Sustainable Operations and Computers, 3,* 275–285. doi:10.1016/j.susoc.2022.05.004

Händel, M., Stephan, M., Gläser-Zikuda, M., Kopp, B., Bedenlier, S., & Ziegler, A. (2022). Digital readiness and its effects on higher education students' socio-emotional perceptions in the context of the COVID-19 pandemic. *Journal of Research on Technology in Education, 54*(2), 267–280. doi:10.1080/15391523.2020.1846147

Hover, A., & Wise, T. (2022). Exploring ways to create 21st century digital learning experiences. *Education 3-13, 50*(1), 40–53. doi:10.1080/03004279.2020.1826993

Kacetl, J., & Klímová, B. (2019). Use of Smartphone Applications in English Language Learning—A Challenge for Foreign Language Education. *Education Sciences, 9*(3), 179. doi:10.3390/educsci9030179

Kajitani, K., Higashijima, I., Kaneko, K., Matsushita, T., Fukumori, H., & Kim, D. (2020). Short-term effect of a smartphone application on the mental health of university students: A pilot study using a user-centered design self-monitoring application for mental health. *PLoS One, 15*(9), e0239592. doi:10.1371/journal.pone.0239592 PMID:32976515

Lei, L. Y.-C., Ismail, M. A.-A., Mohammad, J. A.-M., & Yusoff, M. S. B. (2020). The relationship of smartphone addiction with psychological distress and neuroticism among university medical students. *BMC Psychology, 8*(1), 97. doi:10.118640359-020-00466-6 PMID:32917268

Lin, H., Wan, S., Gan, W., Chen, J., & Chao, H.-C. (2022). Metaverse in Education: Vision, Opportunities, and Challenges. *2022 IEEE International Conference on Big Data (Big Data)*, (pp. 2857–2866). IEEE. 10.1109/BigData55660.2022.10021004

Maatuk, A. M., Elberkawi, E. K., Aljawarneh, S., Rashaideh, H., & Alharbi, H. (2021). The COVID-19 pandemic and E-learning: Challenges and opportunities from the perspective of students and instructors. *Journal of Computing in Higher Education, 34*(1), 21–38. doi:10.100712528-021-09274-2 PMID:33967563

Mahsud, M., Khalaf, A. J. M., Mahsud, Z., Afzal, A., & Afzal, F. (2021). Addiction to smartphones leading to distraction in the classrooms: Effect of different cultures. *Journal of Statistics and Management Systems, 24*(4), 741–754. doi:10.1080/097 20510.2020.1834660

Maqableh, M., & Alia, M. (2021). Evaluation online learning of undergraduate students under lockdown amidst COVID-19 Pandemic: The online learning experience and students' satisfaction. *Children and Youth Services Review, 128*, 106160. doi:10.1016/j.childyouth.2021.106160 PMID:36540702

Maurya, C., Muhammad, T., Maurya, P., & Dhillon, P. (2022). The association of smartphone screen time with sleep problems among adolescents and young adults: Cross-sectional findings from India. *BMC Public Health, 22*(1), 1686. doi:10.118612889-022-14076-x PMID:36064373

Mustafaoglu, R., Yasaci, Z., Zirek, E., Griffiths, M. D., & Ozdincler, A. R. (2021). The relationship between smartphone addiction and musculoskeletal pain prevalence among young population: A cross-sectional study. *The Korean Journal of Pain, 34*(1), 72–81. doi:10.3344/kjp.2021.34.1.72 PMID:33380570

Neger, M., & Uddin, B. (2020). Factors Affecting Consumers' Internet Shopping Behavior During the COVID-19 Pandemic: Evidence From Bangladesh. *The China Business Review, 19*(3). Advance online publication. doi:10.17265/1537-1506/2020.03.003

Nguyen, V. T. (2022). The perceptions of social media users of digital detox apps considering personality traits. *Education and Information Technologies, 27*(7), 9293–9316. doi:10.100710639-022-11022-7 PMID:35370441

Radtke, T., Apel, T., Schenkel, K., Keller, J., & Von Lindern, E. (2022). Digital detox: An effective solution in the smartphone era? A systematic literature review. *Mobile Media & Communication, 10*(2), 190–215. doi:10.1177/20501579211028647

Schmuck, D. (2020). Does Digital Detox Work? Exploring the Role of Digital Detox Applications for Problematic Smartphone Use and Well-Being of Young Adults Using Multigroup Analysis. *Cyberpsychology, Behavior, and Social Networking, 23*(8), 526–532. doi:10.1089/cyber.2019.0578 PMID:32354288

Selvaraj, A., Radhin, V., Ka, N., Benson, N., & Mathew, A. J. (2021). Effect of pandemic based online education on teaching and learning system. *International Journal of Educational Development, 85*, 102444. doi:10.1016/j.ijedudev.2021.102444 PMID:34518732

Tadese, M., Yeshaneh, A., & Mulu, G. B. (2022). Determinants of good academic performance among university students in Ethiopia: A cross-sectional study. *BMC Medical Education, 22*(1), 395. doi:10.118612909-022-03461-0 PMID:35606767

Troll, E. S., Friese, M., & Loschelder, D. D. (2021). How students' self-control and smartphone-use explain their academic performance. *Computers in Human Behavior, 117*, 106624. doi:10.1016/j.chb.2020.106624

Ugur, N. G., & Koc, T. (2015). Time for Digital Detox: Misuse of Mobile Technology and Phubbing. *Procedia: Social and Behavioral Sciences, 195*, 1022–1031. doi:10.1016/j.sbspro.2015.06.491

Wacks, Y., & Weinstein, A. M. (2021). Excessive Smartphone Use Is Associated With Health Problems in Adolescents and Young Adults. *Frontiers in Psychiatry, 12*, 669042. doi:10.3389/fpsyt.2021.669042 PMID:34140904

Wang, J., Li, M., Zhu, D., & Cao, Y. (2020). Smartphone Overuse and Visual Impairment in Children and Young Adults: Systematic Review and Meta-Analysis. *Journal of Medical Internet Research, 22*(12), e21923. doi:10.2196/21923 PMID:33289673

Wang, P. Y., Chen, K. L., Yang, S. Y., & Lin, P. H. (2019). Relationship of sleep quality, smartphone dependence, and health-related behaviours in female junior college students. *PLoS One, 14*(4), e0214769. doi:10.1371/journal.pone.0214769 PMID:30943270

Webster, T. E., & Paquette, J. (2023). "My other hand": The central role of smartphones and SNSs in Korean students' lives and studies. *Computers in Human Behavior, 138*, 107447. doi:10.1016/j.chb.2022.107447

Williams, M. (2022). Virtual reality in ophthalmology education: Simulating pupil examination. *Eye (London, England)*, *36*(11), 2084–2085. doi:10.103841433-022-02078-3 PMID:35538219

Williamson, B. (2021). Making markets through digital platforms: Pearson, edu-business, and the (e)valuation of higher education. *Critical Studies in Education*, *62*(1), 50–66. doi:10.1080/17508487.2020.1737556

Wood, N. T., & Muñoz, C. (2021). UNPLUGGED: DIGITAL DETOX ENHANCES STUDENT LEARNING. *Marketing Education Review*, *31*(1), 14–25. doi:10.1080/10528008.2020.1836973

Yang, R., Zhou, C., Huang, M., Wen, H., & Liang, H.-N. (2021). Design of an Interactive Classroom with Bullet Screen Function in University Teaching. *2021 9th International Conference on Information and Education Technology (ICIET)*, (pp. 47–51). IEEE. 10.1109/ICIET51873.2021.9419627

Yao, N., & Wang, Q. (2023). Technostress from Smartphone Use and Its Impact on University Students' Sleep Quality and Academic Performance. *The Asia-Pacific Education Researcher*, *32*(3), 317–326. doi:10.100740299-022-00654-5

Zarandona, J., Cariñanos-Ayala, S., Cristóbal-Domínguez, E., Martín-Bezos, J., Yoldi-Mitxelena, A., & Hoyos Cillero, I. (2019). With a smartphone in one's pocket: A descriptive cross-sectional study on smartphone use, distraction and restriction policies in nursing students. *Nurse Education Today*, *82*, 67–73. doi:10.1016/j.nedt.2019.08.001 PMID:31445465

Zawacki-Richter, O. (2021). The current state and impact of COVID-19 on digital higher education in Germany. *Human Behavior and Emerging Technologies*, *3*(1), 218–226. doi:10.1002/hbe2.238 PMID:33363276

Zdravkova, K. (2023). Personalised Education for Sustainable Development. *Sustainability (Basel)*, *15*(8), 6901. doi:10.3390u15086901

Zhang, Y., & Ma, Z. F. (2020). Impact of the COVID-19 Pandemic on Mental Health and Quality of Life among Local Residents in Liaoning Province, China: A Cross-Sectional Study. *International Journal of Environmental Research and Public Health*, *17*(7), 2381. doi:10.3390/ijerph17072381 PMID:32244498

Chapter 9

FinTech Frontier:
Navigating the New Horizons and Challenges for Startups

Anju Rohilla
Department of Business Studies, PIET, India

Priya Jindal
Chitkara Business School, Chitkara University, India

ABSTRACT

The adoption of digitalization and favorable regulatory initiatives resulted in the rapid growth of the Fintech sector in recent years. There are limitless opportunities for the person with the right vision and executor plan in the fintech sector from digital payments and peer-to-peer lending to wealth management and insurance. This chapter aims to explore the fintech sector and examines the remarkable new opportunities and significant challenges that fintech firms face as they strive for innovation and expansion. The research aims to provide valuable insights into the factors that contribute to the success or hindrance of fintech startups. The findings of the study show that there is a wide range of potential opportunities available for fintech firms globally, in sectors including lending, wealth management, and digital payments.

INTRODUCTION

The FinTech ecosystem is a vibrant community inside the constantly changing finance industry. The term "fintech" is ephemeral, continuously changing and expanding like a digital phoenix to include a wide range of services that are revolutionizing the way we use

DOI: 10.4018/979-8-3693-1107-3.ch009

and interact with money. Within the sphere of digital technology, FinTech companies not only provide services but also engage in the precise orchestration of financial operations.

The emergence of Fintech Services initially revolved around the provision of payment alternatives, effectively integrating the many aspects of financial transactions. Subsequently, the focus expanded to encompass internet-based financing, wherein loans are originated within the digital marketplace. Mobile applications have emerged as powerful tools, enabling individuals to conveniently access financial resources with a simple tap on their screens. The act of financing takes on the characteristics of a metaphorical pilgrimage, while foreign exchange becomes the form of a worldwide discourse. Remittances exhibit a seamless transnational flow.

MEANING OF FINTECHS

The financial technology (fintech) sector is at the forefront of revolutionary change in a world featured with increasingly connected due to fast technological innovations. Fintech services are becoming increasingly popular in the present day. In 1972, A New York banker has used the term fintech for the first time (Vijai, 2019). The term "financial technology" (or "fintech") is used to describe an industry in which businesses effectively deliver financial services by leveraging technological developments. This sort of service is becoming increasingly popular in the present day. Newly founded firms are endeavoring to substitute conventional transaction processes with current and efficient techniques by applying technology in the financial sectors. Let's us talk about either Peer-to-peer lending or payment services or e-wallets are among the popular technological innovations in financial services which reveals that how technology is changing the way we bank, invest, and transact throughout the world (Pant, 2020). The objective of these initiatives is to enhance the advantages and optimize the efficiency of financial transactions. Furthermore, they contribute to reducing client expenditures.

Nine technologies were identified, with each one representing a distinct element of innovation within the field of Financial Technology (FinTech) (mckinsey.com, 2021). These are as follows:

1. Cloud computing allows information to be stored and accessed remotely.
2. Externalizing processes and services connect the past and the present.
3. Robotic Process Automation (RPA) is widely recognized as a pivotal driver of operational efficiency.
4. Advanced analytics is a sophisticated tool that possesses the ability to predict future financial outcomes.
5. Digital transformation is a transformative process that gives rise to a novel financial landscape.

6. Blockchain, a highly secure and tamper-resistant distributed ledger system.
7. Smart contracts are digital agreements that possess the ability to autonomously enforce themselves.
8. Artificial Intelligence (AI) is a sophisticated technology that plays a crucial role in informing financial decision-making processes.
9. The Internet of Things (IoT) represents a complex network of interconnected devices that collectively contribute to the generation and dissemination of financial narratives.

STATEMENT OF PROBLEM

As the fintech industry changes quickly and has the ability to completely change the way things are done, many new companies have sprung up to use new technologies in financial services. These firms' path to success is, however, greatly impacted by a complicated web of chances and difficulties. The following research questions will be answered in this study.

1. What are the significant opportunities that exist for startups in fintech market, that contribute to their growth and success?
2. What are the main obstacles that fintech firms face that affect their capacity to grow and innovate within the industry?
3. What is the current trend of startup in fintech industry?
4. Who are the key stakeholders of fintech industry?

The objective of this study is to examine the various dimensions of the fintech startup ecosystem, with a particular emphasis on the identification and complete analysis of the opportunities and challenges encountered by these businesses.

The primary focus of this study is to comprehensively examine the complex aspects that contribute to or hinder the development and long-term viability of fintech firms. The objective of this study is to offer significant perspectives that can assist stakeholders, policymakers, and entrepreneurs in effectively navigating the intricate dynamics of the fintech ecosystem and promoting its long-term growth.

LITERATURE REVIEW

Fintech, the most disruptive technology hascurrently adopted by the financial services sector which is undergoing a tremendous transition after its acceptance (Rabbani, 2023). Machine learning, artificial intelligence Cryptocurrencies, data analytics, and blockchain technology are among the fintech services that have significantly impacted the financial sector (Gomber et al., 2018). Some of the Fintech services have witnessed significant levels of adoption such as, savings, peer-to-peer transfers, and investments (Hassan et al., 2022). The significance of Fintech has been demonstrated to such an extent that regulatory bodies have undertaken surveys and implemented actions to address the implications of Fintech (Honisch & Ottenbacher, 2017). Regulatory agencies are under pressure to formulate laws aimed at mitigating the risks associated with Fintech, while simultaneously improving the quality of services offered by these platforms (Aulakh et al., 2023). We have to admit that Fintech has, at this point, sparked a boom in the financial sector, and companies are searching for creative ways to improve the services they already offer (Rabbani et al., 2021). However, it is crucial to conduct thorough examination and research in this area in order to develop new legislation and gain a comprehensive understanding of market dynamics. This will enable us to capitalize on the potential opportunities presented by Fintech while effectively mitigating associated risks, thereby ensuring the preservation of financial stability (Demir et al., 2020). The financial sector has exhibited a consistent trend of intensifying competition and demonstrating agility in response to the evolving dynamics of its ecosystem over several decades (Cheong, 2019).

FINTECH INDUSTRY SEGMENTS

Fintech Industry consists of the various segments which encompasses from traditional financial institutions to modern tech enabled institutions. Not only the financial services provides but it also includes the regulatory bodies which helps in the governance and ensures the legal compliances with the legal requirements. The fintech Industry is classified into Payments, Insurtech, Regtech, Wealthtech, Blockchain/cyrptocurrency and Cybersecurity, digital lending, payments, blockchain and digital wealth management (KPMG, 2021) and on the basis of services provided fintech Industry is classified into Money Transfer and Payments, Savings and Investments, Digital Lending & Lending Marketplaces, Online Insurance & Insurance Marketplaces and Others (Abakah, 2023); 4 major segments of fintechs are Financing, Asset Management, payments and other fintechs. On the basis of available literature on the segments of the Fintechs, the various segments of the fintech industry are depicted in Figure 1.

1. **Traditional Financial Institutions:**
    ○   **Banks:** Fintech is being progressively integrated into traditional banks' activities. To improve their digital offerings, they might collaborate with

Figure 1. Segments of the Fintech industry
Source: Author's Compilation

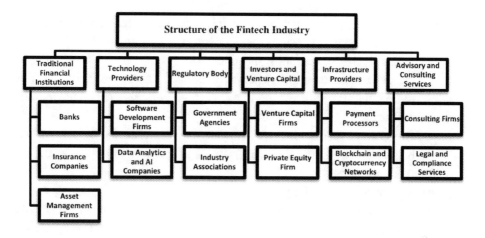

or buy fintech firms. Now the banks offer the digital banking services such as opening and operating the bank digitally, Mobile banking apps, online banking apps,

- ○ **Insurance Companies:** Fintech Services are used by the Insurance companies for improving the customer relations, underwriting, and providing ease in claims settlement processes.
- ○ **Asset Management Firms:** Fintech is used by asset managers for wealth management, algorithmic trading, and portfolio optimization.

2. **Technology Providers:**
- ○ **Software Development Firms:** These are enterprises that focus on creating the infrastructure and software needed for fintech solutions, including payment gateways, cloud services, and cyber security tools
- ○ **Data Analytics and AI Companies:** These are companies that offer machine learning, artificial intelligence, and data analytics solutions that support risk assessment and data-driven decision-making.

3. **Regulatory Bodies:**

Regulatory bodies are the essential component of every system. They ensure the compliances of legal requirements. The Regulatory bodies include the government agencies as well as Industry associations.

- **Government Agencies:** Government agencies play a crucial role in the fintech industry by serving as regulatory authorities that oversee and enforce compliance with financial laws and consumer protection measures. Such as In USA "Financial Industry Regulatory Authority (FINRA) and Securities and Exchange Commission (SEC) are responsible for protecting the interest of fintech investors (Aulakh et al., 2023) and in India Reserve Bank of India, IRDA and SEBI are the regulatory bodies to regulate the fintech market (Srivastava et al., 2023)."
- **Industry Associations:** Industry associations are the group which helps in encouraging the cooperation and adoption of the most suitable practices in their sector.

4. **Investors and Venture Capital:**
   - **Venture Capital Firms:** Venture capital firms are entities that offer financial support to fintech startups and rising enterprises, with the expectation of receiving shares in return. For example, Bain Capital Ventures collaborates with innovative entrepreneurs to accelerate the commercialization of their ideas. The company allocates its resources towards supporting emerging businesses that are revolutionizing several sectors (fintech sector is one among them) throughout their whole lifecycle, starting with the first stage of seed funding and progressing towards sustainable growth. The FinTech portfolio of the Bain Capital Ventures includes a range of companies such as Acorns, AvidXchange, Basecoin, Bench, Billtrust etc (Strom2.com, 2022).
   - **Private Equity Firms:** Private equity firms have the potential to make investments in well-established fintech companies that are seeking to broaden their operations or pursue initial public offerings. For example, Green Visor Capital is an investment firm that focuses on providing funding at various stages of a company's development, including seed, early-stage, and late-stage. The firm's primary objective is to identify and support founders who demonstrate a strong commitment and utilize innovative technology to address significant challenges within the financial services industry. The FinTech portfolio of the company encompasses various entities, namely CreditShop, Cloud Lending, Wefunder, CrowdStreet (Strom2.com, 2022).

5. **Infrastructure Providers:** Infrastructure providers are institutions that are responsible for the provision and maintenance of physical structures and facilities necessary for the functioning of a society or organization. These providers play a crucial role in development of fintech sector.

- ○ **Payment Processors:** Payment processors are firms that handle electronic transactions, encompassing services such as credit card processing and mobile payments such as wingspan, Circle, Big Commerce etc. (Schroer, 2023).
  - ○ **Blockchain and Cryptocurrency Networks:** Blockchain and cryptocurrency networks refer to the decentralised ledger technologies, such as blockchain, that serve as the foundation for cryptocurrencies and digital assets such as Bitcoin Atom, Ripple (Shalender et al., 2023).

6. **Advisory and Consulting Services:** Advisory and consulting services are offered to provide expert guidance and support in several areas.
   - ○ **Consulting Firms:** Consulting businesses provide strategic advisory, regulatory compliance, and technology integration services to fintech enterprises such as CPQi, Summus Group etc (cpqi.com, 2022).
   - ○ **Legal and Compliance Services:** Legal and compliance services encompass law firms that specialize in addressing legal aspects associated to fintech, such as intellectual property, data protection, regulatory compliance, tax planning, contracts, consumer protection (psplab.com, 2022).

7. **Others:**
   - ○ **Educational and Research Institutions:** Educational and research institutions play a significant role in the advancement of knowledge and the development of society. These institutions serve as hubs for learning, intellectual exploration, and the generation of new ideas. They provide a structured environment where students can acquire knowledge, skills.

- **Media and Communication Channels:**
  1. **News Outlets:** News outlets are media organizations that provide coverage and analysis of developments and trends in the field of financial technology.
  2. **Online Communities:** Online communities refer to digital platforms such as forums and social media channels where individuals who are involved in the field of financial technology.These platforms serve as spaces for industry professionals and enthusiasts to exchange ideas and insights pertaining to various fintech subjects.

- **Consumers and Businesses:**
  1. **End Users:** End users refer to both individuals and enterprises who actively engage with fintech products and services, encompassing a wide range of financial activities such as banking, payments, lending, insurance, and other related functions.

2. **Merchants:** Merchants refer to commercial entities that adopt fintech-driven payment solutions, including mobile wallets or online payment gateways.

HISTORY AND GROWTH OF FINTECH INDUSTRY

The fintech sector has undergone a tremendous evolution, marked by changes in consumer behavior, legislative changes, and technology advancements. The history of fintech sector was full of advancement, technological improvement and innovation. Due to this reason the entire fintech sector evolution is divided into 5 main stages as shown in fig. 2.

Early 1990s to Early 2000

a. **Early 1950-60's:** During the period of the 1950s to 1960s, the establishment of electronic financial systems was initiated through the introduction of credit cards and electronic funds transfer.

b. **Origins of Fintech:** In 1970s to the 1980s, automated teller machines (ATMs) had a significant expansion, while electronic trading platforms for stocks emerged, thereby establishing the fundamental infrastructure for the field of digital finance. The 1990s witnessed the emergence of online banking services, which is when fintech first emerged. Consumers have the ability to online verify their account balances, initiate financial transfers, and make electronic payments for bills (Kaur, 2023). This development is the starting stage in the process of digitizing financial services.

c. **Payment Processing Innovations:** During the late 1990s to early 2000s, there were notable advancements in payment processing technologies the emergence of pioneering online brokerage firms, such as E*TRADE. In the year 2000, the word "fintech" experiences a surge in popularity due to the increasing migration of financial services to online platforms (Pant, 2020). The advent of mobile banking and payments is beginning to manifest. PayPal, established in 1998, brought about a significant transformation in the realm of electronic transactions. The company provided secure and convenient mechanisms for money transfer and internet transactions, therefore diminishing the dependence on conventional banking systems (Kaur, 2023).

2000 to 2010

The worldwide economic collapse of 2008 has led many people to doubt the reliability of the banking system and instead seek for new and better ways to manage their money. In 2009, the emergence of blockchain technology and cryptocurrencies was initiated with the introduction of Bitcoin by an unidentified individual named Satoshi Nakamoto. In the year 2010, there was a notable increase in the popularity and acceptance of peer-to-peer lending platforms such as Lending Club and Prosper. These platforms emerged as viable alternatives to conventional banking institutions for individuals seeking personal loans (Pothula, 2022)

2010-2015

In 2011, Square launched a mobile card reader, thereby facilitating the acceptance of card payments by small companies through smart phones or tablets. In 2013, the crowdfunding business witnessed significant expansion following the introduction of platforms such as Kickstarter and Indiegogo, thereby revolutionising the fundraising landscape for companies. In the year 2014, there was a notable increase in the recognition of blockchain technology outside its association with Bitcoin. This led to the initiation of trials exploring its potential uses in many industries, particularly in the realm of finance.

2015-2020

In 2015, the emergence of robo-advisors, exemplified by Betterment (2008) and Wealthfront (2011), grabbed the attention of investors due to their provision of automated investment advice and portfolio management services. In 2016, there was a notable rise in the adoption of peer-to-peer payment applications like as Venmo and Square Cash, particularly among the millennial demographic. These apps gained popularity as they provided a convenient means for individuals to divide expenses and transfer funds. In the year 2017, Initial Coin Offerings (ICOs) emerged as a widely used approach for entrepreneurs to get financial resources by means of selling cryptocurrency tokens. In 2018, the implementation of Open Banking laws, such as the Payment Services Directive 2 (PSD2) in Europe, necessitated that banks offer authorized third-party fintech firms with access to client data.

In 2019, the emergence of digital-only banks, commonly referred to as "challenger banks," such as Revolut and Chime, introduced a disruptive force to the traditional banking sector through the provision of mobile applications that prioritise user-friendliness. Neobanks, alternatively referred to as digital or challenger banks, have developed as financial institutions that provide exclusively online banking services, devoid of physical branch networks. The focal points were placed on interfaces that are easy to navigate for users, reduced fees, and expedited account establishment.

2020-Present

In 2020, the COVID-19 epidemic prompted an expedited uptake of contactless payments and online financial services as a result of the implementation of social distancing protocols. Lemonade, a prominent "insurtech" enterprise, emerged as a leader in the realm of digital insurance by introducing a digital platform for the acquisition of house and renters insurance subsequent to its establishment in 2015. Prominent entities in the digital securities sector, including Coinbase (2012), Bakkt (2018), and Paxos, have established themselves as leader. These companies have assumed leadership positions by offering comprehensive platforms that facilitate the acquisition, sale, and custody of digital assets, including cryptocurrencies and security tokens. The adoption of blockchain technology has facilitated the rise of Decentralised Finance (DeFi) platforms, which have garnered significant attention. These platforms provide users with the opportunity to engage in lending, borrowing, and trading activities, all without the need for conventional intermediaries. The advent of Non-Fungible Tokens (NFTs) has brought forth novel opportunities in the realm of asset ownership and the acquisition of digital collectibles. In recent years, the field of financial technology (fintech) has increasingly incorporated sustainability and Environmental, Social, and Governance (ESG) concepts. This trend is characterised by a heightened emphasis on responsible investing and the development of green finance solutions.

CURRENT TRENDS OF START-UPS IN FINTECH INDUSTRY

In 2019 (the era of COVID-19), the financial technology (fintech) business has undergone transformations and confronting its own special issues. Various drastic changes have been implemented and are now being implemented the financial sector with the idea of ordering everything—from groceries to your newest gadget—online. Simply said, anything that involves money, from payment to banking, will be impacted by these fintech developments.

Nestor Gilbert, in the study "10 Fintech Trends for 2022/2023: Top Predictions" (financesonline, 2023) as shown in Figure 3 the highest number of the digitally active customers are engaged in China i.e. 69% followed by India i.e. 52%, UK (42%) and globally (33%).

Figure 4 depicts that with 87%, China and India have the highest fintech adoption rates, followed by 82% in Russia and South Africa, 76% in Colombia, 75% in Peru,

Figure 2. Timeline of Fintech industry evolution
(e-zigurat.com, 2022)

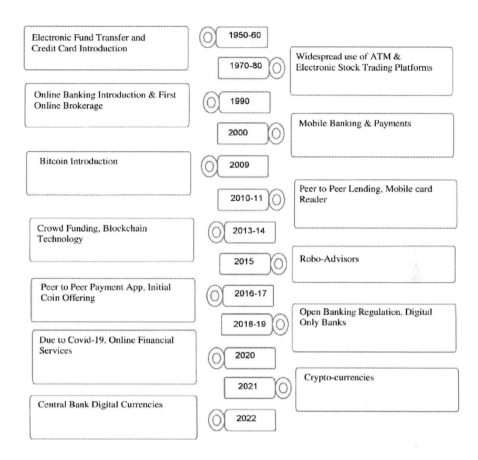

Figure 3. Percentage of digitally active customers using Fintech
Source: financesonline.com (2023)

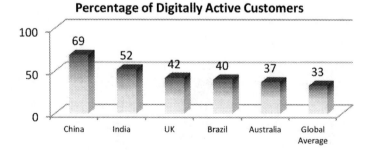

and 71% in the UK. As a result of the high rate of acceptance of financial technology services, it can be concluded that there is ample scope for expansion of the fintech industry.

The rate of fintech adoption among the various segments of fintech sector like Banking and Payment, Financial Management, Financing and Insurance by the various countries represent in Figure 5 China is the leading country with the adoption rate of 92%, 91%, 89%, 62%. Followed By US (52%, 49%, 41%, 31%), Maxico (49%, 36%, 31%, 23%), South Africa (47%, 43%, 34%, 26%) UK (41%, 37%, 34%, 24%).

The global investment made in the Fintech sector is explained in Figure 6. Between 2010 and 2019, the total value of investments made in fintech startups globally

Figure 4. Country- wise customer Fintech adoption rate
Source: financesonline.com (2023)

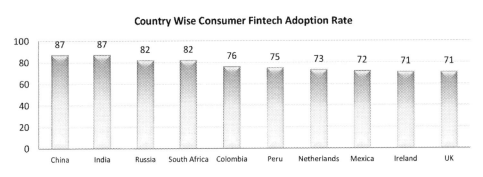

Figure 5. Fintech adoption rate in various segments
Source: financesonline.com (2023)

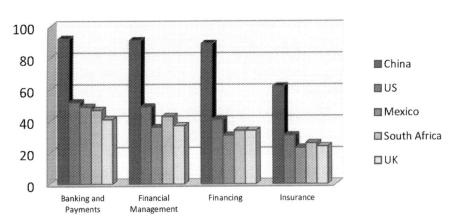

climbed dramatically to reach 216.8 billion U.S. dollars. However, investments in fintech startups fell sharply in 2020—below 140 billion dollars. In 2021, the value of the investment climbed once again, reaching over 247 billion dollars. But 2022 proved to be another slow year for fintech, with investment values falling significantly even though they were still far higher than those recorded in 2020 (Statista, 2023). The first half of 2023 saw a continuation of the declining investment trend, with the global funding value standing at 52.4 billion US dollars. With over half of all investments made in the sector, the Americas were the region drawing the greatest attention (Taherdoost, 2023). Americas has the highest number of fintech startups worldwide with 11,651 startups as per Statista May 2023 Report on Fintech. By contrast, the Asia Pacific region has 5,061 fintech startups, while the EMEA region had 9,681 startups. With almost five times as many fintech unicorns as the United Kingdom (which came in second) in 2023, the United States led the world.

OPPORTUNITIES

The dynamic nature of the fintech business and the growing demand for innovative financial services contribute to the abundance of opportunities available to companies in this sector. The following are significant prospects for entrepreneurial ventures within the financial technology (fintech) industry:

Figure 6. Global level investment in Fintech sector
(financesonline.com, 2023)

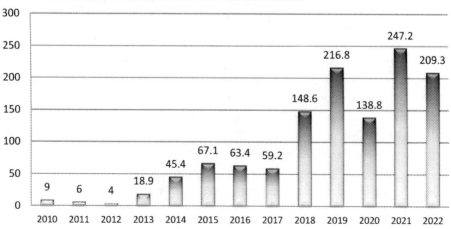

1. **Digital Payments and Wallets**: Online and offline transactions, peer-to-peer transfers, and contactless payments can all be made easier with the help of digital payment platforms and mobile wallet apps and this market can expand in future by 19.6% CAGR (Pant, 2020)). Investigate business potential in developing nations where the use of digital payments is still expanding (Singla et al., 2023).

2. **Neobanking:** The concept of neobanking involves the establishment of digital-only banks, also referred to as neobanks, which provide a comprehensive array of banking services without the presence of physical branch locations (Taherdoost, 2023).. To attract clients, it is imperative to prioritise the development of user-friendly interfaces, implement cheaper fees, and introduce novel services.

3. **Peer-to-Peer Lending:** Establish a platform that allows borrowers to interact with individual lenders and offers quicker loan approval processes along with competitive interest rates.

4. **Robo-Advisors**: Provide automated, low-cost portfolio management and financial advising using algorithm-driven investing platforms. Investment can be done in the startups which integrate investment solutions that encompass Environmental, Social, and Governance (ESG) factors.

5. **Blockchain and Cryptocurrency Services:** Startups can examine business prospects in blockchain technology, such as digital wallets, exchanges for cryptocurrencies, and platforms for decentralised finance (DeFi) (Taherdoost, 2023) as this segment of the fintech sector has the potential to grow by 42.1% CAGR by 2030 (bcg.com, 2023). Startups can also identify niche markets similar to Non-Fungible Token (NFT) marketplaces (Kong & Lin, 2021).

6. **RegTech (Regulatory Technology):** Regulatory Technology (RegTech) encompasses a range of products aimed at assisting financial organisations in effectively adhering to intricate regulatory obligations. There is huge opportunity for the startups to create and implement solutions that facilitate risk management, reporting, and fraud prevention.

7. **InsurTech:** InsurTech refers to the development of digital insurance platforms that attempt to streamline many aspects of insurance operations, including policy management, claims processing, and underwriting. These platforms leverage data analytics and artificial intelligence (AI) techniques to enhance efficiency and effectiveness in the insurance industry.

8. **Personal Finance Management:** Ample opportunity is available for the entrepreneurs to develop the applications or platforms aimed at offering customers a wide range of financial management capabilities, encompassing budgeting, savings, investment tracking, and financial planning.

9. **Cross-Border Payments and Remittances**: Entrepreneurs can seek the opportunity to start their venture by emphasizing on affordable options for

sending money internationally, with a particular focus on migrant employees and companies engaged in international commerce.

10. **Cybersecurity Solutions:** With the rapid increase in the use of fintech services, the need for the security of the data as well as the money is the concern issue (Ferretti & Martino, 2023). There is the need of startups focused towards the cybersecurity solutions to guard against fraud, cyberattacks, and data breaches, develop cybersecurity solutions specifically for fintech and financial institutions.

11. **Biometric Authentication:** The value of Biometics market is 42.9 billion US dollars in 2022 and expected to reach at 82.9 Billion US dollars by 2027 (Grinberg, 2023). There is huge opportunity for the startups to invest in such business whose purpose is to improve security for financial transactions and account access, provide biometric authentication solutions like facial recognition or fingerprint scanning or with some advance technology.

12. **AI-Powered Chatbots and Customer Support:** There exists a significant potential for entrepreneurs to allocate their investments towards businesses that aim to develop AI-powered chatbots and virtual assistants (Ferretti & Martino, 2023). These technological solutions are designed to deliver tailored customer service, optimise client questions, and provide financial guidance.

13. **Sustainable Finance:** Entrepreneurs can also explore the prospects in the field of green and sustainable finance involves the creation of platforms that enable responsible investing, ESG research, and carbon offset solutions (Ryu & KO, 2020).

14. **Financial Inclusion:** The issue of financial inclusion can be effectively addressed by startups through the development of inclusive financial goods and services, such as micro-lending platforms and digital savings accounts, to cater to the requirements of underbanked and unbanked people.

15. **Open banking solutions**: Open banking solutions involve the development of application programming interfaces (APIs) and platforms by entrepreneurs. These tools facilitate secure access and utilisation of financial data by businesses, allowing them to take advantage of the open banking trend.

16. **Healthcare Financial Services:** Startups can be focused towards the integration of financial technology (fintech) with healthcare. These services aim to streamline processes such as medical billing, insurance claims, and healthcare payment plans.

17. **Real Estate Fintech:** This study aims to examine several potential in the field of real estate fintech, specifically focusing on platforms for property investment, real estate crowdfunding, and digital mortgage solutions.

18. **Corporate Finance and Treasury Management:** Among the other opportunities the startups can also find an opportunity to develop financial technology solutions that specifically address the financial requirements of

corporations. These solutions encompass several aspects such as treasury management, supply chain finance, and working capital optimization.

19. **Educational Fintech:** this opportunity is concerned towards the integration of education system with the purpose of creation of the online courses or platforms. In the field of educational financial technology, the startups can be founded with the aim of providing knowledge to both individuals and enterprises on topics such as financial literacy, investment techniques, and financial planning.

20. **Data Analytics and Insights:** Provide business intelligence and data analytics solutions to assist fintech companies and financial institutions in identifying trends, evaluating risk, and making data-driven choices.

21. **Others:** With these entrepreneurs can also seek the opportunities to start or expand their business in Buy Now Pay Later Market which has the potential to grow by 24.3% through online as well as POS (Point of Sale) mode up to 2030 as per the report of Grinberg, 2023. Gamification Market is also providing ample opportunities for the entrepreneurs as the current value of the market is 11.94 billion U.S. dollars. This market has shown ass tremedous growth of 19.45% CAGR in 5 years from 2016 to 2021.

CHALLENGES

1. **Compliance with Regulation:** Ensuring Fintech companies adhere to intricate and dynamic regulatory frameworks is crucial for their effective operations. Ensuring adherence to financial regulations and data protection legislation is of paramount importance and can incur significant expenses and use substantial amounts of time.

2. **Capital requirements:** Capital requirements are a crucial aspect in the creation and expansion of fintech solutions, as they necessitate substantial funds for various purposes such as technology development, regulatory compliance, and marketing efforts. Obtaining financial resources can pose difficulties for startup enterprises, particularly those in their nascent stages.

3. **Security Concerns:** Security concerns arise in the context of fintech companies due to their handling of sensitive financial data and transactions, rendering them susceptible to cyberattacks. The establishment of comprehensive cybersecurity measures and the safeguarding of data protection are of utmost importance.

4. **Market Saturation:** Market saturation is a prevailing condition within the fintech industry, characterized by a high level of competition and a multitude of participants offering comparable solutions. Differentiating oneself and

capturing a larger portion of the market can present considerable difficulties, especially for companies that enter the market later.

5. **Customer Trust:** The establishment of client trust holds significant importance within the realm of financial services. Start-up enterprises encounter the challenge of addressing doubts and mistrust about the security and dependability of their services, particularly when they lack a widely recognized brand.

6. **Competition with Established Players:** Competition from well-established entities, such as traditional financial institutions and huge technology corporations those who entered into the fintech sector, leading to heightened levels of rivalry (Ferretti & Martino, 2023). Start-up enterprises are compelled to engage in competition with well-established brands and avail themselves of limited resources.

7. **Lack of Industry Experience:** One potential challenge faced by fintech founders is the absence of industry experience. It is common for these individuals to possess backgrounds in technology, hence potentially lacking familiarity with the complexities of financial services and regulatory frameworks. Consequently, this dearth of expertise may impede their capacity to traverse the market proficiently.

8. **Scalability Challenges:** As financial technology firms experience growth, they may have challenges pertaining to scalability in terms of their infrastructure, technology, and customer support. Managing higher transaction volumes while ensuring service quality might provide significant difficulties.

9. **Changing Consumer Behavior:** Fintech businesses are required to adjust with the evolving consumer attitudes and behaviors, which can be impacted by several variables like as technical improvements and demographic transitions.

10. **Pressure to Show Fast Growth and High Valuations:** To draw investors, fintech firms may have to contend with pressure to show funding and value pressures. This phenomenon has the potential to result in high-risk expansion tactics and the overestimation of value.

11. **Partnership and Integration Challenges:** Due to variations in technology, culture, and regulatory compliance, working with traditional financial institutions can be challenging. The process of integrating with legacy systems can be both time-consuming and expensive.

12. **Data Privacy and Ethics:** It can be difficult to manage privacy restrictions, thus it is imperative that consumer data be collected and used for risk assessment and personalization in an ethical and compliant manner (Ferretti & Martino, 2023).

13. **Complexity of Global Expansion:** Diverse regulatory frameworks, cultural variances, and competition from regional competitors can all make global expansion challenging.

14. **Operational risks:** Operational risks pose a significant challenge for fintech businesses, encompassing potential issues such as system failures, technical problems, and disruptions in financial markets (Gahlot & Ghosh, 2023). These risks have the potential to result in reputational harm and financial losses for these startups.

15. **Cost Associated with Customer Acquisition:** Customer acquisition costs can be a significant financial burden, especially in highly competitive sectors, due to the expenses associated with acquiring and retaining consumers. The financial burden of acquiring customers can impose significant pressure on the financial resources of a business.

CASE STUDY OF ZEPZ- POINEER FINTECH COMPANY

ZEPZ was established in 2010, the company is headquartered in London, England. Zepz established itself as a pioneer in the field of international e-commerce solutions. The company that is now known as ZEPZ was once known as WorldRemit. Let us examines the establishment, expansion, operational framework, difficulties faced by company, and present status of the company. ZEPZ is a corporation that specialises in delivering digital payment solutions within the financial services sector. The organisation provides secure and expedient services for users to transfer funds to more than 130 countries. These services include several alternatives such as bank deposit, cash collection, mobile airtime top-up, and mobile money. ZEPZ principally caters to the worldwide payments sector.

Catherine Wines, Ismail Ahmed and Richard Igoe are the Co-Founder of the ZEPZ. Breon Corcoran, Philip Doyle and John Henry Vallis are the members of the board of directors of the company. Zepz, a prominent fintech company in Europe, boasts a valuation of $5 billion. The initial investment round took place on July 28, 2010. On August 25, 2020, ZEPZ acquired Sendwave for a total of $500 Million. ZEPZ has raised a grand total of $699.7 million in investment via 12 rounds. On August 23, 2021, a Series E round was held to raise $292 million. Accel, Farallon Capital Management, LeapFrog Investments, and Technology Crossover Ventures are among the top investors.

ZEPZ owns the WorldRemit and Sendwave brands which provides Airtime Top up service, Bank Transfer (transfer money to the bank account), Cash pick ups (send money in cash to receiver) and Mobile money transfer (transfer money to the registered mobile account number). Zipz makes use of 32 technology-related products and services, such as Google Analytics, jQuery, and HTML5. ZEPZ has been recognised as the leader company among a group of 15 others, which includes Revolut, Taptap Send, and PaySend. It offers an exceptional customer experience along with industry-leading speed and accessibility. ZEPZ develop cutting-edge solutions that provide a range of options to address consumer challenges. With its lower prices and quick financial transfers, the business poses a threat to big banks and well-known money transfer providers like Western Union. In order to integrate the newest technologies and industry best practises, it had to continuously update its platform.

CONCLUSION

Fintech sector has emerged as a highly dynamic and swiftly progressing industry in recent times. It is evident from the analysis of the statics available on fintech sector that this sector has the potential for the expansion and growth. The fintech industry has undergone a significant transformation, starting with its modest origins when entrepreneurs aimed to disrupt conventional financial services. This evolution has led to the development of fintech unicorns and saw substantial worldwide investment surges. Consequently, this sector has revolutionized the methods by which an individual or corporate handles their financial resources, conduct payment transactions, and engage in investment activities.

The opportunities within the financial technology (fintech) sector are extensive and varied. Both entrepreneurs and investors have a diverse range of opportunities to consider, including digital payments, neobanking, blockchain, and sustainable finance. The ever-evolving nature of financial technology (fintech) presents a conducive environment for the emergence of novel ideas and solutions. Individuals or entities capable of effectively navigating the hurdles associated with regulatory frameworks, security concerns, and market competitiveness are likely to attain significant benefits and advantages.

Nevertheless, Journey of the Fintech is not without of obstacles. Fintech enterprises are confronted with the intricate challenges associated with ensuring compliance, meeting capital prerequisites, and addressing the persistent menace of cybersecurity vulnerabilities. The individuals or organisations in question are confronted with the formidable challenge of establishing credibility and earning the confidence of customers within a highly competitive market, all the while competing against well-established industry leaders. Furthermore, the requirement for scalability, the ability to adjust to evolving customer behaviours, and the imperative to exhibit swift expansion introduce additional levels of intricacy to the process.

REFERENCES

Abakah, E. J. A., Tiwari, A. K., Lee, C. C., & Ntow-Gyamfi, M. (2023). Quantile price convergence and spillover effects among Bitcoin, Fintech, and artificial intelligence stocks. *International Review of Finance*, 23(1), 187–205. doi:10.1111/irfi.12393

Aulakh, A. (2023). *Fintech Laws and Regulations 2023*. Retrieved from Global Legal Insight. https://www.globallegalinsights.com/practice-areas/fintech-laws-and-regulations

Cheong, C. W. (2019). Cryptocurrencies vs global foreign exchange risk. *The Journal of Risk Finance*, 20(4), 330–351. doi:10.1108/JRF-11-2018-0178

Demir, A., Pesqué-Cela, V., Altunbas, Y., & Murinde, V. (2022). Fintech, financial inclusion and income inequality: A quantile regression approach. *European Journal of Finance*, 28(1), 86–107. doi:10.1080/1351847X.2020.1772335

Ferretti, P., & Martino, P. (2023). FinTech: Challenges and Opportunities for Banks and Financial Markets. *Banking and Financial Markets: New Risks and Challenges from Fintech and Sustainable Finance*, (pp. 73-94). Research Gate.

Gahlot, C. S., & Ghosh, S. (2023). Emerging Opportunities and Challenges in FinTech Industry–A Comparative Study of India With Other Jurisdictions. *Technology, Management and Business: Evolving Perspectives*, (pp. 21-31). Research Gate.

Gomber, P., Kauffman, R. J., Parker, C., & Weber, B. W. (2018). On the fintech revolution: Interpreting the forces of innovation, disruption, and transformation in financial services. *Journal of Management Information Systems*, 35(1), 220–265. doi:10.1080/07421222.2018.1440766

Hassan, M. K., Rabbani, M. R., Khan, S., & Ali, M. A. M. D. (2022). An Islamic Finance Perspective of Crowdfunding and Peer-To-Peer (P2P) Lending. In FinTech in Islamic Financial Institutions: Scope, Challenges, and Implications in Islamic Finance (pp. 263-277). Cham: Springer International Publishing.

Honisch, E., & Ottenbacher, M. (2017). Crowdfunding in restaurants: Setting the stage. *Journal of Culinary Science & Technology*, 15(3), 223–238. doi:10.1080/15428052.2016.1225539

Kaur, G. (2023). *The history and evolution of the fintech industry*. Cointelegraph. https://cointelegraph.com/news/the-history-and-evolution-of-the-fintech-industry

Kong D. R. Lin T. C. (2021). Alternative investments in the Fintech era: The risk and return of Non-Fungible Token (NFT). *Available at* SSRN 3914085. doi:10.2139/ssrn.3914085

KPMG. (2021). *Pulse of Fintech*. KPMG.

Pant, S. K. (2020). Fintech: Emerging trends. *Telecom Business Review*, *13*(1), 47–52.

Rabbani, M. R. (2023). Fintech innovations, scope, challenges, and implications in Islamic Finance: A systematic analysis. *International Journal of Computing and Digital Systems*, *11*(1), 1–28.

Rabbani, M. R., Bashar, A., Atif, M., Jreisat, A., Zulfikar, Z., & Naseem, Y. (2021, December). Text mining and visual analytics in research: Exploring the innovative tools. In *2021 International Conference on Decision Aid Sciences and Application (DASA)* (pp. 1087-1091). IEEE. 10.1109/DASA53625.2021.9682360

Ryu, H. S., & Ko, K. S. (2020). Sustainable development of Fintech: Focused on uncertainty and perceived quality issues. *Sustainability (Basel)*, *12*(18), 7669. doi:10.3390u12187669

Schroer, A. (2023). *41 Top Payment Processing Companies 2023*. Builtin. https://builtin.com/fintech/fintech-payments-companies-examples

Shalender, K., Singla, B., & Sharma, S. (2023). Blockchain Adoption in the Financial Sector: Challenges, Solutions, and Implementation Framework. In *Revolutionizing Financial Services and Markets Through FinTech and Blockchain* (pp. 269–277). IGI Global. doi:10.4018/978-1-6684-8624-5.ch017

Singla, B., Shalender, K., & Sharma, S. (2023). Consumers' Preferences Towards Digital Payments While Online and Offline Shopping Post COVID-19. In *Revolutionizing Financial Services and Markets Through FinTech and Blockchain* (pp. 288–297). IGI Global. doi:10.4018/978-1-6684-8624-5.ch019

Srivastava, A., Srivastava, A., & Maheswari, R. (2023). *Fintech Laws and Regulations 2023- India. Fintech-Worldwide*. Statista. https://www.statista.com/outlook/dmo/fintech/worldwide#users

Taherdoost, H. (2023). Fintech: Emerging trends and the future of finance. *Financial Technologies and DeFi: A Revisit to the Digital Finance Revolution*, 29-39.

Vijai, C. (2019). FinTech in India–opportunities and challenges. *SAARJ Journal on Banking & Insurance Research (SJBIR) Vol, 8.* https://psplab.com/services/fintech-legal-services,2022 https://cpqi.com/top-6-fintech-consulting-firms-2022/ https://www.bcg.com/press/3may2023-fintech-1-5-trillion-industry-by-2030 https://storm2.com/resources/venture-capital/the-leading-venture-capital-firms-for-fintech-startups-in-2022/ https://www.mckinsey.com/cn/our-insights/our-insights/seven-technologies-shaping-the-future-of-fintech https://www.e-zigurat.com/en/blog/evolution-of-fintech,2022

Chapter 10

From Digital Overload to Trading Zen:
The Role of Digital Detox in Enhancing Intraday Trading Performance

Mukul Bhatnagar
Chandigarh University, India

Pawan Kumar
 https://orcid.org/0000-0003-4892-6374
Chandigarh University, India

Sanjay Taneja
 https://orcid.org/0000-0002-3632-4053
Graphic Era University, India

Kiran Sood
 https://orcid.org/0000-0001-6177-

5318
Chitkara Business School, Chitkara University, India & Research Fellow at the Women Researchers Council (WRC), Azerbaijan State University of Economics (UNEC), Azerbaijan

Simon Grima
 https://orcid.org/0000-0003-1523-5120
Department of Insurance, Faculty of Economics Management and Accountancy, University of Malta, Msida, Malta & Faculty of Business, Management and Economics, University of Latvia, Riga, Latvia

ABSTRACT

Because of the urgency and high stakes involved in their trades, intraday traders are especially vulnerable to the perils of information overload in today's digital world. This chapter explores the potential benefits of digital detox programmes for intraday traders. The research uses the statistical programme SMart PLS to do a route analysis using primary data gathered via questionnaire. The results show that taking a break from technology may dramatically lower stress levels, which in turn boosts business efficiency. This correlation is moderated by traders' levels of expertise, however, indicating that newcomers to the market might gain the most from digital

DOI: 10.4018/979-8-3693-1107-3.ch010

detox programmes. The last section of the study emphasises the chapter's central thesis, arguing for the inclusion of digital detox measures in training programmes and workplace rules in order to address the chapter's identified practical ramifications for traders, trading businesses, and regulatory agencies.

INTRODUCTION

In today's technologically advanced society, the phrase "digital detox," short for "digital detoxification," has gained popularity (Schmuck, 2020). It entails taking a time-limited vacation from using things like cellphones, laptops, social media sites, and the internet (Mirbabaie, Braun, et al., 2022). This method was developed to mitigate the harmful effects of excessive screen time on one's health. As people become more dependent on their electronic gadgets, they might benefit from taking a "digital detox" to reclaim their lives (Karlsen, 2023). The main goal of a digital detox is to alleviate the negative consequences of too much time in front of a computer or engaged in online activities, such as increased stress, decreased productivity, disturbed sleep, and a loss in in-person social contacts. Individuals may tailor their digital detox experience to meet their own needs (Purohit et al., 2023). Some people choose to take a prolonged hiatus from all kinds of digital media, a practise known as a "digital sabbatical." For a certain amount of time (which might be days, weeks, or months), you commit to not engaging in things like checking email, social media, and streaming services. Some people may want to ease into it, by including regular breaks from screen time into their routines (Wilcockson et al., 2019). During a digital detox, people often engage in offline activities that are good for their health and wellness instead of spending time on electronic devices. Examples include spending time with loved ones, going outside, reading a physical book, pursuing a hobby, or practising mindfulness (Muench et al., 2020). The idea is to strike a balance between online and offline activities so that people may rediscover their identities and communities. Taking a break from digital devices may have many positive effects. It may help one feel less worried and stressed, work more efficiently, rest more soundly, connect more deeply with others, and savour the present moment. It may also be used as an escape valve for those who are finding the pressures of modern life too much to bear (Szablewicz, 2020).

The term "Trading Zen" refers to the integration of principles from Zen thought with stock market trading. Traders are encouraged to practise mindfulness in order to gain focus, self-control, and equilibrium in their trading. This way of thinking recognises the risks and uncertainties that come with trading and aims to help traders face them with composure and fortitude. Trading Zen takes its cues from Zen Buddhism, which stresses nonattachment to results and living in the now. That's jargon for saying that traders should ignore their gains and losses and concentrate on the act of trading itself. It calls on you to remain in the moment throughout every trade and to make rational, data-driven choices rather than being guided by your emotions. Discipline is a major tenet of Trading Zen. Traders are advised to create and strictly follow a trading strategy. Entry and exit methods, risk management guidelines, and trade selection criteria should all be included in this strategy. Traders may avoid the basic dangers of trading, such as making rash judgements out of fear or greed, by sticking to a well laid out strategy. Trading Zen also places a premium on risk control. There's a strong emphasis on keeping transaction sizes small enough that any losses won't be devastating emotionally. Traders are encouraged to use stop-loss orders and come to terms with the fact that losses will always occur. With this outlook, traders may better manage the emotional ups and downs that always accompany setbacks. The constant pursuit of knowledge and betterment is another theme throughout Trading Zen. Traders should think back on their transactions, break down the wins and losses, and adjust their tactics appropriately. A trader's development and market knowledge might benefit from a healthy dose of introspection and a willingness to learn from failure. Trading Zen stresses the need of patience. Traders are cautioned that they cannot expect to make money on every single deal. Waiting for favourable market circumstances is emphasised rather than rushing into deals. Taking things slow like this might help alleviate some of the tension and worry that comes with trading. In a nutshell, Trading Zen is an approach to the markets that applies the Zen tenets of concentration, self-control, prudence, and patience. It recommends a level-headed and rational approach to trading, with an emphasis on the procedure rather than the results. By adhering to these guidelines, traders may improve their prospects of long-term success in the competitive trading industry while also pursuing a more balanced and rewarding trading experience.

Intraday trading, often known as day trading, is a kind of day trading in which a trader buys and sells securities inside the same trading day (Baldovin et al., 2015; Vella & Ng, 2014). The goal of intraday trading is to capitalise on price variations that occur throughout the course of a single trading session, as opposed to long-term investing's emphasis on keeping assets for a longer time (Ghosh et al., 2022; E. H. Kao & Fung, 2012). This strategy is most often used to tradable assets like stocks, currencies, and commodities (Koch & Maskos, 2020; Malinova & Park, 2014). Positions are started and cancelled within minutes, hours, or even seconds, making speed the defining feature of intraday trading (Darrat et al., 2003; Xin et al., 2019). When looking for chances to make quick money, intraday traders keep a tight eye on price charts, technical indicators, and market news (Boney-Dutra et al., 2013; Chan et al., 2000). In addition to fundamental research, which takes into account things like earnings reports and economic events that might affect prices during the trading day, they often rely on technical analysis to make choices based on previous price data, patterns, and indications. Intraday trading's rapid speed makes risk management all the more important (Balardy, 2022; Ho, 2013; Mishra & Daigler, 2014). To prevent losing too much money, traders use stop-loss orders and create take-profit levels. Intraday traders may better safeguard their cash and keep their trading discipline with the use of sound risk management (Golub et al., 2021; Nguyen et al., 2004, 2005). Intraday traders often use leverage, which magnifies their money to manage bigger holdings with a smaller initial investment. Leverage may double your earnings, but it can also multiply your losses (Arnerić, 2021; Miłobędzki & Nowak, 2018). Traders engaging in intraday activities should exercise caution when employing leverage and should be aware of the dangers involved. Scalping, day trading, and swing trading are just a few of the intraday trading strategies available to investors. To achieve this goal, scalpers engage in several transactions during the trading day. While day traders enter and exit their positions inside the same trading session, swing traders may retain their holdings for many days in an effort to capitalise on bigger price fluctuations (Azzini et al., 2013; Bekiros, 2015; D.-X. Kao et al., 2018; Martens & Steenbeek, 2001). Intraday trading requires extreme mental fortitude. Trading may evoke strong emotions due to the fast decision-making required and the high-stakes nature of prospective earnings or losses. Successful intraday traders are able to keep their emotions in check, trade in accordance with a well-thought-out strategy, and have a level head under pressure. To sum up, intraday trading is a kind of trading that seeks to benefit from very short-term price fluctuations in financial markets. Trading requires a combination of quick decision-making, technical and fundamental analysis, risk management, and mental fortitude. Intraday traders need to keep a close eye on the markets, be able to make snap judgements, and be comfortable with the dangers that come with trading at such a rapid pace. Although it has the potential for immediate gains, sustained success requires a great deal of information, expertise, and self-discipline.

Financial markets and intraday trading are only two areas that have been transformed by the proliferation of digital technologies (Schonert-Hirz, 2017). Traders now have unparalleled access to data thanks to the proliferation of real-time data, sophisticated trading algorithms, and instantaneous communication platforms (Purohit et al., 2020). Digital overload is a problem characterised by an excessive flood of digital information that may lead to cognitive fatigue, lower productivity, and elevated stress levels, despite the numerous benefits of modern technological breakthroughs (Efimova & Semenov, 2020). In light of these considerations, the purpose of the present study, entitled "From Digital Overload to Trading Zen: The Role of Digital Detox in Enhancing Intraday Trading Performance, Mediated by Stress and Moderated by Experience," is to investigate the potential of digital detox as an intervention for mitigating the negative effects of digital overload, with a focus on intraday trading.

Whether positive or negative, past events may profoundly influence how people do business in the future (Gupta, Taneja, et al., 2023; Taneja, Bhatnagar, Kumar, & Rupeika-Apoga, 2023; Taneja & Ozen, 2023). Experience in the financial markets frequently imparts onto traders invaluable insights that inform their strategies going forward (Bansal et al., 2023; H. Kaur et al., 2023; Kumar, Mukul, et al., 2023). Making money from trades and other positive experiences might give traders more confidence in their abilities and judgements (Dangwal, Taneja, et al., 2022; Kumar, Verma, et al., 2023; Taneja, Bhatnagar, Kumar, & Grima, 2023). If they've had success with a certain strategy or risk management technique in the past, they could be inclined to keep using it. On the other side, lessons learned via failure are often more profound than those gained through success (Kumar, Taneja, et al., 2023; V. Singh et al., 2021; Taneja, Gupta, et al., 2023). Losing traders may examine their actions for clues as to what went wrong and formulate plans to prevent a similar outcome in the future (Bhatnagar et al., 2022; Dangwal, Kaur, et al., 2022; Jangir et al., 2023; Taneja, Jaggi, et al., 2022). Trading strategies that emphasise risk management and capital preservation are one possible outcome of such experiences (Bhatnagar et al., 2023; Kumar et al., 2021; Mukul & Pathak, 2021). In addition, following a bad trading experience, many traders seek out formal training and guidance from an experienced professional. Investors might become more cautious, instituting risk restrictions and relying more heavily on stop-loss orders to safeguard their portfolios (Kumar, Özen, et al., 2023; Reepu et al., 2023; A. Singh et al., 2023b; Taneja, Kaur, et al., 2022). A trader's risk tolerance and trading approach might be influenced by their history of losses (Taneja, Grima, et al., 2023; Taneja & Sharma, 2023).

Due to the continual stream of market news, price ticks, and trade notifications, intraday trading, a discipline that requires rapid decisions and constant concentration, poses a heightened risk for digital overload (Jiang & Balaji, 2022). Particularly worrisome is the acute stress caused by digital overload, which may have a negative impact on the mental and emotional health of traders (A. Singh et al., 2023a). As traders under stress are more likely to make illogical judgements that might have far-reaching implications, there are severe concerns regarding trading performance and overall market stability (Syvertsen, 2023).

Existing research on the topic of stress in intraday trading is few and tends to concentrate on superficial remedies like time management or selective attention despite the topic's centrality (Gupta, Arora, et al., 2023). Stress is inextricably linked to the overload of digital stimuli, yet these techniques seldom go to the heart of the problem (Mukul et al., 2023). This research intends to fill this void by investigating the mediating role of digital detox, or time spent away from digital devices and platforms, between digital overload and financial market performance.

In addition, this study broadens the debate by include the moderator role of experience. Experienced traders may be less sensitive to digital overload because they have developed superior coping strategies for dealing with stress, as shown by previous research. This article seeks to add richness to our knowledge of traders' reactions to digital detox therapies by using experience as a moderating element. The goal of this multi-faceted study is to help traders, financial institutions, and policymakers cope with the negative impacts of digital overload by providing empirical insights and practical advice. With a better grasp of digital detox's function, its relationship to stress, and the moderating effect of experience, we want to pave the way for more sustainable trading practises that boost performance without sacrificing well-being.

This study sheds light on the often-overlooked topic of traders' mental health, which is of great value to individual investors. The study prepares individual traders for the problems they may encounter in the fast-paced world of intraday trading by digging into the impact of digital overload and stress on trading performance. Traders may use this information to develop better methods of dealing with stress, which may boost their productivity and decision-making abilities. The report also presents digital detox as an approach to reducing the detrimental effects of technology overuse. The mental and emotional well-being of individual investors may be improved via occasional disconnection from digital gadgets and platforms. Individual investors may benefit from this practical guidance since it equips them to take charge of their trading environment and lessen the impact of stress on their trading performance.

The findings of this study will also be of great use to institutional investors like hedge funds and banks. Today's highly competitive financial environment places a premium on the success of traders employed by institutional investors. The research presented in this study may be used as a foundation for developing training and support systems for traders in financial institutions. Institutional investors may find it useful to use digital detox as a stress management method since it has the potential to minimise turnover and burnout among trading teams. This, in turn, may lead to improved ability to hold on to seasoned traders and more stable long-term investment returns. In addition, the study presents the idea of experience as a moderating element. Realising that more seasoned traders may have developed more robust strategies for dealing with stress, institutional investors might utilise this knowledge to find and cultivate talent within their trading teams. With this knowledge, you can better attract and keep top talent, which will strengthen your business.

In sum, the information presented in this study is an invaluable tool for traders and investors in the financial markets. By explaining the connection between digital overstimulation, stress, and trading performance, this article equips traders to make educated judgements regarding their trading methods, stress-reduction measures, and team-building initiatives. At the end of the day, it might lead to better trading results and a happier financial sector as a whole.

LITERATURE REVIEW

Related Studies

The notion of digital overload, sometimes known as information overflow or cognitive overload, has been widely discussed in academic writing. Many studies have shown that keeping up with digital information such as email, social networking, and market updates may be mentally taxing for humans. Particularly in high-stress contexts like intraday trading, cognitive tiredness may affect decision-making processes and impede overall performance (Hesselberth, 2018).

The impact of stress on traders' results has been known for a long time. Research on the effects of stress on the body and mind in traders has shown elevated heart rates, diminished ability to focus, and impulsive choices. According to studies conducted by Bauwens, traders who are under pressure often make poor choices that hurt their trading results (Bauwens et al., 2019).

Although research on stress management strategies in trading has been conducted, the idea of digital detox as a method is new. The available research on digital detox mostly focuses on the positive effects it has on one's health and well-being. For instance, a recent study by Anrijis found that cutting down on screen time may help with both stress and insomnia. However, further research is needed to see how it may be used in intraday trading and what effect it could have on trading results (Anrijs et al., 2018).

There has been some research on how trading expertise may play a moderating effect in stress management. Those who have been in the market longer may have already developed defences against market anxiety. Experienced traders have an edge since they are more likely to remain calm under pressure, according to research by (Wilcockson et al., 2020). While numerous studies have focused on specific areas of digital overload, stress, and trading performance, there is increasing agreement in the literature that an integrated strategy is required. This method acknowledges the linked nature of these elements and aims to comprehend how therapies like digital detox may efficiently address the core causes of stress and improve trading performance (Gong et al., 2023).

Hypothesis

H1: There is no significant impact of Digital Detoxification on Stress level

The concept that Digital Detoxification significantly impacts stress levels has empirical backing from several research. Cortisol levels, a physiological indicator of stress, were shown to significantly drop when people spent time in nature without digital devices (Khetawat & Steele, 2023). Participants in a one-week digital detox program experienced lower levels of stress (Bertl et al., 2022).

Additionally, a research found that participants' stress levels and subjective well-being improved after a week of not using Facebook. Taken together, these studies provide strong evidence that reducing one's exposure to digital technology might help alleviate stress (Adam et al., 2023).

H2: There is no significant impact of Digital Detoxification on Trading Performance

Digital detoxification has the potential to greatly enhance trading performance, according to a number of studies. Investors who traded less often, limiting their exposure to continual market information, tended to do better than those who traded more regularly, according to a research. This shows that fewer digital interactions could result in more favorable trading results (Roskladka & Baiev, 2021).

Trading performance improved when traders relied less on social media and digital news, according to study by Glaser et al. (2013). This was due in part to traders' increased ability to think critically and avoid making rash judgments. These results indicate that reducing electronic distractions may improve trading performance (Pirogova et al., 2019).

There is also data that shows Digital Detoxification may not always boost trading performance significantly. The possible impacts of digital interaction may be overshadowed by the myriad of other variables that impact trade, such as market circumstances, economic events, and individual trading techniques. Traders who had access to real-time data via digital devices did not perform any better than those who did not, according to research (Pirogova et al., 2020).

H3: There is no significant impact of Stress Level on Trading Performance

There is no statistically significant relationship between stress and trading performance, according to a number of research. Traders with experience did better when subjected to moderate stress levels compared to those working in low-stress environments, according to research (Zehndorfer, 2018). This shows that traders' decision-making skills may be enhanced and their performance enhanced by a certain amount of stress.

In addition, studies conducted suggested that traders who undergo high levels of stress may have a heightened reluctance to take risks and exhibit more conservative trading strategies. Traders' risk management techniques, according to this theory, could lessen the effect of stress on trading performance (Akman et al., 2020).

Alternatively, research suggests that stress may significantly affect trading performance, often to a negative degree. Poor trading results may be the consequence of impulsive and dangerous decision-making brought on by acute stress, according to research (Cohen & Shin, 2013). Traders' cognitive abilities and risk perception are impacted by higher cortisol levels, according to study (Martinez Fernandez et al., 2012).

H4: There is no significant moderation of experience between Digital Detoxification and Stress level Digital Detoxification and Stress level, Digital Detoxification and Trading Performance, Stress Level and Trading Performance.

Digital detoxification may help seasoned traders reduce stress and make better trading choices, according to research. Traders with more experience might better handle the fear of losing access to digital information sources (Mefrouche et al., 2023). However, contrary to popular belief, there is some evidence that prior experience may not considerably mitigate the effects of digital detoxification. For instance, it was discovered that digital detoxification had comparable effects on stress levels and trading performance among both inexperienced and seasoned traders (M. Singh & Bhatnagar, 2023).

A trader's degree of expertise may impact the correlation between Digital Detoxification, stress, and trading success (Banik et al., 2021). Traders with more experience may be better able to handle the pressures of digital isolation because they have developed superior coping mechanisms and decision-making abilities. Nevertheless, there is still a lack of consensus in the research about how much experience influences these associations. One possible moderator of the correlation between stress and trading performance is the trader's degree of experience. Glaser et al. (2009) found that inexperienced traders are more likely to be negatively affected by stress on decision-making than experienced traders. Traders with greater experience may have figured out ways to deal with stress and make their trading tactics more flexible. Weak and contradictory evidence abounds in the research on the moderating roles of experience in the connections among Digital Detoxification, stress, and trading performance (Vella & Ng, 2014). Research has shown mixed results when comparing beginner and experienced traders, with some finding that experience may mitigate these associations and others finding no such difference. Differences in how stress and trading success are defined, as well as the unique circumstances of each trade, might be to blame for the contradictory findings. The amount to which traders' cognitive capacities and risk tolerance vary from one another may also affect how much experience mediates these connections. Finally, the research on digital overload, stress in trading, and the possible role of digital detox in improving intraday trading performance all point to the interaction between these elements as a complicated determinant of trading success (Radtke et al., 2022). While it has been known for some time that stress is a major component in trading, the role that digital overload plays and the advantages of taking a digital detox are more recent areas of research. Furthermore, the moderating effect of experience further complicates the topic. This study fills such knowledge gaps in the literature and adds to our comprehension of intraday trading's complex dynamics.

RESEARCH METHDOLOGY

This study used a quantitative technique to analyse data gathered in Mumbai, India. The data was analysed using the structural equation modelling and high-level statistical analysis software SMART PLS 4. The questionnaire used in the study included reflective components and was scored on a Likert scale. The questionniare was framed after conducting factor analysis. The data was gathered by surveying a representative group of Mumbai residents chosen by random. All participants provided informed permission, and their replies were kept private and anonymous in accordance with ethical standards. Extensive preparation, including data cleaning and outlier identification, was carried out after data collection. Then, other statistical analyses were run using SMART PLS 4, notably structural equation modelling (SEM), to look at the interplay between the variables. Given the questionnaire's usage of reflective notions, we conducted extensive analyses to determine its validity and reliability as a measurement tool. Practical insights pertinent to the Mumbai region and possibly applicable in larger contexts were gleaned from the data analysis and evaluated in light of the existing literature and the study goals. However, it is essential to include any constraints experienced during the research (please explain constraints if any) that may have affected the generalizability of the results. Future research directions were also explored in light of the results of the study.

DATA ANALYSIS

In Table 1, we see the various demographics of the survey takers. Respondents' ages, incomes, marital statuses, sex, work experience, and educational backgrounds are all included. Among those who answered the survey, individuals between the ages of 30 and 39 make up the largest demographic (41.32%), followed by those younger than 30 (25.90%). Those who answered the survey range in age from 40 to 49 (21.49%) to 50 and above (11.29%). Of all respondents, those with monthly incomes of Rs 30,000 to Rs50,000 make up the greatest share (39.94%), followed by those with incomes of Rs50,000 or more (32.51%) and those with incomes of Rs30,000 or less (27.55%). Sixty-four percent of those who answered the survey are married, while thirty-five and a half percent are single. The bulk of responders

Table 1. Demographic file of respondents

Investors' Age (Years)	Count	Percentage	Income (Per Month)	Count	Percentage
Less than 30	94	25.90%	Below 30,000	100	27.55%
Between 30 to 39	150	41.32%	30,000–50,000	145	39.94%
Between 40 to 49	78	21.49%	Above 50,000	118	32.51%
50 and above	41	11.29%			
Total	363	100.00%	Total	363	100.00%
Marital Status			**Experience**		
Married	234	64.46%	Pleasant	198	54.55%
Unmarried	129	35.54%	Unpleasant	165	45.45%
Total	363	100.00%	Total	363	100.00%
Gender			**Qualification**		
Male	270	74.38%	Graduate Level	89	24.52%
Female	93	25.62%	Post Graduate Level	163	44.90%
			Professional	111	30.58%
Total	363	100.00%	Total	363	100.00%

are men (74.38%), while women account for just a quarter of the total (25.62%). In terms of overall satisfaction, 54.55 percent of respondents had a positive experience, while 45.45 percent had a negative one. Finally, when it comes to education levels, Postgraduate Degree holders make up the largest share (44.90%), followed by Professional Degree holders (30.58%) and Graduate Degree holders (24.52%). Understanding the demographic make-up of the sample and extrapolating meaningful information from the survey results is made easier with the help of the information provided in the table below.

Figure 1 shows the results of running PLS-Algorithm on the conceptual model. This step in tabulated and extrapolated in upcoming explanations in the research.

Cronbach's alpha is a measure of internal consistency dependability that examines the degree of agreement between items within a given concept. There is a great degree of internal consistency among the three measures shown in this table, as shown by their high Cronbach's alpha scores. Cronbach's alpha for Digital Detoxification is 0.847, for Stress Levels it's 0.811, and for Trading Performance it's 0.830. In addition, when looking at the composite reliability (rho_a and rho_c) of these constructions, we find that they are all very reliable. Correlation coefficients range from 0.865 to 0.889 for digital detoxification, 0.813 to 0.868 for stress levels, and 0.901 to 0.881 for trading performance. The amount of variation collected by the construct is compared to the measurement error using average variance extracted

Figure 1. PLS- algorithm on conceptual model

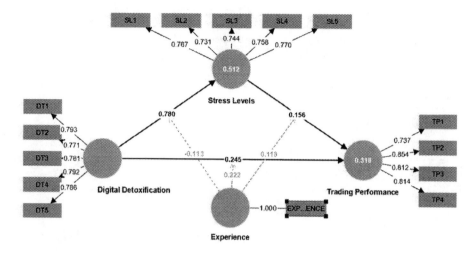

Table 2. Construct reliability and validity

	Cronbach's alpha	Composite reliability (rho_a)	Composite reliability (rho_c)	Average variance extracted (AVE)
Digital Detoxification	0.847	0.865	0.889	0.616
Stress Levels	0.811	0.813	0.868	0.569
Trading Performance	0.83	0.901	0.881	0.649

(AVE). The AVEs for all three constructs are over 0.5, suggesting that they provide reliable and accurate estimates of the target constructs. There is a 0.616 AVE for digital detoxification, a 0.569 AVE for stress levels, and a 0.649 AVE for trading performance. In sum, the table indicates that there is reasonable assurance that the metrics for Digital Detoxification, Stress Levels, and Trading Performance are accurate for study or evaluation purposes.

Discriminant validity between structural model constructs may be evaluated using the HTMT ratios shown in Table 3. The HTMT ratio between pairs of constructs is shown in each column of the table below. A score of 1.0 or near to it implies that the constructs are not distinguishable from one other, whereas a value much below 1.0 shows discriminant validity. If the values in a table are all less than 1.0 (below the diagonal), then the constructs have discriminant validity. Discriminant validity cannot be fully evaluated, however, since values beyond the diagonal are not shown. To verify a measurement model has sufficient discriminant validity, researchers often look at these ratios.

Table 3. HTMT

	Digital Detoxification	Stress Levels	Trading Performance	Experience	Experience x Stress Levels	Experience x Digital Detoxification
Digital Detoxification						
Stress Levels	0.826					
Trading Performance	0.529	0.527				
Experience	0.106	0.052	0.037			
Experience x Stress Levels	0.551	0.793	0.463	0.004		
Experience x Digital Detoxification	0.817	0.549	0.488	0.061	0.696	

Figure 2 shows the results of boot strapping the conceptual model. This step in tabulated and explained in upcoming explanations of the research.

The significance of associations between variables is analysed statistically, and the findings are shown in Table 4. There is a direct correlation between the size of the "T statistics (|O/STDEV|)" column and the strength of the connection being studied. Statistical significance is shown in the "P values" column; P values below 0.05 are often accepted as meaningful. A P value of 0 indicates an extremely strong correlation between "Digital Detoxification" and "Stress Levels" in this table. However, most other relationships, such as "Digital Detoxification" with "Trading

Figure 2. Boot strapping

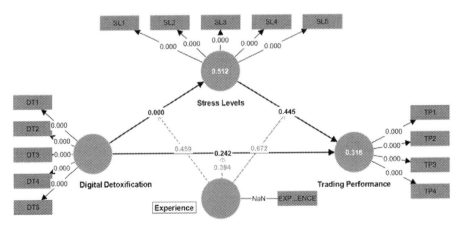

Table 4. Significance of relation between variables

	Original sample (O)	Sample mean (M)	Standard deviation (STDEV)	T statistics (|O/STDEV|)	P values
Digital Detoxification -> Stress Levels	0.78	0.79	0.07	11.083	0
Digital Detoxification -> Trading Performance	0.245	0.24	0.209	1.17	0.242
Stress Levels -> Trading Performance	0.156	0.176	0.204	0.763	0.445
Experience -> Stress Levels	0.144	0.149	0.145	0.989	0.323
Experience -> Trading Performance	0.045	0.049	0.173	0.257	0.797
Experience x Stress Levels -> Trading Performance	0.118	0.071	0.278	0.423	0.672
Experience x Digital Detoxification -> Stress Levels	-0.113	-0.124	0.152	0.74	0.459
Experience x Digital Detoxification -> Trading Performance	0.222	0.237	0.26	0.853	0.394

Performance" and "Experience" with "Stress Levels" and "Trading Performance," do not meet the threshold for statistical significance ($P > 0.05$).

In Table 5, we see the results of a mediation study where we look at how "Digital Detoxification" influences "Trading Performance" through the mediator of "Stress Levels." With a T-Stat of 2.833**, the "Total Effect" reveals a statistically significant overall influence of digital detoxification on trading performance. The "Indirect Effect" (through Stress Levels) is shown to be statistically negligible when looking at the mediation components, which suggests that the link between Digital Detoxification and Trading Performance is not mediated by Stress Levels. Without accounting for the mediator, the "Direct Effect" is similarly statistically negligible. Indirect effects make up 36.84% of the overall impact, as shown by the "VAF" (Variance Accounted For). Although digital detoxification has been shown

Table 5. Mediation analysis- stress level

Type of effect	Effect	Path Coefficient	T-Stats	Remarks
Total Effect	Digital Detoxification -> Trading Performance	0.38	2.833**	Significant Total Effect
Indirect Effect	Digital Detoxification-> Stress Levels -> Trading Performance	0.14	0.741	Insignificant Indirect Effect
Direct Effect	Digital Detoxification -> Trading Performance	0.24	1.17	Insignificant Direct Effect
VAF (Variance Accounted For)	Indirect Effect/Total Effect	36.84%		

to improve trading performance, the mediation analysis reveals that stress levels are not a crucial moderator in this connection.

Your research model's components and interactions may be better understood in light of the supplied data. First, it's clear that the conceptions' reliability and validity have been well examined. All three measures (Digital Detox, Stress, and Trading Performance) have high levels of internal consistency (Cronbach's alpha > 0.7). Furthermore, the average variance extracted (AVE) and composite reliability (rho_a and rho_c) values are consistent with the notion that these constructs are trustworthy and exhibit convergent validity.

It is evident that the diagonal values are all below the required threshold of 0.85, indicating that the constructs are different from each other, which is crucial for construct validity, and we may go on to the discriminant validity tested using the HTMT (Heterotrait-Monotrait) ratio.

The table shows that Digital Detoxification has a high T-statistic and a low p-value, indicating a substantial beneficial influence on Stress Levels. Despite this, there is no evidence linking digital detoxification with improved trading results. There is no clear correlation between stress and trading performance. The intricacy of the linkages you've modelled is shown by the fact that, although Digital Detoxification affect stress levels, it may not have any noticeable effect on trading performance.

The entire impact of digital detoxification on trading performance is also considerable, as shown by a mediation study centering on stress levels. The Stress Levels-mediated indirect impact, however, is determined to be negligible. This suggests that the link between Digital Detoxification and Trading Performance may not be totally mediated by Stress Levels. A score of 36.84% for the variation accounted for (VAF) indicates that Stress Levels only partially explains the whole impact, highlighting the need for further research into other possible mediators or moderators.

In conclusion, the results of this study highlight the significance of Digital Detoxification in affecting Stress Levels, but they also imply a more nuanced link with Trading Performance. In order to fine-tune your research model and investigate other aspects that may affect your Trading Performance, you must first grasp these subtleties. It also emphasises the need of investigating the underlying mechanisms of these connections and the possible moderators that may impact them in future studies.

DISCUSSION

As an investor, you may glean a lot of useful information from the offered data. To begin, it's obvious that Digital Detoxification, the process of limiting your exposure to digital media, may significantly reduce your stress levels (Mohamed et al., 2023). Given the robust positive correlation between them, it's worth noting that cutting less on digital distractions may result in less stress. When emotions run high, it may be difficult to make sound financial decisions. Therefore, it may be beneficial to adopt ways to control digital distractions and decrease stress in order to make better investment decisions and enhance general well-being (Syvertsen & Enli, 2020).

Notably, the data also demonstrates a complicated link in terms of trading success (Schmitt et al., 2021). Although research has associated digital detoxification with less stress, this doesn't seem to translate into improved trading results. This suggests that although limiting screen time might assist with stress management, doing so may not result in improved financial returns (Mirbabaie, Stieglitz, et al., 2022). This underscores the need of incorporating a larger variety of elements, such as market research, risk management, and investing techniques, into your decision-making as an investor (Nguyen, 2022).

Understanding the complexities of these connections is further highlighted by the mediation analysis (Stäheli & Stoltenberg, 2022). This data provides support for the hypothesis that stress levels do not entirely mediate the connection between Digital Detoxification and financial success. This multiplicity of influences highlights the need of avoiding oversimplification while making financial choices.

In sum, the information presented here is helpful for traders as it sheds light on the connections between stress, digital detox, and performance. Stress reduction via less time spent online has many positive health effects, but this shouldn't be your only consideration when making financial decisions. It is still crucial to have a well defined investment plan, adopt efficient risk management measures, and diversify your investment portfolio.

CONCLUSION

Several broad management implications follow from the data analysis. Tailoring goods, services, and marketing tactics requires a thorough understanding of the target audience's demographic profile, which includes factors such as age, income, marital status, gender, experience, and qualification. The credibility of findings is increased and well-informed choices are supported by ensuring the validity and reliability of measuring devices used in data collecting. When working with many variables, it is especially important to evaluate discriminant validity to avoid making hasty inferences. In the context of employee well-being, paying attention to and maybe engaging in treatments that target areas with significant correlations between variables, such as the substantial association between digital detoxification and stress levels is important. Strategies should be developed using the findings of mediation analyses as a guide, with an emphasis on strengthening mediators when indirect effects are considerable. Instead of focusing on just one component, businesses should adopt a more holistic strategy that considers the interplay of several variables. Finally, effective decision-making and rapid response to changing situations need constant monitoring and analysis of data.

REFERENCES

Adam, D., Berschick, J., Schiele, J. K., Bogdanski, M., Schroeter, M., Steinmetz, M., Koch, A. K., Sehouli, J., Reschke, S., Stritter, W., Kessler, C. S., & Seifert, G. (2023). Interventions to reduce stress and prevent burnout in healthcare professionals supported by digital applications: A scoping review. *Frontiers in Public Health, 11*, 1231266. doi:10.3389/fpubh.2023.1231266 PMID:38026413

Akman, M. S., Armstrong, S., Dadush, U., Gonzalez, A., Kimura, F., Nakagawa, J., Rashish, P., Tamura, A., & Primo Braga, C. A. (2020). World Trading System under Stress: Scenarios for the Future. *Global Policy, 11*(3), 360–366. doi:10.1111/1758-5899.12776

Anrijs, S., Bombeke, K., Durnez, W., Van Damme, K., Vanhaelewyn, B., Conradie, P., Smets, E., Cornelis, J., De Raedt, W., Ponnet, K., & De Marez, L. (2018). MobileDNA: Relating physiological stress measurements to smartphone usage to assess the effect of a digital detox. *Communications in Computer and Information Science, 851*, 356–363. doi:10.1007/978-3-319-92279-9_48

Arnerić, J. (2021). Multiple STL decomposition in discovering a multi-seasonality of intraday trading volume. *Croatian Operational Research Review, 12*(1), 61–74. doi:10.17535/crorr.2021.0006

Azzini, A., Dragoni, M., & Tettamanzi, A. G. B. (2013). Short-term market forecasting for intraday trading with neuro-evolutionary modeling. In *Recent Advances in Computational Finance*. Nova Science Publishers, Inc. https://www.scopus.com/inward/record.uri?eid=2-s2.0-84896237644&partnerID=40&md5=4e585a82d4e81a029451948ea0e6545f

Balardy, C. (2022). An Empirical Analysis of the Bid-ask Spread in the Continuous Intraday Trading of the German Power Market. *The Energy Journal (Cambridge, Mass.), 43*(3), 229–255. doi:10.5547/01956574.43.3.cbal

Baldovin, F., Camana, F., Caporin, M., Caraglio, M., & Stella, A. L. (2015). Ensemble properties of high-frequency data and intraday trading rules. *Quantitative Finance, 15*(2), 231–245. doi:10.1080/14697688.2013.867454

Banik, S., Sharma, N., & Sharma, K. P. (2021). Analysis of Regression Techniques for Stock Market Prediction: A Performance Review. *2021 9th International Conference on Reliability, Infocom Technologies and Optimization (Trends and Future Directions), ICRITO 2021*. IEEE. 10.1109/ICRITO51393.2021.9596192

Bansal, N., Bhatnagar, M., & Taneja, S. (2023). Balancing priorities through green optimism: A study elucidating initiatives, approaches, and strategies for sustainable supply chain management. In *Handbook of Research on Designing Sustainable Supply Chains to Achieve a Circular Economy*. IGI Global., doi:10.4018/978-1-6684-7664-2.ch004

Bauwens, J., Thorbjornsson, G. B., & Verstrynge, K. (2019). Unplug Your Life: Digital Detox through a Kierkegaardian Lens. *Kierkegaard Studies*, *24*(1), 415–436. doi:10.1515/kierke-2019-0017

Bekiros, S. D. (2015). Heuristic learning in intraday trading under uncertainty. *Journal of Empirical Finance*, *30*, 34–49. doi:10.1016/j.jempfin.2014.11.002

Bertl, M., Metsallik, J., & Ross, P. (2022). A systematic literature review of AI-based digital decision support systems for post-traumatic stress disorder. *Frontiers in Psychiatry*, *13*, 923613. doi:10.3389/fpsyt.2022.923613 PMID:36016975

Bhatnagar, M., Özen, E., Taneja, S., Grima, S., & Rupeika-Apoga, R. (2022). The Dynamic Connectedness between Risk and Return in the Fintech Market of India: Evidence Using the GARCH-M Approach. *Risks*, *10*(11), 209. doi:10.3390/risks10110209

Bhatnagar, M., Taneja, S., & Rupeika-Apoga, R. (2023). Demystifying the Effect of the News (Shocks) on Crypto Market Volatility. *Journal of Risk and Financial Management*, *16*(2), 136. doi:10.3390/jrfm16020136

Boney-Dutra, V., Guirguis, H., & Mueller, G. R. (2013). Did intraday trading by leveraged and inverse leveraged etfs create excess price volatility? A look at REITs and the broad market. *Journal of Real Estate Portfolio Management*, *19*(1), 1–16. https://www.scopus.com/inward/record.uri?eid=2-s2.0-84881086451&partnerID=40&md5=8399a7e8d2adb28b832fdd34f320c238. doi:10.1080/10835547.2013.12089942

Chan, K., Chockalingam, M., & Lai, K. W. L. (2000). Overnight information and intraday trading behavior: Evidence from NYSE cross-listed stocks and their local market information. *Journal of Multinational Financial Management*, *10*(3–4), 495–509. doi:10.1016/S1042-444X(00)00030-X

Cohen, B. H., & Shin, H. S. (2013). Positive Feedback Trading Under Stress: Evidence from the US Treasury Securities Market. *GLOBAL ECONOMIC REVIEW, 42*(4, SI), 314–345. doi:10.1080/1226508X.2013.860707

Dangwal, A., Kaur, S., Taneja, S., & Taneja, S. (2022). A Bibliometric Analysis of Green Tourism Based on the Scopus Platform. In J. Kaur, P. Jindal, & A. Singh (Eds.), *Developing Relationships, Personalization, and Data Herald in Marketing 5.0* (Vol. i, pp. 1–327). IGI Global. doi:10.4018/978-1-6684-4496-2.ch015

Dangwal, A., Taneja, S., Özen, E., Todorovic, I., & Grima, S. (2022). Abridgement of Renewables: It's Potential and Contribution to India's GDP. *International Journal of Sustainable Development and Planning, 17*(8), 2357–2363. doi:10.18280/ijsdp.170802

Darrat, A. F., Rahman, S., & Zhong, M. (2003). Intraday trading volume and return volatility of the DJIA stocks: A note. *Journal of Banking & Finance, 27*(10), 2035–2043. doi:10.1016/S0378-4266(02)00321-7

Efimova, G. Z., & Semenov, M. Y. (2020). Digital detox of the youth (On the example of social networks). *RUDN Journal of Sociology, 20*(3), 572–581. doi:10.22363/2313-2272-2020-20-3-572-581

Ghosh, P., Neufeld, A., & Sahoo, J. K. (2022). Forecasting directional movements of stock prices for intraday trading using LSTM and random forests. *Finance Research Letters, 46*, 102280. Advance online publication. doi:10.1016/j.frl.2021.102280

Golub, A., Grossmass, L., & Poon, S.-H. (2021). Ultra-short tenor yield curve for intraday trading and settlement. *European Journal of Finance, 27*(4–5), 441–459. doi:10.1080/1351847X.2019.1662821

Gong, Y., Schroeder, A., & Plaisance, P. L. (2023). Digital detox tourism: An Ellulian critique. *Annals of Tourism Research, 103*, 103646. doi:10.1016/j.annals.2023.103646

Gupta, M., Arora, K., & Taneja, S. (2023). Bibliometric analysis on employee engagement and human resource management. In *Enhancing Customer Engagement Through Location-Based Marketing*. IGI Global. doi:10.4018/978-1-6684-8177-6.ch013

Gupta, M., Taneja, S., Sharma, V., Singh, A., Rupeika-Apoga, R., & Jangir, K. (2023). Does Previous Experience with the Unified Payments Interface (UPI) Affect the Usage of Central Bank Digital Currency (CBDC)? *Journal of Risk and Financial Management, 16*(6), 286. doi:10.3390/jrfm16060286

Hesselberth, P. (2018). Connect, disconnect, reconnect historicizing the current gesture towards disconnectivity, from the plug-in drug to the digital detox. *Cinema et Cie, 18*(30), 109 – 118. https://www.scopus.com/inward/record.uri?eid=2-s2.0-85106021759&partnerID=40&md5=d7cc67cb56ff66f648f6d930b591192b

Ho, C. M. (2013). Private information, overconfidence and intraday trading behaviour: Empirical study of the Taiwan stock market. *Applied Financial Economics, 23*(4), 325–345. doi:10.1080/09603107.2012.720012

Jangir, K., Sharma, V., Taneja, S., & Rupeika-Apoga, R. (2023). The Moderating Effect of Perceived Risk on Users' Continuance Intention for FinTech Services. *Journal of Risk and Financial Management, 16*(1), 21. doi:10.3390/jrfm16010021

Jiang, Y., & Balaji, M. S. (2022). Getting unwired: What drives travellers to take a digital detox holiday? *Tourism Recreation Research, 47*(5–6), 453–469. doi:10.10 80/02508281.2021.1889801

Kao, D.-X., Tsai, W.-C., Wang, Y.-H., & Yen, K.-C. (2018). An analysis on the intraday trading activity of VIX derivatives. *Journal of Futures Markets, 38*(2), 158–174. doi:10.1002/fut.21857

Kao, E. H., & Fung, H.-G. (2012). Intraday trading activities and volatility in round-the-clock futures markets. *International Review of Economics & Finance, 21*(1), 195–209. doi:10.1016/j.iref.2011.06.003

Karlsen, F. (2023). The digital detox camp: Practices and motivations for reverse domestication. In *The Routledge Handbook of Media and Technology Domestication.* Taylor and Francis. doi:10.4324/9781003265931-35

Kaur, H., Singh, K., Kumar, P., & Kaur, A. (2023). Assessing the environmental sustainability corridor: An empirical study of Renewable energy consumption in BRICS nation. *IOP Conference Series. Earth and Environmental Science, 1110*(1), 012053. Advance online publication. doi:10.1088/1755-1315/1110/1/012053

Khetawat, D., & Steele, R. G. (2023). Examining the Association Between Digital Stress Components and Psychological Wellbeing: A Meta-Analysis. *Clinical Child and Family Psychology Review, 26*(4), 957–974. doi:10.100710567-023-00440-9 PMID:37432506

Koch, C., & Maskos, P. (2020). Passive balancing through intraday trading: Whether interactions between short-term trading and balancing stabilize Germany's electricity system. *International Journal of Energy Economics and Policy, 10*(2), 101–112. doi:10.32479/ijeep.8750

Kumar, P., Khurana, A., & Sharma, S. (2021). Performance evaluation of public and private sector banks. *World Review of Entrepreneurship, Management and Sustainable Development, 17*(2–3), 306–322. doi:10.1504/WREMSD.2021.114436

Kumar, P., Mukul, Kaur, D., & Kaur, A. (2023). Green Infrastructure- A Roadmap Towards Sustainable Development. *IOP Conference Series. Earth and Environmental Science, 1110*(1), 012060. Advance online publication. doi:10.1088/1755-1315/1110/1/012060

Kumar, P., Özen, E., & Vurur, S. (2023). Adoption of blockchain technology in the financial sector. In *Contemporary Studies of Risks in Emerging Technology, Part A*. Emerald Group Publishing Ltd., doi:10.1108/978-1-80455-562-020231018

Kumar, P., & Taneja, S. Mukul, & Ozen, E. (2023). Digital transformation of the insurance industry - a case of the Indian insurance sector. In *The Impact of Climate Change and Sustainability Standards on the Insurance Market*. Wiley. https://www.scopus.com/inward/record.uri?eid=2-s2.0-85168611885&partnerID=40&md5=6c2fb77610b1390b55b6945d955c0955

Kumar, P., Verma, P., Bhatnagar, M., Taneja, S., Seychel, S., Todorović, I., & Grim, S. (2023). The Financial Performance and Solvency Status of the Indian Public Sector Banks: A CAMELS Rating and Z Index Approach. *International Journal of Sustainable Development and Planning, 18*(2), 367–376. doi:10.18280/ijsdp.180204

Malinova, K., & Park, A. (2014). The impact of competition and information on intraday trading. *Journal of Banking & Finance, 44*(1), 55–71. doi:10.1016/j.jbankfin.2014.03.026

Martens, M., & Steenbeek, O. W. (2001). Intraday trading halts in the Nikkei futures market. *Pacific-Basin Finance Journal, 9*(5), 535–561. doi:10.1016/S0927-538X(01)00023-3

Martinez Fernandez, J., Augusto, J. C., Seepold, R., & Madrid, N. M. (2012). A Sensor Technology Survey for a Stress-Aware Trading Process. *IEEE Transactions on Systems, Man, and Cybernetics. Part C, Applications and Reviews, 42*(6), 809–824. doi:10.1109/TSMCC.2011.2179028

Mefrouche, M. L., Siegmann, E.-M., Boehme, S., Berking, M., & Kornhuber, J. (2023). The Effect of Digital Mindfulness Interventions on Depressive, Anxiety, and Stress Symptoms in Pregnant Women: A Systematic Review and Meta-Analysis. *European Journal of Investigation in Health, Psychology and Education, 13*(9), 1694–1706. doi:10.3390/ejihpe13090122 PMID:37754461

Miłobędzki, P., & Nowak, S. (2018). Intraday Trading Patterns on the Warsaw Stock Exchange. In J. K., L.-J. H., & O. L.T. (Eds.), Springer Proceedings in Business and Economics (pp. 55 – 66). Springer Science and Business Media B.V. doi:10.1007/978-3-319-76228-9_6

Mirbabaie, M., Braun, L.-M., & Marx, J. (2022). Knowledge Work 'Unplugged' - Digital Detox Effects on ICT Demands, Job Performance and Satisfaction. *17th International Conference on Wirtschaftsinformatik, WI 2022*. SCOPUS/ https://www.scopus.com/inward/record.uri?eid=2-s2.0-85152120849&partnerID=40&md5=b7a95d44e0ce0133dbdf35e13e3063b2

Mirbabaie, M., Stieglitz, S., & Marx, J. (2022). Digital Detox. *Business & Information Systems Engineering*, *64*(2), 239–246. doi:10.100712599-022-00747-x

Mishra, S., & Daigler, R. T. (2014). Intraday trading and bidask spread characteristics for SPX and SPY options. *Journal of Derivatives*, *21*(3), 70–84. doi:10.3905/jod.2014.21.3.070

Mohamed, S. M., Abdallah, L. S., & Ali, F. N. K. (2023). Effect of digital detox program on electronic screen syndrome among preparatory school students. *Nursing Open*, *10*(4), 2222–2228. doi:10.1002/nop2.1472 PMID:36373487

Muench, C., Feulner, L., Muench, R., & Carolus, A. (2020). Time to Log Off: An Analysis of Factors Influencing the Willingness to Participate in a Long-Term 'Digital Detox' with the Smartphone. *Communications in Computer and Information Science, 1226 CCIS*, 209 – 216. Springer. doi:10.1007/978-3-030-50732-9_28

Mukul, T. S., Özen, E., Plaha, R., & Zammit, M. L. (2023). Banking, Fintech, BigTech: Emerging challenges for multimedia adoption. In *Intelligent Multimedia Technologies for Financial Risk Management: Trends, Tools and Applications*. Institution of Engineering and Technology. https://www.scopus.com/inward/record.uri?eid=2-s2.0-85166147373&partnerID=40&md5=94818506510d02c90c03db2508d518d3

Mukul, & Pathak, N. (2021). Are the financial inclusion schemes of India developing the nation sustainably? *E3S Web of Conferences, 296*, 06011. IEEE. doi:10.1051/e3sconf/202129606011

Nguyen, V. T. (2022). The perceptions of social media users of digital detox apps considering personality traits. *Education and Information Technologies*, *27*(7), 9293–9316. doi:10.100710639-022-11022-7 PMID:35370441

Nguyen, V. T., Van Ness, B. F., & Van Ness, R. A. (2004). Intraday trading of Island (as reported to the cincinnati stock exchange) and NASDAQ. In *Advances In Quantitative Analysis Of Finance And Accounting - New Series*. World Scientific Publishing Co., doi:10.1142/9789812565457_0006

Nguyen, V. T., Van Ness, B. F., & Van Ness, R. A. (2005). Intraday trading of Island (as reported to the cincinnati stock exchange) and NASDAQ. In *Advances In Quantitative Analysis Of Finance And Accounting - New Series* (Vol. 2). World Scientific Publishing Co., doi:10.1142/9789812701213_0006

Pirogova, O., Makarevich, M., Ilina, O., & Ulanov, V. (2019). Optimizing trading company capital structure on the basis of using bankruptcy logistic models under conditions of economy digitalization. *IOP Conference Series. Materials Science and Engineering*, *497*, 012129. doi:10.1088/1757-899X/497/1/012129

Pirogova, O., Makarevich, M., Khareva, V., & Saveleva, N. (2020). Improving the use effectiveness of trading enterprises intellectual capital at the stages of the life cycle in the context of digitalization. *IOP Conference Series. Materials Science and Engineering*, *940*(1), 012053. doi:10.1088/1757-899X/940/1/012053

Purohit, A. K., Barclay, L., & Holzer, A. (2020). Designing for digital detox: Making social media less addictive with digital nudges. *Conference on Human Factors in Computing Systems - Proceedings*. ACM. 10.1145/3334480.3382810

Purohit, A. K., Raggi, M., & Holzer, A. (2023). How Pricing and Ratings Affect Perceived Value of Digital Detox Apps. *Conference on Human Factors in Computing Systems - Proceedings*. ACM. 10.1145/3544549.3585681

Radtke, T., Apel, T., Schenkel, K., Keller, J., & von Lindern, E. (2022). Digital detox: An effective solution in the smartphone era? A systematic literature review. *Mobile Media & Communication*, *10*(2), 190–215. doi:10.1177/20501579211028647

Reepu, R., Taneja, S., Ozen, E., & Singh, A. (2023). A globetrotter to the future of marketing: Metaverse. In *Cultural Marketing and Metaverse for Consumer Engagement*. IGI Global. doi:10.4018/978-1-6684-8312-1.ch001

Roskladka, A., & Baiev, R. (2021). Digitalization of data analysis tools as the key for success in the online trading markets. *ACCESS-ACCESS TO SCIENCE BUSINESS INNOVATION IN THE DIGITAL ECONOMY*, *2*(3), 222–233. doi:10.46656/access.2021.2.3(2)

Schmitt, J. B., Breuer, J., & Wulf, T. (2021). From cognitive overload to digital detox: Psychological implications of telework during the COVID-19 pandemic. *Computers in Human Behavior*, *124*, 106899. doi:10.1016/j.chb.2021.106899 PMID:34566255

Schmuck, D. (2020). Does digital detox work? exploring the role of digital detox applications for problematic smartphone use and well-being of young adults using multigroup analysis. *Cyberpsychology, Behavior, and Social Networking, 23*(8), 526–532. doi:10.1089/cyber.2019.0578 PMID:32354288

Schonert-Hirz, S. (2017). Digital Balance instead of Digital Detox; [Digitale Balance statt Digital Detox]. *Arbeitsmedizin Sozialmedizin Umweltmedizin, 52*(11), 796 – 800. https://www.scopus.com/inward/record.uri?eid=2-s2.0-85034016206&partn erID=40&md5=f20e31931f3a95938d0045e9371ecc13

Singh, A., Sharma, S., Singh, A., Unanoğlu, M., & Taneja, S. (2023a). Cultural Marketing and Metaverse for Consumer Engagement. In *Cultural Marketing and Metaverse for Consumer Engagement*. IGI Global., doi:10.4018/978-1-6684-8312-1

Singh, A., Sharma, S., Singh, A., Unanoğlu, M., & Taneja, S. (2023b). Preface. In *Cultural Marketing and Metaverse for Consumer Engagement*. IGI Global. https:// www.scopus.com/inward/record.uri?eid=2-s2.0-85162657422&partnerID=40&m d5=1490c94e51004158cb0b33e2dffedda8 doi:10.4018/978-1-6684-8312-1

Singh, M., & Bhatnagar, M. (2023). Sustainability's Symphony: Orchestrating Talent Management for Creating Financial Impact. In Sustainable Investments in Green Finance (pp. 17–48). IGI Global. doi:10.4018/979-8-3693-1388-6.ch002

Singh, V., Taneja, S., Singh, V., Singh, A., & Paul, H. L. (2021). Online advertising strategies in Indian and Australian e-commerce companies:: A comparative study. *Big Data Analytics for Improved Accuracy, Efficiency, and Decision Making in Digital Marketing*, 124–138. doi:10.4018/978-1-7998-7231-3.ch009

Stäheli, U., & Stoltenberg, L. (2022). Digital detox tourism: Practices of analogization. *New Media & Society*. doi:10.1177/14614448211072808

Syvertsen, T. (2023). Framing digital disconnection: Problem definitions, values, and actions among digital detox organisers. *Convergence (London), 29*(3), 658–674. doi:10.1177/13548565221122910

Syvertsen, T., & Enli, G. (2020). Digital detox: Media resistance and the promise of authenticity. *Convergence (London), 26*(5–6), 1269–1283. doi:10.1177/1354856519847325

Szablewicz, M. (2020). From the media fast to digital detox: Examining dominant discourses about technology use. *Communication Teacher, 34*(3), 180–184. doi:10 .1080/17404622.2019.1676913

Taneja, S., Bhatnagar, M., Kumar, P., & Grima, S. (2023). A Panel Analysis of the Effectiveness of the Asset Management in Indian Agricultural Companies. *International Journal of Sustainable Development and Planning, 18*(3), 653–660. doi:10.18280/ijsdp.180301

Taneja, S., Bhatnagar, M., Kumar, P., & Rupeika-Apoga, R. (2023). India's Total Natural Resource Rents (NRR) and GDP: An Augmented Autoregressive Distributed Lag (ARDL) Bound Test. *Journal of Risk and Financial Management, 16*(2), 91. doi:10.3390/jrfm16020091

Taneja, S., Grima, S., Kumar, P., & Ozen, E. (2023). Special Issue: 'Green Asset and Risk Management for Promoting Sustainable Entrepreneurship in the Building of the Green Economy.'. *International Journal of Technology Management & Sustainable Development, 22*(2), 127–130. doi:10.1386/tmsd_00071_7

Taneja, S., Gupta, M., Bhushan, P., Bhatnagar, M., & Singh, A. (2023). Cultural marketing in the digital era. In *Cultural Marketing and Metaverse for Consumer Engagement*. IGI Global., doi:10.4018/978-1-6684-8312-1.ch008

Taneja, S., Jaggi, P., Jewandah, S., & Ozen, E. (2022). Role of Social Inclusion in Sustainable Urban Developments: An Analyse by PRISMA Technique. *International Journal of Design & Nature and Ecodynamics, 17*(6), 937–942. doi:10.18280/ijdne.170615

Taneja, S., Kaur, S., & Özen, E. (2022). Using green finance to promote global growth in a sustainable way. *International Journal of Green Economics, 16*(3), 246–257. doi:10.1504/IJGE.2022.128930

Taneja, S., & Ozen, E. (2023). Impact of the European Green Deal (EDG) on the Agricultural Carbon (CO2) Emission in Turkey. *International Journal of Sustainable Development and Planning, 18*(3), 715–727. doi:10.18280/ijsdp.180307

Taneja, S., & Sharma, V. (2023). Role of beaconing marketing in improving customer buying experience. In *Enhancing Customer Engagement Through Location-Based Marketing*. IGI Global., doi:10.4018/978-1-6684-8177-6.ch012

Vella, V., & Ng, W. L. (2014). Enhancing intraday trading performance of Neural Network using dynamic volatility clustering fuzzy filter. In S. A., M. D., P. V., & A. R.J. (Eds.), *IEEE/IAFE Conference on Computational Intelligence for Financial Engineering, Proceedings (CIFEr)* (pp. 465 – 472). Institute of Electrical and Electronics Engineers Inc. 10.1109/CIFEr.2014.6924110

Wilcockson, T. D. W., Osborne, A. M., & Ellis, D. A. (2019). Digital detox: The effect of smartphone abstinence on mood, anxiety, and craving. *Addictive Behaviors*, *99*, 106013. doi:10.1016/j.addbeh.2019.06.002 PMID:31430621

Wilcockson, T. D. W., Osborne, A. M., & Ellis, D. A. (2020). Corrigendum to 'Digital detox: The effect of smartphone abstinence on mood, anxiety, and craving' (Addictive Behaviors (2019) 99, (S0306460319300681), ()). *Addictive Behaviors, 104*. https://doi.org/ doi:10.1016/j.addbeh.2019.06.002

Xin, L., Lam, K., & Yu, P. L. H. (2019). Effectiveness of filter trading as an intraday trading rule. *Studies in Economics and Finance*, *38*(3), 659–674. doi:10.1108/SEF-09-2018-0294

Zehndorfer, E. (2018). Trading long or short on stress? In PHYSIOLOGY OF EMOTIONAL AND IRRATIONAL INVESTING: CAUSES AND SOLUTIONS (pp. 67–97). ROUTLEDGE. doi:10.4324/9781315269368-3

APPENDIX (CONSTRUCTS AND STATEMENTS)

Digital Detoxification (Independent Variable)

1. To what extent do you actively engage in digital detoxification practices during your intraday trading sessions?
- Strongly Disagree
- Disagree
- Neutral
- Agree
- Strongly Agree

2. How successful are you in limiting your exposure to digital distractions (e.g., social media, news, emails) while trading intraday?
- Not Successful
- Slightly Successful
- Moderately Successful
- Very Successful
- Extremely Successful

3. How often do you consciously set time limits on your digital device usage as a part of your digital detox routine during trading hours?
- Never
- Rarely
- Occasionally
- Often
- Always

4. To what extent do you believe that digital detox practices positively impact your overall well-being as an intraday trader?
- Strongly Disagree
- Disagree
- Neutral
- Agree
- Strongly Agree

5. How would you rate your commitment to reducing digital distractions and focusing on trading during your intraday sessions?
- Very Low
- Low
- Moderate
- High
- Very High

Stress Level (Mediating Variable)

1. How frequently do you experience stress during intraday trading?
   - Very Rarely
   - Rarely
   - Occasionally
   - Frequently
   - Very Frequently

2. How well do you manage your stress levels during intraday trading?
   - Very Ineffectively
   - Ineffectively
   - Neutral
   - Effectively
   - Very Effectively

3. To what extent do external factors, such as market volatility or news events, contribute to your stress levels during intraday trading?
   - Not at All
   - Slightly
   - Moderately
   - Significantly
   - Extremely

4. How much do your stress levels impact your decision-making process during intraday trading?
   - Not at All
   - Slightly
   - Moderately
   - Significantly
   - Extremely

5. How confident are you in your ability to manage stress during intraday trading, regardless of external factors?
   - Not at All Confident
   - Somewhat Confident
   - Neutral
   - Confident
   - Very Confident

Trading Performance (Dependent Variable)

1. How satisfied are you with your overall trading performance in intraday trading?
   - Very Dissatisfied

- Dissatisfied
- Neutral
- Satisfied
- Very Satisfied

2. To what extent do you think your digital detox efforts contribute to your intraday trading results?

- No Contribution
- Minor Contribution
- Moderate Contribution
- Significant Contribution
- Strong Contribution

3. How do you perceive the relationship between your stress levels during trading and your intraday trading performance?

- Negative Relationship
- Slightly Negative Relationship
- No Relationship
- Slightly Positive Relationship
- Positive Relationship

4. To what extent do you believe your experience level influences your trading performance in intraday trading?

- Not at All
- Slightly
- Moderately
- Significantly
- Extremely

Chapter 11

Information Governance Framework to Achieve Information Hygiene in South Africa

Nkholedzeni Sidney Netshakhuma
iD https://orcid.org/0000-0003-0673-7137
University of Cape Town, South Africa

Itumeleng Khadambi
South Africa National Parks, South Africa

ABSTRACT

This chapter aims to develop an information governance framework to achieve information hygiene. In this study, information hygiene is defined as a process to achieve proper information. Information hygiene is developed to prevent any form of fake news. Fake news in this context is defined as misrepresentation of information, created to harm the person. Fake information developed extensively during the spread of COVID-19 in 2019. This chapter will use literature to review the content of the study.

INTRODUCTION

This chapter aims to develop an information governance framework to achieve information hygiene. According to the Collins dictionary, Information hygiene is the careful evaluation of the information that one is consuming and disseminating. In

DOI: 10.4018/979-8-3693-1107-3.ch011

this chapter, information hygiene is defined as a process seeking to achieve authentic and reliable information. The development of Information hygiene is premised on the need to prevent any form of fake news and misinformation. Fake news in this context is considered as the misrepresentation of information created to harm a person or an organisation. Ho, Chan, and Chiu (2022), who draw on the views by Au et al. define "misinformation" as wrong information circulating on the Internet and social media, and "fake news" is "(online) news articles that are intentionally and verifiably false and misleading." The creation of fake news, as noted by Ho, Chan, and Chiu (2022) as found in Morgan, could be a deliberate attempt with a political intention, or based on purely financial incentives as there are possibilities of individual or company earnings of revenue from the deliberate spread of (fake) news and associated advertisements. People with a particular political agenda, not necessarily working on behalf of a government, may spread fake news and misinformation within their communities and across the national borders to influence other countries' politics. Finally, fake news may be deliberately circulated to affirm other people's own beliefs to the detriment of the larger society, as noted during the spread of misinformation during the 2019-2020 spread of Covid-19 while the disease ravaged global communities and continues to up to this day.

The embracing of information as a human right under a democratic principle occurring in various countries has witnessed a surge in demand for access to information. This rise in demand for access to information is based on societal awareness of their rights. An increased access and availability of information enables the achievement of outcomes, identification of opportunities, effective and informed planning, maximisation of value, management of risks, accountability and good governance, the creation, use, maintenance and sharing of information, knowledge creation, problem-solving, and decision making. However, Ryabova and Fesun (2021) argue that the increase in access and availability of information poses a high risk of the spread of fake information in media, and an accidental or on intentional misinformation of society as well as manipulation of public opinion. According to Ho et al. (2022), the Internet has, since the day it was invented, gradually risen to become a powerful means of producing and exchanging information and news. However, as observed by Varynskyi (2020), while technology, the Internet and social media platforms play an enormous role in facilitating access to information, the largest part of the information space of Internet media is fake information. In addition, a considerable part of the adult population receives its news primarily from social media. Thus, the question arises whether information sourced from the media outlets is trustworthy enough and hence, this study's focus on the need to develop an information governance framework to achieve information hygiene.

BACKGROUND OF INFORMATION HYGIENE CONCEPT

The concept of information hygiene as a paradigm, which has been with us for many years and premised on the idea of sanitising information before it is shared to arrest misinformation, is considered as having gained prominence in recent years owing to the viral spread of fake news and misinformation. The recent COVID-19 pandemic is one such global experience that witnessed a massive outbreak of misinformation, disinformation, hoaxes, and conspiracies surrounding this coronavirus. One good example of fake news in the South African context is the story of the Thembisa 10 which alleged that a South African woman gave birth to 10 babies in June 2021. The British Broadcasting Corporation (BBC) notes that the story was first reported by the Independent Online (IOL), a media group that owns the *Pretoria News* and other newspapers and online news sites in South Africa. The story was later reported as fake news and yet, the IOL stood by its reporting. As a result,, more media houses such as the BBC and News24 ran the story and it began to trend in various media platforms and social media. However, the story drew suspicion after *Pretoria News* failed to disclose the hospital where the babies were born and later, a series of hospitals in Gauteng Province of South Africa, came out to deny their involvement. The story was later found to be untrue.

The spread of fake news has reached epidemic level and created anxieties among consumers of news and information. For instance, the rise of fake news during the COVID-19 pandemic lead the World Health Organisation (WHO) and other media and information experts to label the COVID-19 pandemic as an "infodemic"—an epidemic of information. In their February 2020 Novel Coronavirus Situation Report, the WHO noted that the COVID-19 outbreak and response "has been accompanied by a massive 'infodemic'—an over-abundance of information—some accurate and some not—that makes it hard for people to find trustworthy sources and reliable guidance when they need it" (Oer press books pub 2023). As a result, there has been a rise in the viral spread of misinformation and fake news, which has impacted negatively on consumer reception of information.

PROBLEM STATEMENT

There exists research on the significance of clean data in preventing any fake information that was conducted, by Varynskyi et al. (2021), Loukas, Murugesan & Andriole (2022), Tretyak, Ryabova & Fesun (2021) Chisita et al. (2022), Ramkissoon and Goodridge (2022), Ho et al. (2022), Durodolu & Ibenne (2020), Chisita et al. (2022), Molina, Sundar, Le & Lee (2021), Fitzpatrick, Liang, and Straub (2021), Ramkissoon & Goodridge (2022), Mishra, Shukla & Agarwal (2022), Kumar et al.

(2022). The gap identified in this literature is that none of these studies proposed any framework for information hygiene. As a result, there was need to pursue a study that will develop a governance framework to achieve information hygiene that will arrest or detect misinformation or what is known as fake news, which is a threat to humanity post-truth-era. Perpetuating the problem is the growth of technology and social media platforms that facilitate complex transmission and sharing of misinformation across various platforms and place a huge burden on information professionals to design systems for the detection of misinformation and fake news.

PURPOSE

The purpose of the study was to develop an Information Governance framework that can be adopted by organisations to achieve information hygiene.

RESEARCH METHODOLOGY

The study chose the qualitative research method, grounded on content analysis, which allowed the researcher to determine the qualitative features of information hygiene in pursuit of a framework or model that can be used to achieve information hygiene. The researcher reviewed available literature from journal articles and book chapters related to information hygiene to gather the views of other scholars. Observation drawn from the review were used by the researcher to develop a framework that can be used to detect misinformation and fake news.

LITERATURE REVIEW

The study reviewed the literature on information hygiene and arrived at the need for the consideration and adoption of an information governance framework for the detection and sanitisation of misinformation and fake news before its circulation. The reality is such that, misinformation and fake news affect society in a negative way and drives wrong narratives that can cause conflicts that include political unrests, social unrests and health problems. Although it is the responsibility of everyone to verify the authenticity of the information before sharing, special responsibility and awareness are placed on the shoulders of Information professionals to design systems/models or frameworks to achieve high resilience in the detection of fake news, sanitisation and circulation of information. According to Durodolu and Ibenne (2020), as noted in Chisita et al. (2022 p. 36), Librarians should strengthen cooperation among themselves, the government and other key stakeholders, so that they actively participate, as a united front, in national programmes seeking to mitigate and prevent misinformation.

The COVID-19 pandemic is one such phenomenon that that ended up being marked by an infodemic. Moore (2021) notes that the novel human coronavirus disease that started in 2019 (COVID-19) was first reported in Wuhan, China, and subsequently spread globally to become the fifth documented pandemic since the 1918 influenza pandemic. By September 2021, there were more than 200 million confirmed cases and over 4.6 million deaths due to the disease. According to the South African Government News Agency, the first case of COVID-19 was confirmed in South Africa on 05 March 2020. However, the spread of fake news and misinformation became prevalent during the COVID-19 disease period prompting the South African government to issue a warning to the citizens that they should desist from creating and spreading fake news about the Coronavirus COVID-19 with anyone who spread the misinformation being liable for prosecution (www.gov.za). The South African government also encouraged people to verify their information before sharing it. Some of the available literature apportions the blame for the spread of fake news and misinformation y on social media. Durodolu and Ibenne (2020), as noted in Chisita et al. (2022 p. 2), note that the problem of misinformation or fake news is perpetuated by the growing reliance on social media for reporting, and the growth of media inaccuracies that threaten the frontiers of knowledge and trustworthy information. This predicament has resulted in disorderliness in the information ambiance because of the challenges regarding the standardisation of activities on social media, allied to the problem of interfering with the fundamental right of free speech. This reality has led to a new concept in the era of health emergency of Coronavirus known as infodemic, which is an epidemic that was magnified by the inability to access accurate information concerning COVID-19 pandemic (Durodolu & Ibenne, 2020).

The internet plays a significant role in the spread of misinformation. The internet, unlike the traditional means of communication and information sharing such as newspapers and radios which are used by older people, is both a gigantic contributor to information access and sharing, and largely guilty of spreading fake news and misinformation.. For example, a survey of residents of Odesa in Ukraine carried out from May 29 to June 2, 2020 by the sociological group "Rating" shows that most city residents receive information via the Internet (56%) while only 20% use newspapers and radio or extract it from communication with relatives and friends. Almost every person who has access to the Internet enters at least one or two social networks, communicates through them with his friends, and makes various virtual "friends" whom they would have never seen and yet receive a variety of information from these 'unseen' friends. Moreover, the reliability of such information is in great doubt.

Thus, social networks act as both a local communication network of acquaintances and global dynamic way of communication, through which news spreads faster, is directed to a specific recipient, and provides an opportunity to instantly respond to information based on "like – not like" with just one Like buttons (Varynskyi 2020).

INFORMATION HYGIENE FRAMEWORK

A review of related literature shows that, although the originators of misinformation may be malicious entities exploiting social media, "fake news," and conspiracy-theory generators, society as consumers of such information, and our network of people perpetuate misinformation and fake content by sharing without assessing the validity of the content. As a result, we should be part of the solution to ending the spread of fake news. In addition, we should develop and adopt information hygiene practices that contribute to misinformation detection or at the least curb our contribution to its spreading (Loukas, Murugesan & Andriole (2022). The following is the suggested framework that can be adopted to ensure information hygiene:

INFORMATION REGULATION

The regulation of information is seen as an undemocratic practice in that information is considered as a vital agent of change and knowledge creation, and yet many countries have taken initiatives to protect their citizens regarding access to and protection of information. Some governments have enacted legislation that regulates access, use, and circulation of information, as well as the spaces, such as the internet and social media where information is contained. Governments, as noted with the case of Ukraine and China, also regulate the sharing of information to ensure information security and protect national interests and security. According to the Law of Ukraine…, (1992) as noted in Varynskyi (2020), information has actual and potential value, depending on the form and method of filing by the informant and is regulated by law and the state information policy, the main direction of which is "ensuring the information security of Ukraine." In essence these regulations were enacted legislations to arrest fake news and misinformation.

Furthermore, some governments are establishing various infrastructure to ensure information security. The example of Ukraine best shows these attempts at information security. Ukraine built a multi-component paradigm of information security based on the view that information security is "a state of protection of the vital interests of a person, society and the state, in which harm is prevented through incompleteness, timeliness, and inaccuracy of information that is used; negative informational impact; negative consequences of the use of information technology; unauthorized distribution, use, and violation of the integrity, confidentiality, and accessibility of information" (Law of Ukraine..., 2007). The analysis of various legislative acts and scientific publications on the topic indicate that fundamental directions in the study of information security are technical and humanitarian. The first direction is related to issues of technical processes as well as organisational and legal capabilities that ensure the safety of personal, institutional, and state information. The second is focused mainly on the development of problems for improving the mechanisms of regulation and protection of the individual and society as a whole from the negative impact of the information itself, both from the improvement of legal support and by identifying its axiological meaning, relevance, energy impact, emotional influence, and its verbal and non-verbal confidence markers. In this regard, it is important to find a solution to the problem.

Therefore, there is need protect personal data on the network from unauthorised access and dissemination, and to establish protection against inadequate information exposure that could harm physical and mental health, as well as the user's reputation. The second task is related to the hygiene segment in the information space and is of conceptual importance for information security (Varynskyi 2020). Thus, legislation meant to govern information organisations would be required to adopt policies to ensure information hygiene.

TECHNOLOGICAL SOLUTIONS TO SUPPORT DETECTION

The scourge of "fake news", which continues to plague the information environment, resulted in the shifting of attention toward the creation of automated solutions for detecting problematic online content (Molina, Sundar, Le & Lee 2021). According to Fitzpatrick, Liang, and Straub (2021), artificial intelligence (AI) is used throughout modern society and provides a wide variety of benefits as it is associated with technologies that have been used to play games, find software bugs, help the handicapped, detect hackers, and command robots. In addition, Machine learning (ML) systems adaptively learn on their own or utilise an explicit training process while rewards and supplied input and output data are used to direct learning. A study by Ramkissoon and Goodridge (2022) used a system known as Legitimacy which is an ensemble of machine-learning algorithm for fake news detection and prediction. The study noted that the proposed Legitimacy model performed well with an accuracy of 96.9%. The results obtained from the experiments performed indicate that the Legitimacy ensemble learning model performed excellently and as such the study concluded that based on selected datasets, the Legitimacy ensemble learning model is an appropriate method suited for detecting and predicting Credibility-Based Fake

News. Thus, technological solutions were found to have a high rate of success in detecting false news and postings, and yet, the constantly shifting qualities and features of false news on social media networks still pose challenges. In future this study will be helpful for further research in identifying fake news and the development of new models or tools for early detection (Mishra, Shukla & Agarwal 2022). Studies by Loukas, Murugesan and Andriole (2022), and Choras et al. also advocate for the use of technological solutions to help address misinformation at scale and support the user in making faster and more accurate trustworthiness assessments.

Other existing studies are Significant here. There is need to put more emphasis on the use of technology with Kumar et al. (2022) proposing an ensemble-based model for the detection of COVID-19-related misinformation shared through Twitter. He argues that this model achieves high accuracy in comparison with common techniques that do not use the ensemble approach. In addition, the choice of technology has an impact on the aspects of a digital preservation programme. The choice of technology is also influenced by a budget and human resources within an organisation (Corrado & Sandy 2017). The introduction of technology also requires a change in management. This implies that the organisation must develop a change management strategy to ensure access to information. Finally, new technologies require the intervention of various stakeholders with human resources being the most significant assets that organisations have in the contemporary knowledge economy.

Management plays an important role here. It must support the type of technology purchased or acquired by the Information and Communications technology department. This means there is a need for continuous buy-in from management to support the Information communication technology system. Staff from different levels must support the implementation of the type of information technology that would have been purchased. Change management can be a form of management competency and become necessary for management to show the need for transformation in an organisation and to ensure continuous management of the information system. Thererefore, there is a need to receive buy-in from the management and for it to lead in the acceptance of introduction of change regarding the new technology.

An appropriate application of digital preservation is important for the achievement of digital sustainability. Organisations must be aware of continuous change in their entities. Continuous change in organizations ensures that the right information is preserved. They must also note the importance of assessing the sustainability of technology when selecting technologies for permanent preservation. Therefore, organizations should enquire with other organisations so that they choose an appropriate system. It is also important to check the environment to which the system will be applied.

Finally, there is need strengthen the knowledge of recordkeeping systems and the structure of documents (Grace 11, 2002). There is a need to understand the types of recordkeeping systems technology and convention of creation, use, and management of records in the office at specific moments as well as the functioning of the systems. It is also significant to understand the structure of the system to ensure effective management of information. A lack of understanding of any form of fake information poses challenges to any attempts at continuous development of records.

TRUST

The idea that information is completely trustworthy places may reflect professional psyches characterising some archivists and records managers (Cox and Wallace 2002, P 8). Trust is explained as reliance on the integrity, strength, ability, and surety of data. Any information can be trusted if it meets audit and certification standards such as the Data Seal of Approval, DIN 31644, and ISO 16363 (Corrado & Sandy, 2017). The process of auditing and verification of information is significant to avoiding any form of information manipulation. The information must be properly collected and preserved to prove its authenticity, and should be of high quality for decision-making. There is a need to prove or assess whether such information has been changed. In addition, the system must be designed in a way that enables users to get information without any challenges or difficulties within an organisation's digital repository. Employees should also be encouraged to preserve records to ensure long-term preservation of records while quality assurance of data stored in the system should be of high value.

The quality of the information is also important. Repositories assist in establishing the authenticity of information through proper collection and preservation of information created by the organisation (Corrado and Sandy 2017 p.160). It is also important to ensure that the authenticity of information is protected by an organisation continuously. Organisations must develop strategies to ensure that both the information and information system is preserved to ensure that they provide long-term digital preservation of information.

Finally, organizations need to trust their information management systems and technology. Cloud and other information systems need to be trusted before they are implemented. Professionals need to understand the environment in which their organisations operate, and there is need for various stakeholders to be concerned about systems developed within their entities because of various organisational security issues.

FINANCIAL STABILITY

Management's role is to allocate resources to support the development and implementation of the information management system. The trust placed in a cloud or hosted system creates the financial stability in an e organisation providing the service (Corrado and Sandy 2017). In addition, an electronic records management system needs ongoing support and funding as much as any other project requiring the use of long-term digital repositories.

VERIFICATION OF THE AUTHENTICITY OF INFORMATION

According to Digital Minimalism, one of the methods to detect fake news is to verify the authenticity of information chosen for intended use. This burden of information accuracy verification is a burden on all "good" infovores. Tretyak, Ryabova and Fesun (2021) argue that fakes can be different. For example, the news that Prince Harry and Meghan Markle are moving to Zhytomyr, was first published on the humorous news portal and thus, unlikely to cause serious reputational or any other losses to the royal family. At the same time, the news that the Russian bank was preparing to buy Monobank could have serious consequences even though it was quickly denied by the co-founder of Mono. In this context, Tretyak, Ryabova and Fesun (2021) argue that it is important to take into account information from several sources to maintain sobriety of thinking and avoid misconception. After all, the media are y an intermediary between the news and the reader or listener, and interact with business, which has another important goal of its existence – to generate profit. The media can also be used as sources of propaganda that make it possible to broadcast certain views or, conversely, publish stories in support of the popular moods of the target audience. That is why it is extremely important to pay attention to the position of the media and its reputation (Tretyak, Ryabova & Fesun 2021).

Furthermore, information professionals recognised the need for mechanisms or tools for auditing and processes of certification for digital archives to create an overall climate of trust in the ability of the systems to meet their stated goals (Bantin 2016). Process models and standards have been established for designing and certifying trustworthy systems. This means that organisations must develop a roadmap to ensure the verification and authentication of information.

Finally, a trusted digital repository must "provide reliable, long-term access to managed digital resources to its designated community" (Schmidt 2016). Operational data should be permanently stored and the authenticity and integrity of the digital records verified on a continuous basis. Every system must have evidence that it will support all organisational systems capturing, and preserving Information communication technologies, human resources technologies, finance, and assets management systems.

ELECTRONIC RECORDS MANAGEMENT RETENTION SCHEDULE

The expected outcome from the records management system has been to encourage organisations to manage records in line with the records retention schedule. The selection of records for permanent preservation is dependent on the value of each record. The length of time to preserve electronic records is determined by the concerned organisation (McAninch and Cundy 2016). Organisations must develop strategies to retain records or scheduling of records. The organisation should be particularly interested in identifying the challenges and developing methods to facilitate the permanent preservation of records and the creation of preservation-ready files by records creators. As a result, the organisation needs to assure various organisations that trustworthy digital records systems are maintained. In addition, the archive materials must be preserved in a secure environment.

Electronic records management systems include the creation of systems to preserve records for long-term preservation. It also involves a scheduling process and here, records managers of various organisations work with the staff from various organisations, including programmatic personnel, records officers, administrative officials, and managing technologies, to ensure the long-term preservation of archives materials.

ACCESS STRATEGY

The accessibility of digital records depends on the ability to find or discover a digital object (Corrado and Sandy 2017 p. 105). Digital preservation is dependent on the subject and content specialists within the system. There is a need to specify the reason why certain information needs to be preserved or made available to various stakeholders. The right information needs to be preserved and made accessible. As a result, organisation must ensure that information is accessible to various stakeholders. All systems created within the electronic environment should have access consideration building into the framework (Stenson 2016). The system should be built to prevent users from fake news. Information should be accessible to various users. The system must be built in such a way that access to information security would always be maintained. Access can be started by updating the existing framework of access that had long been used in the paper-based environment. The advances in technology requires organisations to ensure access to information regularly. Providing information online offers both opportunities and challenges in that, on the one hand, online information provides opportunities for organisations to search for information online. This means that the organisations are supposed to come up with various strategies to ensure that information is accessible to various stakeholders. On the other hand, fraudsters use online information for criminal activities, if the organisations' systems are weak.

SECURITY AND PRIVACY OF INFORMATION

Digital preservation systems are information technology systems and therefore, organisations should be concerned with security issues (Corrado and Sandy 2017 p. 169). These security matters include theft or damage to hardware, unauthorised access, and disruption of computer systems due to a system compromise or a denial-of-service attack. Organisations dealing with the provision of access to information face challenges such as viruses and malware attacks, and as such, they must ensure a continuous update of their virus and malware detection programmes. It is the responsibility of organisations to develop a governance framework to ensure that the privacy and security of information is protected in compliance with privacy laws.

Furthermore, there is a regulatory dimension to the fight against misinformation and disinformation. As this special issue demonstrates, technology has many answers, but it does not have them all (Loukas, Murugesan & Andriole (2022). Thus, the Protection of Personal Information Act (POPIA), The Regulation of Interception of Communications and Provision of Communication -Related Information Act 70 of 2002 (RICA), The Electronic Communications and Transactions Act 25 of 2002, and the Consumer Protection Acts 68 of 2008 were enacted in South Africa to protect individual rights to privacy and hold organisations to account regarding their guardianship of information. As a result, organisations must ensure that the security of information is in place to protect it from misuse. This implies that systems should be in established e to avoid any leakage of information.

The violation of privacy of information is related to fake news (Pritchard and Verwey 2018). Unauthorized users should not be able to access users' email addresses, bank account numbers, and passwords, because if they gain access to this, they will mislead people, defraud, or engage in a deformation of characters. However, those who violate this legislation may face consequences (McKinley 2016). In addition, there are consequences for both users and the organisations responsible for safeguarding privacy personal data should be accessed without the explicit consent (Pritchard & Verwey 2018). This implies that organisations must collaborate with various stakeholders to ensure that business information is protected from misuse.

The organisations should o ensure that the privacy and security of information is protected. Nonetheless, the challenge with electronic records is that they are dependent on the technical environment to preserve archives materials

Some countries do not allow data to be stored outside of their country environment. There are also various legislations enacted and practices established to prevent any dissemination of information. In the case of organizations, they are required to develop guidelines on websites and owned social media channels that outline the type of information that is accessible. The monitoring of social networks is necessary to identify, locate, and track terrorists and other criminals in the interests of public safety and security (Pritchard & Verwey 2018). Law enforcement may pressurise social networks to hand over biometric data without users' consent when trying to locate criminals and other suspects (Rosenblatt 2016). Nonetheless, there is a need to ensure the rights of individuals for who the information would have been created or the established electronic records were preserved for and made accessible to various stakeholders. This means that organisations must o develop systems to monitor any form of dissemination of information in their system, and ensure that information created on online systems is preserved from any unauthorised use .

DETECTION STRATEGIES

The implementation of detection strategies will address fake news and misinformation. According to Zhou, Zafarani, Shu & Liu (2019), detecting fake news is a complex and multidimensional task due to the characteristics of fake news. The detection strategies exploit multiple news-related (e.g., headline, body text, publisher) and social-related (e.g., feedback, propagation paths, and spreaders) types of information. Each information type can be in the form of text, multimedia or network, and corresponding to various applicable techniques and usable resources. The detection of fake news and misinformation is based on perspectives of knowledge, style, propagation, and credibility. The detection of fake news from a knowledge perspective involves a "comparison" between the relational knowledge extracted from the to-be-verified news articles and that of knowledge bases representing facts/ground truth. Style-based fake news detection captures and quantifies the differences in writing styles between fake and true news while the propagation-based fake news detection uses information provided in news dissemination. Finally, credibility-based fake news detection assesses the credibility of headlines using click-bait detection, publishers based on of source websites, comments using opinion spam detection, and users to indirectly detect fake news. Each perspective carries its own usable set of tools, data sets, and various detection strategies in data mining, machine learning, natural language processing, information retrieval, and social search. Various perspectives can be integrated under a unified framework for fake news analysis, which looks at fake news from the time it is created and published to the time it is disseminated (Zhou, Zafarani, Shu & Liu 2019).

EDUCATION AND AWARENESS

The combination of understanding the problem through literacy, education, and awareness creation, and supporting the users practically with effective technical solutions is a promising direction in the fight against misinformation and the infodemic. Loukas, Murugesan, and Andriole (2022) note that education and awareness are, apart from the use of IT solutions, some of the most promising means for addressing misinformation and fake news. Awareness can be achieved through emphasising the need to improve information presentation styles and information literacy for supporting detection. Massive public awareness campaigns that enable people to note the existence and dangers of fake news and misinformation result in cooperation and collaborations towards finding the right solutions. According to Varynskyi et al. (2021), the denial of fakes makes it possible to avoid various risks. Thus, understanding that the perception of fake information can lead to deviant behaviour highlights the need to "eliminate the consequences" and prevent any misinformation-caused emergency. Therefore, once people begin to believe on the ecotoxicity of information, they will gradually change their worldview and actions, for as noted by (Varynskyi et al. 2021), an awareness of unreliability is the shortest path to reliable knowledge.

The identification of reliable information and its reliable sources is also important because public consciousness is influenced by the phenomenon of the cascade of available information. This cascade of information is the name given to cognitive deformation, in which collective trust in something or belief in something increases with each mention or repetition of a certain statement or fact. Therefore, if specialists that include SMM managers, marketers, psychologists and others who can help "pack" any news are involved in the process of preparing the news before publication in the media, the information will become easier for the target audience to perceive due to its higher level of persuasiveness, argumentation, and expertise.

There also exists a misnomer based on the perception of information by only reading headlines, general descriptions, and fragments of articles. This is especially true for people who mainly take news from social networks since most often the format of delivering information on social networks does not involve reading the news in full. In this way, an illusion of awareness is created in that, a person believes that they are aware of all events and yet, they would not be aware of the details or maybe misinformed (Tretyak, Ryabova & Fesun 2021).

CONCLUSION

This study assessed the state of information management governance. It was noted that an organisation that develops an information governance framework protects itself against the falsification of information. Organisations must ensure that reliable technology is in place to support detection and, they must ensure that the information preserved is authentic, reliable, and complete. Any information communication technology purchased by an organisation should be trusted by various stakeholders. The authenticity of information is supposed to be maintained. However, it is the responsibility of the organisation to ensure that there is financial and human resources support. At the same time, the organizations must ensure that only information or records needed for the operations or continuity of the organisation are preserved, which also demands that the organisations develop strategies to ensure the accessibility of information. Finally, it was also argued that organisations must ensure that information is protected against any form of abuse and that, there is continuous education to raise society's awareness of the significance of information.

IMPLICATIONS

Organisations and individuals rely on records as the basis of valid information and as a result, there is need for an acceptance of records for what they were purported to be and ensure that they would be true and accurate in their content. Fake news or forgeries of information damage the trust within organisations. This means that individuals may not make any information without any decision while organisations cannot make useful or impact decisions with fake information.

AREAS FOR FURTHER STUDIES

This study raises fundamental concerns about the rise of fake news all over the world and particularly in South Africa. There is need for a case study to be conducted in future to assess the state of information in South Africa.

ACKNOWLEDGMENT

This research is supported by the National Institute for the Humanities and Social Sciences of South Africa.

REFERENCES

Bantin, C. P. (2016). Evaluating and Selecting a Trustworthy Repository Theory: Evaluating and Selecting a Trustworthy Repository. In C. B. Phillip (Ed.), *Building Trustworthy Digital Repositories. Theory and Implementation.* Rowman & Littlefield.

BBC. (2021). *South African 10 babies story not true, inquiry finds.*

Butler, W.D, Sargent, A., & Smith, K. (2022). Information Hygiene and Info- in SA. *SA News.* https://www.sanews.gov.za/south-africa/first-case-coronavirus-https://www.pwc.com/ua/en/publications/2021/information-hygiene.html

Choraś, M., Pawlicka, A., Kozik, R., & Woźniak, M. (2022). How Machine Learning May Prevent the Breakdown of Democracy by Contributing to Fake News Detection,&quot. *IT Professional, 24*(2), 25–31. doi:10.1109/MITP.2022.3151312

Corrado, M. E., & Sandy, M. H. (2017). *Digital Preservation for Libraries, Archives, and Museums* (2nd ed.). Rowman & Littlefield.

Cox, J. R., & Wallace, A. D. (2002). *Archives and the Public Good. Accountability and Records in Modern Society.* Quorum Books.

OER. (2020). *Environmentalism.* Oer press books. https://oer.pressbooks.pub/collegeresearch/chapter/info-hygiene- environmentalism/

False Information: A Concept Explication and Taxonomy of Online Content. *American Behavioural Scientist, 65*(2), 180–212. . doi:10.1177/0002764219878224

Fitzpatrick, B., Liang, X., & Straub, J. (2021). Fake news and phishing detection follow in 2022. *Digital Minimalism.* https://digitalminimalism.com/verifying-the-authenticity- Global, USA.

Gracy, B.D (2002). What You Get Is Not What You See: Forgery and the Corruption of Recordkeeping Systems. In Cox, J.R, and Wallace, A.D (eds). *Archives and the Public Good. Accountability and Records in Modern Society.* Quorum Books.

Ho, K. K., Chan, J. Y., & Chiu, K. W. (2022). Fake News and Misinformation During the Pandemic: What We Know and What We Do Not Know. *IT Professional, 24*(2), 19-24. https://www.bbc.com/news/world-africa-57581054

Kumar, A., Singh, J. P., & Singh, A. K. (2022). COVID-19 Fake News Detection Using Ensemble-Based Deep Learning Model. *IT Professional, 24*(2), 32–37. doi:10.1109/MITP.2022.3149140

Lexicall. (2020). information hygiene. *Collins Dictionary.* https://www. collinsdictionary.com/submission/22205/information+hygiene (Accessed Library and Media Roles in Information Hygiene and Managing Information, IGI

Loukas, G., Murugesan, S., & Andriole, S. J. (2022). Information Hygiene: The Fight Against the Misinformation "Infodemic". *IT Professional, 24*(2), 16–18. doi:10.1109/MITP.2022.3163007

McAninch, G., & Cundy, J. (2016). Implementation: Records and Archival Management Strategies for Electronic Records Used by the Kentucky Department for Libraries and Archives. In C. P. Bantin (Ed.), *Building Trustworthy Digital Repositories Theory and Implementation Min Trusts Max.* Rowman & Littlefield.

McKinley, D. T. (2016). *New terrains of privacy in South Africa.* R2K. http://www. r2k.org.za/wp- Content/uploads/Monograph_New_Terrains_of_Privacy_in_South Africa_2016.pdf

Mishra, S. Shukla, P. Agarwal, R. (2022). Analyzing Machine Learning Enabled Fake News Detection Techniques for Diversified Datasets. *Wireless Communications and Mobile Computing.* . doi:10.1155/2022/1575365

Morgan, S. (2018). Fake news, disinformation, manipulation, and online tactics to undermine democracy. *J. Cyber Policy, 3*(1), 39–43. of-any-information-10-rules-to-follow-in-2022/

Pritchard, M., & Verwey, S. (2018). Digital Dynamics and Relational Complexities: Responding to Challenges in the Online Engagement Context. In P. Maritha & K. Sittos (Eds.), *Connect Writing for Online Audiences.* Juta.

Rakich, N. (2020). How does Biden stack up to past Democratic nominees? *FiveThirtyEight.* https://fivethirtyeight.com/features/how-does-biden-stack-up-to-past-democratic-nominees/

Rosenblatt, J. (2016). *Is Facebook's facial-scanning technology invading your privacy rights?* Bloomberg. https://www.bloomberg.com/news/articles/2016-10-26/ is-facebook-s-facial-scanning-technology-invading-your-privacy-rights

Schmidt, L. (2016). Building a Trustworthy System: Ingest Process Theory: Ingest Process. In Bantin C.P (eds). Building Trustworthy Digital Repositories Trust. Theory and Implementation. Rowman & Littlefield. Socionetwork Strat. https:// doi.org/ doi:10.100712626-022-

Stenson, K. (2016). Creating an Access Strategy. Theory: Creating an Access Strategy. In C. P. Bantin (Ed.), *Building Trustworthy Digital Repositories. Theories and Implementation. Min Trust and Max. Theory and Implementation.* Rowman & Littlefield.

Tretyak, A., Ryabova, D., & Fesun, A. (2021). *Fake news and disinformation: what is using a machine learning trained expert system.* arXiv preprint arXiv:2108.08264.

Zhou, X., Zafarani, R., & Shu, K., & Liu, H. (2019). Fake news: Fundamental theories, detection strategies, and challenges. In *Proceedings of the twelfth ACM international conference on web search and data mining.* (pp. 836–837). ACM. 10.1145/3289600.3291382

KEY TERMS AND DEFINITIONS

Authenticity: This is the information, which is original, not manipulated.

COVID-19: It is an infectious disease caused by the SARS- COV 2 virus.

Fake News: This is false or misleading information described as news. The purpose of fake news is to damage the reputation of a person.

Forgery: It is the process of imitating a document, signature.

Information Hygienic: It is a process to achieve authentic and reliable information.

Records Retention Schedule: This is a process of listing of records, records are listed according to its values.

Chapter 12
Journey From FOMO to JOMO by Digital Detoxification

Pretty Bhalla
Lovely Professional University, India

Jaskiran Kaur
(iD) https://orcid.org/0000-0002-4452-1807
Lovely Professional University, India

Sayeed Zafar
College of Business Administration, University of Business and Technology, Jeddah, Saudi Arabia

ABSTRACT

Digital transformation has long been prioritized by corporate companies, both big and small, in almost every sector, due to the urgency of market rivalry. Digital technology is present everywhere nowadays, and it plays a significant role in our daily lives. The fast development of inexpensive and widely available media technologies, together with almost universal internet connection, is profoundly changing how society functions. Digital technology is transforming how we obtain information and communicate with one another more quickly than before. The speed at which digital changes are occurring is having a significant impact on how we live, work, and interact. There seems to be a new cautionary tale about how digital technologies are ruining social life every day. Some of the discussion about the effects of digital technology in recent years has resembled a moral panic.

1. INTRODUCTION

The constant pull of our devices and the fear of missing out (FOMO) on the newest developments, trends, and social interactions are commonplace in today's fast-paced,

DOI: 10.4018/979-8-3693-1107-3.ch012

digitally connected world. But more and more individuals are understanding how important it is to tune out digital distractions to enjoy the pleasure of missing out (JOMO). This transition from FOMO to JOMO is a life-changing event that may lead to better relationships, mental health, and a greater sense of connectedness to the outside world.

1.1 FOMO

The fear of missing out, or FOMO, is a psychological phenomena that is prevalent and often upsetting in the digital era. When individuals feel they are missing out on interesting events, activities, or social interactions that others are having, particularly when they see these things posted on social media or learn about them via their social networks, it is referred to as worry and trepidationStudies have estimated that nearly 70% of adults in developed countries suffer from FOMO

Scholars have looked at the origins of the FOMO concept (2014 Schreckinger). According to research by Lai, Altavilla, Ronconi, and Aceto (2016), FOMO results in increased brain activity, suggesting that it is a result of a neurological drive to belong. Anita Sanz (2015), a clinical psychologist, concurs with Lai et al. (2016)'s conclusions that FOMO is brain-based, but she points to a deeper anthropological explanation. According to her, FOMO has been crucial to human existence since the day of the caveman. We may not survive if we could not discover a clean drinking water source or a food supply. FOMO was thus a major motivator throughout life.

It was during a 1996 focus group research that Dan Herman first learned about the concept of FOMO (Herman, 2011). He defined and clarified the notion of FOMO in a Journal of Brand Management essay that was published four years later (Herman, 2000). Ever since Herman's piece, FOMO has become a much more popular concept. FOMO is described as "a pervasive apprehension that others might be having rewarding experiences from which one is absent" by Przybylski et al. (2013) . FOMO might make you worry that you're missing out on something interesting that's occurring somewhere else.

Key aspects of FOMO include:

- **Social Comparison:** FOMO often results from contrasting one's own life with the lives of others that seem to be more interesting or pleasurable when seen via social media. Feelings of inadequacy and insecurity may result from this.
- **Constant Connectivity:** People may now easily keep informed and connected around-the-clock because to the widespread use of social media and cellphones. Because individuals are always aware of what other people are doing, this continual connectedness might make FOMO worse.

- **Information overload:** Social media and other digital channels provide a steady stream of updates and information that sometimes be too much to handle. FOMO may also be caused by the fear of falling behind on trends, news, or social events.
- **Peer pressure:** FOMO may be significantly impacted by peer pressure. People may be forced to attend events or activities in which they have no true interest only out of dread of the social repercussions of being left out.
- **Impact on Mental Health:** FOMO may have detrimental effects on mental health, including elevated stress, anxiety, and a lowered feeling of self-worth. It may also exacerbate a feeling of detachment from reality.

There are further psychological effects of FOMO on people. According to a 2018 study of first-year college students, FOMO is common among young people and is linked to exhaustion, stress, and difficulty falling asleep. This wasn't limited to the experiences of the marginalized or reclusive. Regardless of how pleasurable the activity they chose was, they nonetheless had a significant sense of missing out, which caused them to feel bad and get distracted when considering or being offered any other options (Milyavskaya et al., 2018). According to Baker et al. (2016), those with greater levels of FOMO had more somatic symptoms, decreased attention, and depressed symptoms. According to Riordan et al. (2015), FOMO may cause people to drink more alcohol. According to a 2011 research by J. Walter Thompson, FOMO makes people feel as if they don't have as much and adds to their general discontent with their social lives. This has a detrimental effect on wellbeing and produces undesirable emotions like boredom and loneliness.

Setting limits with digital gadgets, engaging in mindfulness practices, and putting an emphasis on in-person interactions and experiences are common strategies for overcoming FOMO. The opposite of FOMO is Embracing the Joy of Missing Out (JOMO), where people find satisfaction and pleasure in turning off the digital noise, living in the now, and cherishing their offline experiences.

1.1.1 The FOMO Epidemic

The fear of missing out, or FOMO, is a ubiquitous emotion that has come to be associated with our digital age. We get anxious when we see other people having fun at activities or events that we are not a part of. This sensation is made worse by social media sites, which are constantly posting highlight reels and carefully chosen information. Frequently, we find ourselves engrossed in constant scrolling on our devices because we think we're missing something fascinating.

Studies are being conducted to find out how FOMO affects customers. Even if the previously stated studies show a general lack of pleasure, does this apply to the consuming experience as well?

According to available data, FOMO encourages people to buy the goods they believe they should own that someone else (or many others) is using or to engage in the activity they may feel excluded from.

FOMO has been shown by researchers to enhance consumption. FOMO encourages users to use social media for ostentatious spending. According to Kang et al. (2019), FOMO has also been linked to higher conformance consumption of culturally related products.

1.1.2 The Consequences of FOMO

Constantly experiencing FOMO might be harmful to our mental health. We might become anxious, stressed, and feel inadequate if we are often comparing our lives to the supposedly ideal lives of others on the internet. This might result in a vicious cycle of ongoing discontent and a lowered feeling of value for oneself.

Furthermore, using technology excessively might be harmful to our physical well-being. Heavy screen time is commonly accompanied by a sedentary lifestyle that may cause obesity and musculoskeletal problems. Our sleep habits may be disturbed by the blue light that screens produce, which exacerbates these problems.

FOMO may result in compulsive buying or activity. Research has shown that FOMO may lead to alcohol and smartphone addiction (Wolniewicz et al., 2018; Riordan et al., 2015). FOMO also contributes to impulsive buying, and impulsive buying increases regret after the purchase (Saleh, 2012; Çelik et al., 2019). Bushra and Bilal (2014) investigated whether sales, displays, and marketing methods or internal variables (FOMO, consumerism, etc.) contributed to these regrettable impulsive purchases. They discovered that the obsessive purchase that resulted in regret was being caused by internal causes such as FOMO.

1.2 JOMO

The term "JOMO," or "the Joy of Missing Out," refers to a psychological and cultural phenomenon that describes the sense of fulfilment and enjoyment that comes from purposefully cutting off from social media, electronic gadgets, and other online activities. It's basically the opposite of FOMO (Fear of Missing Out), emphasizing the importance of living in the now and enjoying life away from the screen.

While FOMO has a lot of unfavorable side effects, many people have welcomed the more recent and advantageous JOMO trend. "JOMO, which is basically about being present and content with where you are in life, is the emotionally intelligent counterbalance to FOMO (Fuller, 2018)." Knowing that you choose to be doing precisely what you are doing, rather than engaging in any other activity, fills you with delight and contentment rather than anxiety (Dodgson, 2018a). After having a newborn boy, blogger Anil Dash noticed that bath time with his kid was more enjoyable than anything else, and he used this realization to create the term JOMO in a well-known blog post in 2012 (Dash, 2012).

Key aspects of JOMO include:

1. **Savouring Real-Life encounters:** Without the Distraction of Constant Digital Connectivity: JOMO entails embracing offline encounters. Simple activities like reading a book, conversing with people in person, or spending time in nature provide delight to those who suffer from JOMO.
2. **Mindfulness:** Being completely present and involved in the present moment is a common component of JOMO, and it may improve mental and general well-being. Being attentive enables people to see the richness and beauty of ordinary life.
3. **Creating Digital Boundaries:** People who practice JOMO deliberately establish limits on how much time they spend on digital devices. They set aside specified times to check social media or emails and limit screen use, particularly before bed or at social events.
4. **Putting Self-Care First:** JOMO aficionados place a high value on self-care and give precedence to pursuits that encourage rest, creativity, and personal development. This might be engaging in hobbies, working out, or just spending time with close friends and family.
5. **Minimizing Information Overload:** JOMO recognizes the need of screening out the steady stream of digital noise and information. Those who practice JOMO organize their digital lives to highlight the things that are most important to them and are picky about the stuff they consume.
6. **Building Deep and Meaningful Relationships:** JOMO places a strong emphasis on the value of these kinds of connections. JOMO sufferers are usually more completely present and involved in their relationships with friends and family, which leads to deeper bonds between them.

Like FOMO, it took a few more years for JOMO to become a widely accepted concept. The words "Joy of Missing Out" were projected behind Google CEO Sundar Pichai as he ascended the stage at the company's annual developer conference in the spring of 2018. Many people started to discover this concept of JOMO by the summer. The following publications carried articles: the New York Times, Forbes, Business Insider, Phelan, 2018; Fuller, 2018; Dodgson, 2018a; Cording, 2018; Psychology

Today, Inc. In December 2018, the subject matter was discussed on both the CBS Morning Show and a Younger television episode (Miller, 2018; Seong-yoon, 2019).

JOMO is being marketed as the newest thing in travel (Felepchuk, 2020). Instead of selecting a vacation that would look better on Instagram, travelers are opting for less crowded locations and off-peak times. By choosing pleasant, low-risk activities over high-risk, high-octane pastimes, Subaru is even utilizing it to promote safety (Dhaliwal, 2020).

1.2.1 JOMO Offers Several Benefits, Including

One particular decision to participate in an activity is what defines JOMO. Making the choice to do whatever brings you pleasure, whether it's playing with a pet or going out on a nice night out, is more important than dwelling on the things you won't get to experience (Bradshaw, 2019). JOMO is more about satisfaction, engagement, and connecting and disengaging than FOMO, which is associated with negative emotions like dread, worry, and regret (Dodgson, 2018a; Cording, 2018; Rees, 2017).

- Decreased Stress and Anxiety: Cutting down on digital distractions and FOMO may help cut down on stress and anxiety considerably, which can lead to better mental health.
- Increased Productivity: People who embrace offline activities and establish limits with technology tend to be more focused, innovative, and productive in both their personal and professional life.
- Better Sleep: Refraining from using electronics just before bed may improve the quality of your sleep, which can benefit your general wellbeing.
- Enhanced Satisfaction: As people grow more in sync with their own values and experiences, JOMO may help them enjoy a greater sense of satisfaction, contentment, and pleasure in life.

JOMO is the deliberate decision to discover contentment and enjoyment in the here and now, away from the never-ending flood of online information and social comparisons, in a world overrun with digital distractions. It inspires individuals to make deeper relationships with the world around them and to relish the richness of offline encounters.

2. WHY ADOPT JOMO OVER FOMO

Transforming your fear of missing out (FOMO) into joy of missing out (JOMO) may have a significant and advantageous effect on a number of areas of your life.

Figure 1. FOMO vs. JOMO

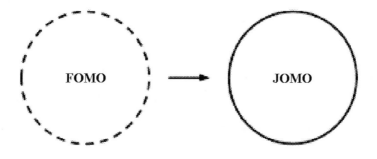

Making this change is advantageous for the following reasons, which are all quite convincing:

- **Decreased tension and Anxiety:** When people worry about missing out on great events and continuously compare themselves to others, FOMO often results in increased levels of tension and anxiety. By embracing JOMO, you may lower your stress levels by letting go of your anxiousness and finding serenity in the here and now.
- **Better Mental Health:** Your mental health may suffer if you constantly try to keep up with the digital world. JOMO encourages self-care and mindfulness, both of which may lead to better mental health and a more upbeat attitude on life.
- **Improved connections:** You may improve your connections with loved ones by unplugging from screens and other electronic distractions. Deeper relationships and more meaningful talks are fostered by being totally present during face-to-face meetings.
- **Enhanced Productivity:** You'll be able to focus more intently on the job at hand when you're not continuously checking your devices for updates and messages. A more balanced work-life dynamic and higher productivity may result from this improved concentration.
- **Improved Sleep:** You may get better sleep by putting electronics away early. Good sleep is crucial for both emotional and physical well-being, and it's simpler to get when you accept JOMO.
- **Personal Development**: You may follow your interests, take up hobbies, and develop your creativity by embracing JOMO. Personal development and a greater feeling of satisfaction may result from this.

- **Reduced Information Overload:** You may relieve yourself of the burden of always being informed by organizing your online space and filtering out digital distractions. Instead of being inundated with stuff, you may focus on the information that is genuinely important to you.
- **Increased Contentment:** JOMO inspires you to embrace the beauty of small, offline encounters and discover happiness and contentment in the here and now. A more meaningful existence and a higher level of happiness result from this.
- **Empowerment and Control:** You can take charge of your digital life by switching from FOMO to JOMO. You are not forced by outside forces to use technology; instead, you choose when and how to use it.
- **Enhanced Self-Awareness:** As you spend more time in the present moment, JOMO promotes introspection and self-awareness. You get a deeper comprehension of your priorities, values, and the things that really make you happy.

Switching from FOMO to JOMO is a deliberate decision to put your relationships, personal development, and wellbeing ahead of the incessant digital chatter and social comparisons. It makes it possible for you to live a more contented, purposeful, and balanced existence in the technologically advanced world of today.

3. TRANSITIONING FROM FOMO TO JOMO

Acknowledging the negative impact FOMO has on our overall health is the first step in starting a digital detox. The following are some crucial tactics to help you go from FOMO to JOMO:

- **Mindful Awareness:** To begin, examine your online behaviors with awareness. Take note of how much time you spend using your gadgets and how it affects your mood. Determine the times when FOMO is most likely to occur.
- **Digital Sabbaticals:** Arrange periodic periods of digital detoxification in which you turn off all electronic gadgets. Make use of this time to concentrate on real-world activities, including engaging in a hobby or spending time with loved ones.
- **Prioritize Offline ties:** Make time for friends and family to strengthen your offline ties. Face-to-face conversations may foster a more profound feeling of satisfaction and connection.

- **Set Boundaries:** Clearly define the limits of your digital use. Set aside certain times to check social media and emails. If you want better sleep, avoid screens at least an hour before going to bed.
- **Accept the Slow Movement:** Decrease your speed and focus on the here and now. Take part in mindfulness-promoting activities like yoga, meditation, or even just taking a stroll in the outdoors.
- **Manage Your Online Presence:** Unfollow or muted accounts that cause FOMO. Establish a digital environment that reflects your hobbies and beliefs. Pay attention to material that uplifts and enhances your life.

3.1 Benefits of JOMO

There are several advantages of accepting JOMO for your physical and emotional well-being:

Better Mental Health: Stress and anxiety may be considerably reduced by letting go of FOMO. You'll start to enjoy the tranquillity that comes with avoiding the continual digital noise, as well as its beauty.

Deeper Connections: Relationships may be strengthened, and a feeling of belonging can be increased by spending quality time with loved ones in person and without the distractions of technology.

Enhanced Productivity: You'll be able to focus better and be more productive at work and in your personal life if there are fewer digital distractions.

Better Sleep: Turning off electronics before bed may enhance the quality of your sleep, waking you up feeling more alert and invigorated.

Rediscovering Interest in Hobbies: JOMO may help you find new interests and creative pursuits that will enable you to explore your passions.

A Richer, More significant Life: You'll discover a greater feeling of satisfaction and purpose in life as you concentrate on the here and now and significant events.

4. PRACTICES ADOPTED BY ORGANISATIONS TO MOVE ON PATH OF JOMO

It might be advantageous for people and businesses to shift from a culture that prioritizes FOMO (Fear of Missing Out) to one that encourages JOMO (Joy of Missing Out). The following are some methods and procedures used by organizations to promote a JOMO culture:

4.1 Promote Work-Life Balance

Motivate staff members to keep a positive work-life balance. This entails honoring their personal time, forbidding overtime, and, if practical, granting flexible work schedules. Stress that turning off your computer after normal business hours is not just OK but recommended.

4.2 Set Clear Communication Expectations

Establish communication standards, particularly for after-hours. Make it clear that non-urgent communications shouldn't interfere with personal time and that staff aren't expected to be accessible all the time. Promote the use of email or other communications services that minimize message urgency by allowing delayed transmission.

4.3 Limit Email and Meeting Overload

Organizations can make an effort to cut out on pointless meetings and email overload since these things might exacerbate FOMO. Promote succinct, unambiguous communication and save meetings for when they are absolutely necessary. Put into practice efficient email management techniques and teach staff members about email best practices..

4.4 Encourage Digital Detoxes

Encourage working through moments of digital detoxification. Encourage staff members to take quick breaks from their devices, especially over lunch or on a regular basis. These pauses may improve wellbeing and productivity in general.

4.5 Provide Opportunities for Mindfulness

Provide staff with meditation or mindfulness training. By engaging in these activities, people might learn to appreciate the present moment and become more conscious of their computer use patterns.

4.6 Flexible Scheduling

When it's feasible, encourage remote work and flexible schedule. This lessens the strain on workers to fit their job into a strict timetable by enabling them to organize their workload around their interests and personal life.

4.7 Encourage In-Person Connections

Encourage in-person communication inside the company. This might be cooperative initiatives that encourage relationships and connections among staff members in the actual world, social gatherings, or team-building exercises.

4.8 Educate About the Importance of JOMO

Offer staff training sessions, conferences, or educational materials to tell them of the advantages of JOMO and the possible drawbacks of excessive digital use. Assist them in realizing the benefits of a balanced approach for increased productivity and well-being.

4.9 Create Technology-Free Zones

There are certain zones in the workplace where using digital devices is either prohibited or restricted. These areas may function as havens where staff members can unplug and rejuvenate.

4.10 Recognize Achievements Beyond Metrics

Instead than focusing only on digital measures to measure productivity, acknowledge and celebrate accomplishments that go beyond numbers. Thank staff members for their contributions to the company and for their inventiveness and originality.

4.11 Lead by Example

By honouring work-life boundaries and exemplifying the advantages of JOMO in their own lives, leaders should lead by example. Employees are more inclined to adopt a balanced approach if they see their leaders doing so.

4.12 Feedback and Open Dialogue

Promote frank discussion about stress levels and digital work practices. Surveys or chances for staff to voice issues and recommendations for improvements should be given. Utilize this criticism to improve organizational procedures.

By putting these strategies into practice, companies may create a work environment where workers' well-being is valued, mindfulness and balance are encouraged, and job happiness, productivity, and creativity are all boosted while the detrimental impacts of FOMO are decreased.

5. CONCLUSION

It takes time to make the transition from FOMO to JOMO, but the effort is rewarded. We may live more balanced and satisfying lives by realizing the detrimental effects of excessive digital usage and making conscious efforts to reclaim control over our online lives. We make room for a fresh feeling of delight in the here and now when we let go of the never-ending flow of information and the fear of missing anything, which eventually strengthens our bonds with the outside world and makes life more fulfilling and interesting.

REFERENCES

Bariso, J. (2018, July 23). *Meet JOMO: The emotionally intelligent response to FOMO*. Inc

Bradley, T. (2022, March 9). The Future Of Work In 2022 And Beyond. *Forbes*. https://www.forbes.com/sites/tonybradley/2022/03/09/the-future-of-work-in-2022-and-beyond/

Bradshaw, F. (2019, September 26). Are you afraid of missing out? replace FOMO with JOMO and rediscover your inner peace. Mind Tools Blog. *Mind Tools*. https://www.mindtools.com/blog/fear-and-joy-of-missing-out/

Çelik, I. K., Eru, O., & Cop, R. (2019). The effects of consumers' FOMO tendencies on impulse buying and the effects of impulse buying on post-purchase regret: An investigation on retail stores. BRAIN. *Broad Research in Artificial Intelligence and Neuroscience*, *10*(3), 124–138.

Chan, S. S., Van Solt, M., Cruz, R. E., Philp, M., Bahl, S., Serin, N., Amaral, N. B., Schindler, R., Bartosiak, A., Kumar, S., & Canbulut, M. (2022, August 13). Social media and mindfulness: From the fear of missing out (FOMO) to the joy of missing out (JOMO). *The Journal of Consumer Affairs*, *56*(3), 1312–1331. doi:10.1111/joca.12476

Cording, J. (2018, July 21). Is the Joy of Missing Out the New Self-Care? *Forbes*.

Dash A. (2012, July 19). JOMO! Retrieved from http://anildash.com/2012/07/19/jom

Decembrele, B. (2018, July 11). *Your workplace guide to summer vacation*. LinkedIn.

Depot, M. S. (2023, January 5). *The Secret to a Digital Detox for Entrepreneurs*. Smart Service. https://www.smartservice.com/smart-service-blog/the-secret-to-a-digital-detox-for-entrepreneurs/

Dhaliwal, N. (2020). From FOMO to JOMO: Why I now prefer a life less risky. *The Guardian*.

Dodgson, L. (2018a, July 26). 'JOMO' is the joy of missing out- here are 3 ways people find happiness in not being involved. *Business Insider*.

Dodgson, L. (2018a, July 26). 'JOMO' is the joy of missing out- here are 3 ways people find happiness in not being involved. *Business Insider*.

Dodgson, L. (2018b, April 24). Here's what's really going on in your brain when you experience 'FOMO'- The fear of missing out. *Business Insider*.

Elhai, J. D., Yang, H., & Montag, C. Fear of missing out (FOMO): overview, theoretical underpinnings, and literature review on relations with severity of negative affectivity and problematic technology use. *Braz J Psychiatry*. http://dx.doi.org/ doi:10.1590/1516-4446-2020-0870

Felepchuk, L. (2020). *What the heck is the new travel trend "JOMO?"* Canada.com. https://o.canada.com/travel/what-the-heck-is-the-new-travel-trend-jomo

FOMO. (2021, July 9). FOMO, JOMO and COVID: How Missing Out and Enjoying Life Are Impacting How We Navigate a Pandemic. *Journal of Organizational Psychology*, *21*(3). doi:10.33423/jop.v21i3.4309

Fuller, K. (2018, July 26). JOMO: The joy of missing out: JOMO is the emotionally intelligent antidote to FOMO. *Psychology Today*.

Fuller, K. (2018, July 26). JOMO: The joy of missing out: JOMO is the emotionally intelligent antidote to FOMO. *Psychology Today*.

Herman, D. (2000). Introducing short-term brands: A new branding tool for a new consumer reality. *Journal of Brand Management*, *7*(5), 330–340. doi:10.1057/ bm.2000.23

Kang, I., Cui, H., & Son, J. (2019). Conformity consumption behavior and FOMO. *Sustainability (Basel)*, *11*(17), 4734. doi:10.3390u11174734

Lai, C., Altavilla, D., Ronconi, A., & Aceto, P. (2016). Fear of missing out (FOMO) is associated with activation of the right middle temporal gyrus during inclusion social cue. *Computers in Human Behavior*, *61*, 516–521. doi:10.1016/j.chb.2016.03.072

Phelan, H. (2018, July 12). How to make this the summer of missing out. *The New York Times*.

Przybylski, A. K., Murayama, K., DeHaan, C. R., & Gladwell, V. (2013). Motivational, emotional, and behavioral correlates of fear of missing out. *Computers in Human Behavior, 29*(4), 1841–1848. doi:10.1016/j.chb.2013.02.014

Rautela, S., & Sharma, S. (2022, February 11). Fear of missing out (FOMO) to the joy of missing out (JOMO): Shifting dunes of problematic usage of the internet among social media users. Journal of Information. *Communication and Ethics in Society, 20*(4), 461–479. doi:10.1108/JICES-06-2021-0057

Rees, M. (2017). *FOMO vs. JOMO: How to embrace the joy of missing out.* Whole Life Challenge.

Riordan, B. C., Flett, J. A., Hunter, J. A., Scarf, D., & Conner, T. S. (2015). Fear of missing out (FoMO): The relationship between FoMO, alcohol use, and alcohol-related consequences in college students. *Journal of Psychiatry and Brain Functions, 2*(1), 9. doi:10.7243/2055-3447-2-9

Riordan, B. C., Flett, J. A., Hunter, J. A., Scarf, D., & Conner, T. S. (2015). Fear of missing out (FoMO): The relationship between FoMO, alcohol use, and alcohol-related consequences in college students. *Journal of Psychiatry and Brain Functions, 2*(1), 9. doi:10.7243/2055-3447-2-9

Saleh, M. A. H. (2012). An investigation of the relationship between unplanned buying and post-purchase regret. *International Journal of Marketing Studies, 4*(4), 106. doi:10.5539/ijms.v4n4p106

Sanz, A. (2015, July 29). *What's the Psychology Behind the Fear of Missing Out?* Slate.

Schreckinger, B. (2014). *The home of FOMO.* Boston Magazine.

Seong-yoon, K. (2019). Younger. Season 6, Ep 12. New York, NY: TVLand.

Wolniewicz, C. A., Tiamiyu, M. F., Weeks, J. W., & Elhai, J. D. (2018). Problematic smartphone use and relations with negative affect, fear of missing out, and fear of negative and positive evaluation. *Psychiatry Research, 262,* 618–623. doi:10.1016/j.psychres.2017.09.058 PMID:28982630

Wolniewicz, C. A., Tiamiyu, M. F., Weeks, J. W., & Elhai, J. D. (2018). Problematic smartphone use and relations with negative affect, fear of missing out, and fear of negative and positive evaluation. *Psychiatry Research, 262,* 618–623. doi:10.1016/j.psychres.2017.09.058 PMID:28982630

Wortham, J. (2012, August 25). Turn off the phone (and the tension). *The New York Times.*

Chapter 13
Life Cycle Analysis of Electric Vehicles

Neha Kamboj
https://orcid.org/0000-0003-1763-7967
IILM University, India

Vinita Choudhary
https://orcid.org/0000-0002-6705-0956
K.R. Mangalam University, India

Sonal Trivedi
VIT Bhopal University, India

ABSTRACT

Due to growing environmental issues, including climate change, urban pollution, and the anticipated scarcity of fossil fuels, societal and political interest in electric mobility has surged recently. When switching from internal combustion engines to alternative drivetrain technologies, such as electric vehicles (EV), there is expected to be a decrease in the usage of fossil fuels and environmental effects. Several nations have already started initiatives to introduce electric vehicles to the market or set goals for the future share of these vehicles. For instance, the European Union wants to reduce the number of vehicles with internal combustion engines in half by 2030 and phase them out entirely in cities by 2050 and by 2030. China and Norway acting as the main drivers. The current chapter examines the LCA studies on electric vehicles and their corresponding batteries that have been published in the previous ten years. Also, the suitability of the employed assessment techniques for addressing the criticality of resources is confirmed.

DOI: 10.4018/979-8-3693-1107-3.ch013

1. INTRODUCTION

Due to growing environmental issues including climate change, urban pollution, and the anticipated scarcity of fossil fuels, communal and governmental concern in power-driven mobility has surged recently. When switching from internal ignition engines to substitute electric driven equipment, such as electrical vehicles, there is expected to be a decrease in the usage of fossil fuels and environmental effects (EV). Several nations have already started initiatives to introduce electric vehicles to the market or fixing aim for the forthcoming stake of these means of transportation (Vassileva & Campillo, 2017; Tchetchik el al., 2020). For instance, the European Union wants to reduce the number of automobiles with internal ignition engines 50% by 2030 and shut them out entirely in towns by 2050. Global sales of electric vehicles are rising, with Norway and China acting as the main pillars (Brdulak et al., 2020).

The main reason for people's concerns regarding the mass market introduction of electric vehicles is the increased demand on resources, such as the usage of lithium in lithium ion batteries (Ghasemi-Marzbali, 2022; Hopkins et al., 2023). The necessity for greater resource efficiency and the industry's rising material consumption are concerns that have received a lot of attention recently. The global patterns of resource usage will change significantly when electric vehicles (EV) replace conventional automobiles (Agusdinata & Liu, 2023; Dlugosch et al., 2022). The demand in particular for the materials needed to produce batteries such as lithium, cobalt, graphite and rare earth elements, is anticipated to rise significantly. The demand for lithium-ion batteries is projected to surge seven folds by 2025 and by 11–13 folds by 2030. A lack of these resources could have an impact on employment and economic growth (Richa et al., 2014; Shafique el al., 2023).

A technique called life cycle assessment (LCA) can be used to look into the environmental effects of different drivetrain systems' resource usage (Mendoza et al., 2020). Quite a few studies have examined the environmental effects of alternative drivetrain technology in comparison to traditional internal combustion engine-powered automobiles over the last ten years. Many techniques have been developed and integrated into LCA to evaluate the resource efficiency of product systems (Zheng & Peng, 2021; Sharma et al., 2011).

The current article offers a summary of Life Cycle Analysis on electric vehicles and their corresponding batteries that have been published in the previous ten years. It examines if and how the assessed publications deal with the "resources" effect category. The publication's primary emphasis is on metals and mineral resources. In order to do so, we looked into the resource use impact assessment techniques used and the general findings of means for electromobility. Furthermore, the suitability of the employed assessment techniques for addressing the criticality of resources is confirmed.

Additionally, the globe has a large fleet of automobiles nowadays. Every country aspires to lessen the significant impact of transport on global greenhouse gas emissions by converting more of its fleet of internal combustion engine (ICE) cars to electric vehicles (EVs). Consequently, this study might be helpful in evaluating electric automobiles.

2. LITERATURE REVIEW

The Table 1 below presents the review based papers in the field of Electric vehicles. Some of the studies are taken to assess about electric vehicles.

3. RESEARCH METHODOLOGY

In this manuscript, Life Cycle Analysis on electric vehicles from 2001 to 2023 was evaluated. To accomplish this objective, the keywords ""life cycle assessment" OR "LCA" AND "electic vehicles" OR "electromobility" were used to search the databases Scopus. Among all of the recognised studies, those that met the following criteria were chosen: A vehicle or a part of a vehicle underwent an LCA; the findings were presented in impact categories, and an interpretation was carried out.

Four steps were used to assess the chosen studies. The following factors were taken into consideration when extracting the research' important information in the first step:

- author(s),
- the publication's title,
- the publishing date,
- the study's objective,
- a useful unit,
- examined vehicle components, life cycle stages, and drivetrain technologies;
- used impact assessment techniques and thought about effect types.

The subsequent stage involved the number of articles produced by journals, Journal's H index, Source clustering through Bradford's Law. Studies examining EV received special attention because they may be a prospective hotspot for the utilisation of essential components in electric transportation. The third important step was looking into the impact assessment techniques used by publications that looked at resource consumption. The final step was drawing broad generalisations about

Table 1. Review based papers published

Authors	Source title	Title	Year	Objectives	Method used	Key findings	Future scope of Research
Farzaneh F., Jung S.	Journal of Cleaner Production	Lifecycle carbon footprint comparison between internal combustion engine versus electric transit vehicle: A case study in the U.S.	2023	Compare carbon emissions and overall environmental impact of EVs and ICEVs.	LCA model	Electricity sources affect emissions of both EVs and ICEVs.	Study of Electric vehicles adoption on urban infrastructure.l
Tao Y., Wang Z., Wu B., Tang Y., Evans S.	Journal of Cleaner Production	Environmental life cycle assessment of recycling technologies for ternary lithium-ion batteries	2023	The goal is to ascertain environment favorable recycling techniques for expired power batteries and assist in decision-making so that end-of-life ternary lithium-ion power batteries could be managed.	LCA model	Various recycling technologies have evolved, raising agenda about their environment favorable recycling technologies.	study about the monetary feasibility and scalability of the environment favorable recycling technologies.
Liu M., Zhang K., Liang Y., Yang Y., Chen Z., Liu W.	Journal of Cleaner Production	Life cycle environmental and economic assessment of electric bicycles with different batteries in China	2023	To Analyze impact of electric bicycles with several kind of batteries in China.	LCA model	The key finding is recycling techniques are environmental friendly for lithium ion batteries.	Further study could assess the application to other related items of batteries
Harnischmacher C., Markefke L., Brendel A.B., Kolbe L.	Journal of Cleaner Production	Two-sided sustainability: Simulating battery degradation in vehicle to grid applications within autonomous electric port transportation	2023	To examine the affect of vehicle lifespan on efficiency balance. l	Regression method	There is direct association between vehicle lifespan on its efficiency	Further study could assess the application to other related items.
Horesh N., Zhou Y., Quinn J.	Journal of Cleaner Production	Home charging for all: Techno-economic and life cycle assessment of multi-unit dwelling electric vehicle charging hubs	2023	To assess the multi-unit dwelling electric vehicle charging hubs	NA	This study found that there is significant impact of multi-unit dwelling electric vehicle charging hubs	Further could explore innovations in multi-unit dwelling electric vehicle charging hubs
Bartolucci L., Cordiner S., Mulone V., Santarelli M., Ortenzi F., Pasquali M.	Journal of Cleaner Production	PV assisted electric vehicle charging station considering the integration of stationary first- or second-life battery storage	2023	To assess carbon emissions of vehicles and Discuss about electric vehicle charging station.	Anova Method	This paper has found that electic vehicles release relatively less carbon emissions per km.	NA

continued on following page

Table 1. Continued

Authors	Source title	Title	Year	Objectives	Method used	Key findings	Future scope of Research
Ou S., Lin Z., Jiang Y., Zhang S.	Journal of Cleaner Production	Quantifying policy gaps for achieving the net-zero GHG emissions target in the U.S. light-duty vehicle market through electrification	2022	To assess carbon emissions of vehicles.	Regression	Transition to electrification leads to the challenge of managing light-duty vehicle market.	Examine potential policy implications and regulatory frameworks for sustainable light-duty vehicle market .
Joshi A., Sharma R., Baral B.	Journal of Cleaner Production	Comparative life cycle assessment of conventional combustion engine vehicle, battery electric vehicle and fuel cell electric vehicle in Nepal	2022	To compare the LCA of Conventional combustion engine vehicles and electric vehicles	LCA model	research depicted that decision-making support for managing end-of-life ternary lithium-ion power batteries is in favor.	Study about battery design that enhance recyclability and minimize environmental impact.
Puricelli S., Costa D., Rigamonti L., Cardellini G., Casadei S., Koroma M.S., Messagie M., Grosso M.	Journal of Cleaner Production	Life Cycle Assessment of innovative fuel blends for passenger cars with a spark-ignition engine: A comparative approach.	2022	LCA of innovative fuel blends for passenger cars with a spark-ignition engine:	LCA model	This paper has found that electic vehicles release relatively less carbon emissions.	Study can be done on private cars or on other modes of transportation
Blömeke S., Scheller C., Cerdas F., Thies C., Hachenberger R., Gonter M., Herrmann C., Spengler T.S.	Journal of Cleaner Production	Material and energy flow analysis for environmental and economic impact assessment of industrial recycling routes for lithium-ion traction batteries	2022	To assess the industrial recycling routes for lithium-ion traction batteries	Survey method	Various recycling technologies have evolved which are environment sustainable.	To study about the monetary feasibility and scalability of the environment favorable recycling technologies.

Source: compiled by authors

213

how resources were used in the research articles that were looked. All passenger electric vehicles will be referred to as "EVs" throughout the duration of this article.

4. RESULTS

The total number of articles was taken 161 for the study. The total scopus articles related to electric vehicles study are 2 in the year 2001, which was 1 in the year 2008.After the recession period, the research on EVs has increased gradually. It was 13, 15, 23 articles published in the years 2017, 2018 and 2019 respectively. In the year 2020, there was a steep decline in scopus published articles i.e. 13. The reason might be covid-19. After that, in the year 2021 and 2022, the published articles were 28 and 28 respectively. In the year 2023 (till February) 5 articles are discussing about EVs (Figure 1).

Figure 2 depicted about Average Citation Per Year. It is clearly visible that the maximum number of citation (373) was achieved in the year 2010 by the article 'Life cycle assessment of lithium-ion batteries for plug-in hybrid electric vehicles-Critical issues' in Journal of Cleaner Production. It has been clearly shown from the evident that the citations has increased after the recession period. From the year 2001 to 2007, the stable trends were existed.

Figure 3 and Table 2 represented about the sum of manuscripts created by each journal. It has been clearly evident that Journal of cleaner production had produced the maximum number of articles i.e. 15, followed by Ecology, Environment & conservation (8). This journal viz pollution research, Nature, Environment and pollution technology and Journal of advanced pharmacy, education & research has produced the same number of manuscripts i.e. three. The figure depicted the most relevant sources related to Electric Vehicles study.

Figure 1. Articles published each year
(compiled by authors)

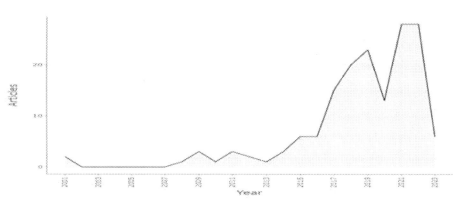

Figure 2. Average citation per year
(compiled by authors)

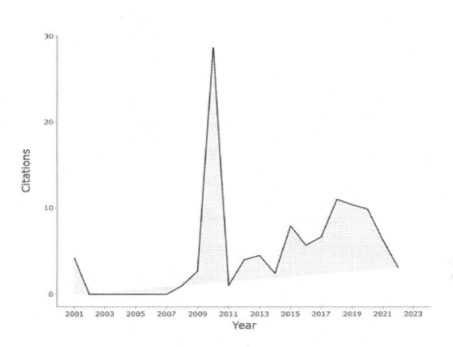

Figure 3. Number of manuscripts formed by journals
(compiled by authors)

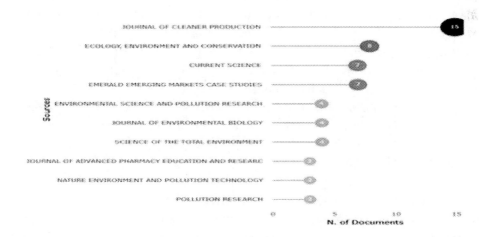

"The utmost value of H at which an author or journal has published at least h papers, each of which has been referenced at least h times", is called out the h-index.

Table 2. Number of articles produced by journals

Sources	Articles
Journal Of Cleaner Production	15
Ecology, Environment And Conservation	8
Current Science	7
Emerald Emerging Markets Case Studies	7
Environmental Science And Pollution Research	4
Journal Of Environmental Biology	4
Science Of The Total Environment	4
Journal Of Advanced Pharmacy Education And Research	3
Nature Environment And Pollution Technology	3
Pollution Research	3

Souce: compiled by authors

The index is intended to outperform less complex components like the total sum of manuscripts or citations. As per figure 4, Journal of Cleaner production has the highest H-index factor followed by the journal Current Science and Environmental Science and Pollution Research. The Journal named Resources, Conservation and Recycling and Science of the Total Environment has same H index which is 3.

The distribution of the literature on a given topic in journals is described by Bradford's law of scattering. The journals which come under Zone 1 are considered as good journals. Table 3 represented the Source clustering through Bradford's Law. Journal of Cleaner Production got rank 1 and comes under Zone 1. It is only journal who has achieved zone 1. All other journals come under Zone 3 category such as International Journal of Recent Technology and Engineering, Technological Forecasting And Social Change, International Journal Of Precision Engineering And Manufacturing - Green Technology etc.

As per Figure 5 and Table 4, India is the most cited country with 1727 number of citations, followed by USA. The Average Article Citation of India is 13.60.

Scientometric Analysis

Table 5 and Figure 6 represented the word cloud of the Articles. A pictorial representation of the frequency of words within a specified piece of text is called a word cloud. They are frequently employed to represent the frequency of words. India is the most frequently used word which occurred 117 times. Sustainable development word is occurred 29 times. All 4 words viz Environmental impact, fly ash, greenhouse gas and waste management words appeared 14 times each.

Figure 4. H index of journals
(*compiled by authors*)

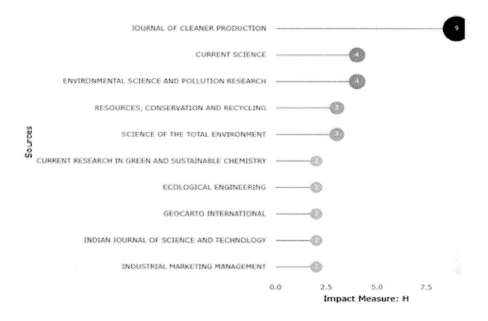

Table 3. Source clustering through Bradford's Law

Journal	Rank	Freq	Cumfreq	Zone
Journal Of Cleaner Production	1	132	132	Zone 1
International Journal Of Recent Technology And Engineering	2	3	135	Zone 3
Technological Forecasting And Social Change	3	3	138	Zone 3
Autotechnology	4	2	140	Zone 3
Clean Technologies And Environmental Policy	5	2	142	Zone 3
Advances In Science, Technology And Engineering Systems	6	1	143	Zone 3
Industrial Management And Data Systems	7	1	144	Zone 3
Industry And Innovation	8	1	145	Zone 3
International Journal Of Automotive Technology And Management	9	1	146	Zone 3
International Journal Of Precision Engineering And Manufacturing - Green Technology	10	1	147	Zone 3

Source: compiled by authors

Figure 7 represented the tree map. Using quadrilaterals of increasingly smaller sizes, the data visualisation practice known as "treemapping" displays hierarchical

Figure 5. Maximum cited countries
(compiled by authors)

Table 4. Maximum cited countries

Country	TC	Average Article Citations
India	1727	13.60
Usa	399	44.33
United Kingdom	152	25.33
Germany	89	22.25
Japan	76	25.33
Lithuania	76	76.00
France	33	33.00
Greece	32	32.00
Spain	32	32.00
Saudi Arabia	28	28.00

Source: compiled by authors

data. India word has maximum association with the words that are sustainable development, recycling, climate change, sustainability and environmental impact. In the same way, other words are associated with another words.

A semantic network, also recognized as a co-occurrence network, is a method for text examination that includes a graphic demonstration of potential relations between entities, clusters, ideas, or other things characterized in textual content. Figure 8 depicted Co occurrence Network analysis of variables. 2 clusters are there Blue and Red. The Red cluster includes Environmental impact, Life cycle assessment,

Table 5. Most frequent words

Words	Occurrences
India	117
sustainable development	29
recycling	22
climate change	17
sustainability	15
environmental impact	14
fly ash	14
greenhouse gas	14
waste management	14

Source: compiled by authors

Figure 6. Word cloud
(compiled by authors)

electric vehicles etc whereas blue cluster includes greenhouse gases, gas emissions, green house emissions etc.

Figure 9 shows the thematic Map. It has been clearly evident that green house gases, gas emissions, secondary batteries have a high relevance with high density and have a motor theme. The words lithium-ion batteries, recycling, and lithium compounds have a niche theme which inferred that these have a high density with low

Figure 7. Tree map
(compiled by authors)

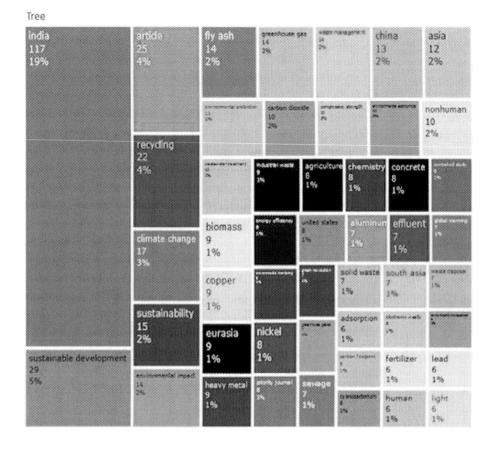

degree of relevance. The terms economic analysis, investments and electric vehicle batteries have low in density and centrality. Moreover, life cycle, environmental impact and electric vehicles have a basic theme inferred high degree of relevance but low degree of development.

5. CONCLUSION

A total of 161 publications were selected for the investigation. The total number of Scopus articles relating to the study of electric vehicles is two in the year 2001, and one in the year 2008. The amount of EV research has gradually expanded since the recession. In the years 2017, 2018, and 2019, there were 13, 15, and 23 articles published, respectively. There was a significant drop in the

Figure 8. Co-occurrence network analysis
(compiled by authors)

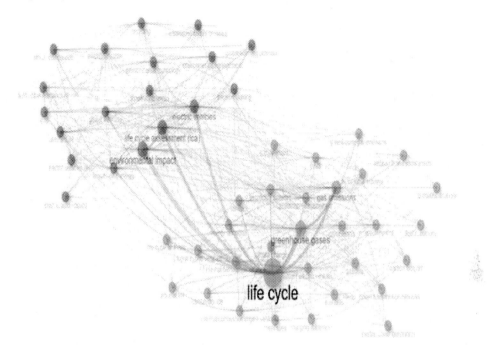

Figure 9. Thematic map
(compiled by authors)

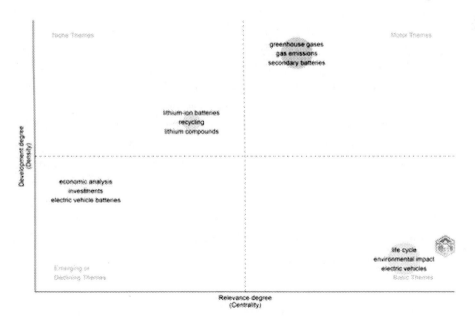

number of publications Scopus published in 2020, to just 13. Covid-19 might be the cause. Following that, there were 28 and 28 articles published in 2021 and 2022, respectively. There are five articles concerning electric vehicles in 2023 (up till February).

Given the general trend towards electric vehicles, it is critical to reduce the gap between more thorough and consistent estimates of the resources needed to support them. Without these evaluations and the appropriate eco-design measures that result from them, EV may not be the best option for sustainable transportation.

6. IMPLICATION OF THE STUDY

A thorough knowledge of the environmental effect of these cars over the course of their full life cycle is provided by the life cycle assessment (LCA) of electric vehicles (EVs), which has numerous significant consequences. It takes into account the complete spectrum of environmental implications connected to EVs in order to assist manufacturers, governments, and consumers in making educated decisions. These include effects that go beyond tailpipe emissions, such as those caused by production, the extraction of raw materials, and end-of-life disposal. Furthermore, LCA enables a direct comparison of the environmental performance of EVs and internal combustion engine cars (ICEVs). This comparison might serve as a roadmap for initiatives to lower transportation's overall carbon impact. Consumers can learn from LCA findings about the wider environmental effects of their car selections. This information may stimulate interest in EVs and promote environmentally friendly modes of transportation. Governments may utilise LCA insights to create efficient regulations that encourage the use of EVs and advance environmentally friendly manufacturing, charging, and recycling methods. Moreover, By taking into account the possible advantages of EVs throughout the course of their entire life cycle, LCA promotes a long-term view. By doing this, "rebound effects"—whereby efficiency improvements are cancelled out by rising usage—can be avoided. By revealing possibilities for reusing, remanufacturing, and recycling of EV components, LCA may aid in the move to a circular economy by minimising waste and resource depletion.

Overall, the effects of completing an LCA of electric cars are extensive and have the potential to positively impact a number of industries, promote sustainable transportation, and have an impact on more general environmental objectives.

REFERENCES

Agusdinata, D. B., & Liu, W. (2023). Global sustainability of electric vehicles minerals: A critical review of news media. *The Extractive Industries and Society*, *13*, 101231. doi:10.1016/j.exis.2023.101231

Bartolucci, L., Cordiner, S., Mulone, V., Santarelli, M., Ortenzi, F., & Pasquali, M. (2023). PV assisted electric vehicle charging station considering the integration of stationary first-or second-life battery storage. *Journal of Cleaner Production*, *383*, 135426. doi:10.1016/j.jclepro.2022.135426

Blömeke, S., Scheller, C., Cerdas, F., Thies, C., Hachenberger, R., Gonter, M., Herrmann, C., & Spengler, T. S. (2022). Material and energy flow analysis for environmental and economic impact assessment of industrial recycling routes for lithium-ion traction batteries. *Journal of Cleaner Production*, *377*, 134344. doi:10.1016/j.jclepro.2022.134344

Brdulak, A., Chaberek, G., & Jagodziński, J. (2020). Development forecasts for the zero-emission bus fleet in servicing public transport in chosen EU member countries. *Energies*, *13*(16), 4239. doi:10.3390/en13164239

Dlugosch, O., Brandt, T., & Neumann, D. (2022). Combining analytics and simulation methods to assess the impact of shared, autonomous electric vehicles on sustainable urban mobility. *Information & Management*, *59*(5), 103285. doi:10.1016/j.im.2020.103285

Farzaneh, F., & Jung, S. (2023). Lifecycle carbon footprint comparison between internal combustion engine versus electric transit vehicle: A case study in the US. *Journal of Cleaner Production*, *390*, 136111. doi:10.1016/j.jclepro.2023.136111

Ghasemi-Marzbali, A. (2022). Fast-charging station for electric vehicles, challenges and issues: A comprehensive review. *Journal of Energy Storage*, *49*, 104136. doi:10.1016/j.est.2022.104136

Harnischmacher, C., Markefke, L., Brendel, A. B., & Kolbe, L. (2023). Two-sided sustainability: Simulating battery degradation in vehicle to grid applications within autonomous electric port transportation. *Journal of Cleaner Production*, *384*, 135598. doi:10.1016/j.jclepro.2022.135598

Hopkins, E., Potoglou, D., Orford, S., & Cipcigan, L. (2023). Can the equitable roll out of electric vehicle charging infrastructure be achieved? *Renewable & Sustainable Energy Reviews*, *182*, 113398. doi:10.1016/j.rser.2023.113398

Horesh, N., Zhou, Y., & Quinn, J. (2023). Home charging for all: Techno-economic and life cycle assessment of multi-unit dwelling electric vehicle charging hubs. *Journal of Cleaner Production, 383*, 135551. doi:10.1016/j.jclepro.2022.135551

Jiang, G., Pan, J., Deng, W., Sun, Y., Guo, J., Che, K., Yang, Y., Lin, Z., Sun, Y., Huang, C., & Zhang, T. (2022). Recovery of high pure pyrolytic carbon black from waste tires by dual acid treatment. *Journal of Cleaner Production, 374*, 133893. doi:10.1016/j.jclepro.2022.133893

Joshi, A., Sharma, R., & Baral, B. (2022). Comparative life cycle assessment of conventional combustion engine vehicle, battery electric vehicle and fuel cell electric vehicle in Nepal. *Journal of Cleaner Production, 379*, 134407. doi:10.1016/j.jclepro.2022.134407

Liu, M., Zhang, K., Liang, Y., Yang, Y., Chen, Z., & Liu, W. (2023). Life cycle environmental and economic assessment of electric bicycles with different batteries in China. *Journal of Cleaner Production, 385*, 135715. doi:10.1016/j.jclepro.2022.135715

Mendoza Beltran, A., Cox, B., Mutel, C., van Vuuren, D. P., Font Vivanco, D., Deetman, S., Edelenbosch, O. Y., Guinée, J., & Tukker, A. (2020). When the background matters: Using scenarios from integrated assessment models in prospective life cycle assessment. *Journal of Industrial Ecology, 24*(1), 64–79. doi:10.1111/jiec.12825

Puricelli, S., Costa, D., Rigamonti, L., Cardellini, G., Casadei, S., Koroma, M. S., Messagie, M., & Grosso, M. (2022). Life Cycle Assessment of innovative fuel blends for passenger cars with a spark-ignition engine: A comparative approach. *Journal of Cleaner Production, 378*, 134535. doi:10.1016/j.jclepro.2022.134535

Richa, K., Babbitt, C. W., Gaustad, G., & Wang, X. (2014). A future perspective on lithium-ion battery waste flows from electric vehicles. *Resources, Conservation and Recycling, 83*, 63–76. doi:10.1016/j.resconrec.2013.11.008

Shafique, M., Akbar, A., Rafiq, M., Azam, A., & Luo, X. (2023). Global material flow analysis of end-of-life of lithium nickel manganese cobalt oxide batteries from battery electric vehicles. *Waste Management & Research, 41*(2), 376–388. doi:10.1177/0734242X221127175 PMID:36373335

Sharma, A., Saxena, A., Sethi, M., Shree, V., & Varun. (2011). Life cycle assessment of buildings: A review. *Renewable & Sustainable Energy Reviews, 15*(1), 871–875. doi:10.1016/j.rser.2010.09.008

Tao, Y., Wang, Z., Wu, B., Tang, Y., & Evans, S. (2023). Environmental life cycle assessment of recycling technologies for ternary lithium-ion batteries. *Journal of Cleaner Production, 389*, 136008. doi:10.1016/j.jclepro.2023.136008

Tchetchik, A., Zvi, L. I., Kaplan, S., & Blass, V. (2020). The joint effects of driving hedonism and trialability on the choice between internal combustion engine, hybrid, and electric vehicles. *Technological Forecasting and Social Change, 151*, 119815. doi:10.1016/j.techfore.2019.119815

Vassileva, I., & Campillo, J. (2017). Adoption barriers for electric vehicles: Experiences from early adopters in Sweden. *Energy, 120*, 632–641. doi:10.1016/j.energy.2016.11.119

Zheng, G., & Peng, Z. (2021). Life Cycle Assessment (LCA) of BEV's environmental benefits for meeting the challenge of ICExit (Internal Combustion Engine Exit). *Energy Reports, 7*, 1203–1216. doi:10.1016/j.egyr.2021.02.039

Chapter 14
New Avenues of Opportunities and Challenges for Start-Ups, MSMEs, the Indian Financial Sector, and the Indian Insurance Sector

Sonal Trivedi
 https://orcid.org/0000-0001-8711-2977
VIT Business School, VIT Bhopal University, India

Vinita Choudhary
 https://orcid.org/0000-0002-6705-0956
K.R. Managalam University, India

Neha Kamboj
 https://orcid.org/0000-0003-1763-7967
IILM University, India

Nirmaljeet Kaur Virk
 https://orcid.org/0000-0002-2000-1073
K.R. Managalam University, India

ABSTRACT

This chapter delves into the evolving landscape of opportunities and challenges for start-ups, micro, small, and medium enterprises (MSMEs), as well as the Indian financial and insurance sectors. It explores the transformations driven by technological advancements, policy shifts, and market dynamics, shedding light on the current scenario of 2022-23. By examining the interplay between these sectors, the chapter aims to provide insights into their symbiotic relationship and prospects for growth.

DOI: 10.4018/979-8-3693-1107-3.ch014

INTRODUCTION

In the dynamic landscape of 2022-23, this research paper delves into the intricate interplay of opportunities and challenges faced by start-ups, Micro, Small, and Medium Enterprises (MSMEs), along with the financial and insurance sectors in India (Farayola et al., 2023). The evolution of these sectors is intricately woven into the fabric of technological advancements, policy shifts, and market dynamics, creating a tapestry that demands careful examination (Allioui & Mourdi, 2023). This study endeavors to unravel the complex web of relationships between these entities, shedding light on how their symbiotic dynamics impact growth trajectories. Technological advancements have been a catalyst for change, driving unprecedented transformations across industries. As start-ups and MSMEs leverage innovative technologies to carve their niche, the financial and insurance sectors witness a ripple effect. Policy shifts at both national and global levels further shape the contours of these industries, influencing the regulatory frameworks that govern their operations (Guckenbiehl & Zubielqui, 2022). Against this backdrop, the research aims to provide a comprehensive snapshot of the current scenario, capturing the pulse of India's economic landscape in the specified timeframe.

This exploration is not merely a retrospective analysis but a forward-looking endeavor to discern the prospects for growth in these sectors. By understanding the synergies and tensions among start-ups, MSMEs, and the financial landscape, the research seeks to illuminate potential pathways for sustainable development. As we navigate this multifaceted terrain, the study stands as a testament to the intricacies and opportunities inherent in India's economic ecosystem during the specified period (Wahyuddin et al., 2022; Kamboj et al., 2023))

In the subsequent discussion, we thoroughly examine the dynamic terrain that encompasses opportunities and challenges within start-ups, Micro, Small, and Medium Enterprises (MSMEs), alongside the Indian financial and insurance sectors. This exploration delves into the ongoing metamorphosis propelled by technological advancements, shifts in policies, and the ever-changing dynamics of the market, offering a nuanced perspective on the prevailing conditions in the year 2022-23. The objective is to illuminate the intricate interplay among these sectors, shedding light on their interconnectedness and presenting valuable insights into the mutualistic relationship they share, all while envisioning potential growth avenues. This analysis not only scrutinizes the current landscape but also extrapolates towards the future by investigating the anticipated benefits, challenges, research trajectories, and transformative potentials that lay ahead.

Objectives of the Study

1. To explore the opportunities and challenges faced by the startups, MSMEs in India.
2. To identify the relationship between Indian financial sector, insurance sector and startups in India.

LITERATURE REVIEW

Micro, small and medium enterprise (MSME) is the kingpin of Indian economy. It contributes to 48% of India's exports and provides employment to 110 million people. This review delves into the challenges and opportunities within the domain of MSMEs and startups (Ahmad & Patra, 2023). The primary objective is to offer valuable insights into the existing body of knowledge, discern prevalent trends, and suggest prospective avenues for the continuous development of this dynamic field. Through a comprehensive examination, the review aims to provide a nuanced understanding of the current Scenario of affairs, shedding light on the intricate challenges and promising opportunities encountered by MSMEs and startups. Ultimately, the goal is to contribute to the ongoing discourse by identifying key trends and proposing forward-looking directions that can shape the future trajectory of these crucial sectors.

START-UPS

Current Scenario

In recent years, India has witnessed a rapid surge in entrepreneurial endeavors, accompanied by policy initiatives supporting start-ups and MSMEs. The financial and insurance sectors have not only facilitated funding and risk management for these entities but have also undergone significant changes in response to digitalization and consumer preferences (Purbasari et al., 2021). This chapter explores the newfound doors of opportunities and challenges that have emerged in this dynamic ecosystem. The past decade has witnessed an extraordinary transformation in India's startup ecosystem. From 2015 to 2022, the nation has surged to become the third-largest global hub for startups, with an impressive count of 1,12,718 DPIIT-recognized startups dispersed across 763 districts as of October 3rd, 2023 (www.pib.gov.in accessed on 8/8/2023). This unprecedented proliferation highlights the decentralized nature of innovation and entrepreneurship in the country. Furthermore, India's startup landscape boasts a remarkable diversity, with innovations spanning across 56 distinct industrial sectors (www.pib.gov.in accessed on 8/8/2023). Beyond sheer numbers, India's innovation prowess is underscored by its global standing in innovation quality. The nation ranks second in this regard, particularly excelling in the quality of scientific publications and the calibre of its universities, a feat particularly noteworthy among middle-income economies (Hurley, 2018). This paper endeavours to not only chronicle this exceptional growth but also to delve into the underlying factors driving it. Through a combination of rigorous data analysis and comprehensive case studies, this research seeks to provide a comprehensive understanding of the dynamics propelling India's startup ecosystem to new heights. The Indian startup ecosystem has undergone a remarkable transformation in recent years, experiencing exponential growth from 2015 to 2022. This period has witnessed a phenomenal 15-fold increase in the total funding garnered by startups, reflecting a surge in investor confidence and interest. Simultaneously, there has been a nine-fold surge in the number of investors, indicating a burgeoning interest in supporting and nurturing innovative ventures. Additionally, the number of incubators has seen a seven-fold rise, providing vital support structures for fledgling startups (www. investindia.gov.in accessed on 10/8/23).

In this dynamic economic landscape, Indian unicorns have emerged as vibrant contributors. These startups not only pioneer groundbreaking solutions and technologies but also serve as substantial generators of employment opportunities. Up until the fiscal year 2016-17, a new unicorn was added to the roster annually. However, over the past four years, starting from fiscal year 2017-18, this growth rate has surged exponentially. Impressively, there has been a staggering 66% year-on-year increase in the number of new unicorns entering the scene. As of October 3rd, 2023, India proudly hosts 111 unicorns, collectively valued at a remarkable $349.67 billion. A noteworthy trend is the exceptional growth observed in 2021, where 45 unicorns were birthed, amassing a total valuation of $102.30 billion. Following suit, 2022 saw the addition of 22 new unicorns, collectively valued at $29.20 billion. The year 2023 introduced Zepto as the latest entrant, standing as the sole unicorn born in that year (www.meity.gov.in accessed on 5/5/2023). This surge in unicorn creation and valuation is indicative of the vibrancy and potential of the Indian startup ecosystem. It showcases the growing maturity and global competitiveness of startups originating from India, solidifying the nation's position as a key player in the global entrepreneurial landscape.

Opportunities for Start-Ups

The Indian start-up ecosystem has become a global player, with innovative ventures spanning across sectors such as technology, healthcare, e-commerce, and renewable energy. The advent of angel investors, venture capital funds, and government schemes like "Start-up India" has provided unprecedented financial backing for budding entrepreneurs. Collaborations between start-ups and established corporations have created synergies, fostering innovation and market penetration (Brown et al., 2019).

Despite the prevailing challenges confronting startups in today's business landscape, there exist numerous advantageous prospects. These opportunities encompass:

- Swift and cost-effective access to a global market.
- Efficient and economical testing of novel concepts.
- Rapid establishment and strengthening of a brand presence.
- Expedited and streamlined capital procurement.

Swift and Cost-Effective Access to a Global Market

Today, startups enjoy a significant edge in their capacity to swiftly and economically access a global market. In the nascent stages of the internet, the process of reaching a global market was prohibitively costly for companies. They were required to construct their own infrastructure and allocate substantial budgets towards expansive advertising campaigns. Presently, owing to the proliferation of social media and a suite of online tools, startups can efficiently tap into a global market at a fraction of the traditional cost. All that's requisite is a compelling concept and a user-friendly website or application, accessible to prospective customers worldwide. This paradigm shift has democratized market access, levelling the playing field for startups irrespective of their size or resources (Ghosh et al., 2021).

Efficient and Economical Testing of Novel Concepts

In the contemporary business landscape, startups possess a significant advantage in their ability to swiftly and affordably test novel concepts. In times past, companies faced substantial expenditures for market research and development when aiming to assess a new product or service. Today, however, thanks to accessible online tools like Google AdWords and Facebook Ads, startups can promptly and cost-effectively pilot new ideas through online advertising campaigns. In the event that an idea resonates with customers, startups can then allocate additional resources to further develop and rapidly scale it. Conversely, if an idea fails to gain traction, they can readily pivot or discontinue it, minimizing financial exposure. This agile testing process empowers startups to refine their offerings in response to real-time feedback, ultimately enhancing their chances of success in the market (Audretsch et al., 2020).

Rapid Establishment and Strengthening of a Brand Presence

Indeed, a substantial advantage for startups in the contemporary landscape lies in their capacity to swiftly establish a robust brand identity. Historically, this process entailed years of concerted effort for companies. However, in today's digital age, platforms like Facebook and Twitter have revolutionized brand-building. Startups can now expedite the creation of a compelling brand identity by generating captivating content and engaging directly with their customer base online. This dynamic interaction not only amplifies brand visibility but also fosters a genuine connection with the audience, propelling startups into the public consciousness at an accelerated pace (Surie, 2017).

Expedited and Streamlined Capital Procurement

Absolutely, another substantial advantage for startups today is their expedited access to capital. In bygone eras, the process of raising funds from venture capitalists or other investors was often protracted, sometimes spanning several years. However, in today's digital age, platforms like Kickstarter and Indiegogo have revolutionized fundraising. Startups can now tap into a diverse array of funding sources swiftly and with relative ease, providing them with the financial resources needed to propel their ventures forward. This democratization of funding avenues has significantly reduced the time and effort required to secure vital capital for startups ((Trautwein, 2021).

Challenges for Start-Ups

While opportunities abound, start-ups face challenges like intense competition, talent acquisition, and regulatory compliance. The process of scaling up often necessitates a delicate balance between rapid growth and financial sustainability. Access to reliable mentorship and guidance remains crucial for steering through uncertainties. Startups today find themselves in a landscape of abundant opportunities coupled with formidable challenges. While they enjoy unprecedented access to resources like capital, skilled talent, and a broad customer base, they also face intense competition in a saturated market. Initiating and sustaining a startup has become more demanding than ever before. Being a startup founder, it's crucial to grasp both the favorable prospects and hurdles in today's business landscape. To leverage the opportunities and navigate the challenges effectively, you need to have a keen awareness of the present scenario and be ready to adjust your business model and go-to-market approach accordingly (Trautwein, 2021).

The present challanges of startups can be encapsulated in three pivotal trends:

1. There is an unprecedented availability of capital.
2. The talent pool is now global and fiercely competitive.
3. The customer base is becoming increasingly diverse and segmented.

   1. **Unprecedented availability of capital:** Over the past decade, one of the most significant shifts in the startup landscape has been the remarkable surge in access to capital. In the early days of the internet, securing funding for startups was a formidable challenge. Venture capitalists were scarce, and many startups had to rely on self-funding. Today, the global landscape boasts over 20,000 active venture capitalists, and startups have a diverse array of funding sources available, ranging from angel investors and incubators to accelerators and crowdfunding platforms. Moreover, the level of investment commitment from backers has seen a substantial uptick. In 2000, the average venture capital deal amounted to $5 million. Nowadays, it's not uncommon for startups to secure $50 million or more in a single financing round (Bikse et al., 2018).

   2. **Unprecedented availability of capital:** The second significant development is the expanding global reach of the talent pool. In the initial stages of internet proliferation, the majority of technical expertise was centralized in Silicon Valley. Nowadays, highly skilled engineers and entrepreneurs can be found across the globe. Consequently, the competition for top-tier talent has intensified considerably (. To secure and retain the finest workforce, startups need to provide competitive compensation and benefits packages while fostering an appealing corporate culture. Additionally, they must be equipped to entice top talent away from well-established firms. Furthermore, startups must be prepared to vie for talent not only against other startups but also against larger corporations (Alawamleh et al., 2023).

   3. **The customer base is becoming increasingly diverse and segmented:** In order to connect with potential customers, startups need to embrace a multi-channel strategy that considers the diverse range of devices and platforms customers utilize. Additionally, they should be ready to customize their products and marketing materials to cater to various markets (Priyanka et al., 2023).

In conclusion, the current business landscape, characterized by global uncertainties and rapid shifts, underscores the crucial role of startups. These emerging ventures bring fresh perspectives, innovative solutions, and a willingness to take risks, setting them apart from established enterprises weighed down by tradition and bureaucracy. Moreover, startups are uniquely positioned to identify and address amplified challenges in times of change, offering a valuable opportunity to provide meaningful solutions.

Their nimbleness and adaptability enable startups to pivot swiftly in response to evolving market conditions, while their integration of cutting-edge technologies confers a competitive edge. Led by passionate, forward-thinking entrepreneurs, startups embody the spirit of innovation that is paramount in today's dynamic economic environment. The ability to envision and execute pandemic-proof business models, coupled with creative and adaptable marketing strategies, ensures that startups not only survive but thrive in this unpredictable landscape.

It embraces video as a powerful communication tool, and maintaining cost-effectiveness through remote work and judicious resource allocation, are essential strategies for startup resilience. Above all, fostering a culture of flexibility and readiness to seize unforeseen opportunities empowers startups to navigate the challenges presented by a pandemic-impacted world.

In essence, startups are not only essential players but also indispensable catalysts for growth and progress in the current business environment. Their capacity to revolutionize industries, adapt to evolving circumstances, and provide innovative solutions makes them integral to shaping the future of global commerce. As the business landscape continues to evolve, startups remain at the forefront, poised to lead the way in innovation and resilience.

MSMEs and Their Prospects

Introduction: Micro, Small, and Medium Enterprises (MSMEs) constitute the backbone of any thriving economy, pivotal in fostering comprehensive development and inclusive progress. MSMEs continue to be the backbone of the Indian economy, contributing significantly to GDP and employment. With technology enabling efficient supply chains, digital marketing, and online sales, MSMEs have a chance to expand their reach and explore global markets. Government initiatives promoting local manufacturing and exports have further elevated their growth potential. In India, this sector boasts an impressive presence, with over 63 million enterprises making substantial contributions – 30% to the nation's GDP, 45% to its manufacturing output, and 40% to its overall exports (Fatima & Akhtar, 2023).

However, despite their undeniable significance, MSMEs often grapple with a myriad of challenges in their pursuit of growth and sustainability. Constraints in resources, difficulties in operational scalability, and a reluctance to adopt modern technology stand as common impediments.

Few of the Challenges Faced by MSMEs Are

Financial and Regulatory Challenges

Obtaining timely access to finance remains a major obstacle for MSMEs in India, with only a limited 16% able to secure funds promptly. This reliance on internal resources often hampers their potential for growth. Even larger enterprises encounter difficulties in obtaining cost-effective credit from formal banking channels. MSMEs also grapple with compliance issues related to taxes and changing labor laws, which can lead to substantial financial burdens. Despite efforts to enhance sector competitiveness, adherence to regulatory and tax requirements continues to be a challenge, resulting in constrained capital and business closures (Hoang & Bui, 2023).

Infrastructure Deficits

Adequate infrastructure is pivotal for the success of the MSME sector, especially in industries reliant on outsourcing. However, the inadequacy of infrastructure in India adversely affects the efficiency and global competitiveness of MSMEs, ultimately limiting their growth prospects.

Productivity Constraints and Innovation Gap

While MSMEs may not always boast high levels of productivity, they offer value through cost-efficient operations and the provision of goods at competitive prices. Nonetheless, their limited scale of production and narrow profit margins can put them at a disadvantage compared to larger enterprises. Many Indian MSMEs continue to rely on outdated technologies, and there is a shortage of entrepreneurial leaders who are willing to adopt and embrace new tools and technologies. This impedes their overall productivity and ability to compete, particularly when compared to larger firms in sectors like e-commerce and call centres (Geeta et al., 2023).

Impact of Technological Changes

MSMEs have grappled with significant technological shifts over time, which have had a notable impact on their potential for growth. Changes in land ownership rights, for instance, have led to issues of mismanagement and reduced productivity, underscoring the importance of adaptability (Geeta et al., 2023).

Competition and Skill Gaps

MSMEs face intense competition, particularly from larger enterprises, a challenge that has been exacerbated by the advent of e-commerce and globalization. Although competition is not a new phenomenon, MSMEs find it increasingly difficult to withstand the pressures, particularly in sectors like agriculture, garments, and tourism. Moreover, Indian MSMEs lag behind their counterparts in other countries in terms of skills. Relying on informal workers with limited technical expertise often hampers productivity and compels smaller enterprises to focus on low-skilled jobs, impeding long-term growth prospects (Agasty et al., 2023).

Absence of Professionalism

A notable number of Indian MSMEs lack professionalism, leaving them vulnerable to corruption and abuses of power. This significantly impacts their business productivity and overall growth trajectory (Agasty et al., 2023).

Lack of Standardized Policies

India currently lacks uniform policies specifically tailored to the MSME sector, resulting in inconsistent development initiatives and entrepreneurship promotion programs. While commendable progress has been made in Delhi, a nationwide concerted effort is imperative for Indian enterprises to effectively compete on a global scale ((Fatima & Akhtar, 2023).

Opportunities for MSMEs in India

In the past two years, the pandemic has presented a multitude of challenges while also offering opportunities for adaptation, growth, and resilience. MSMEs have shown remarkable adaptability by shedding old practices, embracing emerging trends, and integrating cutting-edge technologies. They are increasingly recognizing the transformative potential of digitization and branding, paving the way for new avenues of business development (Gaikwad & Dhokare, 2020).

Prime Minister Narendra Modi, marking the 75th anniversary of India's independence, articulated that the 'Amrit Kaal' signifies the trajectory of the new India for the next 25 years. This period is envisioned as one of national advancement, prosperity, and a time when India will assume a pivotal role in guiding the global course. The Prime Minister emphasized that this heralds only the initial stages of a golden era, highlighting the pivotal role that MSMEs are set to play in propelling India towards its ambition of becoming a $5 trillion economy. As we step into 2023, it is anticipated to be a fruitful year for MSMEs, with the potential to leverage specific trends to catapult their businesses to new heights. Few of the opportunities for MSMEs would be

1. Continued Embrace of Digitalization The integration of digital technologies to reshape existing business models, known as digitalization, presents lucrative opportunities for revenue generation and value creation. The COVID-19 pandemic catalyzed a notable shift in the MSME sector from traditional practices towards digital platforms. CRISIL reports that 53% of SMEs and 47% of micro-enterprises in India adopted digital sales platforms, marking a significant increase from the pre-pandemic figure of 29% (www.kinaracapital. com accessed on 5/8/2023) In 2023, this momentum is poised to persist, as businesses are anticipated to further adopt digital models, aligning with the Government's Digital India initiative. Sectors such as Textiles and Gems & Jewellery are at the forefront of this "digital shift (www.niti.gov.in accessed on 8/9/2023)." A survey by the Endurance International Group reveals that 50% of businesses in these sectors have incorporated technologies like WhatsApp and Video Conferencing tools into their daily operations. Platforms like MSME Global Mart exemplify this transformation, enabling small businesses to engage in global e-commerce, fostering growth, innovation, and economic prosperity. However, many MSMEs remain underutilized and lack proficiency in leveraging technology for optimal results (Singh, et al., 2023). Therefore, providing education in marketing and technology can be immensely beneficial for these enterprises. Consequently, MSMEs are intensifying their adoption of digital technologies to remain competitive and expand their reach to a broader customer base, aligning with the evolving landscape.

2. Formalization of MSMEs Formalization, the process of legally registering businesses, grants previously unrecognized or uncategorized MSMEs access to crucial resources such as government schemes, business credits, and tax benefits. This initiative has empowered many MSME owners to elevate their businesses to new heights. Despite these advantages, an estimated 99.7% of MSMEs in India still operate informally, largely unaware of the potential benefits. To address this, the Ministry of MSME and the Government of India have embarked on an initiative to formalize MSMEs, set to gain traction in 2023. The 'Udyam Registration' portal has been instrumental in this formalization process, with over 1.31 crore MSMEs registered by January 3rd, 2023, and approximately 20,000 new registrations daily. Anticipated to reach 5 crore registrations in 2023, this initiative will open doors to formal and accessible credit for registered MSMEs. This concerted effort, coupled with policy interventions, positions the MSME sector to potentially become the largest

employment generator by 2035 (www.udyamregistration.gov.in accessed on 9/10/2023).

3. Augmented Export Activity India's trade and external sector significantly impact GDP growth and per capita income. Small production units, particularly in MSMEs, play a pivotal role in sectors such as agriculture, textiles, and food processing. India's industrial exports are projected to surpass $1 trillion by 2028, underpinning the country's status as the world's fastest-growing major economy. Increased exports present substantial growth opportunities for MSMEs, with these enterprises traditionally contributing nearly 50% of India's export volume. By expanding export activities, India can create more jobs and opportunities for both semi-skilled and unskilled workers, further bolstering economic prosperity (Gupta & Agarwal, 2023).

4. Diminishing Import Dependency In 2023 and beyond, the Government's emphasis on the "Make in India" initiative aims to curtail imports and foster domestic production. By reducing reliance on foreign imports, MSMEs can play a pivotal role in achieving this goal. Initiatives under the Atmanirbhar Bharat scheme and Raising and Accelerating MSME Performance (RAMP) scheme aim to strengthen India's MSME sector, fostering self-sufficiency in raw materials and reducing dependence on imports. These schemes, when effectively implemented, are poised to elevate India's micro and small entrepreneurship ecosystem to new heights.

5. Surge in Domestic Consumer Demand Consumer demand, driven by purchasing power, is a key determinant of economic growth. In 2023, India is poised to experience a substantial rise in consumer spending, reflecting increased household buying power. This presents a significant opportunity for MSMEs to capitalize on a thriving domestic market. Various sectors, including appliances, consumer electronics, automotive, and food processing, are projected to experience heightened consumer demand, offering a favorable landscape for MSMEs to flourish and expand.

In conclusion, 2023 holds immense promise for the MSME sector in India, which remains a dynamic force in the country's economy. The Government's concerted efforts to create an enabling ecosystem and the industry's adaptability to technological advancements and changing consumer demands are key factors driving this growth. As MSMEs navigate through challenges, such as competition and economic fluctuations, they are leveraging emerging technologies to carve out a distinct identity in the market.

The Ministry of MSME plays a pivotal role in fostering progress, advocating for formalization, and providing essential support to both existing and budding enterprises. Through various schemes and initiatives, MSMEs have access to financial assistance, technological upgrades, infrastructure development, skill enhancement, and market facilitation. This support is critical, especially in the face of escalating technology adoption and raw material costs, which necessitate increased investment in businesses.

Securing adequate capital is fundamental to business development, and seeking a business loan can be instrumental in meeting immediate or planned expenses. Kinara Capital, a leading last-mile lending fintech in India, offers collateral-free business loans with doorstep service and the option to communicate in local languages. Thousands of MSMEs have benefitted from Kinara Capital's streamlined loan application process, often receiving funds within 24 hours. The myKinara App offers a user-friendly way for MSMEs to check their eligibility in just one minute, while a Missed Call to 080-68264454 connects them directly with a Kinara Capital representative. As we step into 2023, the MSME sector is poised for growth, transformation, and continued contributions to India's economic landscape.

MSMEs and Startups: A Symbiotic Relationship

The symbiotic relationship between MSMEs (Micro, Small, and Medium Enterprises) and startups in India is increasingly evident in the current economic landscape. Startups, known for their innovation and agility, are finding valuable partners in established MSMEs, which bring experience, networks, and market presence. Likewise, MSMEs are recognizing the potential for growth and transformation by collaborating with startups, which offer fresh perspectives, cutting-edge technologies, and disruptive business models (Ahmad & Patra, 2023). Startups are leveraging the expertise and market reach of MSMEs to scale their operations swiftly. MSMEs provide startups with a platform to test and refine their products or services in a real-world setting. Additionally, startups benefit from the established customer base, distribution channels, and industry insights that MSMEs bring to the table. This symbiotic relationship allows startups to accelerate their growth trajectories and gain credibility in the market.

Conversely, startups inject innovation and technological advancements into MSMEs, propelling them into the digital era. Startups are adept at leveraging emerging technologies such as AI, IoT, and blockchain, which can revolutionize the operations and offerings of traditional MSMEs. This infusion of technology not only enhances the efficiency and productivity of MSMEs but also enables them to stay competitive in an ever-evolving market. Moreover, startups often operate with leaner structures and a culture of adaptability, which can be a refreshing change for MSMEs looking to infuse a spirit of innovation into their operations. By collaborating with startups, MSMEs can tap into a reservoir of creativity and out-of-the-box thinking, leading to the development of novel products or services and the exploration of new markets (Gaikwad & Dhokare, 2020).

In the current scenario, government initiatives and policies are also fostering this symbiotic relationship. Programs like the "Make in India" and "Digital India" campaigns are creating an enabling environment for both startups and MSMEs to collaborate and thrive. Financial incentives, mentorship programs, and incubation centres are further facilitating partnerships between the two sectors.

In conclusion, the symbiotic relationship between MSMEs and startups in India is poised for significant growth and evolution. As they continue to collaborate and leverage each other's strengths, they contribute not only to their individual success but also to the overall economic development of the country. This synergy is a testament to the dynamic and innovative spirit of the Indian business landscape.

Financial Sector's Evolution

The financial sector has embraced technology through fintech innovations, enhancing access to banking, payment systems, and investment avenues. Peer-to-peer lending, digital wallets, and blockchain-based solutions have redefined customer experiences. However, the challenge lies in ensuring cybersecurity and data privacy in this digital age.

The financial sector in India is undergoing significant evolution as a result of the growth of MSMEs (Micro, Small, and Medium Enterprises) and startups. This transformation is reshaping the way financial institutions operate, innovate, and cater to the diverse needs of these dynamic segments of the economy.

1. **Tailored Financial Products and Services:** To cater to the unique financial requirements of MSMEs and startups, financial institutions are developing specialized products and services. These offerings include tailored lending solutions, working capital loans, venture debt, and customized investment options. This trend is driving innovation in financial product design and delivery.

2. **Digital Transformation and Fintech Integration:** The growth of MSMEs and startups has accelerated the adoption of digital technologies in the financial sector. Fintech companies are playing a crucial role in providing innovative solutions for payments, lending, insurance, and wealth management. This digital transformation is enhancing accessibility, efficiency, and convenience for both businesses and consumers.

3. **Alternative Lending Platforms:** The emergence of peer-to-peer lending platforms and alternative lending models is providing new avenues for MSMEs

and startups to access capital. These platforms facilitate direct lending between individuals or businesses, reducing dependency on traditional banking channels.

4. **Risk Assessment and Credit Scoring:** With the proliferation of data analytics and artificial intelligence, financial institutions are leveraging advanced algorithms to assess creditworthiness. This enables quicker and more accurate decision-making in lending, benefitting MSMEs and startups seeking timely access to capital.

5. **Venture Capital and Angel Investing:** The growth of startups has led to an expansion of the venture capital and angel investing ecosystem. This influx of investment capital is fuelling innovation and growth in the startup sector, providing them with the necessary resources to scale and expand their operations.

6. **Regulatory Reforms and Policy Initiatives:** Regulators and policymakers are recognizing the importance of MSMEs and startups in driving economic growth and job creation. As a result, they are introducing reforms and policies to support these sectors. Initiatives like simplifying compliance procedures, providing financial incentives, and creating dedicated startup hubs are becoming more prevalent.

7. **Collaboration and Ecosystem Building:** Financial institutions are increasingly engaging in partnerships and collaborations with MSMEs and startups. This includes co-lending arrangements, mentorship programs, and co-creation of innovative solutions. These collaborations strengthen the overall business ecosystem and foster mutual growth.

8. **Focus on Financial Inclusion:** The growth of MSMEs and startups has highlighted the importance of financial inclusion. Efforts are being made to expand access to financial services to underserved and unbanked segments, ensuring that they too can participate in the economic growth story (Hoang & Bui, 2023).

In summary, the evolution of the financial sector in India is closely intertwined with the growth of MSMEs and startups. This symbiotic relationship is driving innovation, fostering entrepreneurship, and contributing to the overall dynamism of the Indian economy. As these sectors continue to thrive, the financial landscape will continue to adapt and innovate to meet their evolving needs.

Insurance Sector's Transformation

The Indian insurance sector has embraced digital platforms for sales, claims processing, and customer engagement. Insurtech collaborations have allowed for personalized products and data-driven risk assessment. The pandemic highlighted the importance of health and life coverage, leading to a surge in demand for innovative insurance solutions. The insurance sector in India is experiencing substantial growth in tandem with the expansion of startups and MSMEs (Micro, Small, and Medium Enterprises). This growth is driven by various factors, including the increasing awareness of risk management, regulatory changes, and the evolving needs of businesses in a dynamic economic environment. Insurance companies are adapting to this trend by introducing specialized products, leveraging technology, and expanding their reach to cater to the specific requirements of startups and MSMEs (Hoang & Bui, 2023; Ahmad & Patra, 2023).)..

1. **Tailored Insurance Products:** Insurance companies are developing specialized policies to address the unique risks faced by startups and MSMEs. These products cover areas such as business interruption, cyber liability, product liability, and directors and officers (D&O) insurance. This customization ensures that businesses receive comprehensive coverage that aligns with their specific operations and potential vulnerabilities.

2. **Incubator and Accelerator Programs**: Some insurance companies are actively engaging with startups through incubator and accelerator programs. These initiatives provide startups with access to mentorship, networking opportunities, and funding, in addition to tailored insurance solutions. By nurturing startups in their early stages, insurance companies are fostering long-term partnerships.

3. **Tech-Driven Solutions:** Insurance companies are leveraging technology to streamline processes and enhance customer experiences. Digital platforms and mobile applications are being used for policy issuance, claims processing, and risk assessment. This digitization not only improves efficiency but also provides businesses with real-time access to their insurance information.

4. **Risk Assessment and Data Analytics:** Advanced data analytics tools enable insurance companies to assess risks more accurately. This is particularly beneficial for startups and MSMEs, as it allows insurers to offer competitive premiums based on a detailed understanding of the business's risk profile. Data-driven insights also help businesses identify areas where risk mitigation measures can be implemented.

5. **Partnerships with Insurtech Startups:** Some insurance companies are collaborating with insurtech startups to leverage their innovative technologies and business models. These partnerships lead to the development of cutting-edge solutions, such as on-demand insurance, parametric insurance, and blockchain-based platforms. This collaboration enhances the range of offerings available to startups and MSMEs.

6. **Educational Initiatives:** Insurance companies are conducting workshops, seminars, and webinars to educate startups and MSMEs about the importance of risk management and insurance coverage. These initiatives aim to raise

awareness about the various insurance options available and help businesses make informed decisions about their coverage needs.

7. **Customized Claims Handling:** Insurance companies are adopting more flexible and responsive claims handling processes. This ensures that in the event of a covered loss, startups and MSMEs can receive timely and fair compensation, allowing them to recover and resume operations as quickly as possible.

8. **Expansion of Distribution Channels:** Insurance companies are diversifying their distribution channels to reach startups and MSMEs more effectively. This includes partnerships with industry associations, brokers, online platforms, and digital marketplaces. These efforts expand the accessibility of insurance products to a wider audience (Randive et al., 2023).

There are several real-life examples of Indian insurance companies adapting to the needs of startups and MSMEs:

One prominent example is **Reliance General Insurance**, which has introduced specialized insurance products tailored for startups. They offer policies that cover a range of risks faced by startups, including cyber liability, office protection, and errors and omissions insurance. These policies are designed to provide comprehensive coverage specifically catered to the unique challenges faced by emerging businesses.

Another example is **Bajaj Allianz General Insurance**, which has implemented digital solutions to streamline the insurance process for MSMEs. Their platform offers quick and easy policy issuance, claims processing, and risk assessment through digital channels. This tech-driven approach enhances efficiency and accessibility for businesses seeking insurance coverage (www.bajajallianz.com accessed on 30/10/2023).

Additionally, HDFC Ergo General **Insurance** has partnered with various industry associations and platforms to expand their reach to startups and MSMEs. By collaborating with organizations that have a strong presence in these sectors, HDFC Ergo is able to offer their insurance products through trusted channels, making it more convenient for businesses to access the coverage they need (www.hdfcergo. com accessed on 3/11/2023).

These examples illustrate how Indian insurance companies are proactively adapting their offerings and approaches to cater to the specific requirements of startups and MSMEs. By developing specialized products, leveraging technology, and forming strategic partnerships, these insurers are playing a crucial role in supporting the growth and resilience of small and emerging businesses in India.

In conclusion, the insurance sector in India is actively evolving to meet the specific needs of startups and MSMEs. By offering tailored products, leveraging technology, and engaging in strategic partnerships, insurance companies are contributing to the growth and sustainability of these vital segments of the economy. This collaborative approach ensures that startups and MSMEs have the necessary risk management tools to navigate the challenges and uncertainties of the business landscape.

Symbiotic Relationship

Start-ups and MSMEs rely on the financial sector for funding and expertise, while the financial sector benefits from diversifying its portfolio through investment in these dynamic entities. Similarly, the insurance sector's growth is closely tied to the economic vibrancy of the start-up and MSME ecosystem. The relationship between startups, MSMEs, the financial sector, and the Indian insurance sector is intricately connected and plays a vital role in driving the Indian economy forward. Here's a comprehensive overview of how these elements interact and contribute to economic growth (Ghosh et al., 2021; Audretsch et al., 2020):

Startups and MSMEs as Economic Engines

Startups and MSMEs are dynamic drivers of economic activity in India. They contribute significantly to GDP, create employment opportunities, and foster innovation. Their agility, adaptability, and potential for high growth make them key players in economic development (Sharma & Ritu, 2023).

Financial Sector as Enabler

The financial sector, comprising banks, non-banking financial companies (NBFCs), and other financial institutions, plays a crucial role in providing the necessary capital and financial services to startups and MSMEs. Access to finance is essential for these businesses to innovate, expand operations, and remain competitive.

Role of the Insurance Sector

The insurance sector acts as a risk mitigator for startups and MSMEs. It provides a safety net against unforeseen events or disruptions that could potentially derail their operations. Tailored insurance products designed for specific industries and risks offer businesses the confidence to innovate and invest.

Mitigating Risk and Fostering Growth

Startups and MSMEs inherently face higher levels of risk due to their size and stage of development. Insurance coverage enables them to take calculated risks knowing that they have a safety net in place. This encourages innovation and experimentation, which are critical drivers of economic growth.

Financial Inclusion and Accessibility

The financial sector, including insurance companies, is working towards greater financial inclusion by expanding access to credit and insurance products for startups and MSMEs. This ensures that even businesses in underserved regions or those lacking extensive collateral can participate in the economy.

Innovation in Insurance Products

The growth of startups and MSMEs has spurred innovation in the insurance sector. Insurers are developing specialized products that address the unique risks faced by businesses in emerging industries. This innovation not only supports the growth of startups but also fuels competition and product diversification in the insurance market.

Job Creation and Economic Stability

Startups and MSMEs are significant contributors to job creation, especially in labor-intensive sectors. By providing insurance coverage, businesses can attract and retain talent, knowing that their employees have access to benefits and financial security. This contributes to economic stability and social well-being.

Economic Resilience and Recovery

During periods of economic volatility or unforeseen events (such as the COVID-19 pandemic), startups and MSMEs faced unique challenges. The insurance sector played a crucial role in helping businesses navigate these disruptions by providing coverage for business interruptions, losses, and other contingencies.

In essence, startups, MSMEs, the financial sector, and the insurance sector form an integrated ecosystem that propels economic growth in India. This interdependence fosters innovation, supports job creation, and enhances the overall resilience of the Indian economy in the face of challenges and uncertainties. The collaborative efforts of these sectors are pivotal in shaping a vibrant and sustainable economic future for the country.

Implications of Study and Future Scope

The research paper is a comprehensive study of the interplay between start-ups, MSMEs, and the financial and insurance sectors in India during the dynamic period of 2022-23. Such a study has several **potential implications** and could contribute to shaping the future of these sectors in multiple ways:

Informed Decision-Making

Policymakers, government bodies, and industry stakeholders can use the insights provided in the study to make informed decisions. Understanding the challenges and opportunities in these sectors can aid in crafting policies that foster growth, innovation, and sustainability.

Strategic Planning for Businesses

Start-ups and MSMEs can benefit from the study by gaining a deeper understanding of the current economic landscape and the potential future scenarios. This knowledge can inform their strategic planning, helping them navigate challenges and capitalize on opportunities.

Investment and Funding Decisions

Investors and financial institutions may use the research findings to assess the risk and potential returns associated with investing in start-ups and MSMEs in the Indian market. This can guide investment decisions and influence the allocation of funds.

Educational and Research Initiatives

The study can serve as a valuable resource for academic institutions, researchers, and students interested in understanding the complex dynamics of the Indian economic ecosystem. It may inspire further research and educational initiatives focused on sustainable development.

International Perspective

The research may attract attention from the international community, providing a nuanced perspective on India's economic landscape. It could be used for comparative analyses with other countries and contribute to global discussions on economic development.

Industry Collaboration and Innovation

The study could facilitate collaboration between different sectors. For example, insights into the symbiotic relationship between start-ups, MSMEs, and the financial sector may encourage collaborative efforts to foster innovation and create a more supportive ecosystem.

Policy Advocacy

The findings can be used for advocacy purposes, encouraging the development of policies that support the growth of start-ups and MSMEs. This could include recommendations for regulatory frameworks, incentives, and support mechanisms.

Skill Development Initiatives

Understanding the challenges faced by start-ups and MSMEs can inform skill development initiatives. Tailoring education and training programs to address specific needs identified in the study can contribute to building a more skilled and adaptive workforce (Sindhwani et al., 2023).

In summary, the implications of this type of study are broad and far-reaching, potentially influencing various aspects of policymaking, business strategies, investments, education, and international perceptions of India's economic landscape. The study's value lies not only in its analysis of the current scenario but also in its forward-looking perspective, providing a roadmap for sustainable development in the identified sectors.

CONCLUSION

The new doors of opportunities and challenges in the realms of start-ups, MSMEs, the Indian financial sector, and the insurance sector reflect a multifaceted transformation underway. As technology continues to disrupt traditional models, collaboration and adaptability emerge as the key factors for success. While innovation drives growth, regulatory frameworks need to evolve in tandem. The journey ahead will require a delicate balance between harnessing opportunities and managing risks, shaping a resilient and prosperous landscape for all stakeholders involved. In conclusion, the dynamic evolution of start-ups, MSMEs, the Indian financial sector, and the insurance industry signifies a critical juncture in India's economic journey. This transformative phase has driven by rapid technological advancement, calls for a harmonious blend of innovation, adaptable regulatory frameworks, and collaborative efforts. As businesses navigate this changing landscape, the insurance sector stands as a pillar of support, mitigating risks and enabling calculated experimentation. Striking the right balance between seizing opportunities and managing challenges will be pivotal in shaping a resilient and prosperous economic landscape for all stakeholders. By embracing this transformation with foresight and agility, India is poised to usher in an era of inclusive growth, job creation, and economic prosperity for the entire nation.

REFERENCES

Agasty, S., Tarannum, F., & Narula, S. A. (2023). Sustainability innovation index for micro, small and medium enterprises and their support ecosystems based on an empirical study in India. *Journal of Cleaner Production, 415*, 137793. doi:10.1016/j.jclepro.2023.137793

Ahmad, F., & Patra, M. R. (2023). Role of MSME in Entrepreneurship Development, *Entrepreneurship In India – Issues And Challenges: 1(1)*, 108.

Alawamleh, M., Francis, Y. H., & Alawamleh, K. J. (2023). Entrepreneurship challenges: The case of Jordanian start-ups. *Journal of Innovation and Entrepreneurship, 12*(1), 1–14. doi:10.118613731-023-00286-z PMID:37034301

Allioui, H., & Mourdi, Y. (2023). Exploring the Full Potentials of IoT for Better Financial Growth and Stability: A Comprehensive Survey. *Sensors (Basel), 23*(19), 8015. doi:10.339023198015 PMID:37836845

Audretsch, D., Colombelli, A., Grilli, L., Minola, T., & Rasmussen, E. (2020). Innovative start-ups and policy initiatives. *Research Policy, 49*(10), 104027. doi:10.1016/j.respol.2020.104027

Bikse, V., Lusena–Ezera, I., & Rivza, B. (2018). Innovative start-ups: Challenges and development opportunities in Latvia. *International Journal of Innovation Science, 10*(2), 261–273. doi:10.1108/IJIS-05-2017-0044

Brown, R., Mawson, S., Lee, N., & Peterson, L. (2019). Start-up factories, transnational entrepreneurs and entrepreneurial ecosystems: Unpacking the lure of start-up accelerator programmes. *European Planning Studies, 27*(5), 885–904. doi:10.1080/09654313.2019.1588858

Farayola, O. A., Abdul, A. A., Irabor, B. O., & Okeleke, E. C. (2023). INNOVATIVE BUSINESS MODELS DRIVEN BY AI TECHNOLOGIES: A REVIEW. *Computer Science & IT Research Journal, 4*(2), 85–110. doi:10.51594/csitrj.v4i2.608

Fatima, M., & Akhtar, S. J. (2023). An overview of micro, small and medium enterprises (MSMES) in the state of Uttar Pradesh. [JEBR]. *EPRA International Journal of Economic and Business Review*, *11*(1), 1–10. doi:10.36713/epra12155

Gaikwad, A., & Dhokare, C. S. (2020). India: A Growth opportunities for MSME. *International Journal of Multidisciplinary Research*, *6*(6), 25–30.

Geeta, S. D. T., Mathiraj, S. P., Shanthini, S., Jayanthi, K., & Vidhya, A. A. (2023, November). Issues and challenges faced by micro, small and medium enterprises after goods and services tax implementation. In AIP Conference Proceedings (Vol. 2821, No. 1). AIP Publishing. doi:10.1063/5.0158580

Ghosh, D., Mehta, P., & Avittathur, B. (2021). Supply chain capabilities and competitiveness of high-tech manufacturing start-ups in India. *Benchmarking*, *28*(5), 1783–1808. doi:10.1108/BIJ-12-2018-0437

Guckenbiehl, P., & Corral de Zubielqui, G. (2022). Start-ups' business model changes during the COVID-19 pandemic: Counteracting adversities and pursuing opportunities. *International Small Business Journal*, *40*(2), 150–177. doi:10.1177/02662426211055447 PMID:35250144

Gupta, U., & Agarwal, B. (2023). The role of digital financial services on Indian MSMEs. *Indian Journal of Finance, 17*(2), 08-26.

Hoang, T. G., & Bui, M. L. (2023). Business intelligence and analytic (BIA) stage-of-practice in micro-, small-and medium-sized enterprises (MSMEs). *Journal of Enterprise Information Management*, *36*(4), 1080–1104. doi:10.1108/JEIM-01-2022-0037

Hurley, C. O. (2018). MSME competitiveness in small island economies: A comparative systematic review of the literature from the past 24 years. *Entrepreneurship and Regional Development*, *30*(9-10), 1027–1068. doi:10.1080/08985626.2018.1515822

Kamboj, N., Choudhary, V., & Trivedi, S. (2023). 5 Impact of Macroeconomic Determinants and Corporate Attributes on Firms' Financial Success in India. *Sustainability, Green Management, and Performance of SMEs*, 73.

Priyanka, R., Ravindran, K., Sankaranarayanan, B., & Ali, S. M. (2023). A fuzzy DEMATEL decision modeling framework for identifying key human resources challenges in start-up companies: Implications for sustainable development. *Decision Analytics Journal*, *6*, 100192. doi:10.1016/j.dajour.2023.100192

Purbasari, R., Muttaqin, Z., & Sari, D. S. (2021). Identification of actors and factors in the digital entrepreneurial ecosystem: The case of digital platform-based MSMEs in Indonesia. *Review of Integrative Business and Economics Research*, *10*, 164–187.

Randive, A., Vispute, J., & Goswami, S. (2023). A Study of Perspectives on the Growth, Strategy and Branding in Indian MSMEs. In Indian SMEs and Start-Ups: Growth through Innovation and Leadership (pp. 227-253).

Sharma, A., & Ritu, N. R. (2023). Role of Government Schemes in Supporting Startups in India: A Quantitative Investigation. [EEL]. *European Economic Letters*, *13*(1), 276–280.

Sindhwani, R., Hasteer, N., Behl, A., Varshney, A., & Sharma, A. (2023). Exploring "what," "why" and "how" of resilience in MSME sector: A m-TISM approach. *Benchmarking*, *30*(6), 1884–1911. doi:10.1108/BIJ-11-2021-0682

Singh, S., Chamola, P., Kumar, V., Verma, P., & Makkar, N. (2023). Explaining the revival strategies of Indian MSMEs to mitigate the effects of COVID-19 outbreak. *Benchmarking*, *30*(1), 121–148. doi:10.1108/BIJ-08-2021-0497

Surie, G. (2017). Creating the innovation ecosystem for renewable energy via social entrepreneurship: Insights from India. *Technological Forecasting and Social Change*, *121*, 184–195. doi:10.1016/j.techfore.2017.03.006

Trautwein, C. (2021). Sustainability impact assessment of start-ups–Key insights on relevant assessment challenges and approaches based on an inclusive, systematic literature review. *Journal of Cleaner Production*, *281*, 125330. doi:10.1016/j.jclepro.2020.125330

Wahyuddin, W., Marzuki, M., Khaddafi, M., Ilham, R. N., & Sinta, I. (2022). A Study of Micro, Small and Medium Enterprises (MSMEs) during Covid-19 Pandemic: An Evidence using Economic Value-Added Method. *Journal of Madani Society*, *1*(1), 1–7. doi:10.56225/jmsc.v1i1.123

ENDNOTES

1. https://pib.gov.in/PressReleaseIframePage.aspx?PRID=1913977
2. https://udyamregistration.gov.in/
3. https://www.bajajallianz.com/blog/announcements/digital-care-for-you-in-the-digital-age.html
4. https://www.hdfcergo.com/
5. https://www.investindia.gov.in/indian-unicorn-landscape

6.   https://www.meity.gov.in/writereaddata/files/india_trillion-dollar_digital_ opportunity.pdf

7.   https://kinaracapital.com/5-key-trends-and-developments-that-msmes-cannot-ignore-in-2023/

8.   https://www.niti.gov.in/sites/default/files/2023-03/Three-Year-Action-Agenda-2017-19.pdf

Chapter 15

Recharging Creativity:
Embracing Digital Detox for Entrepreneurial Excellence

Jaskiran Kaur
iD https://orcid.org/0000-0002-4452-1807
Lovely Professional University, India

Amit Dutt
Lovely Professional University, India

Pretty Bhalla
Lovely Professional University, India

Vishal Kumar Poddar
Lovely Professional University, India

Varun Kumra
Lovely Professional University, India

ABSTRACT

Over the last few decades, it has become nearly impossible to imagine a workspace without highly integrated technology. Ever since cell phones entered the scene, co-workers have been able to collaborate on projects, no matter where in the world they are. Digital meeting spaces have allowed companies to stay connected across countries and even continents. Although these advancements have improved productivity and connectivity, it may be time for a step back. Since the global pandemic took over the world, working from home has been the norm. In a bid to keep operations moving and businesses flourishing, companies are doing everything in their captivity to make remote working as feasible as possible. Implementing digital detox strategies, such as setting boundaries on technology usage and promoting mindfulness practices, can empower entrepreneurs to maintain a healthier work-life balance and make more informed business decisions. This abstract explores meaning, importance, impact, and strategies of digital detoxification to mitigate the negative impacts of excessive digital engagement.

DOI: 10.4018/979-8-3693-1107-3.ch015

1. INTRODUCTION

"Do you frequently catch yourself scrolling aimlessly on your smartphone screen as hours pass by? It's not just you. According to research, 61% of adults admit to being dependent on the internet and their electronic devices. Even worse, having a continual connection might degrade your quality of life and overstimulate your senses. It may thus be beneficial for both your mental and physical health to take a vacation from your various social media applications and spend some time away from screens. A digital detox can help with that. You deliberately cut back on the amount of time you spend online on your gadgets during this time. Even choosing to entirely unplug is an option. Smartphones are widely used today. We use our cellphones for around three hours each day on average (Markowetz, 2015). Smartphones, in contrast to other electronic devices, allow the use of such functions essentially whenever and wherever, with countless implications for our everyday life.

Smartphones provide advantages, including the ability to stay in touch with friends at all times, enjoy engaging leisure activities, have access to an inexhaustible supply of information online, and have favourable effects on knowledge exchange (Lepp et al., 2013; Omar et al., 2016). On the other hand, using a smartphone can have a negative impact on wellbeing, a development that has drawn a lot of attention from the general public and academics. For instance, studies have demonstrated that smartphone use has an impact on social connections, performance, and health and well-being. According to research on health-related issues, smartphone usage is linked to greater rates of depression and anxiety (Lepp et al., 2014), trouble sleeping (Thomée, 2018), and musculoskeletal issues in cases of smartphone misuse (Nal et al., 2015). Additionally, a large body of empirical evidence suggests a negative relationship between smartphone usage and academic achievement (Amez & Baert, 2020), which is consistent with findings indicating excessive smartphone use is linked to reduced engagement and productivity at work (e.g., Duke & Montag, 2017). Additionally, when people focus on their personal cellphones during social encounters (a practise known as phubbing; McDaniel & Radesky, 2018; Nuez et al., 2020), it lowers the quality of conversations and raises negative affect or tension.

Smartphone users are worried about their personal smartphone usage, even if some of the negative correlations between using digital technology and health and well-being are slight (Dienlin & Johannes, 2020; Orben & Przybylski, 2019a; Orben & Przybylski, 2019b). For instance, studies have shown that smartphone users write blogs about the need to take breaks from their devices (Jorge, 2019; Kuntsman & Miyake, 2016), or even look for tips on how to better manage their online time, such as with the aid of apps like iOS Screen Time, Android Digital Well-Being, Moment, Forest, Quality Time, Detox, Space, or OffTime. Additionally, organisations have planned a yearly National (and Global) Day of Unplugging that has been observed for a number of years and has a large following (National Day of Unplugging, n.d.). Therefore, it is not unexpected that the media portrays switching off from cellphones as a hip approach to lessen its adverse effects on health-related results. Many different venues, including social media, websites, and books with titles like 24/6: The value of unplugging one day a week (Price, 2018; Shlain, 2019; Syvertsen, 2017), provide self-help advice. These messages' concerns are reflective of broader worries about smartphone use, and suggestions are made on how to rebalance one's life by cutting back on smartphone use (Syvertsen, 2017). Similar to this, travel agencies advertise "mobile free" vacations and so-called digital detox camps or centres. All of them try to aid individuals in escaping regular digital connectivity. Such celebrations and activities are particularly popular in Asia (Collier, 2009; Dickinson et al., 2016; Syvertsen, 2017).

1.1 Digital Detox Definition

When it comes to not using electronic gadgets, both the general population and the scientific community utilise several words. Common phrases include abstinence, break, disconnect, detox, timeout, or unplugging (Brown & Kuss, 2020; Fioravanti et al., 2019). The crucial feature these phrases have is that they all refer to a time when using digital devices, such as tablets, is prohibited. In our evaluation, we referred to all of these concepts collectively as "digital detox." 2012 saw the first mention of the phrase (Felix & Dean, 2012). A "period of time during which a person refrains from using their electronic devices, such as smartphones, regarded as an opportunity to reduce stress or focus on social interaction in the physical world" is referred to as a "digital detox" (Oxford Dictionaries, 2019). According to this description, a digital detox involves fasting-like brief abstention from electronic gadgets in order to purify oneself. As a result, digital detox is different from detoxification therapies that encourage long-term abstinence from alcohol or illegal substances (Syvertsen & Enli, 2019). This term also emphasises a distinction when contrasted to TV abstinence, which was promoted in the 1990s and early 2000s. While giving up TV was encouraged owing to unfavourable assessments of the medium and its content, digital detox emphasises an attempt to increase awareness of excessive usage and strengthen self-optimization to minimise stress (Syvertsen & Enli, 2019). Regarding the following factors, the concept of digital detox (Oxford Dictionaries, 2019) is still ambiguous. No inference can be made as to whether (a) a person can take a timeout from only one device (for example, the smartphone) or whether, in accordance with the definition, all devices may no longer be used, (b) it entails only intentionally avoiding using digital devices or whether it also includes involuntary, forced abstinence, (c) avoiding any specific content is relevant, or (d) digital detox refers to a complete timeout from electronic devices only. So, we recommend broadening the definition.

According to the hierarchical computer-mediated communication taxonomy (Meier & Reinecke, 2020), the term "digital detox" should be expanded to include a time period during which people abstain from using (a) electronic devices and (b) specific application types (such as social media), branded media (such as unplugging from Facebook), and special features (such as disconnecting from c). Meier and Reinecke (2020) state that the six levels' distinctions are more than pertinent for systematically capturing all the many facets of using electronic media. We secondly propose that digital detox comprises both breaks from just one gadget and from all digital devices based on this taxonomy. Thirdly, we define digital detox as a voluntary and intentional limited removal of this aversive stimulus, namely digital devices and/or specific subsets of smartphone use, to encourage health behaviour change. This definition is consistent with the taxonomy of behaviour change techniques (BCTs; BCT 7.5) from Michie et al. Given that research has demonstrated that people's intents and motives are crucial for effective health behaviour change (e.g., Hardcastle et al., 2015; Miller & Rollnick, 2013; Vitinius et al., 2018), we presume it is vital to add the phrases voluntary and purposeful."

1.2 Why Do You Need a Digital Detox?

According to one research, 25% of smartphone owners between the ages of 18 and 44 can't recall the last time their phone wasn't in their immediate vicinity.

All that time online can cause:

- Self-image problems
- Low self-esteem
- Sleep problems
- Depression
- Anxiety
- Weight gain
- Unhealthy eating
- Lack of exercise
- Lack of time management
- Work ethic problems

2. LITERATURE REVIEW

Although people can't always completely eradicate the factors that cause cognitive overload, they can learn coping mechanisms to lessen the negative effects of overload. Prolonged stress and low productivity at work can have detrimental long-term effects on individuals' psychological well-being as well as the financial health of organisations (De Jonge et al., 2012). Though mostly as buzzwords in popular-science blogs, self-help books, lifestyle websites, and social media, ideas like digital minimalism and digital detox have gained more attention recently to address cognitive overload and its possible effects (Syvertsen & Enli, 2019). They promote a particular "philosophy of technology use" that is minimalistic (Newport, 2019). These ideas' overarching notion is to intentionally disconnect from digital media by concentrating on clearly "non-digital" activities that include the real world (Syvertsen & Enli, 2019).

Numerous research streams indicate that these tactics have beneficial effects: Improving self-control, for example, turning off alerts and shutting off electronics at a set time in the evening, appears to boost both the quantity and quality of sleep, which in turn increases productivity at work the next day (Lanaj et al., 2014). The possible negative impacts of social networking sites on young people's wellbeing can also be avoided by using digital detox applications, which help users monitor and set time limits for using their smartphones (Schmuck, 2020). According to other research, limiting your response time to set times each day for emails will help you operate less stressfully (Kushlev & Dunn, 2015). When considered collectively, these results suggest that methods for digital detoxification may generally improve feelings of wellbeing.

The concept of digital detoxification has garnered significant interest in the fields of academics, popular culture, and self-help. "A process or period of time in which one abstains from or rids the body of toxic or unhealthy substances" is what the term "detox" itself describes (Oxford Languages 2021). The scientific basis for detoxification in medicine is debatable; it's more likely to be viewed as a marketing term for medical supplies (Cohen 2007). However, the efficacy of detoxification techniques is currently being examined in the context of digital media. Existing research on digital detoxification dates back to approximately (Ugur & Koc, 2015), and it is scattered over a number of academic fields, including media and communication studies (Syvertsen and Enli 2019), psychology (Schmuck 2020), and IS (Mirbabaie et al. 2020).

Figure 1. Conceptualisation of digital detox in organisations

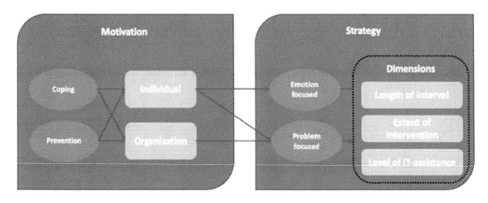

3. CONCEPTUAL FRAMEWORK

For two reasons, this idea will be helpful in future studies on digital detoxification. First off, the concept of digital detox is useful for understanding technostress and related literature because it broadens the chain of causality that is often accepted in current research, which goes from stressors, strain, and consequences to coping mechanisms and prevention tactics. Secondly, it makes it possible for further studies to grade different digital detoxification techniques. This implies that every measure may be evaluated and compared along the three dimensions, whether they are preventative or coping in nature.

4. THE BENEFITS OF A DIGITAL DETOX

- "Finding out if technology is preventing you from living your best life may be done by participating in a digital detox. Unplugging may have a variety of positive effects, from increasing job productivity to improving your connections with friends and family. Your quality of life may be improved by unplugging from your electronics or making an attempt to use them less by
- Feel relaxed and satisfied. Taking a regular vacation from using your smartphone or other electronic gadget can lessen your stress levels, according to many social research. It may also enable you to sharpen your attention to the present and your surroundings.
- Increase your output. It takes time to scroll, like, publish, or just browse the internet. It can take time away from your obligations. You'll be able to concentrate better on the tasks at hand if you put your phone away.

- Have a better self-image. You regularly compare yourself to others via social media applications. That could change the way you view yourself. Your self-image and self-esteem may improve if you reduce your phone usage.
- Become more fit. Eye strain, dry eyes, fuzzy vision, teary eyes, and headaches might result from staring at your smartphone for numerous hours. Additionally, you could slouch over when staring down at the phone or screen. Neck and lower back issues may result from this. Different portions of your body might feel better after disconnecting.
- Better sleep. Your brain produces melatonin when your body signals that it is time to sleep to promote relaxation and sleepiness. Before going to bed, looking at your phone keeps your brain busy and awake and slows the production of melatonin. Long-term sleep deprivation can have an impact on your health and happiness. • Sharper focus. A digital detox might assist your body in better controlling your sleep patterns. According to Prewitt, it's simple to become preoccupied with your electronics' constant beeps and pop-up messages and lose focus on your surroundings. You could discover that you pay more attention to your immediate surroundings while on a digital detox. Your ability to focus on your work is much improved.
- Less anxiety. Too much knowledge might be distressing for some people. Prewitt recalls numerous coworkers who had been really agitated after viewing hours of news. They felt more at ease after they stopped reading the news and started doing something else.
- Improved relationships with others. By getting rid of digital distractions, you have more chances to focus on those around you. For instance, when there aren't any electronics around at dinner, you naturally engage and bond with your family more. You may also have the opportunity to make new friends in the checkout queue if your face isn't buried in your smartphone. You're also more likely to pick up the phone to call a buddy if texting is prohibited.
- More time management. Have you ever had a strong temptation to check your phone or visit social media? It's not just you. Americans check their cellphones 96 times every day on average, and they spend almost two hours on social media. Many individuals have a reflexive, non-necessary need to check their phone or social media anytime they have a few spare minutes. You may fight obsessive usage of digital gadgets and media by taking a break from them."

5. HOW TO GET STARTED?

"It could be time for a digital detox if you believe that your use of technology is negatively affecting your physical and mental health, taking time away from tasks you need to do, or both. You don't have to completely give up using electronics; simply decide what suits your lifestyle the best. This can be putting your phone away for a few hours every now and again, determining how little you actually need to use it, or turning off your internet connection entirely for a day or longer.

In order to begin your digital detox:

- Be mindful of your feelings when using your phone. To better understand your connection with your phone, be careful of how you use it. Ask yourself why you use your phone at various times of the day.

Are you bored? Does it pertain to your job? Do you feel like you're lacking in comparison to others? Does looking at your phone improve or worsen your mood? According to experts, improving your emotional awareness might help you better manage your phone use. If it's hurting you, attempt to limit how much time you spend using it each day.

- Set aside time to unplug from your phone. Setting aside times when you won't check your phone is one technique to detox if you use your smartphone constantly and you suspect addictive behaviour. Try to check your phone, for instance, just every 15 or 30 minutes.

An easy tip to follow, according to experts, is to put your phone aside during mealtimes. You may find it easier to pay attention to your surroundings if you do this. Try to keep your phone out of sight in another room or out of easy reach if you find it difficult to put it down so you can concentrate on your meal.

- Use applications to measure your usage. You may also schedule periods when you won't use it, like as when you're out for a stroll, at a social event, or after a particular hour at night. Want to monitor your regular phone usage? There is an app for that if your phone can't do it for you. Some applications can also offer you a thorough report on what you're spending too much time on or temporarily ban your access to social networking websites. This might help you regain some control by reducing your dependency on your phone.
- Disconnect before going to bed at night. Try to disconnect or turn off your phone before going to bed if you can, or establish a time like 9 p.m. or 10 p.m. to unplug as phone use might interfere with your sleep patterns. You may establish a bedtime routine and obtain better sleep by doing this.
- Disable alerts. It would be a good idea to turn off notifications in your phone settings if you find yourself responding to every text alert, email, or ping from

your social media applications. This may lessen the need to react to every sound it produces. The do not disturb function is another option."

6. WAYS TO DO A DIGITAL DETOX (WITHOUT PULLING THE PLUG ENTIRELY)

"The majority of people won't give up technology entirely. According to Carol Vidal, MD, PhD, MPH, an associate professor of psychiatry and behavioural sciences at the Johns Hopkins University School of Medicine in Baltimore, "cutting down seems like a more realistic approach," in 2023.

Make a strategy, advises Brittany Becker, a certified mental health counsellor located in New York City and the director of the Dorm, an all-encompassing mental health treatment facility, to accomplish this. Decide which of your harmful behaviours you wish to modify after identifying them. "I think it is really helpful to get a clear picture of your tech use and review the time spent on your phone," adds Becker. "A great place to start is how that time is divided up with different applications, and then you can identify which areas to start limiting."

Here are seven tips to help you control your technology use and test out a digital detox on your own.

- Plan Screen-Free Time Throughout the Day. It's hard to ignore screens when working at a computer, so prioritising breaks is all the more crucial. To remember to take a stroll or eat lunch somewhere other than your desk, schedule a time in your calendar or set an alarm on your phone, advises Becker. Also, don't forget to put your phone away.
- Take a Break From Technology Occasionally. Breaks can lower stress, especially for heavy users, according to Vidal. She claims that additional study is necessary before explicit suggestions can be made about what digital abstinence looks like and how long it should endure. However, it can entail participating with people who are dedicated to disconnecting at occasions like those hosted by Digital Detox (a business that organises tech-free getaways) or erasing harmful applications from your phone, either permanently or temporarily.
- "If you frequently click on the Facebook app and find yourself scrolling through for long periods of time, getting rid of the app and having to use the search browser takes an extra step and gives you a chance to pause and consider whether this activity is appropriate at this time," says Becker.
- Upgrade Your Phone Less. Eliminate the distractions by switching from your smartphone to a basic mobile phone that does not support applications if you

are having problems remaining present. If at all feasible, downgrading from a smartphone may be quite beneficial, according to Boca Raton, Florida-based social professional Jennifer Kelman, LCSW. In actuality, she employs this with her own kids. They only have basic call or text functions, according to her.

- Put Your Phone Away at a Specific Hour. Try turning off the electricity before dinner and till the next morning. Users of Apple and Android devices may activate do-not-disturb settings to block calls, notifications, and alarms. Utilise the tools that are already there on your devices, advises Becker.

- Limit some apps by changing your phone's settings. Users of Apple iPhones may plan Downtime, during which only calls or particular applications are permitted and those apps have a time limit, and establish restrictions with Screen Time (located in your phone's settings). For Google devices, Digital Wellbeing functions similarly. According to a research analysis, those who didn't utilise these features were more likely to have problematic smartphone use and poorer wellbeing than those who did.

- Establish no-phone zones. It's thought that blocking particular apps doesn't always work. Instead, she advises quitting using devices altogether. You can prevent devices from disrupting your sleep by, for example, banning phones and screens from the bedroom. Additionally, if you have to use a gadget in a separate room or area of your house, it could stop you from mindlessly scrolling.

- Think about contacting a mental health professional. We all use technology continuously, so it might be challenging to determine when there is a problem or not, according to Becker. It could be time to seek professional assistance if your actions or attitudes towards technology or particular applications and websites start to interfere with how you live your life, according to Becker. It's also time to talk to someone if your self-esteem suffers or you start to experience anxiety or sadness."

7. SIGNS YOU NEED TO PUT DOWN THE DEVICES

"Wondering if you need a digital detox? If using electronic media causes you to have any of the following experiences, it's a sign that you may need to disconnect:

- Depressed mood.
- Increased irritability, frustration or anger.
- Feeling insecure.
- Loss of sleep or interrupted sleep.

- Feeling obligated to consume, respond, react or check in.

You should also be mindful of how your usage of digital media affects other aspects of your life. Prewitt advises thinking about a digital detox if you find yourself neglecting obligations at home or at work as a result of how much time you spend online. Another warning sign is if you stop wanting to interact with people in person in favour of doing it online."

8. HOW TO DO A DIGITAL DETOX?

"If you're ready to begin a digital detox, follow these steps:

1. Choose a new behaviour to adopt: First, identify the problem. Are you always logged onto your smartphone? Do the headlines make you anxious? Do you use social media for an excessive amount of time? Decide which activities you wish to cut back on or completely abandon.
2. Set objectives: Decide if you want to limit or completely stop using a certain gadget or form of media while setting a goal for yourself. Make it particular. Will it happen all day or only at particular hours? For instance, you may opt to limit your time on social media to 15 minutes each day, keep your phone away from you at night, or forgo technology on Sundays.
3. Commit the necessary amount of time: It takes time to break lifelong digital habits. Consider dedicating at least two weeks. You want to reach the sensation of having stopped the habit.
4. Obtain assistance: It's beneficial to have a spouse, relative, or close friend who can motivate you and serve as an accountability partner. Tell those who will support you about your aims. Even better, you may ask them for suggestions on how to stop your desired behaviour.
5. Evaluate your development: After a few days of beginning your digital detox, see how it's going. Avoid switching from one digital habit to another. You might want to think about giving up social media altogether, for instance, if you find that you are spending more time on Instagram since leaving Facebook.
6. Take long-term changes into account: Pay attention to the advantages and difficulties you encountered throughout the digital detox. What transpired after three hours without monitoring the news? When you weren't using Facebook or Instagram, how did you feel? Was it harder or simpler than you anticipated? After that, pick which parts of the modification you want to carry ahead. For instance, establishing a home rule prohibiting the use of digital devices during

meals with the family. Or, now that you've accomplished your first digital detox, try to change more of your digital behaviours.

Doing a digital detox is about taking charge of how you spend your time and energy and what you give your attention to. It helps you realize what you want more and less of so you can break unhelpful habits and create new, more meaningful ones."

7. MOTIVATIONS TO START DETOX

"Motivations to start a digital detox include:

- Concern about developing addictive behavior that some identify as an Internet addiction disorder
- Aiming to reduce stress and anxiety caused by the over-use of technology
- Re-focusing offline social interactions and actions
- Re-connecting with nature
- Increasing mindfulness
- Improving one's learning ability by decreasing distractions and eliminating multi-tasking"

8. DISCUSSIONS

As entrepreneurs, we understand the relentless demands of the digital world, but there comes a time when we need to pause, recharge, and reconnect with what truly matters. That's where a digital detox retreat comes in – a transformative experience that allows you to distance yourself from technology and immerse in a world of rejuvenation, focus, and personal growth.

Within the current entrepreneurial environment, when digital connectivity is frequently regarded as essential, the concept of "Recharging Creativity" by intentionally embracing "Digital Detox" becomes an intriguing and relevant topic of study. Digital device addiction has become the norm for businesses, creating a constant feeling of connectivity that ironically could hinder rather than promote creativity. Constant notifications, the need for immediate reactions, and the deluge of information can all lead to cognitive overload, which impairs an entrepreneur's capacity for creative thought. The purpose of this study article is to analyse the complex relationship between entrepreneurial creativity and digital saturation, highlighting the various effects of constant connectedness.

Examining the literature reveals that previous research has demonstrated the detrimental effects of digital overload on cognitive processes, with attention fatigue and diminished problem-solving abilities being common results. But by examining the advantages of embracing a purposeful digital detox, our research aims to move the conversation in the direction of a solution-oriented viewpoint. Disconnecting from the digital world can benefit entrepreneurs by improving their mental health, increasing their focus, and revitalising their creative ideation process. This study highlights the potential benefits of a digital detox for achieving entrepreneurial excellence through an analysis of successful case studies. It also provides practical implementation tactics. As we explore the nexus between technology, creativity, and entrepreneurship, it becomes clear that setting out deliberate time for disconnecting could be the secret to discovering a creative wellspring of unrealized potential that could eventually lead business owners to achieve previously unheard-of heights of success.

REFERENCES

Amez, S., & Baert, S. (2020). Smartphone use and academic performance: A literature review. *International Journal of Educational Research*, *103*, 101618. doi:10.1016/j.ijer.2020.101618

Bradley, T. (2022). The Future Of Work In 2022 And Beyond. *Forbes*. https://www.forbes.com/sites/tonybradley/2022/03/09/the-future-of-work-in-2022-and-beyond/

Brown, L., & Kuss, D. J. (2020). Fear of missing out, mental wellbeing, and social connectedness: A seven-day social media abstinence trial. *International Journal of Environmental Research and Public Health*, *17*(12), 4566. doi:10.3390/ijerph17124566 PMID:32599962

Cohen, M. (2007). 'Detox': Science or sales pitch? *Australian Family Physician*, *36*(12). PMID:18075624

Collier, R. (2009). *Virtual detox: Inpatient therapy for Internet addicts.*

de Jonge, J., Spoor, E., Sonnentag, S., Dormann, C., & van den Tooren, M. (2012). "Take a break?!" Off-job recovery, job demands, and job resources as predictors of health, active learning, and creativity. *European Journal of Work and Organizational Psychology*, *21*(3), 321–348. doi:10.1080/1359432X.2011.576009

Depot, M. S. (2023). The Secret to a Digital Detox for Entrepreneurs. *Smart Service*. https://www.smartservice.com/smart-service-blog/the-secret-to-a-digital-detox-for-entrepreneurs/

Dickinson, J. E., Hibbert, J. F., & Filimonau, V. (2016). Mobile technology and the tourist experience:(Dis) connection at the campsite. *Tourism Management, 57,* 193–201. doi:10.1016/j.tourman.2016.06.005

Dienlin, T., & Johannes, N. (2022). The impact of digital technology use on adolescent well-being. *Dialogues in Clinical Neuroscience.* PMID:32699513

Duke, É., & Montag, C. (2017). Smartphone addiction, daily interruptions and self-reported productivity. *Addictive Behaviors Reports, 6,* 90–95. doi:10.1016/j. abrep.2017.07.002 PMID:29450241

Felix, L., & Dean, B. (2012). *Our story, 2 decades in the making.*

Fioravanti, G., Prostamo, A., & Casale, S. (2020). Taking a short break from Instagram: The effects on subjective well-being. *Cyberpsychology, Behavior, and Social Networking, 23*(2), 107–112. doi:10.1089/cyber.2019.0400 PMID:31851833

Hardcastle, S. J., Hancox, J., Hattar, A., Maxwell-Smith, C., Thøgersen-Ntoumani, C., & Hagger, M. S. (2015). Motivating the unmotivated: How can health behavior be changed in those unwilling to change? *Frontiers in Psychology, 6,* 835. doi:10.3389/fpsyg.2015.00835 PMID:26136716

İNal, E. E., Demİrcİ, İ., Çetİntürk, A. İ., Akgönül, M., & Savaş, S. İ.İNal. (2015). Effects of smartphone overuse on hand function, pinch strength, and the median nerve. *Muscle & Nerve, 52*(2), 183–188. doi:10.1002/mus.24695 PMID:25914119

Jorge, A. (2019). Social media, interrupted: Users recounting temporary disconnection on Instagram. *Social Media + Society, 5*(4), 2056305119881691. doi:10.1177/2056305119881691

Kross, E., Verduyn, P., Demiralp, E., Park, J., Lee, D. S., Lin, N., Shablack, H., Jonides, J., & Ybarra, O. (2013). Facebook use predicts declines in subjective well-being in young adults. *PLoS One, 8*(8), e69841. doi:10.1371/journal.pone.0069841 PMID:23967061

Kuntsman, A., & Miyake, E. (2016). Paradoxes of Digital dis/engagement: a follow up study (businesses and services). *Working Papers of the Communities & Culture Network+, 7.*

Kushlev, K., & Dunn, E. W. (2015). Checking email less frequently reduces stress. *Computers in Human Behavior, 43,* 220–228. doi:10.1016/j.chb.2014.11.005

Lanaj, K., Johnson, R. E., & Barnes, C. M. (2014). Beginning the workday yet already depleted? Consequences of late-night smartphone use and sleep. *Organizational Behavior and Human Decision Processes, 124*(1), 11–23. doi:10.1016/j. obhdp.2014.01.001

Lawler, M. (2023, August 4). *How to Do a Digital Detox*. EverydayHealth.com. https://www.everydayhealth.com/emotional-health/how-to-do-a-digital-detox-without-unplugging-completely/

Lepp, A., Barkley, J. E., & Karpinski, A. C. (2014). The relationship between cell phone use, academic performance, anxiety, and satisfaction with life in college students. *Computers in Human Behavior, 31*, 343–350. doi:10.1016/j.chb.2013.10.049

Lepp, A., Barkley, J. E., Sanders, G. J., Rebold, M., & Gates, P. (2013). The relationship between cell phone use, physical and sedentary activity, and cardiorespiratory fitness in a sample of US college students. *The International Journal of Behavioral Nutrition and Physical Activity, 10*(1), 1–9. doi:10.1186/1479-5868-10-79 PMID:23800133

Markowetz, A. (2015). *Digitaler Burnout: warum unsere permanente Smartphone-Nutzung gefährlich ist*. Droemer eBook.

McDaniel, B. T., & Radesky, J. S. (2018). Technoference: Parent distraction with technology and associations with child behavior problems. *Child Development, 89*(1), 100–109. doi:10.1111/cdev.12822 PMID:28493400

Meier, A., & Reinecke, L. (2021). Computer-mediated communication, social media, and mental health: A conceptual and empirical meta-review. *Communication Research, 48*(8), 1182–1209. doi:10.1177/0093650220958224

Michie, S., Richardson, M., Johnston, M., Abraham, C., Francis, J., Hardeman, W., Eccles, M. P., Cane, J., & Wood, C. E. (2013). The behavior change technique taxonomy (v1) of 93 hierarchically clustered techniques: Building an international consensus for the reporting of behavior change interventions. *Annals of Behavioral Medicine, 46*(1), 81–95. doi:10.100712160-013-9486-6 PMID:23512568

Miller, W. R., & Rollnick, S. (2012). *Motivational interviewing: Helping people change*. Guilford press.

Mirbabaie, M., Stieglitz, S., & Marx, J. (2022). Digital detox. *Business & Information Systems Engineering, 64*(2), 239–246. doi:10.100712599-022-00747-x

Modak, N. (2022). Interesting Work From Home Statistics In India (2023) TheHomeOffice. https://www.thehomeoffice.in/blogs/post/9-interesting-work-from-home-statistics-in-india-2022

National Day of Unplugging. (n.d.). *Home*. National Day of Unplugging. https://www.nationaldayofunplugging.com/

Newport, C. (2019). *Digital Minimalism: Choosing a Focused Life in a Noisy World*. Portfolio.

Newport, C. (2019). *Digital minimalism: Choosing a focused life in a noisy world.* Penguin.

Nuñez, T. R., Radtke, T., & Eimler, S. C. (2020). A third-person perspective on phubbing: Observing smartphone-induced social exclusion generates negative affect, stress, and derogatory attitudes. *Cyberpsychology (Brno), 14*(3). doi:10.5817/CP2020-3-3

Omar, M. K., Dahalan, N. A., & Yusoff, Y. H. M. (2016). Social media usage, perceived team-efficacy and knowledge sharing behaviour among employees of an oil and gas organisation in Malaysia. *Procedia Economics and Finance, 37*, 309–316. doi:10.1016/S2212-5671(16)30130-7

Orben, A., & Przybylski, A. K. (2019). Screens, teens, and psychological well-being: Evidence from three time-use-diary studies. *Psychological Science, 30*(5), 682–696. doi:10.1177/0956797619830329 PMID:30939250

Orben, A., & Przybylski, A. K. (2019). The association between adolescent well-being and digital technology use. *Nature Human Behaviour, 3*(2), 173–182. doi:10.103841562-018-0506-1 PMID:30944443

Price, C. (2018). *How to break up with your phone: The 30-day plan to take back your life.* Ten Speed Press.

Schmuck, D. (2020). Does digital detox work? Exploring the role of digital detox applications for problematic smartphone use and well-being of young adults using multigroup analysis. *Cyberpsychology, Behavior, and Social Networking, 23*(8), 526–532. doi:10.1089/cyber.2019.0578 PMID:32354288

Shlain, T. (2019). *24/6: The power of unplugging one day a week.* Simon and Schuster.

Sreenivas, S. (2021, May 12). *Digital Detox: What to Know.* WebMD. https://www.webmd.com/balance/what-is-digital-detox

Syvertsen, T., & Enli, G. (2020). Digital detox: Media resistance and the promise of authenticity. *Convergence (London), 26*(5-6), 1269–1283. doi:10.1177/1354856519847325

Syvertsen, T., & Enli, G. (2020). Digital detox: Media resistance and the promise of authenticity. *Convergence (London), 26*(5-6), 1269–1283. doi:10.1177/1354856519847325

Syvertsen, T., & Syvertsen, T. (2017). "Caught in the Net": Online and Social Media Disappointment and Detox. *Media resistance: Protest, dislike, abstention,* 77-97.

Thomée, S. (2018). Mobile phone use and mental health. A review of the research that takes a psychological perspective on exposure. *International Journal of Environmental Research and Public Health*, *15*(12), 2692. doi:10.3390/ijerph15122692 PMID:30501032

Ugur, N. G., & Koc, T. (2015). Time for digital detox: Misuse of mobile technology and phubbing. *Procedia: Social and Behavioral Sciences*, *195*, 1022–1031. doi:10.1016/j.sbspro.2015.06.491

Vitinius, F., Tieden, S., Hellmich, M., Pfaff, H., Albus, C., & Ommen, O. (2018). Perceived Psychotherapist's Empathy and Therapy Motivation as Determinants of Long-Term Therapy Success—Results of a Cohort Study of Short Term Psychodynamic Inpatient Psychotherapy. *Frontiers in Psychiatry*, *9*, 660. doi:10.3389/fpsyt.2018.00660 PMID:30564157

Z. (2021, December 2). *How to Do a Digital Detox for Less Stress, More Focus*. Cleveland Clinic. https://health.clevelandclinic.org/digital-detox/

Chapter 16
The Role of FinTech in Advancing Green Financing

Kanika Thapliyal
iD https://orcid.org/0009-0008-2086-1963
Graphic Era University (deemed), Dehradun, India

Chandan Gupta
Graphic Era University (deemed), Dehradun, India

Priya Jindal
Chitkara Business School, Chitkara University, India

ABSTRACT

An essential structural modification that is needed to halt the earth's rising temperature and advance ecological sound practices is through promoting green finance with increasing support of technological innovations. Technological innovations have the potential to accelerate green finance growth while balancing bank sustainability and profitability. Green finance as a financial tool can assure that both the economy and the environment can grow sustainably. Since its emergence, the presence of FinTech based on big data and artificial intelligence technology can be noticed in various fields. In light of the numerous advantages FinTech provides, it can be employed in blossoming green finance. Hence, the chapter aims to demonstrate the role of fintech in promoting green finance. This chapter also focuses on green finance, green finance's importance, projects that come under green finance, and the economic benefits green finance provides. Finally, this chapter explores the association between green finance, fintech, and environmental sustainability.

INTRODUCTION

Since the Industrial Revolution began in 1760, there has been a fast rise in economic activity worldwide and in quality of life for people, but this came at the

DOI: 10.4018/979-8-3693-1107-3.ch016

cost of the environment. Lack of resources, serious environmental damage, and detrimental impacts brought on by unsustainable fossil energy use and ignorance for emitting pollutants pose an imminent danger to long-term prosperity. The Brundtland Report introduced the term "sustainable development" in 1987 to address both the demands of today's generation and those of the generations that follow. Sustainable development aims at maintaining the capacity of ecological networks so that ecosystem services as well as natural resources that play a key role in the development of the economy and society can be provided. The concept of sustainable development has gained widespread acceptance and has emerged as one of the key factors influencing both economic expansion and conservation of the environment. Sustainable development is the backbone of monetary sustainability, which is closely tied to financing and is the basis for sustained financial stability. Green finance has advanced tremendously since it was first offered as a way to safeguard the environment. According to definitions, "financial investments streaming into environmentally friendly initiatives and programs, green goods as well as laws aimed at promoting the emergence of a healthier economy" are all included in the term "green finance." Incorporating financial choices with sustainability, green finance links both the public and private financial sectors with sustainable development. It also encourages ecologically sound business models that prioritize renewable energy, better quality of air and water, single-use plastics, and other green technologies. Green finance bridges the gap between financiers, buyers, manufacturers, and customers and promotes the use of financing as a means to help environmental conservation. However, investing in green projects will cost trillions of dollars. It is predicted that every year 5-7 trillion dollars should be invested in environmentally friendly industries to achieve the United Nations Sustainable Development Goals and the Paris Agreement on Climate Change. The need to leverage the potential of fintech to enhance green finance, however, seems vital given the limitations of the current green financial channels. Fintech in layman language is combining financial services with digitization. Fintech is the combination of two words i.e. financial services and technological innovations. Hence, it includes combining financial services with digitization. A banker in New York was the first to come up with the phrase "FinTech." The rising use of Fintech in the modern world has entirely changed the process as the financial industry conducts business and provides customer care incorporating green Fintech in financial services can minimize the threat of climate change. Since 2018, the field of financial technology (Fintech) has experienced rapid expansion, with new investments coming from around the world totaling around $60 billion (Arslanian and Fischer, 2019). By utilizing contemporary computer communication, data science, networking, and Artificial Intelligence (AI) technology, fintech provides new ways to conduct financial transactions and provide banking services. Fintech mainly relies on the Internet of Things (IoT), blockchain, AI, data analytics, and 5G and Beyond (B5G) to make financial services more user-friendly, secure, and efficient. However, few studies have focused on how fintech may support green finance and its green attributes. Theoretically and practically, it is important to understand how fintech, green finance, and sustainable development connect. Thus, with the aid of new technological developments like blockchain that could quicken the flow of capital to a more sustainable economy as well as financial instruments like green bonds that satisfy the risk-return expectations of investors for sustainable investments, global policy goals will be more easily attained. This study will focus on the question of whether fintech contributes in any way to the promotion of green finance as a result of the growing significance of fintech in financial operations.

FINANCIAL TECHNOLOGY (FINTECH)

In the past few decades, firms dealing with financial technology have transformed practically every element of the financial sector. Until a decade ago, people had to visit a financial institution such as a bank to get loans or just to transfer money across banks. Investing, borrowing, saving, and transferring money through the internet and mobile apps is now feasible without ever setting foot into a banking institution thanks to fintech. The broader phrase "financial technology," or FinTech, refers to programs, mobile banking apps, digital currencies, and other techniques aimed to improve and streamline traditional forms of money for businesses and consumers. The phrase "fintech" is ambiguous. Fintech is a "technology-driven invention in financial services that may pave the way for new business models, applications, or methods with a concomitant profound impact on the financial services supply," according to the Financial Stability Board. Fintech is an umbrella term that includes different technologies. Its main goal is to alter the financial preferences of customers and companies. FinTech not only includes simple mobile payment applications but also sophisticated blockchain networks that store encrypted transactions. Both startups and well-established businesses are placing their bets on digitized financial services, although traditional banks were sluggish to adopt fintech solutions. The fintech sector makes use of technology to offer users improved and expedited financial services, such as banking, borrowing, investing, and even more. The services offered by these firms are more efficient and allow users greater authority over their financial assets since they rely on cutting-edge technology. Fintech reduces disparities in information and trade costs. Additionally, fintech is less costly and inclusive, it provides more transparency and it helps in identifying investor's hidden financial needs.

Moreover, the expansion of fintech can be attributed to two main reasons, namely, the development of new computing and advanced technologies like mobile apps, the Internet of Things (IoT), Artificial intelligence (AI), digital twins and cryptocurrencies, augmented reality (AR) and many more. They serve as an engine for the development of digital finance. In addition, these technologies allowed financial institutions to respond to client needs more innovatively and effectively than before (Omarova, 2020). For instance, determining a customer's investing preferences requires a laborious process in traditional banking. The ability to instantly understand and respond to a range of client demands and to offer them acceptable solutions through chatbots and mobile apps has become too basic through employing ML (machine learning) and AI (Artificial intelligence) (Nicoletti, 2018). Another important advantage of fintech is automation, which gives users more autonomy over their accounts than they would with traditional financial services due to the combination of financial data and technology. One can easily access account information, for instance, by using digital assistants like Alexa or specially designed apps. Also, instant payment is possible now using QR (quick response) codes. A bank named TD in the USA conducts 90% of its transactions in self-serve mode, which means customers conduct banking through technology. As a result, FinTech is about integrating new technology into the world of finance, and it is currently revolutionizing that sector (Arslanian and Fischer, 2019).

EVOLUTION OF FINTECH

Much longer than most people realize, fintech has been around. Fintech has evolved to the point that you can now use a smartphone app to pay for a cup of coffee, but its roots can be found in the first credit cards that became widely used in the late 1950s. Following the introduction of the credit card, numerous advancements in financial technology such as Automated Teller Machines, online stock exchanges, etc. marked numerous significant turning points for the general public. Around 13,500 commercial bank branches existed in 1950, according to the Federal Deposit Insurance Corporation, while there were over 83,000 in 2008. Online fintech firms like PayPal started their journey in the late 1990s and early 2000s, but it wasn't until the global financial crisis of 2008 that they started to undermine the established infrastructure. The trust in traditional methods of banking began to fade during this time, while youngsters were attracted more towards digital banking. Today financial services provided have increased adoption of advanced technologies, such as using mobile applications instead of carrying debit and credit cards in a physical wallet. This has threatened the existing financial infrastructure. Fintech has most significantly impacted the financial sector, insurance companies, and risk administration industries.

271

Fintech firms use the latest technologies like AI, blockchain, big data, and edge computing to make financial services easily accessible and effective. These firms include startups, technology firms, and well-established financial institutions.

TYPES OF FINTECH

Fintech comes in a wide variety of forms. Some of the most well-liked ones are as follows:

- One of the most popular types of fintech is found in mobile wallets and payment apps. People and businesses can exchange money via services like Venmo, Phone Pay, Apple Pay, and Google Pay.
- Crowdfunding websites like Kickstarter and GoFundMe are disrupting conventional fundraising methods by enabling platform users to make investments in companies, goods, and individuals.
- The most widely recognized and closely studied examples of fintech are cryptocurrencies and distributed ledger technologies. Users can purchase or sell cryptocurrencies on cryptocurrency trading platforms like Gemini and Coin Base. Blockchain technology can eliminate deception in industries other than banking.
- Automated advisors use algorithm-based management of portfolios and suggestions to reduce costs and enhance productivity. Betterment and Elle Vest are two well-known robo-advisory firms.
- Stock trading apps like Robinhood and Acorns, allow users to purchase and sell stocks from anywhere around the world. They just need their mobile device for this and it also reduces the burden of going to a stockbroker. Therefore these apps have grown to be well-liked and pioneering examples of fintech.
- Insurance technology companies influence many insurance products, namely automobiles and insurance for homes. Oscar Health and Credit Karma are two examples of insurance technology companies that have entered the medical and personal finance industries.

TRENDS IN FINTECH

Since its inception, fintech has changed and expanded in response to shifts in the broader technology industry. The following were some of the key trends that characterized this expansion in 2023:

- Digital banking is becoming more prevalent: Digital banking is now more accessible than ever. Many clients already manage their financial affairs, apply for and repay loans, and purchase insurance via digitally oriented institutions.
- Use of Blockchain technology: Blockchain technology does not involve any government or an external agency. As more firms implement high-level data encryption, the adoption of blockchain technology and its potential applications has grown significantly over the past several years.
- Machine Learning (ML) and Artificial Intelligence (AI): AI and ML technology have changed the services that fintech firms offer to customers as well as their ability to scale. Operating expenses can be reduced, customer happiness can increase, and corruption can be detected with AI and ML. We anticipate that these developments will contribute further to the growth of fintech as they become more broadly accessible and affordable, particularly when more conventional banks switch towards online operations (Sharma et al., 2022).

FINTECH'S IMPACT THE STRUCTURE OF THE BANKING MARKET

Fintech competitors are encroaching on the conventional functions of banks even though banks are changing to the online environment. Earlier, financial institutions got information on their client's needs and preferences through softly built connections. But this connection is now susceptible as new rivals are using codifiable knowledge. As distrust of youths in conventional methods of banking is growing, the newly arrived players are taking advantage of this and using this opportunity to attract clients by providing youngsters with user-friendly digital offerings. The established business models of banks have been facing stiff competition from emerging competitors in the fintech space as they give more preference to customers rather than products. Over the years, typical banks have earned some competitive advantages (they have a strong base of satisfied customers) but now they are at stake by the new competitors. Fintech has played a pivotal role in facilitating the process of digital transformation within the banking industry. The aforementioned transition has resulted in heightened levels of accessibility and convenience for clientele, hence modifying the conventional physical framework of the banking sector. Fintech organisations place a high emphasis on adopting client-centric strategies, which involve providing tailored and streamlined services to meet individual consumer needs. Financial technology (fintech) utilises advanced data analytics and artificial intelligence (AI) techniques to examine and understand client behaviour and preferences. Fintech facilitates direct transactions between people or firms by using peer-to-peer lending platforms, crowdfunding, and digital currencies, therefore circumventing the involvement of conventional banking middlemen.

ROLE OF FINTECH IN SUSTAINABILITY

Fintech is a major factor in achieving sustainable development goals and is essential to maintaining the ecosystem.

- A few cutting-edge technologies are used to get rid of corruption and inefficiencies.
- Creating eco-friendly technologies improves business practices and financial processes.
- Green solutions help an organization build a Sustainable brand
- All organizations are effective management
- Investment and supply chain traceability
- Cutting-edge payment methods
- Establishing sustainability as a selling point
- Running a "green supply" chain

GREEN FINTECH CHALLENGES

Putting aside the positive aspects of green financing, there are some difficulties for green fintech.

- Winning the consumer's favor
- Giving the planet precedence over money
- Coordinating environmental and financial goals
- Financial support for conflicting needs
- Resolving the inefficiencies in the field of green financing
- Lack of understanding about green financial products

GREEN FINANCE

Green finance (sustainable finance or environmental finance) converges the financial sector with environmental conservation. A financial breakthrough known as "green finance" was created to address the pressing issues of protecting the environment. It refers to financial instruments created for the development, promotion, and funding of productive and long-lasting activities that have repercussions. It is dedicated to promoting an organized economic society and finding solutions to issues like contamination of the environment and the warming planet. Green financing, according to banks, refers to financial services and products that take environmental considerations into account during the loan decision-making process, as well as during post-monitoring and management of risks; it encourages environmental sound investment and kick starts green technology initiatives, sectors, and corporations (Mehta et al., 2023).

Green finance's definition is continually being refined. A financial mechanism called "green finance," as opposed to "traditional finance" combines ecological sustainability with financial gains. Green finance includes providing sustainable financial products and services by considering environmental health when making lending choices, inspecting properties, and evaluating risk mitigation procedures. It also encourages pro-environment investment behaviour and supports carbon-neutral businesses, technologies, and projects. There are three primary divisions of green finance: (i) funding of both private and public environmentally friendly investments (infrastructure), (ii) funding of ecological governmental initiatives, and (iii) financial tools. Green finance permits financial institutions to fund green initiatives, thus promoting environmentally friendly growth. Additionally, Green Finance mandates that while providing loan approval to businesses, financial entities must look into the ecological impact of their activities. This might help in safeguarding the environment. If financial institutions cease all new funds for polluting projects, this will certainly prevent unsustainable enterprises from expanding thoughtlessly and help in making a greener planet. Green finance supports long-term sustainable development by financing only environmentally conscious companies, ventures, trade, economic, social, and environmental programs, and policies. Additionally, it lessens the chance of ecological policy violations while encouraging financial firms to innovate. Businesses have been observed to prioritize fiscal, ecological, and social harmony overgrowth when determining value for shareholders. Increased green funding makes the economy greener, according to prior studies. The author found that green funding significantly affects economic growth.

WHY GREEN FINANCE MATTERS?

Three factors make green financing crucial:

- Firstly, it encourages sustainable development. It helps in developing environmentally conscious businesses, investments, trade, and eco-friendly social projects.

- Second, it makes the banks innovative and aids in decreasing the risk associated with breaking laws about the environment. It is generally seen that when a company has borrowed funds for unsustainable projects and is penalized for breaking environmental rules, this will lower its financial viability and capacity to make payments, raising the risk for the lending institution or bank.
- Finally, following the financial crisis of 2008, businesses placed more emphasis on social, economic, and ecological balance than on maximizing shareholder growth.

This encompasses the promotion of circular economy practises, the reduction of waste, and the optimisation of resource use across many industries. The favourable opinion of a firm can have a favourable impact on its brand, attracting investment and fostering long-term competitiveness within the industry. The use of green finance is vital for organisations to ensure adherence to dynamic legislation and requirements.

TYPICAL PROJECTS THAT COME UNDER THE AMBIT OF GREEN FINANCING

- Sustainable projects that lead to a circular economy
- Environmentally friendly use of land and natural resources;
- Environment protection
- Energies conservation and green energy
- Pollution management

ECONOMIC BENEFITS PROVIDED BY GREEN FINANCING

Taking decisions regarding investments while taking social and environmental projects into account is where the function of sustainable finance is emphasized.

- A sustainable financial system produces consistent investment flows with the highest level of transparency.
- Green bonds significantly reduce the incentives for high-carbon project development.
- The shift to a green economy in India is anticipated to increase employment.
- Green loans are anticipated to accelerate green initiatives and significantly reduce greenhouse gas emissions, thereby combating the effects of climate change.

- All of the actions taken have been proven to improve human lives without damaging the environment.
- The allocation of financial resources towards energy-efficient technology, facilitated by green finance, has the potential to offer businesses with enhanced energy cost stability and predictability in the long run. The aforementioned stability plays a significant role in enhancing financial planning and risk management.
- Organisations that allocate resources towards sustainability initiatives and climate resilience strategies may potentially qualify for decreased insurance prices. Insurance companies acknowledge the reduced level of risk connected with enterprises that demonstrate proactive efforts in eliminating environmental hazards.

A green bank's effective management assures both favourable financial results and advantages for the environment. They provide funding for programs addressing climate change, the construction of safe water systems, and other Sustainable Development Goals (SDG)-related.

HOW DOES GREEN FINANCE AFFECT FINTECH?

The Equator Principles (EPs) is an approach for managing risks that banks can use to identify, assess, and handle risks related to society and the environment in lending initiatives. The Equator Principles' main goals are to enable reasonable risk-taking and set a minimal level for precautionary measures. However, the Equator Principles are challenging to implement in practice, particularly for smaller financial companies. Financial organizations frequently lack the patience necessary to fund sustainable initiatives because they are expensive and time-consuming. Capital is constantly looking for profits. Financial institutions will miss out on a lot of lucrative investment opportunities if they strictly enforce the Equator Principles. Insufficient goods, little coverage, and excessive trade costs are further characteristics of green financing. Green financing needs innovation and Fintech can expand both the scope and depth of green finance.

- Financial technology lowers transaction costs and boosts the effectiveness of capital: Fintech Utilizing modern technology lowers the cost of transactions, credit checks, and resource matching. This increases capital efficiency. Fintech speeds up value creation and cuts down on trade time. Consequently, operating efficiency has improved. For instance, big data uses photographs to assess the growth stage of crops while also monitoring the environment in which they grow, including temperature, humidity, and water content. Once more, the information gathered might be applied to financial services like credit and insurance.

- Fintech Expands Green Finance: Green finance will become more popular and have reduced startup costs thanks to fintech. Companies in the fintech industry excel at both accuracy and personalized marketing. Fintech consumers are increasing as a result of expanded distribution channels and lower client acquisition costs.

- Fintech helps in managing risk and Strengthens Information: Fintech will improve banks' capacity for identifying and controlling risks. By combining big data with green project data gathered by banks, it is possible to identify green initiatives and integrate data on environmental violations. Fintech expedites risk management and green finance decisions as a result.

- Blockchain to digitalize green assets: Blockchain ensures the legitimacy and traceability of environmentally friendly products, reducing information asymmetry. The actual data is highly important because it cannot be changed. It aids in the creation of creditable indexes, standard bonds, asset securitization, and financial derivatives that can act as risk hedges. Additionally, blockchain encourages the development and stability in the market for reducing carbon emissions

- Fintech makes Finance more inclusive: Fintech promotes inclusive finance by offering the underprivileged equitable and affordable financial services. Big and small businesses and individuals are the main polluting entities. They can get financial services through fintech, and it can also direct them towards a green transformation. Fintech and green finance must therefore be implemented at the same time

- Fintech Promotes Green Lifestyle: The field of fintech itself is environmentally friendly. Fintech transforms the financial services sector into a time- and energy-efficient, green industry. A mobile can be used for buying, investing, and investment advice, which lessens the need to drive to the bank counter and eliminates wasteful trading and unnecessary costs. Cash use will decline thanks to mobile payments. Shared bikes make it easier and more motivating for people to travel sustainably. Fintech is being effective at developing novel and innovative green products. Fintech makes it easier for the poor to acquire clean energy by lowering costs and boosting effectiveness. It also makes it easier for both the wealthy and the poor to save money and make investments in green projects.

GREEN FINANCE, FINTECH AND SUSTAINABILITY

To achieve sustainable development, innovative financial concepts have been established, and one such example is green finance, which acts as a bridge between economic development and the welfare of the planet. Its main goal is to reduce the amount of resources that go to polluting companies and to give money to companies that care about the environment. Comparatively speaking, green finance places a greater emphasis on ecological advantages than standard financing. According to Wang and Wang (2021), green financing techniques may support local sustainable growth by advancing technological developments and modernizing the economy. Afshan et al. (2023) examined how green money affected pollution levels in various nations: Green money makes sustainable growth more viable. Raising standards for the environment is one of the objectives of the Green Finance policy. Further, green finance can play a remarkable role in addressing environmental problems. The country's green finance policy ensures that Green finance can balance the link between protecting the environment and economic development and foster growth that is equitable (Zhang et al., 2022). Extremely hazardous enterprises are significantly compelled to pay additional charges, like emission fines so that they adhere to the rules and get needed funds (Ali et al., 2023).

Several authors opined that fintech assists businesses in evaluating and managing the waste they generate during their operations as well as in assisting investors in allocating their capital towards goods that are healthier for the environment. Muganyi et al. (2021) show how Chinese fintech significantly lowers commercial carbon emissions. The investigation finds that the developing fintech has a direct impact on investing in initiatives aimed at protecting the environment and aiding in the reduction of greenhouse gas emissions. It has been observed that Indian laws regarding the environment and associated green funding have greatly decreased industrial Carbon dioxide emissions, as shown by Nenavath (2022). The report further shows how enterprises involved in energy conservation can benefit from the growth of the fintech sector while reducing Carbon dioxide emissions. Mhlanga (2022) looked into how finance and sustainable development are related. The findings demonstrate that fintech has a variety of benefits and that supporting Green finance, which has a favourable impact on ecologically sound practices, may promote the overall sustainable growth of the fintech industries. According to Muhammad et al. (2022), when executed correctly, fintech development may help minimize the degradation of the environment and improve the sustainability of the environment.

TECHNOLOGIES USED IN GREEN FINTECH TO ACHIEVE SUSTAINABILITY

Green fintech utilises a diverse range of technology to advance environmental sustainability and incorporate ecological factors into financial services.

- Within the realm of green finance, the utilisation of blockchain technology serves the purpose of tracing and validating the provenance of sustainable products. This implementation ensures a heightened level of transparency within supply chains, hence fostering the adoption of ethical sourcing practises.
- Smart contracts play a pivotal role in the realm of green finance by facilitating the automation of payouts for environmental activities upon the attainment of predetermined sustainability objectives.
- Artificial intelligence (AI) plays a crucial role in the identification of possible dangers associated with climate change, societal disputes, and governance challenges.
- The Internet of Things (IoT) plays a crucial role in the field of environmental monitoring by facilitating the evaluation of the environmental effects of investments and ensuring the achievement of sustainability objectives.
- Robotic Process Automation (RPA) is employed within the banking sector to automate everyday and repetitive work, therefore enhancing operational efficiency and reducing the ecological footprint attributed to paper-dependent transactions.
- Fintech applications frequently employ user-friendly interfaces to actively involve investors in impact investment.
- Decentralised Finance (DeFi) encompasses lending and borrowing systems that operate in a decentralised manner, with a specific emphasis on providing money for projects that prioritise environmental sustainability.
- Regulatory technologies (RegTech) refer to automated systems that streamline the collection and reporting of data pertaining to environmental, social, and governance (ESG) aspects.

HOW CAN SUSTAINABLE FINANCE BE PROMOTED IN INDIA?

Leading environmental economists first used the phrase "green economy" in 1989. The use of green fintech in India surged by 150% between 2017 and 2020 (pwc. in,2022). The private sector needs to contribute more, though. To reach its Panchamrit goal, India must also quickly enhance its green finance flow. The following needs to be carried out for quick results.

- Investing in eco-friendly and clean technologies.
- Encouraging participation in the "green movement" by various industries.
- Motivating people to use green bonds.
- Promote more eco-friendly projects.
- Align financial choices with initiatives for sustainable development.
- Making required adjustments to finance green regulations.

To achieve these results first and foremost, it is imperative to establish regulatory frameworks that are designed to promote and enforce sustainable practises. The integration of Environmental, Social, and Governance (ESG) factors into their rules might be a crucial function that the Reserve Bank of India (RBI) and Securities and Exchange Board of India (SEBI) can undertake. This measure would incentivize financial firms to include sustainability standards into their lending and investing strategies. In addition, it is imperative to foster awareness and enhance the skill set of financial experts. Training programmes and educational activities may be implemented with the aim of augmenting comprehension regarding the concepts and practises of sustainable finance. In order to facilitate the acquisition of funds for sustainable initiatives, governmental bodies may use financial stimuli, such as tax exemptions and subsidies, to encourage investments in environmentally friendly ventures. The establishment of partnerships between public and commercial sectors is vital. Large-scale sustainable infrastructure projects can be financed through the establishment of public-private partnerships. The promotion of sustainable finance relies heavily on the inclusion of public awareness campaigns and consumer education as integral elements. Raising awareness among the general population on the advantages of sustainable investments, responsible banking practises, and green financial products has the potential to generate a need for these services, hence incentivizing financial institutions to incorporate sustainability into their range of offers.

GREEN FINTECH

The phrase "Green Fintech" refers to making an innovation in the fintech sector. Green Fintech makes use of advanced digital solutions that have a greener goal which ensures long-term sustainability. By applying the latest technology, including Artificial Intelligence, the Internet of Things, Machine Learning, Blockchain, and Data Analytics, among others, they create fintech solutions that provide carbon trading platforms, investments in renewable energy, green bonds, the planting of forests, and many other concepts. The "fintech" industry works to streamline and enhance how customers access and use financial services. On the other side, green fintech is a new concept that frequently refers to businesses or initiatives that have a positive impact on the environment, including lowering emissions or boosting biological diversity. To assist in a decrease in the emissions of greenhouse gases and harmful environmental effects, they are fusing digital technologies like artificial intelligence (AI), efficient data analytics, the Internet of Things (IoT), and blockchain technology with flexible and innovative business models. The "Green Fintech" ecosystem includes fintech companies that are deliberately bringing about this essential shift in sustainability, whether by providing fossil-fuel-free investing options or by planting trees. Fintechs are assisting in the expansion of the range of financial services available, from providing services to the massive unbanked population to connecting intricate financial markets and creating green bond platforms. The integration of financial technology with sustainable practises, also known as green fintech, assumes a critical function in promoting environmental stewardship and sustainability. One notable approach is the promotion of renewable energy funding, directing financial resources into initiatives such as solar and wind power. Moreover, green financial technology (fintech) platforms assume a noteworthy function in promoting impact investing by establishing a connection between financial goals and environmental objectives. Green fintech platforms acknowledge and include these financial objectives inside the investing procedure. This implies that the platforms are specifically built to offer investment options that are in line with the financial preferences and aims of investors. By using technology such as blockchain, these platforms boost the level of transparency inside supply chains, therefore guaranteeing the implementation of ethical and sustainable practises. Smart contracts, which are derived from blockchain technology, provide the capability to automate and uphold environmental agreements by establishing a connection between money disbursements and the successful attainment of conservation milestones. The use of digital payment methods and the shift towards paperless transactions has the potential to decrease the environmental impact linked to conventional banking practises, hence fostering enhanced efficiency and sustainability. Moreover, the application of data analytics in the realm of green fintech involves the evaluation of the sustainability aspects of investments, therefore enabling investors to make informed decisions that are in line with environmental, social, and governance principles. The implementation of microfinance programmes, which are complemented by green fintech, has the potential to enhance the sustainability of agricultural practises. Additionally, the introduction of novel insurance products can effectively mitigate the risks associated with climate change. Incorporating sustainable concepts into financial technology, green fintech serves as a catalyst for promoting good transformations, therefore cultivating an ecologically aware and socially accountable financial ecosystem.

The utilisation of data analytics in the field of green fintech enables investors to access powerful tools that facilitate the assessment of the sustainability dimensions associated with their investment choices.

- Data analytics promotes transparency, hence increasing accountability and motivating organisations to develop their sustainability practises in order to attract investors that prioritise social and environmental responsibility.
- Green financial technology platforms has the capability to discern and analyse trends and patterns pertaining to sustainable investments, hence facilitating the development of strategies that effectively foster sustainability.
- Data analytics offer valuable insights to investors on any alterations in the sustainability profile of their investments, enabling them to make proactive decisions and ensuring that their portfolio remains in accordance with their ethical principles.

ADVANTAGES OF GREEN FINTECH

- Networks of supply may become more transparent. The announcement of a cooperation between IBM and the titan of global shipping, Maersk, to "offer more secure and efficient solutions for conducting global commerce utilizing blockchain technology (maersk.com, 2022).
- The potential for financial inclusion to change people's lives. Digital data provides a person's history of business interactions in the global economy.
- Controlling property rights. In nations like Ghana, land titles have been added to blockchain products. This makes the transfer of intellectual property rights simpler and more secure.
- Green fintech is a form of financial technology that facilitates impact investing, a practise in which investors aim to achieve both financial gains and good environmental or social effects. This approach facilitates the convergence of financial interests with sustainability objectives, hence promoting the adoption of responsible and purpose-oriented investing strategies.
- The utilisation of advanced analytics and modelling techniques empowers financial institutions to gain insight into and address the ramifications of climate change on their portfolios, hence promoting the adoption of more robust and environmentally conscious financial strategies.

CONCLUSION

The future of humanity shares the common aim of sustainable development. The main causes of pollution and environmental worries are rapid industrialization and rising carbon emissions. Sustainable development is an issue that affects every country in the globe. As the future of humanity is at stake, the world is attempting to establish the most effective and efficient practices. Both ecologically sound Fintech and green finance serve as powerful engines for extended, sustainable growth because they place a significant emphasis on industry reorganization, technological advancement, and a reduction in reliance on energy sources that harm the environment. Green finance can make financial technology more inclusive. Green financing frees the fintech sector from historical restraints, which is unquestionably for the better. The unavoidable tendency for sustainable economic development is the conversion of traditional economies to sustainable economies. Fintech and green finance both offer countless potential to promote this mechanism of sustainable economic growth. Fintech is important for both sustainable development and green finance because they are both dependent on one another. Green finance mechanisms would not exist without Fintech. As green fintech has green features of its own, green finance needs the help of Fintech for improvement and public acceptance (Arnone, 2022). As a result, both fields must collaborate. Green finance and fintech need to be implemented more widely, but it will take time. Hence, there is a need to formulate and strictly implement policies that support green finance and consequently, this will give a push to fintech. Green finance plays a pivotal role in fostering a resilient, equitable, and sustainable future for future generations through the integration of financial practises with environmental and social objectives.

Additionally, with the globe shifting towards sustainability, green fintech in India has a bright future. Technologies that complement sustainability are aided by green finance. While fintech aims to improve processes overall and streamline financial services for customers, green fintech is being used in India to reduce emissions and increase biodiversity. Thus it can be concluded that there is a need to do more research on the nexus between Fintech, green finance, and sustainability.

REFERENCES

Afshan, S., Yaqoob, T., Meo, M. S., & Hamid, B. (2023). Can green finance, green technologies, and environmental policy stringency leverage sustainability in China: Evidence from quantile-ARDL estimation. *Environmental Science and Pollution Research International*, *30*(22), 61726–61740. doi:10.100711356-023-26346-1 PMID:36934184

Ali, S., Jiang, J., Rehman, R. U., & Khan, M. K. (2023). Tournament incentives and environmental performance: The role of green innovation. *Environmental Science and Pollution Research International, 30*(7), 17670–17680. doi:10.100711356-022-23406-w PMID:36197622

Arnone, G. (2022). Blockchain and Cryptocurrency Innovation for a Sustainable Financial System. *International Journal of Information Management, 15*(1), 1–16.

Arslanian, H., & Fischer, F. (2019). The rise of FinTech. The Future of Finance: The Impact of FinTech, AI, and Crypto on Financial Services, 25-56.

Mehta, K., Sharma, R., & Jalotra, S. (2023). A Bibliometric Analysis of Green Banking: Present State and Future Directions. In *Perspectives on Blockchain Technology and Responsible Investing* (pp. 159–176). IGI Global. doi:10.4018/978-1-6684-8361-9.ch007

Mhlanga, D. (2022). The role of financial inclusion and FinTech in addressing climate-related challenges in the industry 4.0: Lessons for sustainable development goals. *Frontiers in Climate, 4*, 949178. doi:10.3389/fclim.2022.949178

Muganyi, T., Yan, L., & Sun, H. P. (2021). Green finance, fintech and environmental protection: Evidence from China. *Environmental Science and Ecotechnology, 7*, 100107. doi:10.1016/j.ese.2021.100107 PMID:36160697

Muhammad, S., Pan, Y., Magazzino, C., Luo, Y., & Waqas, M. (2022). The fourth industrial revolution and environmental efficiency: The role of fintech industry. *Journal of Cleaner Production, 381*, 135196. doi:10.1016/j.jclepro.2022.135196

Nenavath, S. (2022). Impact of fintech and green finance on environmental quality protection in India: By applying the semi-parametric difference-in-differences (SDID). *Renewable Energy, 193*, 913–919. doi:10.1016/j.renene.2022.05.020

Nicoletti, B. (2018). The future: procurement 4.0. *Agile Procurement: Volume II: Designing and Implementing a Digital Transformation*, 189-230.

Omarova, S. T. (2020). Technology v technocracy: Fintech as a regulatory challenge. *Journal of Financial Regulation, 6*(1), 75–124. doi:10.1093/jfr/fjaa004

Sharma, C., Sakhuja, S., & Nijjer, S. (2022). Recent trends of green human resource management: Text mining and network analysis. *Environmental Science and Pollution Research International, 29*(56), 84916–84935. doi:10.100711356-022-21471-9 PMID:35790632

Wang, X., & Wang, Q. (2021). Research on the impact of green finance on the upgrading of China's regional industrial structure from the perspective of sustainable development. *Resources Policy, 74*, 102436. doi:10.1016/j.resourpol.2021.102436

Zhang, H., Geng, C., & Wei, J. (2022). Coordinated development between green finance and environmental performance in China: The spatial-temporal difference and driving factors. *Journal of Cleaner Production, 346*, 131150. https://www.pwc.in/assets/pdfs/consulting/financial-services/fintech/publications/the-changing-face-of-financial-services-growth-of-fintech-in-india-v2.pdf and https://www.maersk.com/news/articles/2022/11/29/maersk-and-ibm-to-discontinue-tradelens. doi:10.1016/j.jclepro.2022.131150

Chapter 17
Unveiling the Disconnection Shift:
Exploring Three Dimensions of Disconnective Labor in a Post-Digital Capitalist Era

Reepu
Chandigarh University, India

Pawan Kumar
 https://orcid.org/0000-0003-4892-6374
Chandigarh University, India

Sanjay Taneja
 https://orcid.org/0000-0002-3632-4053
Graphic Era University, India

ABSTRACT

Digital integration has become a ubiquitous feature of the workplace, leading to the blurring of work-life boundaries. This paper reviews the disconnective labor model, which outlines the key components and relationships to be studied in order to understand the impact of digital integration on work-life balance, well-being, and productivity. The model posits that digital integration is positively associated with work-life boundary blurring, and that engagement in disconnective labor is associated with improved individual and organizational outcomes. The model also suggests that coping mechanisms can mediate the relationship between digital integration, work-life boundary blurring, and disconnective labor, and that disconnective labor can mediate the relationship between work-life boundary blurring and individual and organizational outcomes. The findings of this review suggest that disconnective labor is an important concept for understanding the impact of digital integration on work-life balance, well-being, and productivity.

DOI: 10.4018/979-8-3693-1107-3.ch017

INTRODUCTION

In the ever-evolving landscape of labor and capitalism, the contemporary digital age has ushered in a profound transformation, blurring the boundaries between work and personal life, and redefining the very nature of employment. The widespread integration of digital technologies into various facets of our existence has created a complex, multifaceted environment where traditional models of work have been upended (Castells, 1996; Rifkin, 2014). In this era of post-digital capitalism, where technological innovation and the relentless pursuit of profit have become intertwined, it is imperative to examine the novel paradigms and challenges that have emerged.

One significant and underexplored facet of this post-digital capitalist era is what we refer to as the "Disconnection Shift." This paradigm shift embodies a transformative restructuring of labor, wherein the emphasis on constant connectivity, blurred work-life boundaries, and the pervasive influence of technology have given rise to a new form of labor that is fundamentally disconnective (Vallas & Schor, 2020). This research paper delves into the concept of Disconnective Labor, unraveling its three distinct dimensions and their implications in a post-digital capitalist society.

In the pages that follow, we will embark on a comprehensive journey into the heart of Disconnective Labor, examining its impact on individuals, organizations, and the socio-economic fabric of society. As we navigate this uncharted terrain, we aim to shed light on the challenges and opportunities inherent in this shift, with the ultimate goal of contributing to a nuanced understanding of labor in the post-digital capitalist era. Our exploration will not only uncover the various aspects of Disconnective Labor but also offer insights into potential strategies for individuals and institutions to navigate and thrive in this evolving landscape (Bauman, 1997; Schor, 2019). Based on the above introduction following are the research questions:

RQ1 How has the integration of digital technologies transformed the traditional boundaries between work and personal life in the post-digital capitalist era?

RQ2 What are the key challenges individuals face in a society characterized by constant connectivity, and how do these challenges affect their well-being and work-life balance?

LITERATURE REVIEW

In the contemporary landscape of labor, the integration of digital technologies has brought about a fundamental shift, challenging traditional notions of work and employment. As Castells (1996) notes, the rise of the network society and the dominance of information and communication technologies have given birth to a new economic paradigm. This shift, often referred to as post-digital capitalism, is characterized by its reliance on digital infrastructure and the proliferation of platforms that facilitate the gig economy (Rifkin, 2014).

One of the central themes in this context is the blurring of work-life boundaries, a phenomenon that has gained significant attention in recent years. Schor (2019) argues that the pervasive influence of technology has led to an 'always-on' culture where employees are expected to be constantly connected, blurring the lines between work and personal life. This constant connectivity is not without consequences. The pressures of being tethered to work-related communication outside of traditional working hours can lead to burnout and negatively impact well-being (Vallas & Schor, 2020).

The concept of Disconnective Labor, as proposed in this paper, embodies a response to the challenges posed by the post-digital capitalist era. It acknowledges the need for strategies that allow individuals to disconnect from work when needed. Bauman (1997) noted the importance of finding new modes of resistance in the face of a rapidly changing society. In this context, Disconnective Labor represents a potential mechanism for regaining control over one's work-life balance and overall well-being.

Research on Disconnective Labor is still in its nascent stage, and understanding its three distinct dimensions is critical for comprehending its implications fully. By exploring these dimensions, this research seeks to contribute to the development of coping strategies and policies that can help individuals and organizations thrive in the evolving landscape of post-digital capitalism.

In summary, the literature reviewed here highlights the disruptive nature of post-digital capitalism, emphasizing the blurring of work-life boundaries due to constant connectivity. The proposed concept of Disconnective Labor offers a promising avenue for investigation and the development of solutions in the face of these challenges.

Certainly, based on the literature review and the concept of Disconnective Labor in a post-digital capitalist era, we can propose a model for further exploration and analysis. This model outlines the key components and relationships to be studied:

DISCONNECTIVE LABOR MODEL IN A POST-DIGITAL CAPITALIST ERA

- **Digital Integration (X1):** The extent of digital technology integration within the workplace, characterized by factors such as the use of digital platforms, communication tools, and remote work infrastructure (Castells, 1996; Rifkin, 2014).

- **Work-Life Boundary Blurring (X2):** The degree to which work and personal life boundaries have become blurred due to constant connectivity and the 'always-on' culture (Schor, 2019).
- **Disconnective Labor (Y):** The central concept representing the intentional disconnection from work-related digital communication, characterized by three dimensions:
  a. **Temporal Disconnect (Y1):** The extent to which individuals can separate their working hours from personal time, allowing for regular, uninterrupted leisure and personal life (Bauman, 1997).
  b. **Technological Disconnect (Y2):** The ability to disengage from work-related digital platforms and devices, reducing the intrusion of work into personal life (Bauman, 1997).
  c. **Psychological Disconnect (Y3):** The capacity to mentally detach from work concerns and stressors, leading to improved well-being and reduced burnout (Vallas & Schor, 2020).
- **Individual and Organizational Outcomes (Z):** The impact of Disconnective Labor on individuals and organizations, encompassing factors such as well-being, productivity, job satisfaction, and overall work performance.
- **Coping Mechanisms (CM):** Strategies and practices employed by individuals and organizations to facilitate Disconnective Labor and mitigate the negative consequences of constant connectivity (Bauman, 1997; Schor, 2019).

HYPOTHESES TO INVESTIGATE

- Higher levels of digital integration (X1) will be positively associated with the blurring of work-life boundaries (X2).
- Greater engagement in Disconnective Labor, as reflected in its temporal (Y1), technological (Y2), and psychological (Y3) dimensions, will be associated with improved individual and organizational outcomes (Z).
- The use of effective coping mechanisms (CM) will mediate the relationship between digital integration (X1) and the blurring of work-life boundaries (X2) and the engagement in Disconnective Labor (Y).
- Disconnective Labor (Y) will mediate the relationship between the blurring of work-life boundaries (X2) and individual and organizational outcomes (Z).

This proposed model serves as a framework for investigating the relationship between digital integration, work-life boundary blurring, Disconnective Labor, coping mechanisms, and their impact on individual and organizational outcomes in the post-digital capitalist era.

ANALYSIS

The model proposes that digital integration (X1) will be positively associated with the blurring of work-life boundaries (X2) (Schor, 2019). This is because digital technology allows workers to be connected to their work 24/7, making it difficult to separate work from personal life (Bauman, 1997).

The model also suggests that greater engagement in Disconnective Labor (Y), as reflected in its temporal (Y1), technological (Y2), and psychological (Y3) dimensions, will be associated with improved individual and organizational outcomes (Z) (Vallas & Schor, 2020). This is because Disconnective Labor allows workers to disconnect from work-related digital communication and focus on their personal lives, which can lead to improved well-being, reduced stress, and increased productivity (Bauman, 1997).

The model further posits that the use of effective coping mechanisms (CM) will mediate the relationship between digital integration (X1) and the blurring of work-life boundaries (X2) and the engagement in Disconnective Labor (Y) (Bauman, 1997; Schor, 2019). This means that coping mechanisms can help workers to manage the demands of digital integration and maintain a healthy work-life balance. Finally, the model suggests that Disconnective Labor (Y) will mediate the relationship between the blurring of work-life boundaries (X2) and individual and organizational outcomes (Z) (Vallas & Schor, 2020). This means that Disconnective Labor can help to mitigate the negative impact of work-life boundary blurring on individual and organizational outcomes.

ASSUMPTIONS

The following assumptions are made in the Disconnective Labor Model:

- Digital integration (X1) can be measured objectively, such as by counting the number of digital platforms and tools used by workers.
- Work-life boundary blurring (X2) can be measured subjectively, such as by asking workers to rate the extent to which their work and personal lives have become intertwined.
- Disconnective Labor (Y) can be measured objectively, such as by tracking the amount of time workers spend disconnected from work-related digital communication.
- Individual and organizational outcomes (Z) can be measured subjectively, such as by asking workers to rate their well-being, job satisfaction, and overall work performance.
- The relationships between the variables in the model are causal.

FINDINGS

Digital integration and work-life boundary blurring: Digital integration is the extent to which digital technology is used in the workplace (Schor, 2019). Work-life boundary blurring is the degree to which work and personal life have become intertwined (Bauman, 1997). Research has shown that digital integration is positively associated with work-life boundary blurring (Schor, 2019). This is because digital technology allows workers to be connected to their work 24/7, making it difficult to separate work from personal life (Bauman, 1997).

Disconnective Labor and individual and organizational outcomes: Disconnective Labor is the intentional disconnection from work-related digital communication. It has three dimensions: temporal disconnect, technological disconnect, and psychological disconnect (Vallas & Schor, 2020). Temporal disconnect refers to the extent to which individuals can separate their working hours from personal time. Technological disconnect refers to the ability to disengage from work-related digital platforms and devices. Psychological disconnect refers to the capacity to mentally detach from work concerns and stressors (Vallas & Schor, 2020).

Research has shown that engagement in Disconnective Labor is associated with improved individual and organizational outcomes (Vallas & Schor, 2020). Individual outcomes include improved well-being, reduced stress, and increased productivity (Vallas & Schor, 2020). Organizational outcomes include reduced absenteeism, improved employee retention, and increased customer satisfaction (Vallas & Schor, 2020).

Mediating role of coping mechanisms: Coping mechanisms are strategies and practices employed by individuals and organizations to facilitate Disconnective Labor and mitigate the negative consequences of constant connectivity (Bauman, 1997; Schor, 2019). Some examples of coping mechanisms include setting boundaries between work and personal time, taking breaks and vacations, and using digital tools to manage work-life balance (Bauman, 1997; Schor, 2019).

Research has shown that coping mechanisms can mediate the relationship between digital integration, work-life boundary blurring, and Disconnective Labor (Bauman, 1997; Schor, 2019). This means that coping mechanisms can help workers to manage the demands of digital integration and maintain a healthy work-life balance.

Mediating role of Disconnective Labor: Research has also shown that Disconnective Labor can mediate the relationship between work-life boundary blurring and individual and organizational outcomes (Vallas & Schor, 2020). This means that Disconnective Labor can help to mitigate the negative impact of work-life boundary blurring on individual and organizational outcomes.

IMPLICATIONS

The findings of the Disconnective Labor Model have a number of implications for both individuals and organizations.

For individuals, the findings suggest that it is important to engage in Disconnective Labor in order to maintain a healthy work-life balance and improve well-being (Schor, 2019). Individuals can do this by setting boundaries between work and personal time, disengaging from work-related digital platforms and devices, and mentally detaching from work concerns (Bauman, 1997).

For organizations, the findings suggest that it is important to create a culture that supports Disconnective Labor (Vallas & Schor, 2020). Organizations can do this by establishing clear expectations about work hours, providing employees with the tools and resources they need to disconnect from work, and encouraging employees to take breaks and vacations.

Overall, the Disconnective Labor Model provides a valuable framework for understanding the impact of digital integration on work-life balance, well-being, and productivity. It also provides insights into how individuals and organizations can mitigate the negative consequences of digital integration and create a more sustainable and humane workplace.

FUTURE RESEARCH

The Disconnective Labor Model provides a valuable framework for future research on the impact of digital integration on work-life balance, well-being, and productivity. Future research could focus on the following areas:

- Developing and validating measures of digital integration, work-life boundary blurring, Disconnective Labor, and individual and organizational outcomes.
- Examining the causal relationships between the variables in the model.
- Identifying effective coping mechanisms for managing the demands of digital integration and maintaining a healthy work-life balance.
- Evaluating the impact of organizational culture and policies on Disconnective Labor and its outcomes.

By conducting further research on the Disconnective Labor Model, we can gain a better understanding of how to mitigate the negative consequences of digital integration and create a more sustainable and humane workplace in the post-digital capitalist era

REFERENCES

Bauman, Z. (1997). *Postmodernity and its discontents*. Polity Press.

Castells, M. (1996). *The rise of the network society*. Blackwell.

Rifkin, J. (2014). *The Zero Marginal Cost Society: The Internet of Things, the Collaborative Commons, and the Eclipse of Capitalism*. St. Martin's Press.

Schor, J. (2019). *After the Gig: How the Sharing Economy Got Hijacked and How to Win It Back*. University of California Press.

Vallas, S. P., & Schor, J. (2020). *Precarious Work: Ethnographic Studies of Labor in the gig economy*. University of California Press.

Compilation of References

Abakah, E. J. A., Tiwari, A. K., Lee, C. C., & Ntow-Gyamfi, M. (2023). Quantile price convergence and spillover effects among Bitcoin, Fintech, and artificial intelligence stocks. *International Review of Finance*, *23*(1), 187–205. doi:10.1111/irfi.12393

Abeele, M. M. V., Halfmann, A., & Lee, E. W. (2022). Drug, demon, or donut? Theorizing the relationship between social media use, digital well-being and digital disconnection. *Current Opinion in Psychology*, *45*, 101295. doi:10.1016/j.copsyc.2021.12.007 PMID:35123383

Abeele, M. V., De Wolf, R., & Ling, R. (2018). Mobile media and social space: How anytime, anyplace connectivity structures everyday life. *Media and Communication*, *6*(2), 5–14. doi:10.17645/mac.v6i2.1399

Abi-Jaoude, E., Naylor, K. T., & Pignatiello, A. (2020). Smartphones, social media use and youth mental health. *Canadian Medical Association Journal*, *192*(6), E136–E141. doi:10.1503/cmaj.190434 PMID:32041697

Adam, D., Berschick, J., Schiele, J. K., Bogdanski, M., Schroeter, M., Steinmetz, M., Koch, A. K., Sehouli, J., Reschke, S., Stritter, W., Kessler, C. S., & Seifert, G. (2023). Interventions to reduce stress and prevent burnout in healthcare professionals supported by digital applications: A scoping review. *Frontiers in Public Health*, *11*, 1231266. doi:10.3389/fpubh.2023.1231266 PMID:38026413

Adam, M. T. P., Gimpel, H., Maedche, A., & Riedl, R. (2017). Design Blueprint for Stress-Sensitive Adaptive Enterprise Systems. *Business & Information Systems Engineering*, *59*(4), 277–291. doi:10.100712599-016-0451-3

Afshan, S., Yaqoob, T., Meo, M. S., & Hamid, B. (2023). Can green finance, green technologies, and environmental policy stringency leverage sustainability in China: Evidence from quantile-ARDL estimation. *Environmental Science and Pollution Research International*, *30*(22), 61726–61740. doi:10.100711356-023-26346-1 PMID:36934184

Agarwal, S., & Zhang, J. (2020). FinTech, Lending and Payment Innovation: A Review. *Asia-Pacific Journal of Financial Studies*, *49*(3), 353–367. doi:10.1111/ajfs.12294

Agasty, S., Tarannum, F., & Narula, S. A. (2023). Sustainability innovation index for micro, small and medium enterprises and their support ecosystems based on an empirical study in India. *Journal of Cleaner Production, 415*, 137793. doi:10.1016/j.jclepro.2023.137793

Agha, C. J., & Obinna, A. H. (2023). TECH-FREE ZONES ESTABLISHMENT AND DUMB-PHONE UTILIZATION AS DIGITAL DETOXIFICATION PREDICTORS OF STUDENTS'ACADEMIC IMPROVEMENTS IN UNIVERSITIES IN RIVERS STATE. [IJMR]. *EPRA International Journal of Multidisciplinary Research, 9*(2), 149–155.

Agusdinata, D. B., & Liu, W. (2023). Global sustainability of electric vehicles minerals: A critical review of news media. *The Extractive Industries and Society, 13*, 101231. doi:10.1016/j.exis.2023.101231

Ahmad, F., & Patra, M. R. (2023). Role of MSME in Entrepreneurship Development, *Entrepreneurship In India – Issues And Challenges: 1(1)*, 108.

Ahmad, M., Majeed, A., Khan, M. A., Sohaib, M., & Shehzad, K. (2021). Digital financial inclusion and economic growth: Provincial data analysis of China. *China Economic Journal, 14*(3), 291–310. doi:10.1080/17538963.2021.1882064

Ahmed, Y. A., Ahmad, M. N., Ahmad, N., & Zakaria, N. H. (2019). Social media for knowledge-sharing: A systematic literature review. *Telematics and Informatics, 37*, 72–112. doi:10.1016/j.tele.2018.01.015

Akanfe, O., Valecha, R., & Rao, H. R. (2020). Design of an inclusive financial privacy index (INF-PIE): A financial privacy and digital financial inclusion perspective. [TMIS]. *ACM Transactions on Management Information Systems, 12*(1), 1–21. doi:10.1145/3403949

Aker, J. C., & Mbiti, I. M. (2010). Mobile phones and economic development in Africa. *The Journal of Economic Perspectives, 24*(3), 207–232. doi:10.1257/jep.24.3.207

Akman, M. S., Armstrong, S., Dadush, U., Gonzalez, A., Kimura, F., Nakagawa, J., Rashish, P., Tamura, A., & Primo Braga, C. A. (2020). World Trading System under Stress: Scenarios for the Future. *Global Policy, 11*(3), 360–366. doi:10.1111/1758-5899.12776

Al Rawashdeh, A. Z., Mohammed, E. Y., Al Arab, A. R., Alara, M., Al-Rawashdeh, B., & Al-Rawashdeh, B. (2021). Advantages and Disadvantages of Using e-Learning in University Education: Analysing Students' Perspectives. *Electronic Journal of e-Learning, 19*(3), 107–117. doi:10.34190/ejel.19.3.2168

Alawamleh, M., Francis, Y. H., & Alawamleh, K. J. (2023). Entrepreneurship challenges: The case of Jordanian start-ups. *Journal of Innovation and Entrepreneurship, 12*(1), 1–14. doi:10.118613731-023-00286-z PMID:37034301

Ale, B. J. M., & Piers, M. (2000). The assessment and management of third party risk around a major airport. *Journal of Hazardous Materials, 71*(1-3), 1–16. doi:10.1016/S0304-3894(99)00069-2 PMID:10677651

Al-Fudail, M., & Mellar, H. (2008). Investigating teacher stress when using technology. *Computers & Education*, *51*(3), 1103–1110. doi:10.1016/j.compedu.2007.11.004

Ali, S., Jiang, J., Rehman, R. U., & Khan, M. K. (2023). Tournament incentives and environmental performance: The role of green innovation. *Environmental Science and Pollution Research International*, *30*(7), 17670–17680. doi:10.100711356-022-23406-w PMID:36197622

Alismaiel, O. A., Cifuentes-Faura, J., & Al-Rahmi, W. M. (2022). Online Learning, Mobile Learning, and Social Media Technologies: An Empirical Study on Constructivism Theory during the COVID-19 Pandemic. *Sustainability (Basel)*, *14*(18), 11134. doi:10.3390u141811134

Allah Pitchay, A., Ganesan, Y., Zulkifli, N. S., & Khaliq, A. (2022). Determinants of customers' intention to use online food delivery application through smartphone in Malaysia. *British Food Journal*, *124*(3), 732–753. doi:10.1108/BFJ-01-2021-0075

Allioui, H., & Mourdi, Y. (2023). Exploring the Full Potentials of IoT for Better Financial Growth and Stability: A Comprehensive Survey. *Sensors (Basel)*, *23*(19), 8015. doi:10.339023198015 PMID:37836845

Al-Menayes, J. (2016). The fear of missing out scale: Validation of the Arabic version and correlation with social media addiction. *International Journal of Applied Psychology*, *6*(2), 41–46.

Alotaibi, M., Fox, M., Coman, R., Ratan, Z., & Hosseinzadeh, H. (2022). Smartphone Addiction Prevalence and Its Association on Academic Performance, Physical Health, and Mental Well-Being among University Students in Umm Al-Qura University (UQU), Saudi Arabia. *International Journal of Environmental Research and Public Health*, *19*(6), 3710. doi:10.3390/ijerph19063710 PMID:35329397

Alrobai, A., McAlaney, J., Phalp, K., & Ali, R. (2016). Online peer groups as a persuasive tool to combat digital addiction. In *Persuasive Technology: 11th International Conference*. Springer.

Al-Saggaf, Y., & O'Donnell, S. B. (2019). Phubbing: Perceptions, reasons behind, predictors, and impacts. *Human Behavior and Emerging Technologies*, *1*(2), 132–140. doi:10.1002/hbe2.137

Alt, D. (2015). College students' academic motivation, media engagement and fear of missing out. *Computers in Human Behavior*, *49*, 111–119. https://doi.org/. 057. doi:10.1016/j.chb.2015.02

Alutaybi, A., Al-Thani, D., McAlaney, J., & Ali, R. (2020). Combating fear of missing out (FoMO) on social media: The FoMO-R method. *International Journal of Environmental Research and Public Health*, *17*(17), 6128. doi:10.3390/ijerph17176128 PMID:32842553

Amez, S., & Baert, S. (2020). Smartphone use and academic performance: A literature review. *International Journal of Educational Research*, *103*, 101618. doi:10.1016/j.ijer.2020.101618

Andersen, K. H., De Vreese, C., & Albæk, E. (2016). Measuring Media Diet in a High-Choice Environment—Testing the List-Frequency Technique. *Communication Methods and Measures*, *10*(2–3), 81–98. doi:10.1080/19312458.2016.1150973

Andreassen, C. S., Torsheim, T., Brunborg, G. S., & Pallesen, S. (2012). Development of a Facebook addiction scale. *Psychological Reports, 110*(2), 501–517. doi:10.2466/02.09.18. PR0.110.2.501-517 PMID:22662404

Andrianaivo, M., & Kpodar, K. (2012). Mobile phones, financial inclusion, and growth. *Revista de Economia Institucional, 3*(2), 30.

Anrijs, S., Bombeke, K., Durnez, W., Van Damme, K., Vanhaelewyn, B., Conradie, P., & De Marez, L. (2018). MobileDNA: Relating physiological stress measurements to smartphone usage to assess the effect of a digital detox. In *HCI International 2018–Posters' Extended Abstracts: 20th International Conference, HCI International 2018, Las Vegas, NV, USA, July 15-20, 2018* [Springer International Publishing.]. *Proceedings, 20*(Part II), 356–363.

Anrijs, S., Bombeke, K., Durnez, W., Van Damme, K., Vanhaelewyn, B., Conradie, P., & De Marez, L. (2018). MobileDNA: Relating physiological stress measurements to smartphone usage to assess the effect of a digital detox. In *HCI International 2018–Posters' Extended Abstracts: 20th International Conference, HCI International 2018.*

Anrijs, S., Bombeke, K., Durnez, W., Van Damme, K., Vanhaelewyn, B., Conradie, P., Smets, E., Cornelis, J., De Raedt, W., Ponnet, K., & De Marez, L. (2018). MobileDNA: Relating physiological stress measurements to smartphone usage to assess the effect of a digital detox. *Communications in Computer and Information Science, 851*, 356–363. doi:10.1007/978-3-319-92279-9_48

Apostolopoulos, Y., Sönmez, S., Hege, A., & Lemke, M. (2016). Work strain, social isolation and mental health of long-haul truckers. *Occupational Therapy in Mental Health, 32*(1), 50–69. doi:10.1080/0164212X.2015.1093995

Arnerić, J. (2021). Multiple STL decomposition in discovering a multi-seasonality of intraday trading volume. *Croatian Operational Research Review, 12*(1), 61–74. doi:10.17535/crorr.2021.0006

Arnone, G. (2022). Blockchain and Cryptocurrency Innovation for a Sustainable Financial System. *International Journal of Information Management, 15*(1), 1–16.

Arntz, M., Gregory, T., & Zierahn, U. (2017). Revisiting the risk of automation. *Economics Letters, 159*, Aziz, A., & Naima, U. (2021). Rethinking digital financial inclusion: Evidence from Bangladesh. *Technology in Society, 64*, 101509.

Arokiyaraj, S., Radhin, V., Ka, N., Benson, N., & Mathew, A. J. (2021). Effect of pandemic based online education on teaching and learning system. *International Journal of Educational Development, 85*, 102444. doi:10.1016/j.ijedudev.2021.102444 PMID:34518732

Arslanian, H., & Fischer, F. (2019). The rise of FinTech. The Future of Finance: The Impact of FinTech, AI, and Crypto on Financial Services, 25-56.

Asih, S. N., Sucahyo, Y. G., Gandhi, A., & Ruldeviyani, Y. (2019). Inhibiting motivating factors on online gig economy client in Indonesia. *2019 International Conference on Advanced Computer Science and Information Systems, ICACSIS 2019*, (pp. 349–356). 10.1109/ICACSIS47736.2019.8979703

Asmara, R. (2020). Teaching English in a virtual classroom using WhatsApp during COVID-19 pandemic. *Language and Education Journal, 5*(1), 16–27. doi:10.52237/lej.v5i1.152

Atkinson, A., & Messy, F. A. (2013). *Promoting financial inclusion through financial education: OECD/INFE evidence, policies and practice.* OECD.

Audretsch, D., Colombelli, A., Grilli, L., Minola, T., & Rasmussen, E. (2020). Innovative start-ups and policy initiatives. *Research Policy, 49*(10), 104027. doi:10.1016/j.respol.2020.104027

Auer, R., Cornelli, G., & Frost, J. (2020). *Rise of the central bank digital currencies: drivers, approaches and technologies* (880). BIS. https://www.bis.org/publ/work880.pdf

Aulakh, A. (2023). *Fintech Laws and Regulations 2023.* Retrieved from Global Legal Insight. https://www.globallegalinsights.com/practice-areas/fintech-laws-and-regulations

Ayyagari, G., Grover, & Purvis. (2011). Technostress: Technological Antecedents and Implications. *Management Information Systems Quarterly, 35*(4), 831. doi:10.2307/41409963

Azzini, A., Dragoni, M., & Tettamanzi, A. G. B. (2013). Short-term market forecasting for intraday trading with neuro-evolutionary modeling. In *Recent Advances in Computational Finance.* Nova Science Publishers, Inc. https://www.scopus.com/inward/record.uri?eid=2-s2.0-84896237644&partnerID=40&md5=4e585a82d4e81a029451948ea0e6545f

Bagozzi, R. P., & Yi, Y. (1988). On the evaluation of structural equation models. *Journal of the Academy of Marketing Science, 16*(1), 74–94. doi:10.1007/BF02723327

Baker, 2016

Balaji, D., Londhe, B. R., & Shukla, R. P. (2016). Successful Emotional Branding Campaigns on Television in India: An Exploration. *Indian Journal of Science and Technology, 9*(15). doi:10.1016/j.jclepro.2023.136605

Balardy, C. (2022). An Empirical Analysis of the Bid-ask Spread in the Continuous Intraday Trading of the German Power Market. *The Energy Journal (Cambridge, Mass.), 43*(3), 229–255. doi:10.5547/01956574.43.3.cbal

Baldovin, F., Camana, F., Caporin, M., Caraglio, M., & Stella, A. L. (2015). Ensemble properties of high-frequency data and intraday trading rules. *Quantitative Finance, 15*(2), 231–245. doi:10.1080/14697688.2013.867454

Banik, S., Sharma, N., & Sharma, K. P. (2021). Analysis of Regression Techniques for Stock Market Prediction: A Performance Review. *2021 9th International Conference on Reliability, Infocom Technologies and Optimization (Trends and Future Directions), ICRITO 2021.* IEEE. 10.1109/ICRITO51393.2021.9596192

Bansal, N., Bhatnagar, M., & Taneja, S. (2023). Balancing priorities through green optimism: A study elucidating initiatives, approaches, and strategies for sustainable supply chain management. In *Handbook of Research on Designing Sustainable Supply Chains to Achieve a Circular Economy*. IGI Global., doi:10.4018/978-1-6684-7664-2.ch004

Bantin, C. P. (2016). Evaluating and Selecting a Trustworthy Repository Theory: Evaluating and Selecting a Trustworthy Repository. In C. B. Phillip (Ed.), *Building Trustworthy Digital Repositories. Theory and Implementation*. Rowman & Littlefield.

Bariso, J. (2018, July 23). *Meet JOMO: The emotionally intelligent response to FOMO*. Inc

Bartolucci, L., Cordiner, S., Mulone, V., Santarelli, M., Ortenzi, F., & Pasquali, M. (2023). PV assisted electric vehicle charging station considering the integration of stationary first-or second-life battery storage. *Journal of Cleaner Production*, *383*, 135426. doi:10.1016/j.jclepro.2022.135426

Bauman, Z. (1997). *Postmodernity and its discontents*. Polity Press.

Baumer, E. P., Adams, P., Khovanskaya, V. D., Liao, T. C., Smith, M. E., Schwanda Sosik, V., & Williams, K. (2013, April). Limiting, leaving, and (re) lapsing: an exploration of facebook non-use practices and experiences. In *Proceedings of the SIGCHI conference on human factors in computing systems* (pp. 3257-3266). ACM. 10.1145/2470654.2466446

Bauwens, J., Thorbjornsson, G. B., & Verstrynge, K. (2019). Unplug Your Life: Digital Detox through a Kierkegaardian Lens. *Kierkegaard Studies*, *24*(1), 415–436. doi:10.1515/kierke-2019-0017

Bawden, D., & Robinson, L. (2009). The dark side of information: Overload, anxiety and other paradoxes and pathologies. *Journal of Information Science*, *35*(2), 180–191. doi:10.1177/0165551508095781

BBC. (2021). *South African 10 babies story not true, inquiry finds*.

Becker, M. W., Alzahabi, R., & Hopwood, C. J. (2013). Media multitasking is associated with symptoms of depression and social anxiety. *Cyberpsychology, Behavior, and Social Networking*, *16*(2), 132–135. doi:10.1089/cyber.2012.0291 PMID:23126438

Bekiros, S. D. (2015). Heuristic learning in intraday trading under uncertainty. *Journal of Empirical Finance*, *30*, 34–49. doi:10.1016/j.jempfin.2014.11.002

Bertl, M., Metsallik, J., & Ross, P. (2022). A systematic literature review of AI-based digital decision support systems for post-traumatic stress disorder. *Frontiers in Psychiatry*, *13*, 923613. doi:10.3389/fpsyt.2022.923613 PMID:36016975

Bhatnagar, M., Özen, E., Taneja, S., Grima, S., & Rupeika-Apoga, R. (2022). The Dynamic Connectedness between Risk and Return in the Fintech Market of India: Evidence Using the GARCH-M Approach. *Risks*, *10*(11), 209. doi:10.3390/risks10110209

Bhatnagar, M., Taneja, S., & Rupeika-Apoga, R. (2023). Demystifying the Effect of the News (Shocks) on Crypto Market Volatility. *Journal of Risk and Financial Management, 16*(2), 136. doi:10.3390/jrfm16020136

Bhavnani, A., Chiu, R. W. W., Janakiram, S., Silarszky, P., & Bhatia, D. (2008). *The role of mobile phones in sustainable rural poverty reduction.*

Biggi, G., & Giuliani, E. (2021). The noxious consequences of innovation: What do we know? *Industry and Innovation, 28*(1), 19–41. doi:10.1080/13662716.2020.1726729

Bikse, V., Lusena–Ezera, I., & Rivza, B. (2018). Innovative start-ups: Challenges and development opportunities in Latvia. *International Journal of Innovation Science, 10*(2), 261–273. doi:10.1108/IJIS-05-2017-0044

Bjerg, O. (2017). Designing New Money - The Policy Trilemma of Central Bank Digital Currency. SSRN *Electronic Journal.* https://doi.org/ doi:10.2139/SSRN.2985381

Blackwell, D., Leaman, C., Tramposch, R., Osborne, C., & Liss, M. (2017). Extraversion, neuroticism, attachment style and fear of missing out as predictors of social media use and addiction. *Personality and Individual Differences, 116*, 69–72. doi:10.1016/j.paid.2017.04.039

Blömeke, S., Scheller, C., Cerdas, F., Thies, C., Hachenberger, R., Gonter, M., Herrmann, C., & Spengler, T. S. (2022). Material and energy flow analysis for environmental and economic impact assessment of industrial recycling routes for lithium-ion traction batteries. *Journal of Cleaner Production, 377*, 134344. doi:10.1016/j.jclepro.2022.134344

Boar, C., Holden, H., & Wadsworth, A. (2020). Impending arrival – a sequel to the survey on central bank digital currency. *BIS Papers.* www.bis.org

Boguszewicz, C., Boguszewicz, M., Iqbal, Z., Khan, S., Gaba, G. S., Suresh, A., & Pervaiz, B. (2021). The fourth industrial revolution-cyberspace mental wellbeing: Harnessing science & technology for humanity. *Global foundation for cyber studies and research.*

Bol, N., Helberger, N., & Weert, J. C. (2018). Differences in mobile health app use: A source of new digital inequalities? *The Information Society, 34*(3), 183–193. doi:10.1080/01972243.2018.1438550

Bolt, W., Lubbersen, V., & Wierts, P. (2022). *GETTING THE BALANCE RIGHT: Crypto, stablecoin and CBDC* (736). https://www.dnb.nl/media/jo3h1dlu/working_paper_no-_736.pdf

Boney-Dutra, V., Guirguis, H., & Mueller, G. R. (2013). Did intraday trading by leveraged and inverse leveraged etfs create excess price volatility? A look at REITs and the broad market. *Journal of Real Estate Portfolio Management, 19*(1), 1–16. https://www.scopus.com/inward/record.uri?eid=2-s2.0-84881086451&partnerID=40&md5=8399a7e8d2adb28b832fdd34f320c238. doi:10.1080/10835547.2013.12089942

Bordo, M. D. (2021). *Central Bank Digital Currency In Historical Perspective: Another Crossroad In Monetary History* (29171). NBER. https://www.nber.org/system/files/working_papers/w29171/w29171.pdf

Bordo, M. D., & Levin, A. T. (2017). Central Bank Digital Currency and the Future of Monetary Policy. In *National Bureau of Economic Research Working Paper Series* (23711). NBER. doi:10.3386/w23711

Bossu, W., Itatani, M., Margulis, C., Rossi, A., Weenink, H., & Yoshinaga, A. (2020). Legal Aspects of Central Bank Digital Currency: Central Bank and Monetary Law Considerations. SSRN *Electronic Journal*. https://papers.ssrn.com/sol3/papers.cfm?abstract_id=3758088 doi:10.5089/9781513561622.001

Bozan, V., & Treré, E. (2023). When digital inequalities meet digital disconnection: Studying the material conditions of disconnection in rural Turkey. *Convergence (London)*, *135485652311745*. Advance online publication. doi:10.1177/13548565231174596

Bradley, T. (2022). The Future Of Work In 2022 And Beyond. *Forbes*. https://www.forbes.com/sites/tonybradley/2022/03/09/the-future-of-work-in-2022-and-beyond/

Bradley, T. (2022, March 9). The Future Of Work In 2022 And Beyond. *Forbes*. https://www.forbes.com/sites/tonybradley/2022/03/09/the-future-of-work-in-2022-and-beyond/

Bradshaw, F. (2019, September 26). Are you afraid of missing out? replace FOMO with JOMO and rediscover your inner peace. Mind Tools Blog. *Mind Tools*. https://www.mindtools.com/blog/fear-and-joy-of-missing-out/

Braukmann, J., Schmitt, A., Ďuranová, L., & Ohly, S. (2018). Identifying ICT-Related Affective Events Across Life Domains and Examining their Unique Relationships with Employee Recovery. *Journal of Business and Psychology*, *33*(4), 529–544. doi:10.100710869-017-9508-7

Brdulak, A., Chaberek, G., & Jagodziński, J. (2020). Development forecasts for the zero-emission bus fleet in servicing public transport in chosen EU member countries. *Energies*, *13*(16), 4239. doi:10.3390/en13164239

Brown, L., & Kuss, D. J. (2020). Fear of missing out, mental wellbeing, and social connectedness: A seven-day social media abstinence trial. *International Journal of Environmental Research and Public Health*, *17*(12), 4566. doi:10.3390/ijerph17124566 PMID:32599962

Brown, R., Mawson, S., Lee, N., & Peterson, L. (2019). Start-up factories, transnational entrepreneurs and entrepreneurial ecosystems: Unpacking the lure of start-up accelerator programmes. *European Planning Studies*, *27*(5), 885–904. doi:10.1080/09654313.2019.1588858

Bryman, A. (2016). *Social research methods* (5th ed.). Oxford University Press.

Brynjolfsson, E., Horton, J., Ozimek, A., Rock, D., Sharma, G., & TuYe, H.-Y. (2020). *COVID-19 and Remote Work: An Early Look at US Data* (w27344; p. w27344). National Bureau of Economic Research. doi:10.3386/w27344

Bucci, S., Schwannauer, M., & Berry, N. (2019). The digital revolution and its impact on mental health care. *Psychology and Psychotherapy: Theory, Research and Practice, 92*(2), 277–297. doi:10.1111/papt.12222 PMID:30924316

Bucher, E., Fieseler, C., & Suphan, A. (2013). The stress potential of social media in the workplace. *Information Communication and Society, 16*(10), 1639–1667. doi:10.1080/1369118X.2012.710245

Butler, W.D, Sargent, A., & Smith, K. (2022). Information Hygiene and Info-in SA. *SA News.* https://www.sanews.gov.za/south-africa/first-case-coronavirus-https://www.pwc.com/ua/en/publications/2021/information-hygiene.html

Bzo, I. (2023). *Fintech trends worth following in 2023 and beyond.* Fintech Nexus. https://www.fintechnexus.com/fintech-trends-worth-following-in-2023-and-beyond/

Cascio, W. F., & Montealegre, R. (2016). How technology is changing work and organizations. *Annual Review of Organizational Psychology and Organizational Behavior, 3*(1), 349–375. doi:10.1146/annurev-orgpsych-041015-062352

Castells, M. (1996). *The rise of the network society.* Blackwell.

Çelik, I. K., Eru, O., & Cop, R. (2019). The effects of consumers' FOMO tendencies on impulse buying and the effects of impulse buying on post-purchase regret: An investigation on retail stores. BRAIN. *Broad Research in Artificial Intelligence and Neuroscience, 10*(3), 124–138.

Chan, K., Chockalingam, M., & Lai, K. W. L. (2000). Overnight information and intraday trading behavior: Evidence from NYSE cross-listed stocks and their local market information. *Journal of Multinational Financial Management, 10*(3–4), 495–509. doi:10.1016/S1042-444X(00)00030-X

Chan, S. S., Van Solt, M., Cruz, R. E., Philp, M., Bahl, S., Serin, N., Amaral, N. B., Schindler, R., Bartosiak, A., Kumar, S., & Canbulut, M. (2022, August 13). Social media and mindfulness: From the fear of missing out (FOMO) to the joy of missing out (JOMO). *The Journal of Consumer Affairs, 56*(3), 1312–1331. doi:10.1111/joca.12476

Chaum, D., Grothoff, C., & Moser, T. (2021). How to Issue a Central Bank Digital Currency. *Ideas.* https://ideas.repec.org/p/arx/papers/2103.00254.html

Chen, Y. R. R., & Schulz, P. J. (2016). The effect of information communication technology interventions on reducing social isolation in the elderly: A systematic review. *Journal of Medical Internet Research, 18*(1), e4596. doi:10.2196/jmir.4596 PMID:26822073

Cheong, C. W. (2019). Cryptocurrencies vs global foreign exchange risk. *The Journal of Risk Finance, 20*(4), 330–351. doi:10.1108/JRF-11-2018-0178

Cherry, M. A. (2009). Working for (Virtually) Minimum Wage: Applying the Fair Labor Standards act in Cyberspace. *Alabama Law Review, 60*(5), 1077–1110.

Cho, J. (2015). Roles of Smartphone App Use in Improving Social Capital and Reducing Social Isolation. *Cyberpsychology, Behavior, and Social Networking, 18*(6), 350–355. (). doi:10.1089/cyber.2014.0657

Choi, S. B., & Lim, M. S. (2016). Effects of social and technology overload on psychological well-being in young South Korean adults: The mediatory role of social network service addiction. *Computers in Human Behavior, 61*, 245–254. doi:10.1016/j.chb.2016.03.032

Choraś, M., Pawlicka, A., Kozik, R., & Woźniak, M. (2022). How Machine Learning May Prevent the Breakdown of Democracy by Contributing to Fake News Detection,& quot. *IT Professional, 24*(2), 25–31. doi:10.1109/MITP.2022.3151312

Chou, A. (2019). What's in the Black Box: Balancing Financial Inclusion and Privacy in Digital Consumer Lending. *Duke Law Journal, 69*, 1183.

Cijan, A., Jenič, L., Lamovšek, A., & Stemberger, J. (2019). How digitalization changes the workplace. *Dynamic relationships management journal, 8*(1), 3-12.

Coca-Stefaniak, J. A. (2021). Beyond smart tourism cities – towards a new generation of "wise" tourism destinations. *Journal of Tourism Futures, 7*(2), 251–258. doi:10.1108/JTF-11-2019-0130

Cohen, B. H., & Shin, H. S. (2013). Positive Feedback Trading Under Stress: Evidence from the US Treasury Securities Market. *GLOBAL ECONOMIC REVIEW, 42*(4, SI), 314–345. doi:10.1080/1226508X.2013.860707

Cohen, M. (2007). 'Detox': Science or sales pitch? *Australian Family Physician, 36*(12). PMID:18075624

Collier, R. (2009). *Virtual detox: Inpatient therapy for Internet addicts.*

Cording, J. (2018, July 21). Is the Joy of Missing Out the New Self-Care? *Forbes.*

Corrado, M. E., & Sandy, M. H. (2017). *Digital Preservation for Libraries, Archives, and Museums* (2nd ed.). Rowman & Littlefield.

Cox, J. R., & Wallace, A. D. (2002). *Archives and the Public Good. Accountability and Records in Modern Society.* Quorum Books.

Csibi, S., Griffiths, M. D., Demetrovics, Z., & Szabo, A. (2021). Analysis of Problematic Smartphone Use Across Different Age Groups within the 'Components Model of Addiction'. *International Journal of Mental Health and Addiction, 19*(3), 616–631. doi:10.100711469-019-00095-0

Cukierman, A. (2019). Welfare and Political Economy Aspects of a Central Bank Digital Currency. *Federal Reserve Bank of Dallas, Globalization Institute Working Papers, 2019*(355). Reserve Bank of Dallas. doi:10.24149/gwp355

Curran, V., Matthews, L., Fleet, L., Simmons, K., Gustafson, D. L., & Wetsch, L. (2017). A review of digital, social, and mobile technologies in health professional education. *The Journal of Continuing Education in the Health Professions*, *37*(3), 195–206. doi:10.1097/CEH.0000000000000168 PMID:28834849

Czyżowska, N., & Gurba, E. (2022). Enhancing meaning in life and psychological well-being among a european cohort of young adults via a gratitude intervention. *Frontiers in Psychology*, *12*, 751081. doi:10.3389/fpsyg.2021.751081 PMID:35058837

Dangwal, A., Kaur, S., Taneja, S., & Taneja, S. (2022). A Bibliometric Analysis of Green Tourism Based on the Scopus Platform. In J. Kaur, P. Jindal, & A. Singh (Eds.), *Developing Relationships, Personalization, and Data Herald in Marketing 5.0* (Vol. i, pp. 1–327). IGI Global. doi:10.4018/978-1-6684-4496-2.ch015

Dangwal, A., Taneja, S., Özen, E., Todorovic, I., & Grima, S. (2022). Abridgement of Renewables: It's Potential and Contribution to India's GDP. *International Journal of Sustainable Development and Planning*, *17*(8), 2357–2363. doi:10.18280/ijsdp.170802

Darrat, A. F., Rahman, S., & Zhong, M. (2003). Intraday trading volume and return volatility of the DJIA stocks: A note. *Journal of Banking & Finance*, *27*(10), 2035–2043. doi:10.1016/S0378-4266(02)00321-7

DashA. (2012, July 19). JOMO! Retrieved from http://anildash.com/2012/07/19/jom

Daud, S. N. M., & Ahmad, A. H. (2023). Financial inclusion, economic growth and the role of digital technology. *Finance Research Letters*, *53*(103602), 157–160. doi:10.1016/j.frl.2022.103602

David, M. E., & Roberts, J. A. (2021). Smartphone Use during the COVID-19 Pandemic: Social Versus Physical Distancing. *International Journal of Environmental Research and Public Health*, *18*(3), 1034. doi:10.3390/ijerph18031034 PMID:33503907

Davis, M., Kumiega, A., & Van Vliet, B. (2013). Ethics, finance, and automation: A preliminary survey of problems in high frequency trading. *Science and Engineering Ethics*, *19*(3), 851–874. doi:10.100711948-012-9412-5 PMID:23138232

Day, G. S. (2011). Closing the marketing capabilities gap. *Journal of Marketing*, *75*(4), 183–195. doi:10.1509/jmkg.75.4.183

De Jonge, J., Spoor, E., Sonnentag, S., Dormann, C., & van den Tooren, M. (2012). "Take a break?!" Off-job recovery, job demands, and job resources as predictors of health, active learning, and creativity. *European Journal of Work and Organizational Psychology*, *21*(3), 321–348. doi:10.1080/1359432X.2011.576009

Decembrele, B. (2018, July 11). *Your workplace guide to summer vacation*. LinkedIn.

Dedrick, J., Gurbaxani, V., & Kraemer, K. L. (2003). Information technology and economic performance: A critical review of the empirical evidence. *ACM Computing Surveys*, *35*(1), 1–28. doi:10.1145/641865.641866

Demir, A., Pesqué-Cela, V., Altunbas, Y., & Murinde, V. (2022). Fintech, financial inclusion and income inequality: A quantile regression approach. *European Journal of Finance, 28*(1), 86–107. doi:10.1080/1351847X.2020.1772335

Demirci, K., Akgönül, M., & Akpinar, A. (2015). Relationship of € smartphone use severity with sleep quality, depression, and anxiety in university students. *Journal of Behavioral Addictions, 4*(2), 85–92. doi:10.1556/2006.4.2015.010 PMID:26132913

Demirgüç-Kunt, A., Klapper, L. F., Singer, D., & Van Oudheusden, P. (2015). The global findex database 2014: Measuring financial inclusion around the world. *World Bank Policy Research Working Paper*, No. 7255.

Depot, M. S. (2023). The Secret to a Digital Detox for Entrepreneurs. *Smart Service.* https://www.smartservice.com/smart-service-blog/the-secret-to-a-digital-detox-for-entrepreneurs/

Depot, M. S. (2023, January 5). *The Secret to a Digital Detox for Entrepreneurs.* Smart Service. https://www.smartservice.com/smart-service-blog/the-secret-to-a-digital-detox-for-entrepreneurs/

Desai, V., & Vidyapee, B. (2019). Digital Marketing: A Review. *International Journal of Trend in Scientific Research and Development, Special Issue*(Special Issue-FIIIIPM2019), 196–200. doi:10.31142/ijtsrd23100

Dev, S. M. (2006). Financial inclusion: Issues and challenges. *Economic and Political Weekly*, 4310–4313.

Dhaliwal, N. (2020). From FOMO to JOMO: Why I now prefer a life less risky. *The Guardian.*

Dhir, A., Yossatorn, Y., Kaur, P., & Chen, S. (2018). Online social media fatigue and psychological wellbeing—A study of compulsive use, fear of missing out, fatigue, anxiety and depression. *International Journal of Information Management, 40*, 141–152. doi:10.1016/j.ijinfomgt.2018.01.012

Díaz-Meneses, G., & Estupinán-Ojeda, M. (2022). The Outbreak of Digital Detox Motives and Their Public Health Implications for Holiday Destinations. *International Journal of Environmental Research and Public Health, 19*(3), 1548. doi:10.3390/ijerph19031548 PMID:35162570

Dickinson, J. E., Hibbert, J. F., & Filimonau, V. (2016). Mobile technology and the tourist experience:(Dis) connection at the campsite. *Tourism Management, 57*, 193–201. doi:10.1016/j.tourman.2016.06.005

Dickinson, L. (1995). Autonomy and motivation a literature review. *System, 23*(2), 165–174. doi:10.1016/0346-251X(95)00005-5

Dictionaries, O. (2023, September 16). *Definition of digital detox noun from the Oxford Advanced Learner's Dictionary.* Oxford Press. https://www.oxfordlearnersdictionaries.com/definition/english/digital-detox

Dienlin, T., & Johannes, N. (2022). The impact of digital technology use on adolescent well-being. *Dialogues in Clinical Neuroscience.* PMID:32699513

Digital Assets Worldwide. (2023). Statista. https://www.statista.com/outlook/dmo/fintech/digital-assets/worldwide#revenue

Dixon, S. J. (2021). *Number of worldwide social network users 2027.* Statista. https://www.statista.com/statistics/278414/number-of-worldwide-social-network-users/

Dlugosch, O., Brandt, T., & Neumann, D. (2022). Combining analytics and simulation methods to assess the impact of shared, autonomous electric vehicles on sustainable urban mobility. *Information & Management, 59*(5), 103285. doi:10.1016/j.im.2020.103285

Dodgson, L. (2018a, July 26). 'JOMO' is the joy of missing out- here are 3 ways people find happiness in not being involved. *Business Insider.*

Dodgson, L. (2018b, April 24). Here's what's really going on in your brain when you experience 'FOMO'- The fear of missing out. *Business Insider.*

Dryglas, D., & Klimkiewicz, K. (2023). Emerging trends in employee competencies in Polish therapeutic tourism enterprises. *International Journal of Spa and Wellness, 6*(1), 157–175. doi:10.1080/24721735.2022.2152849

Duke, É., & Montag, C. (2017). Smartphone addiction, daily interruptions and self-reported productivity. *Addictive Behaviors Reports, 6*, 90–95. doi:10.1016/j.abrep.2017.07.002 PMID:29450241

Dutt, B. (2023). Wellbeing Amid Digital Risks: Implications of Digital Risks, Threats, and Scams on Users' Wellbeing. *Media and Communication, 11*(2), 355–366. doi:10.17645/mac.v11i2.6480

Ediagbonya, V., & Tioluwani, C. (2023). The role of fintech in driving financial inclusion in developing and emerging markets: Issues, challenges and prospects. *Technological Sustainability, 2*(1), 100–119. doi:10.1108/TECHS-10-2021-0017

Edmunds, A., & Morris, A. (2000). The problem of information overload in business organisations: A review of the literature. *International Journal of Information Management, 20*(1), 17–28. doi:10.1016/S0268-4012(99)00051-1

Efimova, G. Z., & Semenov, M. Y. (2020). Digital detox of the youth (On the example of social networks). *RUDN Journal of Sociology, 20*(3), 572–581. doi:10.22363/2313-2272-2020-20-3-572-581

Egger, I., Lei, S. I., & Wassler, P. (2020). Digital free tourism – An exploratory study of tourist motivations. *Tourism Management, 79*, 104098. doi:10.1016/j.tourman.2020.104098

Elhai, J. D., Gallinari, E. F., Rozgonjuk, D., & Yang, H. (2020). Depression, anxiety and fear of missing out as correlates of social, non-social and problematic smartphone use. *Addictive Behaviors, 105*, 106335. https://doi.org/. 106335. doi:10.1016/j.addbeh.2020

Elhai, J. D., Yang, H., & Montag, C. Fear of missing out (FOMO): overview, theoretical underpinnings, and literature review on relations with severity of negative affectivity and problematic technology use. *Braz J Psychiatry.* http://dx.doi.org/ doi:10.1590/1516-4446-2020-0870

Elhai, J. D., Dvorak, R. D., Levine, J. C., & Hall, B. J. (2017). Problematic smartphone use: A conceptual overview and systematic review of relations with anxiety and depression psychopathology. *Journal of Affective Disorders, 207*, 251–259. doi:10.1016/j.jad.2016.08.030 PMID:27736736

Elhai, J. D., Levine, J. C., Alghraibeh, A. M., Alafnan, A. A., Aldraiweesh, A. A., & Hall, B. J. (2018). Fear of missing out: Testing relationships with negative affectivity, online social engagement, and problematic smartphone use. *Computers in Human Behavior, 89*, 289–298. doi:10.1016/j.chb.2018.08.020

Elhai, J. D., Levine, J. C., Dvorak, R. D., & Hall, B. J. (2016). Fear of missing out, need for touch, anxiety and depression are related to problematic smartphone use. *Computers in Human Behavior, 63*, 509–516. doi:10.1016/j.chb.2016.05.079

Elhai, J. D., Yang, H., Fang, J., Bai, X., & Hall, B. J. (2020). Depression and anxiety symptoms are related to problematic smartphone use severity in Chinese young adults: Fear of missing out as a mediator. *Addictive Behaviors, 101*, 105962. doi:10.1016/j.addbeh.2019.04.020 PMID:31030950

El-Khoury, J., Haidar, R., Kanj, R. R., Ali, L. B., & Majari, G. (2021). Characteristics of social media 'detoxification' in university students. *The Libyan Journal of Medicine, 16*(1), 1846861. doi:10.1080/19932820.2020.1846861 PMID:33250011

EngertW.FungB. S. C. (2017). *Central Bank Digital Currency: Motivations and Implications.* Bank of Canada. doi:10.34989/SDP-2017-16

Eppler, M. J., & Mengis, J. (2008). The Concept of Information Overload-A Review of Literature from Organization Science, Accounting, Marketing, MIS, and Related Disciplines (2004). *The Information Society: An International Journal, 20*(5), 271–305.

False Information: A Concept Explication and Taxonomy of Online Content. *American Behavioural Scientist, 65*(2), 180–212. . doi:10.1177/0002764219878224

Farayola, O. A., Abdul, A. A., Irabor, B. O., & Okeleke, E. C. (2023). INNOVATIVE BUSINESS MODELS DRIVEN BY AI TECHNOLOGIES: A REVIEW. *Computer Science & IT Research Journal, 4*(2), 85–110. doi:10.51594/csitrj.v4i2.608

Farzaneh, F., & Jung, S. (2023). Lifecycle carbon footprint comparison between internal combustion engine versus electric transit vehicle: A case study in the US. *Journal of Cleaner Production, 390*, 136111. doi:10.1016/j.jclepro.2023.136111

Fatima, M., & Akhtar, S. J. (2023). An overview of micro, small and medium enterprises (MSMES) in the state of Uttar Pradesh. [JEBR]. *EPRA International Journal of Economic and Business Review, 11*(1), 1–10. doi:10.36713/epra12155

Fearn, A., & Saunders, C. (2022). *Individuals holding cryptoassets: uptake and understanding.* Skadden. https://www.skadden.com/-/media/files/publications/2022/09/cryptoasset-seizures-and-forfeitures/individuals_holding_cryptoassets_uptake_and_understanding.pdf

Feenberg, A. (2010). Ten Paradoxes of Technology. *Techné: Research in Philosophy and Technology, 14*(1).

Feghali, K., Mora, N., & Nassif, P. (2021). Financial inclusion, bank market structure, and financial stability: International evidence. *The Quarterly Review of Economics and Finance, 80,* 236–257. doi:10.1016/j.qref.2021.01.007

Felepchuk, L. (2020). *What the heck is the new travel trend "JOMO?"* Canada. com. https://o.canada.com/travel/what-the-heck-is-the-new-travel-trend-jomo

Felix, L., & Dean, B. (2012). *Our story, 2 decades in the making.*

Felix, L., & Dean, B. (2012). *Our story, 2 decades in the making.* Digital Detox. https://www.digitaldetox.com/our-story

Fernández-Villaverde, J., Schilling, L., & Uhlig, H. (2020). Central Bank Digital Currency: When Price and Bank Stability Collide. SSRN *Electronic Journal.* https://papers.ssrn.com/sol3/papers.cfm?abstract_id=3753955 doi:10.2139/ssrn.3606226

Ferretti, P., & Martino, P. (2023). FinTech: Challenges and Opportunities for Banks and Financial Markets. *Banking and Financial Markets: New Risks and Challenges from Fintech and Sustainable Finance,* (pp. 73-94). Research Gate.

Financial Services Global Market Report 2023. (2023). Report Linker. https://www.reportlinker.com/p06277918/Financial-Services-Global-Market-Report.html?utm_source=GNW

FinTech – Worldwide, Statista Market Forecast. (2023). Statista. https://www.statista.com/outlook/dmo/fintech/worldwide

Fioravanti, G., Prostamo, A., & Casale, S. (2019). Taking a short break from Instagram: The effects on subjective well-being. *Cyberpsychology, Behavior, and Social Networking.* doi:10.1089/cyber.2019.0400 PMID:31851833

Firmansyah, R. O., Hamdani, R. A., & Kuswardhana, D. (2020). The use of smartphone on learning activities: Systematic review. *IOP Conference Series. Materials Science and Engineering, 850*(1), 012006. doi:10.1088/1757-899X/850/1/012006

Fitzpatrick, B., Liang, X., & Straub, J. (2021). Fake news and phishing detection follow in 2022. *Digital Minimalism.* https://digitalminimalism.com/verifying-the-authenticity- Global, USA.

Florackis, C., Louca, C., Michaely, R., & Weber, M. (2023). Cybersecurity risk. *Review of Financial Studies*, *36*(1), 351–407. doi:10.1093/rfs/hhac024

FOMO. (2021, July 9). FOMO, JOMO and COVID: How Missing Out and Enjoying Life Are Impacting How We Navigate a Pandemic. *Journal of Organizational Psychology*, *21*(3). doi:10.33423/jop.v21i3.4309

Fornell, C., & Larcker, D. F. (1981). Evaluating structural equation models with unobservable variables and measurement error. *JMR, Journal of Marketing Research*, *18*(1), 39–50. doi:10.1177/002224378101800104

Franchina, V., Vanden Abeele, M., Van Rooij, A. J., Lo Coco, G., & De Marez, L. (2018). Fear of missing out as a predictor of problematic social media use and phubbing behavior among Flemish adolescents. *International Journal of Environmental Research and Public Health*, *15*(10), 2319. doi:10.3390/ijerph15102319 PMID:30360407

Friedline, T., Naraharisetti, S., & Weaver, A. (2020). Digital redlining: Poor rural communities' access to fintech and implications for financial inclusion. *Journal of Poverty*, *24*(5-6), 517–541. doi:10.1080/10875549.2019.1695162

Fuller, K. (2018, July 26). JOMO: The joy of missing out: JOMO is the emotionally intelligent antidote to FOMO. *Psychology Today*.

Gahlot, C. S., & Ghosh, S. (2023). Emerging Opportunities and Challenges in FinTech Industry–A Comparative Study of India With Other Jurisdictions. *Technology, Management and Business: Evolving Perspectives*, (pp. 21-31). Research Gate.

Gaikwad, A., & Dhokare, C. S. (2020). India: A Growth opportunities for MSME. *International Journal of Multidisciplinary Research*, *6*(6), 25–30.

Gallego-Losada, M. J., Montero-Navarro, A., García-Abajo, E., & Gallego-Losada, R. (2023). Digital financial inclusion. Visualizing the academic literature. *Research in International Business and Finance*, *64*, 101862. doi:10.1016/j.ribaf.2022.101862

Garad, A., Al-Ansi, A. M., & Qamari, I. N. (2021). THE ROLE OF E-LEARNING INFRASTRUCTURE AND COGNITIVE COMPETENCE IN DISTANCE LEARNING EFFECTIVENESS DURING THE COVID-19 PANDEMIC. *Cakrawala Pendidikan: Jurnal Ilmiah Pendidikan*, *40*(1), 81–91. doi:10.21831/cp.v40i1.33474

Geeta, S. D. T., Mathiraj, S. P., Shanthini, S., Jayanthi, K., & Vidhya, A. A. (2023, November). Issues and challenges faced by micro, small and medium enterprises after goods and services tax implementation. In AIP Conference Proceedings (Vol. 2821, No. 1). AIP Publishing. doi:10.1063/5.0158580

Ghasemi-Marzbali, A. (2022). Fast-charging station for electric vehicles, challenges and issues: A comprehensive review. *Journal of Energy Storage*, *49*, 104136. doi:10.1016/j.est.2022.104136

Ghosh, D., Mehta, P., & Avittathur, B. (2021). Supply chain capabilities and competitiveness of high-tech manufacturing start-ups in India. *Benchmarking, 28*(5), 1783–1808. doi:10.1108/BIJ-12-2018-0437

Ghosh, P., Neufeld, A., & Sahoo, J. K. (2022). Forecasting directional movements of stock prices for intraday trading using LSTM and random forests. *Finance Research Letters, 46*, 102280. Advance online publication. doi:10.1016/j.frl.2021.102280

Gil, F., Chamarro, A., & Oberst, U. (2015). PO-14: Addiction to online social networks: A question of "fear of missing out"? *Journal of Behavioral Addictions, 4*(S1), 51–52.

Golub, A., Grossmass, L., & Poon, S.-H. (2021). Ultra-short tenor yield curve for intraday trading and settlement. *European Journal of Finance, 27*(4–5), 441–459. doi:10.1080/135184 7X.2019.1662821

Gomber, P., Kauffman, R. J., Parker, C., & Weber, B. W. (2018). On the fintech revolution: Interpreting the forces of innovation, disruption, and transformation in financial services. *Journal of Management Information Systems, 35*(1), 220–265. doi:10.1080/07421222.2018.1440766

Gong, Y., Schroeder, A., & Plaisance, P. L. (2023). Digital detox tourism: An Ellulian critique. *Annals of Tourism Research, 103*, 103646. doi:10.1016/j.annals.2023.103646

González-PadillaP. (2022). *Tourist behavior and demand for digital disconnection: A review.* doi:10.34623/TP23-A945

Gorman, M. E. (2002). Types of knowledge and their roles in technology transfer. *The Journal of Technology Transfer, 27*(3), 219–231. doi:10.1023/A:1015672119590

Gracy, B.D (2002). What You Get Is Not What You See: Forgery and the Corruption of Recordkeeping Systems. In Cox, J.R, and Wallace, A.D (eds). *Archives and the Public Good. Accountability and Records in Modern Society.* Quorum Books.

Griffiths, M. D. (1996). Internet addiction: An issue for clinical psychology? *Clinical Psychology Forum, 97*(97), 32–36. doi:10.53841/bpscpf.1996.1.97.32

Griffiths, M. D. (1998). Internet addiction: Does it really exist? In J. Gackenbach (Ed.), *Psychology and the internet: Intrapersonal, interpersonal, and transpersonal implications.* Academic Press.

Grisé, M. L., & Gallupe, R. B. (1999). Information overload: Addressing the productivity paradox in face-to-face electronic meetings. *Journal of Management Information Systems, 16*(3), 157–185. doi:10.1080/07421222.1999.11518260

Guckenbiehl, P., & Corral de Zubielqui, G. (2022). Start-ups' business model changes during the COVID-19 pandemic: Counteracting adversities and pursuing opportunities. *International Small Business Journal, 40*(2), 150–177. doi:10.1177/02662426211055447 PMID:35250144

Gui, M., & Büchi, M. (2019). From Use to Overuse: Digital Inequality in the Age of Communication Abundance. *Social Science Computer Review*, 1–17. doi:10.1177/0894439319851163

Gui, M., Fasoli, M., & Carradore, R. (2017). Digital well-being. Developing a new theoretical tool for media literacy research. *Italian Journal of Sociology of Education*, 9(1), 155–173.

Gupta, U., & Agarwal, B. (2023). The role of digital financial services on Indian MSMEs. *Indian Journal of Finance, 17*(2), 08-26.

Gupta, M., Arora, K., & Taneja, S. (2023). Bibliometric analysis on employee engagement and human resource management. In *Enhancing Customer Engagement Through Location-Based Marketing*. IGI Global. doi:10.4018/978-1-6684-8177-6.ch013

Gupta, M., Taneja, S., Sharma, V., Singh, A., Rupeika-Apoga, R., & Jangir, K. (2023). Does Previous Experience with the Unified Payments Interface (UPI) Affect the Usage of Central Bank Digital Currency (CBDC)? *Journal of Risk and Financial Management, 16*(6), 286. doi:10.3390/jrfm16060286

Hair, J. F., Black, W. C., Babin, B. J., Anderson, R. E., & Tatham, R. L. (2010). *Multivariate data analysis* (7th ed.). Prentice Hall.

Haleem, A., Javaid, M., Qadri, M. A., & Suman, R. (2022). Understanding the role of digital technologies in education: A review. *Sustainable Operations and Computers*, 3, 275–285. doi:10.1016/j.susoc.2022.05.004

Händel, M., Stephan, M., Gläser-Zikuda, M., Kopp, B., Bedenlier, S., & Ziegler, A. (2022). Digital readiness and its effects on higher education students' socio-emotional perceptions in the context of the COVID-19 pandemic. *Journal of Research on Technology in Education, 54*(2), 267–280. doi:10.1080/15391523.2020.1846147

Hardcastle, S. J., Hancox, J., Hattar, A., Maxwell-Smith, C., Thøgersen-Ntoumani, C., & Hagger, M. S. (2015). Motivating the unmotivated: How can health behavior be changed in those unwilling to change? *Frontiers in Psychology*, 6, 835. doi:10.3389/fpsyg.2015.00835 PMID:26136716

Harmon, J., & Duffy, L. (2023). Turn off to tune in: Digital disconnection, digital consciousness, and meaningful leisure. *Journal of Leisure Research*, 1–21. doi:10.1080/00222216.2023.2246042

Harnischmacher, C., Markefke, L., Brendel, A. B., & Kolbe, L. (2023). Two-sided sustainability: Simulating battery degradation in vehicle to grid applications within autonomous electric port transportation. *Journal of Cleaner Production*, 384, 135598. doi:10.1016/j.jclepro.2022.135598

Hassan, M. K., Rabbani, M. R., Khan, S., & Ali, M. A. M. D. (2022). An Islamic Finance Perspective of Crowdfunding and Peer-To-Peer (P2P) Lending. In FinTech in Islamic Financial Institutions: Scope, Challenges, and Implications in Islamic Finance (pp. 263-277). Cham: Springer International Publishing.

Hayes, A. F. (2013). *Introduction to mediation, moderation, and conditional process analysis: A regression-based approach*. Guilford Press.

Healy, T. (2012). The unanticipated consequences of technology. *Nanotechnology: ethical and social Implications*, 155-173.

Heeks, R. (2008). Development Informatics. In *Development (Vol. 32)*. University of Manchester. http://www.digitale-chancen.de/transfer/downloads/MD280.pdf

Herman, D. (2000). Introducing short-term brands: A new branding tool for a new consumer reality. *Journal of Brand Management*, *7*(5), 330–340. doi:10.1057/bm.2000.23

Hesselberth, P. (2018). Connect, disconnect, reconnect historicizing the current gesture towards disconnectivity, from the plug-in drug to the digital detox. *Cinema et Cie*, *18*(30), 109 – 118. https://www.scopus.com/inward/record.uri?eid=2-s2.0-85106021 759&partnerID=40&md5=d7cc67cb56ff66f648f6d930b591192b

Hitlin, P. (2018). Internet, social media use and device ownership in U.S. have plateaued after years of growth [Internet]. Pew Research. https://www.pewresearch.org/fact-tank/2018/09/28/internet-so cial-media-use-and-device-ownership-in-u-s-have-plateaued-af ter-years-of-growth/ » https://www.pewresearch.org/fact-tank/2018/09/28/internet-so cial-media-use-and-device-ownership-in-u-s-have-plateaued-af ter-years-of-growth/

Ho, K. K., Chan, J. Y., & Chiu, K. W. (2022). Fake News and Misinformation During the Pandemic: What We Know and What We Do Not Know. *IT Professional*, *24* (2), 19-24. https://www.bbc.com/news/world-africa-57581054

Hoang, Q., Cronin, J., & Skandalis, A. (2023). Futureless vicissitudes: Gestural anti-consumption and the reflexively impotent (anti-)consumer. *Marketing Theory*, *14705931231153*1(4), 585–606. Advance online publication. doi:10.1177/14705931231153193

Hoang, T. G., & Bui, M. L. (2023). Business intelligence and analytic (BIA) stage-of-practice in micro-, small-and medium-sized enterprises (MSMEs). *Journal of Enterprise Information Management*, *36*(4), 1080–1104. doi:10.1108/JEIM-01-2022-0037

Hoang, T. G., Nguyen, G. N. T., & Le, D. A. (2022). Developments in financial technologies for achieving the Sustainable Development Goals (SDGs): FinTech and SDGs. In *Disruptive technologies and eco-innovation for sustainable development* (pp. 1–19). IGI Global. doi:10.4018/978-1-7998-8900-7.ch001

Ho, C. M. (2013). Private information, overconfidence and intraday trading behaviour: Empirical study of the Taiwan stock market. *Applied Financial Economics*, *23*(4), 325–345. doi:10.1080 /09603107.2012.720012

Honisch, E., & Ottenbacher, M. (2017). Crowdfunding in restaurants: Setting the stage. *Journal of Culinary Science & Technology*, *15*(3), 223–238. doi:10.1080/15428052.2016.1225539

Hopkins, E., Potoglou, D., Orford, S., & Cipcigan, L. (2023). Can the equitable roll out of electric vehicle charging infrastructure be achieved? *Renewable & Sustainable Energy Reviews*, *182*, 113398. doi:10.1016/j.rser.2023.113398

Horesh, N., Zhou, Y., & Quinn, J. (2023). Home charging for all: Techno-economic and life cycle assessment of multi-unit dwelling electric vehicle charging hubs. *Journal of Cleaner Production*, *383*, 135551. doi:10.1016/j.jclepro.2022.135551

Hover, A., & Wise, T. (2022). Exploring ways to create 21st century digital learning experiences. *Education 3-13, 50*(1), 40–53. doi:10.1080/03004279.2020.1826993

HOW MANY SMARTPHONES ARE IN THE WORLD ? (2023). Bank My Cell.Com. https://www.bankmycell.com/blog/how-many-phones-are-in-the-world#:~:text=How

Hsi & Potts. (2000, October). Studying the evolution and enhancement of software features. In *Proceedings 2000 International Conference on Software Maintenance* (pp. 143-151). IEEE.

Huang, H., Mbanyele, W., Fan, S., & Zhao, X. (2022). Digital financial inclusion and energy-environment performance: What can learn from China. *Structural Change and Economic Dynamics*, *63*, 342–366. doi:10.1016/j.strueco.2022.10.007

Hurley, C. O. (2018). MSME competitiveness in small island economies: A comparative systematic review of the literature from the past 24 years. *Entrepreneurship and Regional Development*, *30*(9-10), 1027–1068. doi:10.1080/08985626.2018.1515822

İnal, E. E., Demİrcİ, İ., Çetİntürk, A. İ., Akgönül, M., & Savaş, S. İ. (2015). Effects of smartphone overuse on hand function, pinch strength, and the median nerve. *Muscle & Nerve, 52*(2), 183–188. doi:10.1002/mus.24695 PMID:25914119

International Labour Organization. (2018). *The architecture of digital labour platforms: Policy recommendations on platform design for worker well-being*. ILO. www.ilo.org/publns

Irimiás, A. (2023). The Young Tourist and Social Media. In A. Irimiás, The Youth Tourist: Motives, Experiences and Travel Behaviour (pp. 63–81). Emerald Publishing Limited. doi:10.1108/978-1-80455-147-920231005

Jadli, A., Hain, M., & Hasbaoui, A. (2023). Artificial intelligence-based lead propensity prediction. *IAES International Journal of Artificial Intelligence, 12*(3), 1281–1290. doi:10.11591/ijai.v12.i3.pp1281-1290

Jangir, K., Sharma, V., Taneja, S., & Rupeika-Apoga, R. (2023). The Moderating Effect of Perceived Risk on Users' Continuance Intention for FinTech Services. *Journal of Risk and Financial Management*, *16*(1), 21. doi:10.3390/jrfm16010021

Jaramillo, L. E. S. (2018). Malware detection and mitigation techniques: Lessons learned from Mirai DDOS attack. *Journal of Information Systems Engineering & Management*, *3*(3), 19. doi:10.20897/jisem/2655

Jiang, D., Kalyuga, S., & Sweller, J. (2021). Comparing face-to-face and computer-mediated collaboration when teaching EFL writing skills. *Educational Psychology*, *41*(1), 5–24. doi:10.1080/01443410.2020.1785399

Jiang, G., Pan, J., Deng, W., Sun, Y., Guo, J., Che, K., Yang, Y., Lin, Z., Sun, Y., Huang, C., & Zhang, T. (2022). Recovery of high pure pyrolytic carbon black from waste tires by dual acid treatment. *Journal of Cleaner Production*, *374*, 133893. doi:10.1016/j.jclepro.2022.133893

Jiang, Y., & Balaji, M. S. (2022). Getting unwired: What drives travellers to take a digital detox holiday? *Tourism Recreation Research*, *47*(5–6), 453–469. doi:10.1080/02508281.2021.1889801

Ji, X., Wang, K., Xu, H., & Li, M. (2021). Has digital financial inclusion narrowed the urban-rural income gap: The role of entrepreneurship in China. *Sustainability (Basel)*, *13*(15), 8292. doi:10.3390u13158292

Jorge, A. (2019). Social media, interrupted: Users recounting temporary disconnection on Instagram. *Social Media + Society*, *5*(4), 2056305119881691. doi:10.1177/2056305119881691

Joshi, A., Sharma, R., & Baral, B. (2022). Comparative life cycle assessment of conventional combustion engine vehicle, battery electric vehicle and fuel cell electric vehicle in Nepal. *Journal of Cleaner Production*, *379*, 134407. doi:10.1016/j.jclepro.2022.134407

Juncal, B., Vides, G., Matos, P., & Sousa, B. B. (2022). Digital Detox, Trends, and Segmentation in Tourism. In C. M. Q. Ramos, S. Quinteiro, & A. R. Gonçalves (Eds.), (pp. 155–169). Advances in Business Strategy and Competitive Advantage. IGI Global. doi:10.4018/978-1-7998-8165-0.ch010

Kacetl, J., & Klímová, B. (2019). Use of Smartphone Applications in English Language Learning—A Challenge for Foreign Language Education. *Education Sciences*, *9*(3), 179. doi:10.3390/educsci9030179

Kahn, C., & Rivadeneyra, F. (2020). *Security and convenience of a central bank digital currency*. Publications. https://publications.gc.ca/collections/collection_2020/banque-bank-canada/FB3-7-2020-21-eng.pdf

Kajitani, K., Higashijima, I., Kaneko, K., Matsushita, T., Fukumori, H., & Kim, D. (2020). Short-term effect of a smartphone application on the mental health of university students: A pilot study using a user-centered design self-monitoring application for mental health. *PLoS One*, *15*(9), e0239592. doi:10.1371/journal.pone.0239592 PMID:32976515

Kamboj, N., Choudhary, V., & Trivedi, S. (2023). 5 Impact of Macroeconomic Determinants and Corporate Attributes on Firms' Financial Success in India. *Sustainability, Green Management, and Performance of SMEs*, 73.

Kang, I., Cui, H., & Son, J. (2019). Conformity consumption behavior and FOMO. *Sustainability (Basel)*, *11*(17), 4734. doi:10.3390u11174734

Kao, D.-X., Tsai, W.-C., Wang, Y.-H., & Yen, K.-C. (2018). An analysis on the intraday trading activity of VIX derivatives. *Journal of Futures Markets*, *38*(2), 158–174. doi:10.1002/fut.21857

Kao, E. H., & Fung, H.-G. (2012). Intraday trading activities and volatility in round-the-clock futures markets. *International Review of Economics & Finance*, *21*(1), 195–209. doi:10.1016/j.iref.2011.06.003

Karadas, T., Dilci, T., & Sagbas, N. Ö. (2023). Life in the Digital World. In R. Sine Nazlı & G. Sari (Eds.), (pp. 192–216). Advances in Human and Social Aspects of Technology. IGI Global. doi:10.4018/978-1-6684-8397-8.ch013

Karlsen, F. (2023). The digital detox camp: Practices and motivations for reverse domestication. In *The Routledge Handbook of Media and Technology Domestication*. Taylor and Francis. doi:10.4324/9781003265931-35

Karlsen, F., & Syvertsen, T. (2016). You can't smell roses online: Intruding Media and Reverse Domestication. *Nordicom Review*, *37*(1), 25–39. doi:10.1515/nor-2016-0021

Karr-Wisniewski, P., & Lu, Y. (2010). When more is too much: Operationalizing technology overload and exploring its impact on knowledge worker productivity. *Computers in Human Behavior*, *26*(5), 1061–1072. doi:10.1016/j.chb.2010.03.008

Karsay, K., Schmuck, D., Matthes, J., & Stevic, A. (2019). Longitudinal effects of excessive smartphone use on stress and loneliness: The moderating role of self-disclosure. *Cyberpsychology, Behavior, and Social Networking*, *22*(11), 706–713. doi:10.1089/cyber.2019.0255 PMID:31697600

Katsumata, P., Hemenway, J., & Gavins, W. (2010, October). Cybersecurity risk management. In *2010-MILCOM 2010 Military Communications Conference* (pp. 890-895). IEEE.

Kaur, G. (2023). *The history and evolution of the fintech industry*. Cointelegraph. https://cointelegraph.com/news/the-history-and-evolution-of-the-fintech-industry

Kaur, H., Singh, K., Kumar, P., & Kaur, A. (2023). Assessing the environmental sustainability corridor: An empirical study of Renewable energy consumption in BRICS nation. *IOP Conference Series. Earth and Environmental Science*, *1110*(1), 012053. Advance online publication. doi:10.1088/1755-1315/1110/1/012053

Kelikume, I. (2021). Digital financial inclusion, informal economy and poverty reduction in Africa. *Journal of Enterprising Communities: People and Places in the Global Economy*, *15*(4), 626–640. doi:10.1108/JEC-06-2020-0124

Kent, R. (2020). Self-tracking health over time: From the use of Instagram to perform optimal health to the protective shield of the digital detox. *Social Media + Society*, *6*(3), 2056305120940694. doi:10.1177/2056305120940694

Khare, A., Awasthi, G., & Shukla, R. P. (2019). Do mall events affect mall traffic and image? A qualitative study of Indian mall retailers. *Asia Pacific Journal of Marketing and Logistics, 32*(2), 343–365. doi:10.1108/APJML-01-2019-0021

Khera, P., Ng, S., Ogawa, S., & Sahay, R. (2022). Measuring digital financial inclusion in emerging market and developing economies: A new index. *Asian Economic Policy Review*, *17*(2), 213–230. doi:10.1111/aepr.12377

Khetawat, D., & Steele, R. G. (2023). Examining the Association Between Digital Stress Components and Psychological Wellbeing: A Meta-Analysis. *Clinical Child and Family Psychology Review, 26*(4), 957–974. doi:10.100710567-023-00440-9 PMID:37432506

King, A. L. S., Valença, A. M., Silva, A. C., Sancassiani, F., Machado, S., & Nardi, A. E. (2014). Nomophobia: Impact of cell phone use interfering with symptoms and emotions of individuals with panic disorder compared with A control group. *Clinical Practice and Epidemiology in Mental Health, 10*(1), 28–35. doi:10.2174/1745017901410010028 PMID:24669231

Kirsh, D. (2000). A Few Thoughts on Cognitive Overload. *Intellectica, 30*(1), 19–51. doi:10.3406/intel.2000.1592

Kline, R. B. (2005). *Principles and practice of structural equation modeling* (2nd ed.). The Guilford Press.

Ko, C. H., Yen, J. Y., Yen, C. F., Chen, C. S., & Chen, C. C. (2012). The association between internet addiction and psychiatric disorder: A review of the literature. *European Psychiatry, 27*(1), 1–8. doi:10.1016/j.eurpsy.2010.04.011 PMID:22153731

Koch, C., & Maskos, P. (2020). Passive balancing through intraday trading: Whether interactions between short-term trading and balancing stabilize Germany's electricity system. *International Journal of Energy Economics and Policy, 10*(2), 101–112. doi:10.32479/ijeep.8750

Kofman, P., & Payne, C. (2021). Digital financial inclusion of women: An ethical appraisal. *Handbook on ethics in finance*, 133-157.

Koh, F., Phoon, K. F., & Ha, C. D. (2018). Digital financial inclusion in Southeast Asia. In Handbook of Blockchain, Digital Finance, and Inclusion, Volume 2 (pp. 387-403). Academic Press.

KongD. R.LinT. C. (2021). Alternative investments in the Fintech era: The risk and return of Non-Fungible Token (NFT). *Available at* SSRN 3914085. doi:10.2139/ssrn.3914085

Kour, G. (2016). Digital Detoxification: A content analysis of user generated videos uploaded on Youtube by Facebook Quitters. *Media Watch, 7*(1), 75–83.

KPMG. (2021). *Pulse of Fintech*. KPMG.

Kross, E., Verduyn, P., Demiralp, E., Park, J., Lee, D. S., Lin, N., Shablack, H., Jonides, J., & Ybarra, O. (2013). Facebook use predicts declines in subjective well-being in young adults. *PLoS One, 8*(8), e69841. doi:10.1371/journal.pone.0069841 PMID:23967061

Kumar, P., & Taneja, S. Mukul, & Ozen, E. (2023). Digital transformation of the insurance industry - a case of the Indian insurance sector. In *The Impact of Climate Change and Sustainability Standards on the Insurance Market*. Wiley. https://www.scopus.com/inward/record.uri?eid=2-s2.0-85168611885&partnerID=40&md5=6c2fb77610b1390b55b6945d955c0955

Kumar, A., Singh, J. P., & Singh, A. K. (2022). COVID-19 Fake News Detection Using Ensemble-Based Deep Learning Model. *IT Professional, 24*(2), 32–37. doi:10.1109/MITP.2022.3149140

Kumar, P., Khurana, A., & Sharma, S. (2021). Performance evaluation of public and private sector banks. *World Review of Entrepreneurship, Management and Sustainable Development*, *17*(2–3), 306–322. doi:10.1504/WREMSD.2021.114436

Kumar, P., Mukul, Kaur, D., & Kaur, A. (2023). Green Infrastructure- A Roadmap Towards Sustainable Development. *IOP Conference Series. Earth and Environmental Science*, *1110*(1), 012060. Advance online publication. doi:10.1088/1755-1315/1110/1/012060

Kumar, P., Özen, E., & Vurur, S. (2023). Adoption of blockchain technology in the financial sector. In *Contemporary Studies of Risks in Emerging Technology, Part A*. Emerald Group Publishing Ltd., doi:10.1108/978-1-80455-562-020231018

Kumar, P., Verma, P., Bhatnagar, M., Taneja, S., Seychel, S., Todorović, I., & Grim, S. (2023). The Financial Performance and Solvency Status of the Indian Public Sector Banks: A CAMELS Rating and Z Index Approach. *International Journal of Sustainable Development and Planning*, *18*(2), 367–376. doi:10.18280/ijsdp.180204

Kumar, S., Talukder, M. B., Kabir, F., & Kaiser, F. (2023). Challenges and Sustainability of Green Finance in the Tourism Industry: Evidence from Bangladesh. In S. Taneja, P. Kumar, S. Grima, E. Ozen, & K. Sood (Eds.), (pp. 97–111). Advances in Finance, Accounting, and Economics. IGI Global. doi:10.4018/979-8-3693-1388-6.ch006

Kuntsman, A., & Miyake, E. (2016). Paradoxes of Digital dis/engagement: a follow up study (businesses and services). *Working Papers of the Communities & Culture Network+, 7*.

Kushlev, K., & Dunn, E. W. (2015). Checking email less frequently reduces stress. *Computers in Human Behavior*, *43*, 220–228. doi:10.1016/j.chb.2014.11.005

Kuss, D. J., & Griffiths, M. D. (2017). Social networking sites and addiction: Ten lessons learned. *International Journal of Environmental Research and Public Health*, *14*(3), 311. doi:10.3390/ijerph14030311 PMID:28304359

Kwon, H. E., So, H., Han, S. P., & Oh, W. (2016). Excessive dependence on mobile social apps: A rational addiction perspective. *Information Systems Research*, *27*(4), 919–939. doi:10.1287/isre.2016.0658

Labonte, M., Nelson, R. M., & Perkins, D. W. (2020). *Financial Innovation: Central Bank Digital Currencies*. Every CRS Report. https://www.everycrsreport.com/files/2020-03-20_IF11471_deb8 3c3c9793651d65de8303485538b6f979962e.pdf

Lai, C., Altavilla, D., Ronconi, A., & Aceto, P. (2016). Fear of missing out (FOMO) is associated with activation of the right middle temporal gyrus during inclusion social cue. *Computers in Human Behavior*, *61*, 516–521. doi:10.1016/j.chb.2016.03.072

Lanaj, K., Johnson, R. E., & Barnes, C. M. (2014). Beginning the workday yet already depleted? Consequences of late-night smartphone use and sleep. *Organizational Behavior and Human Decision Processes*, *124*(1), 11–23. doi:10.1016/j.obhdp.2014.01.001

Lawler, M. (2023, August 4). *How to Do a Digital Detox*. EverydayHealth. com. https://www.everydayhealth.com/emotional-health/how-to-do-a-digital-detox-without-unplugging-completely/

Lee, C. C., Lou, R., & Wang, F. (2023). Digital financial inclusion and poverty alleviation: Evidence from the sustainable development of China. *Economic Analysis and Policy, 77*, 418–434. doi:10.1016/j.eap.2022.12.004

Lee, C. C., Wang, F., & Lou, R. (2022). Digital financial inclusion and carbon neutrality: Evidence from non-linear analysis. *Resources Policy, 79*, 102974. doi:10.1016/j.resourpol.2022.102974

Lee, D. K. C., Yan, L., & Wang, Y. (2021). A global perspective on central bank digital currency. *China Economic Journal, 14*(1), 52–66. doi:10.1080/17538963.2020.1870279

Lee, I., & Shin, Y. J. (2018). Fintech: Ecosystem, business models, investment decisions, and challenges. *Business Horizons, 61*(1), 35–46. doi:10.1016/j.bushor.2017.09.003

Lei, L. Y.-C., Ismail, M. A.-A., Mohammad, J. A.-M., & Yusoff, M. S. B. (2020). The relationship of smartphone addiction with psychological distress and neuroticism among university medical students. *BMC Psychology, 8*(1), 97. doi:10.118640359-020-00466-6 PMID:32917268

Lepp, A., Barkley, J. E., & Karpinski, A. C. (2014). The relationship between cell phone use, academic performance, anxiety, and satisfaction with life in college students. *Computers in Human Behavior, 31*, 343–350. doi:10.1016/j.chb.2013.10.049

Lepp, A., Barkley, J. E., Sanders, G. J., Rebold, M., & Gates, P. (2013). The relationship between cell phone use, physical and sedentary activity, and cardiorespiratory fitness in a sample of U.S. college students. *The International Journal of Behavioral Nutrition and Physical Activity, 10*(1), 79. doi:10.1186/1479-5868-10-79 PMID:23800133

Lexicall. (2020). information hygiene. *Collins Dictionary*. https://www.collinsdictionary.com/submission/22205/informati on+hygiene (Accessed Library and Media Roles in Information Hygiene and Managing Information, IGI

Li, L., Griffiths, M. D., Niu, Z., & Mei, S. (2020). The trait-state fear of missing out scale: Validity, reliability, and measurement invariance in a Chinese sample of university students. *Journal of Affective Disorders, 274*, 711–718. https://doi.org/. jad.2020.05.103. doi:10.1016/j

Li, B., & Xu, Z. (2021). Insights into financial technology (FinTech): A bibliometric and visual study. *Financial Innovation, 7*(1), 1–28. doi:10.118640854-021-00285-7 PMID:35024290

Lim, S. S., Cho, H., & Sanchez, M. R. (2009). Online privacy, government surveillance and national ID cards. *Communications of the ACM, 52*(12), 116–120. doi:10.1145/1610252.1610283

Lin, H., Wan, S., Gan, W., Chen, J., & Chao, H.-C. (2022). Metaverse in Education: Vision, Opportunities, and Challenges. *2022 IEEE International Conference on Big Data (Big Data)*, (pp. 2857–2866). IEEE. 10.1109/BigData55660.2022.10021004

Lips, A. M. B., Taylor, J. A., & Organ, J. (2009). Managing citizen identity information in E-government service relationships in the UK: The emergence of a surveillance state or a service state? *Public Management Review*, *11*(6), 833–856. doi:10.1080/14719030903318988

Liu, M., Zhang, K., Liang, Y., Yang, Y., Chen, Z., & Liu, W. (2023). Life cycle environmental and economic assessment of electric bicycles with different batteries in China. *Journal of Cleaner Production*, *385*, 135715. doi:10.1016/j.jclepro.2022.135715

Liu, Y., Luan, L., Wu, W., Zhang, Z., & Hsu, Y. (2021). Can digital financial inclusion promote China's economic growth? *International Review of Financial Analysis*, *78*, 101889. doi:10.1016/j.irfa.2021.101889

Logacheva, V., Dementieva, D., Ustyantsev, S., Moskovskiy, D., Dale, D., Krotova, I., & Panchenko, A. (2022, May). Paradetox: Detoxification with parallel data. In *Proceedings of the 60th Annual Meeting of the Association for Computational Linguistics (Volume 1: Long Papers)* (pp. 6804-6818).

Lohmeier, L. (2023). *Statistics on internet usage in Germany*. Statista. https://de.statista.com/themen/2033/internetnutzung-in-deutschland/#topicOverview

Loukas, G., Murugesan, S., & Andriole, S. J. (2022). Information Hygiene: The Fight Against the Misinformation "Infodemic". *IT Professional*, *24*(2), 16–18. doi:10.1109/MITP.2022.3163007

Lu, X., Lai, Y., & Zhang, Y. (2023). Digital financial inclusion and investment diversification: Evidence from China. *Accounting and Finance*, *63*(S2), 2781–2799. doi:10.1111/acfi.13043

Maatuk, A. M., Elberkawi, E. K., Aljawarneh, S., Rashaideh, H., & Alharbi, H. (2021). The COVID-19 pandemic and E-learning: Challenges and opportunities from the perspective of students and instructors. *Journal of Computing in Higher Education*, *34*(1), 21–38. doi:10.100712528-021-09274-2 PMID:33967563

Madianou, M. M., Longboan, L., & Ong, J. C. (2015). *Finding a voice through 'humanitarian technologies'?* Communication technologies and participation in disaster recovery.

Mahalle, A., Yong, J., & Tao, X. (2019, October). Protecting privacy in digital era on cloud architecture for banking and financial services industry. In *2019 6th International Conference on Behavioral, Economic and Socio-Cultural Computing (BESC)* (pp. 1-6). IEEE. 10.1109/BESC48373.2019.8963459

Mahsud, M., Khalaf, A. J. M., Mahsud, Z., Afzal, A., & Afzal, F. (2021). Addiction to smartphones leading to distraction in the classrooms: Effect of different cultures. *Journal of Statistics and Management Systems*, *24*(4), 741–754. doi:10.1080/09720510.2020.1834660

Malinova, K., & Park, A. (2014). The impact of competition and information on intraday trading. *Journal of Banking & Finance*, *44*(1), 55–71. doi:10.1016/j.jbankfin.2014.03.026

Malladi, C. M., Soni, R. K., & Srinivasan, S. (2021). Digital financial inclusion: Next frontiers—Challenges and opportunities. *CSI Transactions on ICT*, 9(2), 127–134. doi:10.100740012-021-00328-5

Manohar, S., Mittal, A., & Marwah, S. (2020). Service innovation, corporate reputation and word-of-mouth in the banking sector: A test on multigroup-moderated mediation effect. *Benchmarking*, 27(1), 406–429. doi:10.1108/BIJ-05-2019-0217

Maqableh, M., & Alia, M. (2021). Evaluation online learning of undergraduate students under lockdown amidst COVID-19 Pandemic: The online learning experience and students' satisfaction. *Children and Youth Services Review*, 128, 106160. doi:10.1016/j.childyouth.2021.106160 PMID:36540702

Markowetz, A. (2015). *Digitaler Burnout: warum unsere permanente Smartphone-Nutzung gefährlich ist.* Droemer eBook.

Marshall, A. (2023). *Global Fintech 2023: Reimagining the Future of Finance.* QED Investors. https://www.qedinvestors.com/blog/global-fintech-2023-reimagining-the-future-of-finance

Martens, M., & Steenbeek, O. W. (2001). Intraday trading halts in the Nikkei futures market. *Pacific-Basin Finance Journal*, 9(5), 535–561. doi:10.1016/S0927-538X(01)00023-3

Martinez Fernandez, J., Augusto, J. C., Seepold, R., & Madrid, N. M. (2012). A Sensor Technology Survey for a Stress-Aware Trading Process. *IEEE Transactions on Systems, Man, and Cybernetics. Part C, Applications and Reviews*, 42(6), 809–824. doi:10.1109/TSMCC.2011.2179028

Maurya, C., Muhammad, T., Maurya, P., & Dhillon, P. (2022). The association of smartphone screen time with sleep problems among adolescents and young adults: Cross-sectional findings from India. *BMC Public Health*, 22(1), 1686. doi:10.118612889-022-14076-x PMID:36064373

McAninch, G., & Cundy, J. (2016). Implementation: Records and Archival Management Strategies for Electronic Records Used by the Kentucky Department for Libraries and Archives. In C. P. Bantin (Ed.), *Building Trustworthy Digital Repositories Theory and Implementation Min Trusts Max.* Rowman & Littlefield.

McDaniel, B. T., & Radesky, J. S. (2018). Technoference: Parent distraction with technology and associations with child behavior problems. *Child Development*, 89(1), 100–109. doi:10.1111/cdev.12822 PMID:28493400

McKinley, D. T. (2016). *New terrains of privacy in South Africa.* R2K. http://www.r2k.org.za/wp-Content/uploads/Monograph_New_Terrains_of_Privacy_in_South Africa_2016.pdf

Mefrouche, M. L., Siegmann, E.-M., Boehme, S., Berking, M., & Kornhuber, J. (2023). The Effect of Digital Mindfulness Interventions on Depressive, Anxiety, and Stress Symptoms in Pregnant Women: A Systematic Review and Meta-Analysis. *European Journal of Investigation in Health, Psychology and Education*, 13(9), 1694–1706. doi:10.3390/ejihpe13090122 PMID:37754461

Mehta, K., Sharma, R., & Jalotra, S. (2023). A Bibliometric Analysis of Green Banking: Present State and Future Directions. In *Perspectives on Blockchain Technology and Responsible Investing* (pp. 159–176). IGI Global. doi:10.4018/978-1-6684-8361-9.ch007

Meier, A., & Reinecke, L. (2021). Computer-mediated communication, social media, and mental health: A conceptual and empirical meta-review. *Communication Research, 48*(8), 1182–1209. doi:10.1177/0093650220958224

Mendoza Beltran, A., Cox, B., Mutel, C., van Vuuren, D. P., Font Vivanco, D., Deetman, S., Edelenbosch, O. Y., Guinée, J., & Tukker, A. (2020). When the background matters: Using scenarios from integrated assessment models in prospective life cycle assessment. *Journal of Industrial Ecology, 24*(1), 64–79. doi:10.1111/jiec.12825

Mhlanga, D. (2022). The role of financial inclusion and FinTech in addressing climate-related challenges in the industry 4.0: Lessons for sustainable development goals. *Frontiers in Climate, 4*, 949178. doi:10.3389/fclim.2022.949178

Michie, S., Richardson, M., Johnston, M., Abraham, C., Francis, J., Hardeman, W., Eccles, M. P., Cane, J., & Wood, C. E. (2013). The behavior change technique taxonomy (v1) of 93 hierarchically clustered techniques: Building an international consensus for the reporting of behavior change interventions. *Annals of Behavioral Medicine, 46*(1), 81–95. doi:10.100712160-013-9486-6 PMID:23512568

Miksch, L., & Schulz, C. (2018). Disconnect to reconnect: The phenomenon of digital detox as a reaction to technology overload.

Milicevic, M. (2015). Contemporary education and digital technologies. *International Journal of Social Science and Humanity, 5*(7), 656–659. doi:10.7763/IJSSH.2015.V5.535

Miller, W. R., & Rollnick, S. (2012). *Motivational interviewing: Helping people change*. Guilford press.

Miłobędzki, P., & Nowak, S. (2018). Intraday Trading Patterns on the Warsaw Stock Exchange. In J. K., L.-J. H., & O. L.T. (Eds.), Springer Proceedings in Business and Economics (pp. 55 – 66). Springer Science and Business Media B.V. doi:10.1007/978-3-319-76228-9_6

Milyavskaya, M., Saffran, M., Hope, N., & Koestner, R. (2018). Fear of missing out: Prevalence, dynamics, and consequences of experiencing FOMO. *Motivation and Emotion, 42*(5), 725–737. doi:10.100711031-018-9683-5

Mirbabaie, M., Braun, L.-M., & Marx, J. (2022). Knowledge Work 'Unplugged' - Digital Detox Effects on ICT Demands, Job Performance and Satisfaction. *17th International Conference on Wirtschaftsinformatik, WI 2022.* SCOPUS/ https://www.scopus.com/inward/record.uri?eid=2-s2.0-85152120849&partnerID=40&md5=b7a95d44e0ce0133dbdf35e13e3063b2

Mirbabaie, M., Marx, J., Braun, L. M., & Stieglitz, S. (2020). Digital Detox—Mitigating Digital Overuse in Times of Remote Work and Social Isolation. *arXiv preprint arXiv:2012.09535.*

Compilation of References

Mirbabaie, M., Stieglitz, S., & Marx, J. (2022). Digital Detox. *Business & Information Systems Engineering*, *64*(2), 239–246. doi:10.100712599-022-00747-x

Mishra, S. Shukla, P. Agarwal, R. (2022). Analyzing Machine Learning Enabled Fake News Detection Techniques for Diversified Datasets. *Wireless Communications and Mobile Computing*. . doi:10.1155/2022/1575365

Mishra, S., & Daigler, R. T. (2014). Intraday trading and bidask spread characteristics for SPX and SPY options. *Journal of Derivatives*, *21*(3), 70–84. doi:10.3905/jod.2014.21.3.070

Modak, N. (2022). Interesting Work From Home Statistics In India (2023) TheHomeOffice. https://www.thehomeoffice.in/blogs/post/9-interesting-work-f rom-home-statistics-in-india-2022

Mohamed, S. M., Abdallah, L. S., & Ali, F. N. K. (2023). Effect of digital detox program on electronic screen syndrome among preparatory school students. *Nursing Open*, *10*(4), 2222–2228. doi:10.1002/nop2.1472 PMID:36373487

Mohammad, B. T., & Mokarram Hossain, M. (2021). Prospects of future tourism in Bangladesh: An evaluative study. *I-Manager's. Journal of Management*, *15*(4), 31. doi:10.26634/jmgt.15.4.17495

Monge Roffarello, A., & De Russis, L. (2019, May). The race towards digital wellbeing: Issues and opportunities. In *Proceedings of the 2019 CHI conference on human factors in computing systems* (pp. 1-14). ACM. 10.1145/3290605.3300616

Montag, C., & Walla, P. (2016). Carpe diem instead of losing your social mind: Beyond digital addiction and why we all suffer from digital overuse. *Cogent Psychology*, *3*(1), 1157281. doi:1 0.1080/23311908.2016.1157281

Morford, M. (2010). Oh my God you are so missing out [Internet]. SF Gate. https://www.sfgate.com/entertainment/morford/article/Oh-my-G od-you-are-so-missing-out-2536241.php

Morgan, S. (2018). Fake news, disinformation, manipulation, and online tactics to undermine democracy. *J. Cyber Policy*, *3*(1), 39–43. of-any-information-10-rules-to-follow-in-2022/

Mubarak, M. F., & Petraite, M. (2020). Industry 4.0 technologies, digital trust and technological orientation: What matters in open innovation? *Technological Forecasting and Social Change*, *161*, 120332. doi:10.1016/j.techfore.2020.120332

Muench, C., Feulner, L., Muench, R., & Carolus, A. (2020). Time to Log Off: An Analysis of Factors Influencing the Willingness to Participate in a Long-Term 'Digital Detox' with the Smartphone. *Communications in Computer and Information Science, 1226 CCIS*, 209 – 216. Springer. doi:10.1007/978-3-030-50732-9_28

Muganyi, T., Yan, L., & Sun, H. P. (2021). Green finance, fintech and environmental protection: Evidence from China. *Environmental Science and Ecotechnology*, *7*, 100107. doi:10.1016/j. ese.2021.100107 PMID:36160697

Muhammad, S., Pan, Y., Magazzino, C., Luo, Y., & Waqas, M. (2022). The fourth industrial revolution and environmental efficiency: The role of fintech industry. *Journal of Cleaner Production, 381,* 135196. doi:10.1016/j.jclepro.2022.135196

Mukul, & Pathak, N. (2021). Are the financial inclusion schemes of India developing the nation sustainably? *E3S Web of Conferences, 296,* 06011. IEEE. doi:10.1051/e3sconf/202129606011

Mukul, T. S., Özen, E., Plaha, R., & Zammit, M. L. (2023). Banking, Fintech, BigTech: Emerging challenges for multimedia adoption. In *Intelligent Multimedia Technologies for Financial Risk Management: Trends, Tools and Applications.* Institution of Engineering and Technology. https://www.scopus.com/inward/record.uri?eid=2-s2.0-85166147 373&partnerID=40&md5=94818506510d02c90c03db2508d518d3

Müller, J., & Kerényi, Á. (2019). The Need for Trust and Ethics in the Digital Age–Sunshine and Shadows in the FinTech World. *Financial and Economic Review, 18*(4), 5–34. doi:10.33893/FER.18.4.534

Mustafaoglu, R., Yasaci, Z., Zirek, E., Griffiths, M. D., & Ozdincler, A. R. (2021). The relationship between smartphone addiction and musculoskeletal pain prevalence among young population: A cross-sectional study. *The Korean Journal of Pain, 34*(1), 72–81. doi:10.3344/kjp.2021.34.1.72 PMID:33380570

Mutsvairo, B., Ragnedda, M., & Mabvundwi, K. (2022). 'Our old pastor thinks the mobile phone is a source of evil.' Capturing contested and conflicting insights on digital wellbeing and digital detoxing in an age of rapid mobile connectivity. *Media International Australia,* 1329878X2210909. doi:10.1177/1329878X221090992

Mutsvairo, B., Ragnedda, M., & Mabvundwi, K. (2022). 'Our old pastor thinks the mobile phone is a source of evil.' Capturing contested and conflicting insights on digital wellbeing and digital detoxing in an age of rapid mobile connectivity. *Media International Australia,* 1329878X221090992.

National Day of Unplugging. (n.d.). *Home.* National Day of Unplugging. https://www.nationaldayofunplugging.com/

Naumenkova, S., Mishchenko, S., & Dorofeiev, D. (2019). Digital financial inclusion: Evidence from Ukraine. *Investment Management & Financial Innovations, 16*(3), 194–205. doi:10.21511/imfi.16(3).2019.18

Neger, M., & Uddin, B. (2020). Factors Affecting Consumers' Internet Shopping Behavior During the COVID-19 Pandemic: Evidence From Bangladesh. *The China Business Review, 19*(3). Advance online publication. doi:10.17265/1537-1506/2020.03.003

Nelson, M. R. (1994). We have the information you want, but getting it will cost you! held hostage by information overload. *XRDS: Crossroads. The ACM Magazine for Students, 1*(1), 11–15.

Compilation of References

Nenavath, S. (2022). Impact of fintech and green finance on environmental quality protection in India: By applying the semi-parametric difference-in-differences (SDID). *Renewable Energy, 193*, 913–919. doi:10.1016/j.renene.2022.05.020

Newport, C. (2019). *Digital minimalism: Choosing a focused life in a noisy world*. Penguin.

Newport, C. (2019). *Digital Minimalism: Choosing a Focused Life in a Noisy World*. Portfolio.

Nguyen, M. H., Büchi, M., & Geber, S. (2022). Everyday disconnection experiences: Exploring people's understanding of digital well-being and management of digital media use. *new media & society*, 14614448221105428.

Nguyen, D. K., Sermpinis, G., & Stasinakis, C. (2023). Big data, artificial intelligence and machine learning: A transformative symbiosis in favour of financial technology. *European Financial Management, 29*(2), 517–548. doi:10.1111/eufm.12365

Nguyen, V. T. (2022). The perceptions of social media users of digital detox apps considering personality traits. *Education and Information Technologies, 27*(7), 9293–9316. doi:10.100710639-022-11022-7 PMID:35370441

Nguyen, V. T., Van Ness, B. F., & Van Ness, R. A. (2004). Intraday trading of Island (as reported to the cincinnati stock exchange) and NASDAQ. In *Advances In Quantitative Analysis Of Finance And Accounting - New Series*. World Scientific Publishing Co., doi:10.1142/9789812565457_0006

Nicoletti, B. (2018). The future: procurement 4.0. *Agile Procurement: Volume II: Designing and Implementing a Digital Transformation*, 189-230.

Niu, G., Jin, X., Wang, Q., & Zhou, Y. (2022). Broadband infrastructure and digital financial inclusion in rural China. *China Economic Review, 76*, 101853. doi:10.1016/j.chieco.2022.101853

Number of global mobile users since 2010. (2023). Statista. https://www.statista.com/statistics/218984/number-of-global-mobile-users-since-2010/#statisticContainer

Nuñez, T. R., Radtke, T., & Eimler, S. (2020). Third-person perspective on phubbing: Observing smartphone-induced social exclusion generates negative affect, stress, and derogatory attitudes. *Cyberpsychology (Brno), 14*(3). doi:10.5817/CP2020-3-3

O'Connell, C. (2020). How FOMO (Fear of missing out), the smartphone, and social media may be affecting university students in the Middle East. *North American Journal of Psychology, 22*(1).

Obar, J. A., & Wildman, S. (2015). Social media definition and the governance challenge: An introduction to the special issue. *Telecommunications Policy, 39*(9), 745–750. doi:10.1016/j.telpol.2015.07.014

Oberst, U., Wegmann, E., Stodt, B., Brand, M., & Chamarro, A. (2017). Negative consequences from heavy social networking in adolescents: The mediating role of fear of missing out. *Journal of Adolescence, 55*(1), 51–60. doi:10.1016/j.adolescence.2016.12.008 PMID:28033503

Obiora, K., & Ozili, P. K. (2023). Benefits of digital-only financial inclusion. In *The Impact of AI Innovation on Financial Sectors in the Era of Industry 5.0* (pp. 261–269). IGI Global.

Oehler, A., & Wendt, S. (2018). Trust and financial services: The impact of increasing digitalisation and the financial crisis. In *The Return of Trust? Institutions and the Public after the Icelandic Financial Crisis* (pp. 195–211). Emerald Publishing Limited. doi:10.1108/978-1-78743-347-220181014

OER. (2020). *Environmentalism*. Oer press books. https://oer.pressbooks.pub/collegeresearch/chapter/info-hygi ene- environmentalism/

Omar, M. K., Dahalan, N. A., & Yusoff, Y. H. M. (2016). Social media usage, perceived team-efficacy and knowledge sharing behaviour among employees of an oil and gas organisation in Malaysia. *Procedia Economics and Finance*, *37*, 309–316. doi:10.1016/S2212-5671(16)30130-7

Omarova, S. T. (2020). Technology v technocracy: Fintech as a regulatory challenge. *Journal of Financial Regulation*, *6*(1), 75–124. doi:10.1093/jfr/fjaa004

Onik, M. M. H., Chul-Soo, K. I. M., & Jinhong, Y. A. N. G. (2019, February). Personal data privacy challenges of the fourth industrial revolution. In *2019 21st International Conference on Advanced Communication Technology (ICACT)* (pp. 635-638). IEEE. 10.23919/ICACT.2019.8701932

Orben, A., & Przybylski, A. K. (2019). Screens, teens, and psychological well-being: Evidence from three time-use-diary studies. *Psychological Science*, *30*(5), 682–696. doi:10.1177/0956797619830329 PMID:30939250

Orben, A., & Przybylski, A. K. (2019). The association between adolescent well-being and digital technology use. *Nature Human Behaviour*, *3*(2), 173–182. doi:10.103841562-018-0506-1 PMID:30944443

Orlikowski, W. J., Scott, S. V., & Elgar, E. (2016). MIT Open Access Articles Digital Work: A Research Agenda DIGITAL WORK: A RESEARCH AGENDA. *A Research Agenda for Management and Organization Studies*, 88–96. https://dspace.mit.edu/bitstream/handle/1721.1/108411/Digita l

Ouma, S. A., Odongo, T. M., & Were, M. (2017). Mobile financial services and financial inclusion: Is it a boon for savings mobilization? *Review of development finance, 7*(1), 29-35.

Ouwehand, K., Kroef, A. V. D., Wong, J., & Paas, F. (2021, September). Measuring cognitive load: Are there more valid alternatives to Likert rating scales? [). Frontiers Media SA.]. *Frontiers in Education*, *6*, 702616. doi:10.3389/feduc.2021.702616

Oxford Dictionaries. (2019, January 30). Definition of *digital detox* in English. Oxford Press. http://www.oxforddictionaries.com/definition/english/digital-detox

Ozili, P. K. (2022). Central bank digital currency research around the world: a review of literature. *Journal of Money Laundering Control*. https://doi.org/https://doi.org/10.1108/JMLC-11-2021-0126

Ozili, P. K. (2020). Contesting digital finance for the poor. *Digital Policy. Regulation & Governance*, 22(2), 135–151. doi:10.1108/DPRG-12-2019-0104

Ozili, P. K. (2021a). Financial inclusion research around the world: A review. *The Forum for Social Economics*, 50(4), 457–479. doi:10.1080/07360932.2020.1715238

Ozili, P. K. (2021b). Financial inclusion-exclusion paradox: How banked adults become unbanked again. *Financial Internet Quarterly*, 17(2), 44–50. doi:10.2478/fiqf-2021-0012

Ozili, P. K. (2022). Digital financial inclusion. In *Big Data: A game changer for insurance industry* (pp. 229–238). Emerald Publishing Limited. doi:10.1108/978-1-80262-605-620221015

Ozili, P. K. (2023a). CBDC, Fintech and cryptocurrency for financial inclusion and financial stability. *Digital Policy. Regulation & Governance*, 25(1), 40–57. doi:10.1108/DPRG-04-2022-0033

Ozili, P. K., & Mhlanga, D. (2023b). Why is financial inclusion so popular? An analysis of development buzzwords. *Journal of International Development*, jid.3812. doi:10.1002/jid.3812

Ozturk, I., & Ullah, S. (2022). Does digital financial inclusion matter for economic growth and environmental sustainability in OBRI economies? An empirical analysis. *Resources, Conservation and Recycling*, 185, 106489. doi:10.1016/j.resconrec.2022.106489

Pandita, R., Xiao, X., Yang, W., Enck, W., & Xie, T. (2013). {WHYPER}: Towards automating risk assessment of mobile applications. In *22nd USENIX Security Symposium (USENIX Security 13)* (pp. 527-542).

Pant, S. K. (2020). Fintech: Emerging trends. *Telecom Business Review*, 13(1), 47–52.

Peng, P., & Mao, H. (2023). The effect of digital financial inclusion on relative poverty among urban households: A case study on China. *Social Indicators Research*, 165(2), 377–407. doi:10.100711205-022-03019-z

Peric, K. (2015). Digital financial inclusion. *Journal of Payments Strategy & Systems*, 9(3), 212–214.

Pflügner, K., Maier, C., Mattke, J., & Weitzel, T. (2021). Personality Profiles that Put Users at Risk of Perceiving Technostress: A Qualitative Comparative Analysis with the Big Five Personality Traits. *Business & Information Systems Engineering*, 63(4), 389–402. doi:10.100712599-020-00668-7

Pflugner, K., Maier, C., & Weitzel, T. (2020). The direct and indirect influence of mindfulness on techno-stressors and job burnout: A quantitative study of white-collar workers. *Computers in Human Behavior*, 106566.

Phelan, H. (2018, July 12). How to make this the summer of missing out. *The New York Times*.

Pinto, A., Cardinale, Y., Dongo, I., & Ticona-Herrera, R. (2022). An Ontology for Modeling Cultural Heritage Knowledge in Urban Tourism. *IEEE Access : Practical Innovations, Open Solutions*, 10, 61820–61842. doi:10.1109/ACCESS.2022.3179664

Pirogova, O., Makarevich, M., Ilina, O., & Ulanov, V. (2019). Optimizing trading company capital structure on the basis of using bankruptcy logistic models under conditions of economy digitalization. *IOP Conference Series. Materials Science and Engineering, 497*, 012129. doi:10.1088/1757-899X/497/1/012129

Pirogova, O., Makarevich, M., Khareva, V., & Saveleva, N. (2020). Improving the use effectiveness of trading enterprises intellectual capital at the stages of the life cycle in the context of digitalization. *IOP Conference Series. Materials Science and Engineering, 940*(1), 012053. doi:10.1088/1757-899X/940/1/012053

Pontes, H. M., Szabo, A., & Griffiths, M. D. (2015). The impact of Internet-based specific activities on the perceptions of Internet addiction, quality of life, and excessive usage: A cross-sectional study. *Addictive Behaviors Reports, 1*, 19–25. doi:10.1016/j.abrep.2015.03.002 PMID:29531976

Portwood-Stacer, L. (2013). Media refusal and conspicuous non-consumption: The performative and political dimensions of Facebook abstention. *New Media & Society, 15*(7), 1041–1057. doi:10.1177/1461444812465139

Poushter, J., Bishop, C., & Chwe, H. (2018). *Social media use continues to rise in developing countries but plateaus across developed ones.* Pew Research. https://www.pewglobal.org/2018/06/19/social-media-use-contin ues-to-rise-in-developing-countries-but-plateaus-across-deve loped-ones/

Prasad, A., & Quinones, A. (2020). Digital overload warnings-"the right amount of shame"? In *Human-Computer Interaction. Human Values and Quality of Life: Thematic Area.* Springer.

Price, C. (2018). *How to break up with your phone: The 30-day plan to take back your life.* Ten Speed Press.

Pritchard, M., & Verwey, S. (2018). Digital Dynamics and Relational Complexities: Responding to Challenges in the Online Engagement Context. In P. Maritha & K. Sittos (Eds.), *Connect Writing for Online Audiences.* Juta.

Priyanka, R., Ravindran, K., Sankaranarayanan, B., & Ali, S. M. (2023). A fuzzy DEMATEL decision modeling framework for identifying key human resources challenges in start-up companies: Implications for sustainable development. *Decision Analytics Journal, 6*, 100192. doi:10.1016/j.dajour.2023.100192

Przybylski, A. K., Murayama, K., DeHaan, C. R., & Gladwell, V. (2013). Motivational, emotional, and behavioral correlates of fear of missing out. *Computers in Human Behavior, 29*(4), 1841–1848. doi:10.1016/j.chb.2013.02.014

Przybylski, A. K., Nguyen, T. V. T., Law, W., & Weinstein, N. (2021). Does taking a short break from social media have a positive effect on well-being? Evidence from three preregistered field experiments. *Journal of Technology in Behavioral Science, 6*(3), 507–514. doi:10.100741347-020-00189-w

Purbasari, R., Muttaqin, Z., & Sari, D. S. (2021). Identification of actors and factors in the digital entrepreneurial ecosystem: The case of digital platform-based MSMEs in Indonesia. *Review of Integrative Business and Economics Research, 10,* 164–187.

Puricelli, S., Costa, D., Rigamonti, L., Cardellini, G., Casadei, S., Koroma, M. S., Messagie, M., & Grosso, M. (2022). Life Cycle Assessment of innovative fuel blends for passenger cars with a spark-ignition engine: A comparative approach. *Journal of Cleaner Production, 378,* 134535. doi:10.1016/j.jclepro.2022.134535

Purohit, A. K., Barclay, L., & Holzer, A. (2020, April). Designing for digital detox: Making social media less addictive with digital nudges. In *Extended Abstracts of the 2020 CHI Conference on Human Factors in Computing Systems* (pp. 1-9).

Purohit, A. K., Barclay, L., & Holzer, A. (2020). Designing for digital detox: Making social media less addictive with digital nudges. *Conference on Human Factors in Computing Systems - Proceedings.* ACM. 10.1145/3334480.3382810

Purohit, A. K., Raggi, M., & Holzer, A. (2023). How Pricing and Ratings Affect Perceived Value of Digital Detox Apps. *Conference on Human Factors in Computing Systems - Proceedings.* ACM. 10.1145/3544549.3585681

Rabbani, M. R. (2023). Fintech innovations, scope, challenges, and implications in Islamic Finance: A systematic analysis. *International Journal of Computing and Digital Systems, 11*(1), 1–28.

Rabbani, M. R., Bashar, A., Atif, M., Jreisat, A., Zulfikar, Z., & Naseem, Y. (2021, December). Text mining and visual analytics in research: Exploring the innovative tools. In *2021 International Conference on Decision Aid Sciences and Application (DASA)* (pp. 1087-1091). IEEE. 10.1109/DASA53625.2021.9682360

Radtke, T., Apel, T., Schenkel, K., Keller, J., & Von Lindern, E. (2022). Digital detox: An effective solution in the smartphone era? A systematic literature review. *Mobile Media & Communication, 10*(2), 190–215. doi:10.1177/20501579211028647

Ragu-Nathan, T. S., Tarafdar, M., Ragu-Nathan, B. S., & Tu, Q. (2008). The Consequences of Technostress for End Users in Organizations: Conceptual Development and Empirical Validation. *Information Systems Research, 19*(4), 417–433. doi:10.1287/isre.1070.0165

Rakich, N. (2020). How does Biden stack up to past Democratic nominees? *FiveThirtyEight.* https://fivethirtyeight.com/features/how-does-biden-stack-up-to-past-democratic-nominees/

Randive, A., Vispute, J., & Goswami, S. (2023). A Study of Perspectives on the Growth, Strategy and Branding in Indian MSMEs. In Indian SMEs and Start-Ups: Growth through Innovation and Leadership (pp. 227-253).

Rathebe, P. C., & Mosoeu, L. G. (2023). Fruits and vegetables contaminated with particles of heavy metals: A narrative review to explore the use of electromagnetic fields as an alternative treatment method. *Cogent Food & Agriculture*, *9*(1), 2231686. doi:10.1080/23311932.2023.2231686

Rautela, S., & Sharma, S. (2022, February 11). Fear of missing out (FOMO) to the joy of missing out (JOMO): Shifting dunes of problematic usage of the internet among social media users. Journal of Information. *Communication and Ethics in Society*, *20*(4), 461–479. doi:10.1108/JICES-06-2021-0057

Reepu, R., Taneja, S., Ozen, E., & Singh, A. (2023). A globetrotter to the future of marketing: Metaverse. In *Cultural Marketing and Metaverse for Consumer Engagement*. IGI Global. doi:10.4018/978-1-6684-8312-1.ch001

Rees, M. (2017). *FOMO vs. JOMO: How to embrace the joy of missing out*. Whole Life Challenge.

Richa, K., Babbitt, C. W., Gaustad, G., & Wang, X. (2014). A future perspective on lithium-ion battery waste flows from electric vehicles. *Resources, Conservation and Recycling*, *83*, 63–76. doi:10.1016/j.resconrec.2013.11.008

Rifkin, J. (2014). *The Zero Marginal Cost Society: The Internet of Things, the Collaborative Commons, and the Eclipse of Capitalism*. St. Martin's Press.

Riksbank Sveriges. (2023). *E-krona report E-krona pilot, phase 3*. Risbank. https://www.riksbank.se/globalassets/media/rapporter/e-krona/2023/e-krona-pilot-phase-3.pdf

Riordan, B. C., Flett, J. A., Hunter, J. A., Scarf, D., & Conner, T. S. (2015). Fear of missing out (FoMO): The relationship between FoMO, alcohol use, and alcohol-related consequences in college students. *Journal of Psychiatry and Brain Functions*, *2*(1), 9. doi:10.7243/2055-3447-2-9

Roberts, A. L., Fisher, A., Smith, L., Heinrich, M., & Potts, H. W. (2017). Digital health behaviour change interventions targeting physical activity and diet in cancer survivors: A systematic review and meta-analysis. *Journal of Cancer Survivorship: Research and Practice*, *11*(6), 704–719. doi:10.100711764-017-0632-1 PMID:28779220

Roberts, J. A., & David, M. E. (2020). The social media party: Fear of missing out (FOMO), social media intensity, connection, and well-being. *International Journal of Human-Computer Interaction*, *36*(4), 386–392. doi:10.1080/10447318.2019.1646517

Robertson, D. J., Malin, J., Martin, S., Butler, S. H., John, B., Graff, M., & Jones, B. C. (2023). Social media use: attitudes, 'detox', and craving in typical and frequent users.

Rod, N. H., Dissing, A. S., Clark, A., Gerds, T. A., & Lund, R. (2018). Overnight smartphone use: A new public health challenge? A novel study design based on high-resolution smartphone data. *PLoS One*, *13*(10), e0204811. doi:10.1371/journal.pone.0204811 PMID:30325929

Rodriguez-Ruiz, A., Lång, K., Gubern-Merida, A., Broeders, M., Gennaro, G., Clauser, P., Helbich, T. H., Chevalier, M., Tan, T., Mertelmeier, T., Wallis, M. G., Andersson, I., Zackrisson, S., Mann, R. M., & Sechopoulos, I. (2019). Stand-Alone Artificial Intelligence for Breast Cancer Detection in Mammography: Comparison With 101 Radiologists. *Journal of the National Cancer Institute, 111*(9), 916–922. doi:10.1093/jnci/djy222 PMID:30834436

Rosenblatt, J. (2016). *Is Facebook's facial-scanning technology invading your privacy rights?* Bloomberg. https: //www.bloomberg.com/news/articles/2016-10-26/is-faceb ook-s-facial-scanning-technology-invading-your-privacy-right s

Rosen, L., & Samuel, A. (2015). Conquering digital distraction. *Harvard Business Review, 93*(6), 110–113.

Roskladka, A., & Baiev, R. (2021). Digitalization of data analysis tools as the key for success in the online trading markets. *ACCESS-ACCESS TO SCIENCE BUSINESS INNOVATION IN THE DIGITAL ECONOMY, 2*(3), 222–233. doi:10.46656/access.2021.2.3(2)

Rust, R. T. (2020). The future of marketing. *International Journal of Research in Marketing, 37*(1), 15–26. doi:10.1016/j.ijresmar.2019.08.002

Ryu, E. J., Choi, K. S., Seo, J. S., & Nam, B. W. (2004). The relationships of Internet addiction, depression, and suicidal ideation in adolescents. *Taehan Kanho Hakhoe Chi, 34*(1), 102–110. doi:10.4040/jkan.2004.34.1.102 PMID:15314344

Ryu, H. S., & Ko, K. S. (2020). Sustainable development of Fintech: Focused on uncertainty and perceived quality issues. *Sustainability (Basel), 12*(18), 7669. doi:10.3390u12187669

Sahay, M. R., von Allmen, M. U. E., Lahreche, M. A., Khera, P., Ogawa, M. S., Bazarbash, M., & Beaton, M. K. (2020). *The promise of fintech: Financial inclusion in the post COVID-19 era.* International Monetary Fund.

Saleh, M. A. H. (2012). An investigation of the relationship between unplanned buying and post-purchase regret. *International Journal of Marketing Studies, 4*(4), 106. doi:10.5539/ijms.v4n4p106

Sanz, A. (2015, July 29). *What's the Psychology Behind the Fear of Missing Out?* Slate.

Saritepeci, M. (2021). Multiple screen addiction scale: Validity and reliability study. *Instructional Technology and Lifelong Learning, 2*(1), 1–17.

Scheppe, M. M., & Seiffen, A. L. (2022). Is it time for a Social Media Detox? *Understanding the journey of intermittent discontinuance of Instagram among Gen Y.*

Schilling, L. (2019). Risks Involved with CBDCs: On Cash, Privacy, and Information Centralization. SSRN *Electronic Journal*. doi:10.2139/ssrn.3479035

Schmidt, L. (2016). Building a Trustworthy System: Ingest Process Theory: Ingest Process. In Bantin C.P (eds). Building Trustworthy Digital Repositories Trust. Theory and Implementation. Rowman & Littlefield. Socionetwork Strat. https://doi.org/ doi:10.100712626-022-

Schmitt, J. B., Breuer, J., & Wulf, T. (2021). From cognitive overload to digital detox: Psychological implications of telework during the COVID-19 pandemic. *Computers in Human Behavior, 124*, 124. doi:10.1016/j.chb.2021.106899 PMID:34566255

Schmuck, D. (2020). Does digital detox work? Exploring the role of digital detox applications for problematic smartphone use and well-being of young adults using multigroup analysis. *Cyberpsychology, Behavior, and Social Networking, 23*(8), 526–532. doi:10.1089/cyber.2019.0578 PMID:32354288

Schonert-Hirz, S. (2017). Digital Balance instead of Digital Detox; [Digitale Balance statt Digital Detox]. *Arbeitsmedizin Sozialmedizin Umweltmedizin, 52*(11), 796 – 800. https://www.scopus.com/inward/record.uri?eid=2-s2.0-85034016 206&partnerID=40&md5=f20e31931f3a95938d0045e9371ecc13

Schor, J. (2019). *After the Gig: How the Sharing Economy Got Hijacked and How to Win It Back.* University of California Press.

Schreckinger, B. (2014). *The home of FOMO.* Boston Magazine.

Schroer, A. (2023). *41 Top Payment Processing Companies 2023.* Builtin. https://builtin.com/fintech/fintech-payments-companies-examp les

Scott, N., Batchelor, S., Ridley, J., & Jorgensen, B. (2004). The impact of mobile phones in Africa. *Commission for africa, 19*(04).

Seong-yoon, K. (2019). Younger. Season 6, Ep 12. New York, NY: TVLand.

Shafique, M., Akbar, A., Rafiq, M., Azam, A., & Luo, X. (2023). Global material flow analysis of end-of-life of lithium nickel manganese cobalt oxide batteries from battery electric vehicles. *Waste Management & Research, 41*(2), 376–388. doi:10.1177/0734242X221127175 PMID:36373335

Shaikh, A. A., Glavee-Geo, R., Karjaluoto, H., & Hinson, R. E. (2023). Mobile money as a driver of digital financial inclusion. *Technological Forecasting and Social Change, 186*, 122158. doi:10.1016/j.techfore.2022.122158

Shalender, K., Singla, B., & Sharma, S. (2023). Blockchain Adoption in the Financial Sector: Challenges, Solutions, and Implementation Framework. In *Revolutionizing Financial Services and Markets Through FinTech and Blockchain* (pp. 269–277). IGI Global. doi:10.4018/978-1-6684-8624-5.ch017

Sharma, A., & Ritu, N. R. (2023). Role of Government Schemes in Supporting Startups in India: A Quantitative Investigation. [EEL]. *European Economic Letters, 13*(1), 276–280.

Sharma, A., Saxena, A., Sethi, M., Shree, V., & Varun. (2011). Life cycle assessment of buildings: A review. *Renewable & Sustainable Energy Reviews, 15*(1), 871–875. doi:10.1016/j.rser.2010.09.008

Sharma, C., Sakhuja, S., & Nijjer, S. (2022). Recent trends of green human resource management: Text mining and network analysis. *Environmental Science and Pollution Research International*, *29*(56), 84916–84935. doi:10.100711356-022-21471-9 PMID:35790632

Sharma, M. K., Anand, N., Ahuja, S., Thakur, P. C., Mondal, I., Singh, P., Kohli, T., & Venkateshan, S. (2020). Digital burnout: COVID-19 lockdown mediates excessive technology use stress. *World Social Psychiatry*, *2*(2), 171–172. doi:10.4103/WSP.WSP_21_20

Shen, Y., Hueng, C. J., & Hu, W. (2020). Using digital technology to improve financial inclusion in China. *Applied Economics Letters*, *27*(1), 30–34. doi:10.1080/13504851.2019.1606401

Shen, Y., Hu, W., & Hueng, C. J. (2021). Digital financial inclusion and economic growth: A cross-country study. *Procedia Computer Science*, *187*, 218–223. doi:10.1016/j.procs.2021.04.054

Shepherd-Banigan, M., Bell, J. F., Basu, A., Booth-LaForce, C., & Harris, J. R. (2015). Workplace Stress and Home Influence Depressive Symptoms Among Employed Women with Young Children. *International Journal of Behavioral Medicine*, *23*(1), 102–111. doi:10.100712529-015-9482-2 PMID:25894581

Shlain, T. (2019). *24/6: The power of unplugging one day a week*. Simon and Schuster.

Sindhwani, R., Hasteer, N., Behl, A., Varshney, A., & Sharma, A. (2023). Exploring "what," "why" and "how" of resilience in MSME sector: A m-TISM approach. *Benchmarking*, *30*(6), 1884–1911. doi:10.1108/BIJ-11-2021-0682

Singh, M., & Bhatnagar, M. (2023). Sustainability's Symphony: Orchestrating Talent Management for Creating Financial Impact. In Sustainable Investments in Green Finance (pp. 17–48). IGI Global. doi:10.4018/979-8-3693-1388-6.ch002

Singh, V., Taneja, S., Singh, V., Singh, A., & Paul, H. L. (2021). Online advertising strategies in Indian and Australian e-commerce companies:: A comparative study. *Big Data Analytics for Improved Accuracy, Efficiency, and Decision Making in Digital Marketing*, 124–138. doi:10.4018/978-1-7998-7231-3.ch009

Singh, A., Sharma, S., Singh, A., Unanoğlu, M., & Taneja, S. (2023a). Cultural Marketing and Metaverse for Consumer Engagement. In *Cultural Marketing and Metaverse for Consumer Engagement*. IGI Global., doi:10.4018/978-1-6684-8312-1

Singh, S., Chamola, P., Kumar, V., Verma, P., & Makkar, N. (2023). Explaining the revival strategies of Indian MSMEs to mitigate the effects of COVID-19 outbreak. *Benchmarking*, *30*(1), 121–148. doi:10.1108/BIJ-08-2021-0497

Singla, B., Shalender, K., & Sharma, S. (2023). Consumers' Preferences Towards Digital Payments While Online and Offline Shopping Post COVID-19. In *Revolutionizing Financial Services and Markets Through FinTech and Blockchain* (pp. 288–297). IGI Global. doi:10.4018/978-1-6684-8624-5.ch019

Sood, K., Kaur, B., & Grima, S. (2022). Revamping Indian non-life insurance industry with a trusted network: Blockchain technology. In *Big Data: A game changer for insurance industry* (pp. 213–228). Emerald Publishing Limited. doi:10.1108/978-1-80262-605-620221014

Sreenivas, S. (2021, May 12). *Digital Detox: What to Know.* WebMD. https://www.webmd.com/balance/what-is-digital-detox

Srivastava, A., Srivastava, A., & Maheswari, R. (2023). *Fintech Laws and Regulations 2023- India. Fintech-Worldwide.* Statista. https://www.statista.com/outlook/dmo/fintech/worldwide#users

Stäheli, U., & Stoltenberg, L. (2022). Digital detox tourism: Practices of analogization. *New Media & Society.* doi:10.1177/14614448211072808

Statista.com. (2021). *Number of smartphone users worldwide from 2016 to 2021 (in billions).* Statista. https://www.statista.com/statistics/330695/number-ofsmartphoneusers-worldwide/

Stenson, K. (2016). Creating an Access Strategy. Theory: Creating an Access Strategy. In C. P. Bantin (Ed.), *Building Trustworthy Digital Repositories. Theories and Implementation. Min Trust and Max. Theory and Implementation.* Rowman & Littlefield.

Stewart, A., & Stanford, J. (2017). Regulating work in the gig economy: What are the options? *Economic and Labour Relations Review, 28*(3), 420–437.

Stewart, C. (2021). *Negative effect of tech on employee's well-being in the UK 2019 | Statista.* Statista. https://www.statista.com/statistics/1134262/negative-effect-of-tech-on-employee-s-well-being-in-the-uk/

Surie, G. (2017). Creating the innovation ecosystem for renewable energy via social entrepreneurship: Insights from India. *Technological Forecasting and Social Change, 121,* 184–195. doi:10.1016/j.techfore.2017.03.006

Suryono, R. R., Budi, I., & Purwandari, B. (2020). Challenges and Trends of Financial Technology (Fintech): A Systematic Literature Review. *Information, 11*(12), 590. doi:10.3390/info11120590

Sutton, T. (2017). Disconnect to reconnect: The food/technology metaphor in digital detoxing. *First Monday, 22*(6). doi:10.5210/fm.v22i6.7561

Sweller, J. (1994). Cognitive load theory, learning difficulty, and instructional design. *Learning and Instruction, 4*(4), 295–312. doi:10.1016/0959-4752(94)90003-5

Syvertsen, T., & Syvertsen, T. (2017). "Caught in the Net": Online and Social Media Disappointment and Detox. *Media resistance: Protest, dislike, abstention,* 77-97.

Syvertsen, T. (2023). Framing digital disconnection: Problem definitions, values, and actions among digital detox organisers. *Convergence (London), 29*(3), 658–674. doi:10.1177/13548565221122910

Syvertsen, T., & Enli, G. (2019). Digital Detox: Media Resistance and the Promise of Authenticity. *Convergence (London),* 1–15. doi:10.1177/1354856519847325

Szablewicz, M. (2020). From the media fast to digital detox: Examining dominant discourses about technology use. *Communication Teacher*, *34*(3), 180–184. doi:10.1080/17404622.2019.1676913

Tadese, M., Yeshaneh, A., & Mulu, G. B. (2022). Determinants of good academic performance among university students in Ethiopia: A cross-sectional study. *BMC Medical Education*, *22*(1), 395. doi:10.118612909-022-03461-0 PMID:35606767

Taherdoost, H. (2023). Fintech: Emerging trends and the future of finance. *Financial Technologies and DeFi: A Revisit to the Digital Finance Revolution*, 29-39.

Talukder, M., Shakhawat Hossain, M., & Kumar, S. (2022). Blue Ocean Strategies in Hotel Industry in Bangladesh: A Review of Present Literatures' Gap and Suggestions for Further Study. SSRN *Electronic Journal*. doi:10.2139/ssrn.4160709

Talukder, M. B. (2020). The Future of Culinary Tourism: An Emerging Dimension for the Tourism Industry of Bangladesh. I-Manager's. *Journal of Management*, *15*(1), 27. doi:10.26634/jmgt.15.1.17181

Talukder, M. B. (2021). An assessment of the roles of the social network in the development of the Tourism Industry in Bangladesh. *International Journal of Business, Law, and Education*, *2*(3), 85–93. doi:10.56442/ijble.v2i3.21

Talukder, M. B., Kumar, S., Sood, K., & Grima, S. (2023). Information Technology, Food Service Quality and Restaurant Revisit Intention. *International Journal of Sustainable Development and Planning*, *18*(1), 295–303. doi:10.18280/ijsdp.180131

Tandon, U., Jhamb, B., & Chand, P. (2022). Hedonic Pleasure, Cyber-Dating, Live-In Relationship, and Social Acceptance Amongst IT Professionals. *International Journal of Human Capital and Information Technology Professionals*, *13*(1), 1–18. doi:10.4018/IJHCITP.300311

Taneja, S., Bhatnagar, M., Kumar, P., & Grima, S. (2023). A Panel Analysis of the Effectiveness of the Asset Management in Indian Agricultural Companies. *International Journal of Sustainable Development and Planning*, *18*(3), 653–660. doi:10.18280/ijsdp.180301

Taneja, S., Bhatnagar, M., Kumar, P., & Rupeika-Apoga, R. (2023). India's Total Natural Resource Rents (NRR) and GDP: An Augmented Autoregressive Distributed Lag (ARDL) Bound Test. *Journal of Risk and Financial Management*, *16*(2), 91. doi:10.3390/jrfm16020091

Taneja, S., Grima, S., Kumar, P., & Ozen, E. (2023). Special Issue: 'Green Asset and Risk Management for Promoting Sustainable Entrepreneurship in the Building of the Green Economy.'. *International Journal of Technology Management & Sustainable Development*, *22*(2), 127–130. doi:10.1386/tmsd_00071_7

Taneja, S., Gupta, M., Bhushan, P., Bhatnagar, M., & Singh, A. (2023). Cultural marketing in the digital era. In *Cultural Marketing and Metaverse for Consumer Engagement*. IGI Global., doi:10.4018/978-1-6684-8312-1.ch008

Taneja, S., Jaggi, P., Jewandah, S., & Ozen, E. (2022). Role of Social Inclusion in Sustainable Urban Developments: An Analyse by PRISMA Technique. *International Journal of Design & Nature and Ecodynamics*, *17*(6), 937–942. doi:10.18280/ijdne.170615

Taneja, S., Kaur, S., & Özen, E. (2022). Using green finance to promote global growth in a sustainable way. *International Journal of Green Economics*, *16*(3), 246–257. doi:10.1504/IJGE.2022.128930

Taneja, S., & Ozen, E. (2023). Impact of the European Green Deal (EDG) on the Agricultural Carbon (CO2) Emission in Turkey. *International Journal of Sustainable Development and Planning*, *18*(3), 715–727. doi:10.18280/ijsdp.180307

Taneja, S., & Sharma, V. (2023). Role of beaconing marketing in improving customer buying experience. In *Enhancing Customer Engagement Through Location-Based Marketing*. IGI Global., doi:10.4018/978-1-6684-8177-6.ch012

Tao, Y., Wang, Z., Wu, B., Tang, Y., & Evans, S. (2023). Environmental life cycle assessment of recycling technologies for ternary lithium-ion batteries. *Journal of Cleaner Production*, *389*, 136008. doi:10.1016/j.jclepro.2023.136008

Tarafdar, M., Tu, Q., Ragu-Nathan, B. S., & Ragu-Nathan, T. S. (2014). The Impact of Technostress on Role Stress and Productivity. *Journal of Management Information Systems*, *24*(1), 301–328. doi:10.2753/MIS0742-1222240109

Tarafdar, M., Tu, Q., & Ragu-Nathan, T. S. (2010). Impact of technostress on end-user satisfaction and performance. *Journal of Management Information Systems*, *27*(3), 303–334. doi:10.2753/MIS0742-1222270311

Tay, L. Y., Tai, H. T., & Tan, G. S. (2022). Digital financial inclusion: A gateway to sustainable development. *Heliyon*, *8*(6), e09766. doi:10.1016/j.heliyon.2022.e09766 PMID:35785228

Tchetchik, A., Zvi, L. I., Kaplan, S., & Blass, V. (2020). The joint effects of driving hedonism and trialability on the choice between internal combustion engine, hybrid, and electric vehicles. *Technological Forecasting and Social Change*, *151*, 119815. doi:10.1016/j.techfore.2019.119815

Theoharidou, M., Papanikolaou, N., Pearson, S., & Gritzalis, D. (2013, December). Privacy risk, security, accountability in the cloud. In *2013 IEEE 5th International Conference on Cloud Computing Technology and Science* (Vol. 1, pp. 177-184). IEEE. 10.1109/CloudCom.2013.31

Thomas, O., Hagen, S., Frank, U., Recker, J., Wessel, L., Kammler, F., Zarvic, N., & Timm, I. (2020). Global Crises and the Role of BISE. *Business & Information Systems Engineering*, *62*(4), 385–396. doi:10.100712599-020-00657-w

Thomée, S. (2018). Mobile phone use and mental health: A review of the research that takes a psychological perspective on exposure. *International Journal of Environmental Research and Public Health*, *15*(12), 2692. doi:10.3390/ijerph15122692 PMID:30501032

Trautwein, C. (2021). Sustainability impact assessment of start-ups–Key insights on relevant assessment challenges and approaches based on an inclusive, systematic literature review. *Journal of Cleaner Production, 281*, 125330. doi:10.1016/j.jclepro.2020.125330

Tretyak, A., Ryabova, D., & Fesun, A. (2021). *Fake news and disinformation: what is using a machine learning trained expert system.* arXiv preprint arXiv:2108.08264.

Tripathi, A. (2017). Impact of internet addiction on mental health: An integrative therapy is needed. *Integrative Medicine International, 4*(3–4), 215–222.

Troll, E. S., Friese, M., & Loschelder, D. D. (2021). How students' self-control and smartphone-use explain their academic performance. *Computers in Human Behavior, 117*, 106624. doi:10.1016/j.chb.2020.106624

Ugur, N. G., & Koc, T. (2015). Time for digital detox: Misuse of mobile technology and phubbing. *Procedia: Social and Behavioral Sciences, 195*, 1022–1031. doi:10.1016/j.sbspro.2015.06.491

Vallas, S. P., & Schor, J. (2020). *Precarious Work: Ethnographic Studies of Labor in the gig economy.* University of California Press.

Value of global P2P loans 2012-2025. (2015). Statista. https://www.statista.com/statistics/325902/global-p2p-lendin g/

Van-Den-Eijnden, R., Doornwaard, S., & Ter Bogt, T. (2017). OP117: Are smartphone dependence symptoms related to FOMO, craving and withdrawal symptoms during smartphone abstinence? Findings from a natural experiment. *Journal of Behavioral Addictions, 6*(S1), 56–57.

Vassileva, I., & Campillo, J. (2017). Adoption barriers for electric vehicles: Experiences from early adopters in Sweden. *Energy, 120*, 632–641. doi:10.1016/j.energy.2016.11.119

Vella, V., & Ng, W. L. (2014). Enhancing intraday trading performance of Neural Network using dynamic volatility clustering fuzzy filter. In S. A., M. D., P. V., & A. R.J. (Eds.), *IEEE/IAFE Conference on Computational Intelligence for Financial Engineering, Proceedings (CIFEr)* (pp. 465 – 472). Institute of Electrical and Electronics Engineers Inc. 10.1109/CIFEr.2014.6924110

Verhoef, P. C., Kannan, P. K., & Inman, J. J. (2015). From Multi-Channel Retailing to Omni-Channel Retailing. Introduction to the Special Issue on Multi-Channel Retailing. *Journal of Retailing, 91*(2), 174–181. doi:10.1016/j.jretai.2015.02.005

Vialle, S. J., Machin, T., & Abel, S. (2023). Better than scrolling: Digital detox in the search for the ideal self. *Psychology of Popular Media.*

Vijai, C. (2019). FinTech in India–opportunities and challenges. *SAARJ Journal on Banking & Insurance Research (SJBIR) Vol, 8.* https://psplab.com/services/fintech-legal-services,2022 https://cpqi.com/top-6-fintech-consulting-firms-2022/ https://www.bcg.com/press/3may2023-fintech-1-5-trillion-industry-b y-2030 https://storm2.com/resources/venture-capital/the-leading-venture-capital-firms-for-fintech-startups-in-2022/ https://www.mckinsey.com/cn/our-insights/our-insights/seven-technologies-shaping-the-future-of-fintech https://www.e-zigurat.com/en/blog/evolution-of-fintech,2022

Vinuesa, R., Azizpour, H., Leite, I., Balaam, M., Dignum, V., Domisch, S., Felländer, A., Langhans, S. D., Tegmark, M., & Fuso Nerini, F. (2020). The role of artificial intelligence in achieving the Sustainable Development Goals. *Nature Communications, 11*(1), 1–10. doi:10.103841467-019-14108-y PMID:31932590

Vishwakarma, M. (2022). Social media: An addiction in disguise. *Peer Reviewed and UGC-CARE Listed Bilingual Journal of Rajasthan Sociological Association*, 85.

Vitinius, F., Tieden, S., Hellmich, M., Pfaff, H., Albus, C., & Ommen, O. (2018). Perceived Psychotherapist's Empathy and Therapy Motivation as Determinants of Long-Term Therapy Success—Results of a Cohort Study of Short Term Psychodynamic Inpatient Psychotherapy. *Frontiers in Psychiatry, 9*, 660. doi:10.3389/fpsyt.2018.00660 PMID:30564157

Vitunskaite, M., He, Y., Brandstetter, T., & Janicke, H. (2019). Smart cities and cyber security: Are we there yet? A comparative study on the role of standards, third party risk management and security ownership. *Computers & Security, 83*, 313–331. doi:10.1016/j.cose.2019.02.009

Vollmann, T. E. (1991). Cutting the Gordian knot of misguided performance measurement. *Industrial Management & Data Systems, 91*(1), 24–26. doi:10.1108/02635579110138126

Vos, S. R., Clark-Ginsberg, A., Puente-Duran, S., Salas-Wright, C. P., Duque, M. C., Herrera, I. C., Maldonado-Molina, M. M., Castillo, M. N., Lee, T. K., Garcia, M. F., Fernandez, C. A., Hanson, M., Scaramutti, C., & Schwartz, S. J. (2021). The family crisis migration stress framework: A framework to understand the mental health effects of crisis migration on children and families caused by disasters. *New Directions for Child and Adolescent Development, 2021*(176), 41–59. doi:10.1002/cad.20397 PMID:33634569

Wacks, Y., & Weinstein, A. M. (2021). Excessive Smartphone Use Is Associated With Health Problems in Adolescents and Young Adults. *Frontiers in Psychiatry, 12*, 669042. doi:10.3389/fpsyt.2021.669042 PMID:34140904

Wagner, I., & Boiten, E. (2018). Privacy risk assessment: from art to science, by metrics. In *Data Privacy Management, Cryptocurrencies and Blockchain Technology: ESORICS 2018 International Workshops* Springer..

Wahyuddin, W., Marzuki, M., Khaddafi, M., Ilham, R. N., & Sinta, I. (2022). A Study of Micro, Small and Medium Enterprises (MSMEs) during Covid-19 Pandemic: An Evidence using Economic Value-Added Method. *Journal of Madani Society*, *1*(1), 1–7. doi:10.56225/jmsc.v1i1.123

Wangen, G., Shalaginov, A., & Hallstensen, C. (2016). Cyber security risk assessment of a ddos attack. In Information Security: 19th International Conference. Springer.

Wang, J., Li, M., Zhu, D., & Cao, Y. (2020). Smartphone Overuse and Visual Impairment in Children and Young Adults: Systematic Review and Meta-Analysis. *Journal of Medical Internet Research*, *22*(12), e21923. doi:10.2196/21923 PMID:33289673

Wang, P. Y., Chen, K. L., Yang, S. Y., & Lin, P. H. (2019). Relationship of sleep quality, smartphone dependence, and health-related behaviours in female junior college students. *PLoS One*, *14*(4), e0214769. doi:10.1371/journal.pone.0214769 PMID:30943270

Wang, P., Wang, X., Nie, J., Zeng, P., Liu, K., Wang, J., Guo, J., & Lei, L. (2019). Envy and problematic smartphone use: The mediating role of FOMO and the moderating role of student-student relationship. *Personality and Individual Differences*, *146*, 136–142. doi:10.1016/j.paid.2019.04.013

Wang, X., & Wang, Q. (2021). Research on the impact of green finance on the upgrading of China's regional industrial structure from the perspective of sustainable development. *Resources Policy*, *74*, 102436. doi:10.1016/j.resourpol.2021.102436

Wang, Y., & Li, M. (2021). Family identity bundles and holiday decision making. *Journal of Travel Research*, *60*(3), 486–502. doi:10.1177/0047287520930091

Wang, Y., Xiuping, S., & Zhang, Q. (2021). Can fintech improve the efficiency of commercial banks?—An analysis based on big data. *Research in International Business and Finance*, *55*, 101338. doi:10.1016/j.ribaf.2020.101338

We are Social. (2018). *Digital in 2018 in western Asia*. Slideshare. https://www.slideshare.net/wearesocial/digital-in-2018-inwes tern-asia-part-1-northwest86865983

Webster, T. E., & Paquette, J. (2023). "My other hand": The central role of smartphones and SNSs in Korean students' lives and studies. *Computers in Human Behavior*, *138*, 107447. doi:10.1016/j.chb.2022.107447

Weinstein, A., Dorani, D., Elhadif, R., Bukovza, Y., Yarmulnik, A., & Dannon, P. (2015). Internet addiction is associated with social anxiety in young adults. *Annals of Clinical Psychiatry*, *27*(1), 4–9. PMID:25696775

Whitley, E. A. (2013). Perceptions of government technology, surveillance and privacy: the UK identity cards scheme. In *New directions in surveillance and privacy* (pp. 133–156). Willan.

Wilcockson, T. D., Osborne, A. M., & Ellis, D. A. (2019). Digital detox: The effect of smartphone abstinence on mood, anxiety, and craving. *Addictive Behaviors*, *99*, 106013. doi:10.1016/j.addbeh.2019.06.002 PMID:31430621

Williams, M. (2022). Virtual reality in ophthalmology education: Simulating pupil examination. *Eye (London, England), 36*(11), 2084–2085. doi:10.103841433-022-02078-3 PMID:35538219

Williamson, B. (2021). Making markets through digital platforms: Pearson, edu-business, and the (e)valuation of higher education. *Critical Studies in Education, 62*(1), 50–66. doi:10.1080/17508487.2020.1737556

Wolniewicz, C. A., Rozgonjuk, D., & Elhai, J. D. (2020). Boredom proneness and fear of missing out mediate relations between depression and anxiety with problematic smartphone use. *Human Behavior and Emerging Technologies, 2*(1), 61–70. doi:10.1002/hbe2.159

Wolniewicz, C. A., Tiamiyu, M. F., Weeks, J. W., & Elhai, J. D. (2018). Problematic smartphone use and relations with negative affect, fear of missing out, and fear of negative and positive evaluation. *Psychiatry Research, 262*, 618–623. doi:10.1016/j.psychres.2017.09.058 PMID:28982630

Wood, N. T., & Muñoz, C. (2021). Unplugged: Digital detox enhances student learning. *Marketing Education Review, 31*(1), 14–25. doi:10.1080/10528008.2020.1836973

Woodstock, L. (2014). The news-democracy narrative and the unexpected benefits of limited news consumption: The case of news resisters. *Journalism, 15*(7), 834–849. doi:10.1177/1464884913504260

Wortham, J. (2012, August 25). Turn off the phone (and the tension). *The New York Times.*

Xia, M., Shao, H., Williams, D., Lu, S., Shu, L., & de Silva, C. W. (2021). Intelligent fault diagnosis of machinery using digital twin-assisted deep transfer learning. *Reliability Engineering and System Safety, 215.* doi:10.1016/j.ress.2021.107938

Xin, L., Lam, K., & Yu, P. L. H. (2019). Effectiveness of filter trading as an intraday trading rule. *Studies in Economics and Finance, 38*(3), 659–674. doi:10.1108/SEF-09-2018-0294

Yang, R., Zhou, C., Huang, M., Wen, H., & Liang, H.-N. (2021). Design of an Interactive Classroom with Bullet Screen Function in University Teaching. *2021 9th International Conference on Information and Education Technology (ICIET)*, (pp. 47–51). IEEE. 10.1109/ICIET51873.2021.9419627

Yao, N., & Wang, Q. (2023). Technostress from Smartphone Use and Its Impact on University Students' Sleep Quality and Academic Performance. *The Asia-Pacific Education Researcher, 32*(3), 317–326. doi:10.100740299-022-00654-5

Young, K. S. (1997, August). What makes the internet addictive: Potential explanations for pathological Internet use. In *105th annual conference of the American Psychological Association (Vol. 15*, pp. 12–30). APA.

Young, K. (1996). Psychology of computer use: XL. Addictive use of the internet: A case that breaks the stereotype. *Psychological Reports, 79*(3), 899–902. doi:10.2466/pr0.1996.79.3.899 PMID:8969098

Yu, X., Anaya, G. J., Miao, L., Lehto, X., & Wong, I. A. (2018). The impact of smartphones on the family vacation experience. *Journal of Travel Research*, *57*(5), 579–596. doi:10.1177/0047287517706263

Z. (2021, December 2). *How to Do a Digital Detox for Less Stress, More Focus.* Cleveland Clinic. https://health.clevelandclinic.org/digital-detox/

Zarandona, J., Cariñanos-Ayala, S., Cristóbal-Domínguez, E., Martín-Bezos, J., Yoldi-Mitxelena, A., & Hoyos Cillero, I. (2019). With a smartphone in one's pocket: A descriptive cross-sectional study on smartphone use, distraction and restriction policies in nursing students. *Nurse Education Today*, *82*, 67–73. doi:10.1016/j.nedt.2019.08.001 PMID:31445465

Zawacki-Richter, O. (2021). The current state and impact of COVID-19 on digital higher education in Germany. *Human Behavior and Emerging Technologies*, *3*(1), 218–226. doi:10.1002/hbe2.238 PMID:33363276

Zdravkova, K. (2023). Personalised Education for Sustainable Development. *Sustainability (Basel)*, *15*(8), 6901. doi:10.3390u15086901

Zehndorfer, E. (2018). Trading long or short on stress? In PHYSIOLOGY OF EMOTIONAL AND IRRATIONAL INVESTING: CAUSES AND SOLUTIONS (pp. 67–97). ROUTLEDGE. doi:10.4324/9781315269368-3

Zhang, H., Geng, C., & Wei, J. (2022). Coordinated development between green finance and environmental performance in China: The spatial-temporal difference and driving factors. *Journal of Cleaner Production*, *346*, 131150. https://www.pwc.in/assets/pdfs/consulting/financial-services /fintech/publications/the-changing-face-of-financial-service s-growth-of-fintech-in-india-v2.pdf and https://www. maersk.com/news/articles/2022/11/29/maersk-and-i bm-to-discontinue-tradelens. doi:10.1016/j.jclepro.2022.131150

Zhang, Y., & Ma, Z. F. (2020). Impact of the COVID-19 Pandemic on Mental Health and Quality of Life among Local Residents in Liaoning Province, China: A Cross-Sectional Study. *International Journal of Environmental Research and Public Health*, *17*(7), 2381. doi:10.3390/ijerph17072381 PMID:32244498

Zhao, Z., Shi, D., Qi, X., Shan, Y., & Liu, X. (2023). Family travel among people with autism: Challenges and support needs. *International Journal of Contemporary Hospitality Management*, *35*(11), 3743–3763. doi:10.1108/IJCHM-10-2022-1229

Zheng, G., & Peng, Z. (2021). Life Cycle Assessment (LCA) of BEV's environmental benefits for meeting the challenge of ICExit (Internal Combustion Engine Exit). *Energy Reports*, *7*, 1203–1216. doi:10.1016/j.egyr.2021.02.039

Zhou, X., Zafarani, R., & Shu, K., & Liu, H. (2019). Fake news: Fundamental theories, detection strategies, and challenges. In *Proceedings of the twelfth ACM international conference on web search and data mining.* (pp. 836–837). ACM. 10.1145/3289600.3291382

Zook, M., & Graham, M. (2018). Hacking code/space: Confounding the code of global capitalism. *Transactions of the Institute of British Geographers, 43*(3), 390–404. doi:10.1111/tran.12228

About the Contributors

Simon Grima, PhD, is the Deputy Dean of the Faculty of Economics, Management and Accountancy and Associate Professor and Head of the Insurance and Risk Management Department at the University of Malta, Msida, Malta. He coordinates the MA and MSc Insurance and Risk Management degrees and the undergraduate degree program in Insurance. He is also a Professor at the University of Latvia, Faculty of Business, Management and Economics and a visiting Professor at Università Cattolica del Sacro Cuore, Milan, Italy. He served as the President of the Malta Association of Risk Management and President of the Malta Association of Compliance Officers. In addition, he is the chairman of the Scientific Education Committee of the Public Risk Management Organization (PRIMO) and the Federation of European Risk Managers (FERMA).. His research focuses on governance, regulations, and internal controls. He has over 35 years of varied experience in financial services, academia, and public entities. He has acted as co-chair and is a member of the scientific program committees at several international conferences. He is also a chief editor, editor, and review editor of several journals and book series. He has been awarded outstanding reviewer for the Journal of Financial Regulation and Compliance Emerald Literati Awards in 2017 and 2022. Professor Grima acts as an independent director for financial services firms; sits on risk, compliance, procurement, investment, and audit committees; and carries out duties as a compliance officer, internal auditor, and risk manager.

Shilpa Chaudhary is working as an Assistant Professor at Mittal School of Business, Lovely Professional University, Punjab. She has 11 years of teaching experience. She has presented various papers in national and international conferences. Her research mainly focuses on social capital, Absorptive capacity, Innovation, innovation capabilities and various contemporaneous issues

Kiran Sood, an esteemed professor at Chitkara Business School, Chitkara University, India, holds degrees in commerce and a Ph.D. in Commerce, specializing in the Product Portfolio Performance of General Insurance Companies. With 19

years of comprehensive experience across four distinguished organizations, she assumed her role at Chitkara in 2019. Dr. Sood's research, featured in reputable international conferences and journals, delves into the intricate domains of regulations, marketing, finance in insurance, and innovation management. As an editor for prestigious journals such as IJBST and JCGIRM, she significantly contributes to academic discourse. Moreover, Dr. Sood, serving as a Research Fellow at the Women Researchers Council (WRC) at Azerbaijan State University of Economics (UNEC), further underscores her commitment to advancing scholarly knowledge in insurance and related disciplines.

Sanjeev Kumar is an accomplished expert in Food and Beverage. He currently holds the positions of Professor at the Lovely Professional University, Punjab, India. With over a decade of experience in the field, food Service Industry, his research focuses on Alcoholic beverages, Event management and Sustainable Management Practices, Metaverse and Artificial Intelligence. He has published more than 35 research papers, articles and chapters in Scopus Indexed, UGC Approved and peer reviewed Journals and books. Dr. Sanjeev Kumar participated and acted as resource person in various National and International conferences, seminars, research workshops and industry talks and his work has been widely cited.

***

Shivani Agarwal received her PhD in the area of Organizational Behavior and Human Resource Management from Indian Institute of Technology, Roorkee. She holds a MBA degree in HRM and IT from Guru Gobind Singh University, India and B.Sc. degree from Charan Singh University (formerly Meerut University), India. She is a recipient of prestigious UGC Junior Research Fellowship and has several years of experience as a faculty in management institutes. She has presented and published papers at national and international conferences. She is the corresponding author.

Pretty Bhalla has experience of more than 15 years in teaching, consultancy, conducting workshops

Niti Chatterji is currently associated with Doctoral Research Centre, Chikara Business School, Chitkara University (Punjab). Prior to this she was associated with Amity Business School, Amity University, Haryana and LMThapar School of Management, Thapar University, Patiala. She has completed her Ph.D from Thapar University, Patiala. Her research area is higher education, intellectual capital, human capital, performance and universities. Currently she is doing research in contemporary areas in HR like career development, burnout and turnover intention. She has more than a decade of rich teaching experience across subjects like Organizational Behavior, Human Resource Management, Change Management, Leadership, Strategic Human Resource Management and Global Human Resource Management. She has published papers in reputed international journals indexed in ABDC, SSCI and Scopus. Few journals of international repute where her research has been published include International Journal of Educational Development, Journal of Marketing for Higher Education and Journal of Intellectual Capital. Other academic contributions are writing book chapters and being the reviewer for reputed journals like Journal of Marketing for Higher Education and Studies in Higher Education.

Vinita Choudhary has a PhD in finance(october2020) have done M.Sc. (Mathematics), MBA (Finance/IT) with a qualitative experience of 4+ years in Education Field Currently working as an Assistant Professor in the School of Management and Commerce, K.R.MANGALAM UNIVERSITY,GURGAON HARYANA,INDIA Since 2011 she has taught many courses to under graduate (UG) and post graduate (PG) students of business administration programme at reputed management College. She is teaching various Financial and Mathematical subjects like Financial Management Business mathematics, Business Statistics, Operation Research to BBA, B.Com, MBA students. She has participated in various national and international workshops, seminars, conferences, Faculty Development Programs to keep herself updated and well equipped with latest innovations and changes in the field of Finance and management.

Amit Dutt is a Professor and Associate Dean, in Lovely Professional University. As a tenured professor at Lovely Professional University, he has made indelible contributions to the academic landscape. His research spans a wide array of topics within operations management, His work has been published in prestigious journals. His research is characterized by its innovative thinking, rigorous empirical methodologies, and real-world applicability. Their publications have not only advanced theoretical frameworks but have also provided actionable insights for organizations seeking to enhance their operational efficiency and effectiveness.

Anshul Garg is experienced Senior Lecturer with a demonstrated history of working in the higher education industry. Skilled in Research, MS-Office, Quantitative Research, SPSS, AMOS, Self Service Technologies, Service Quality, Service Clues, Hospitality Service, Risk and Crisis Management in Hospitality & Tourism and Tourist Risk Perception. Strong education background with earned Doctorate (Hospitality & Tourism) and MSc (Tourism) from Taylor's University, Malaysia, MBA (Hotel Management) from CSM Institute of Graduate Studies, Canada and a Bachelor of Hotel Management degree from the University of Mangalore, India.

Earned certifications like Certified Hospitality Educator (CHE), Certification in Hotel Industry Analytics (CHIA) from American Hotel & Lodging Educational Institute (AHLEI) and International Certification in Wine & Spirits (Intermediate Level) With over 22 years of work experience in Academia and industry while working with various leading educational institutions and hotel brands. Successfully published research work in various SCOPUS and Web of Science indexed journals, book chapters in books published by highly recognised publishers (Emerald, CABI, IGI-Global). Presented research at various international conferences as a plenary speaker and a presenter in Malaysia, India, Japan, Vietnam, and the Philippines, served as the session chair/moderator for various conferences in India, Malaysia, Japan, and the United States of America. Member of the editorial review board for multiple journals and the international advisory board member for conferences held in various countries.

Chandan Gupta is Sr. Assistant Professor, Department of Commerce, Graphic Era Deemed to be University, Dehradun, India. He holds a master degree in commerce and management and earned his Doctorate in management. He has also qualified UGC NET in Commerce. He has been teaching marketing, accounting and finance in several universities and has gained an experience of 12 years in academics and teaching. He is supervising 3 Ph.D. research scholars under him, he has published several research papers and Book chapter in the leading journals and conferences. Dr. Gupta also has industry experience and having worked in marketing and insurance sector. He is appreciated to translate academic research into practical applications.

Priya Jindal is currently working as an Associate Professor at Chitkara Business School, Chitkara University, Punjab, India and holds a master degree in commerce and economics. She earned her doctorate in management. She has contributed more than 16 years in teaching. She supervised four Ph.D. research scholars and two M.Phil candidates.There are numerous research papers to her credit in leading journals among them seven research paper has been published in Scopus Indexed Journal. Her areas of research included Banking, Finance and insurance. She has filed more than 21 patents and two copyright. She is the editor of two books under IGI publications and the book got indexed in Scopus.

Firoj Kabir is a Lecturer, Department of Tourism and Hospitality Management, Daffodil Institute of IT (DIIT). He has completed his Graduation from University of Dhaka of Bangladesh.

Neha Kamboj is working as an Assistant Professor in the School of Management and Commerce, K.R. Mangalam University, Gurugram. She has chaired 2 conferences and filed 6 Patents. She is also reviewer of various Scopus indexed journals. Since 2013 she has taught many courses to under graduate (UG) and post graduate (PG) students of business administration programme at reputed management. She is teaching various Finance subjects like Financial Management, Corporate Accounting, Accounting for Business, Financial Reporting & Analysis, Multinational Financial Management, Capital Market, Elements of Banking and Indian Financial System & Financial Markets, to BBA, B.Com, MBA students. She has participated in various national and international workshops, seminars, conferences, Faculty Development Programs to keep herself updated and well equipped with latest innovations and changes in the field of Finance and Banking.

Ms. Megha Kukreja holds a Master's degree in Business Administration with Finance as her specialization. With over 9 years of teaching experience, she has taught accounting and finance papers to undergraduate students. Currently, she is working as an Assistant Professor at Centre for Management Studies, Jain (Deemed-to-be University), Bangalore, India and pursuing her Ph.D in Management.

Mr Thanga Kumar R is currently working as Assistant Professor at Center for Management Studies, Jain (Deemed-to-be University) has completed his M.Com, PGDMM, MBA(FIN), MBA(HR), and presently pursuing his Ph.D. He is an expert in Finance and Accounting with a deep passion for teaching all facets of finance for more than 15 years. He includes practice and application of the fundamentals into Corporate and Cost Management Accounting. He has demonstrated excellence in teaching and also maintained exceptional standards in education. He has assisted in designing and developing the Finance Course Curriculum. His area of research is Inventory Analysis and Inventory control. He is a regular trader & investor for the past 10 years, he has expertise in Fundamental & Technical Analysis.

Pawan Kumar is having academic experience of 15 years and have done hus phd from Kurukshetra university, Kurukshetra.He have done 20 publications in national and international journals and had presented papers in 15 National & International seminars and confrences.

Farhana Yeasmin Lina is a dedicated Lecturer in the Department of Tourism & Hospitality Management within the Faculty of Business & Entrepreneurship at Daffodil International University. Currently pursuing an MPhil degree at the University of Dhaka in the same department, Lina holds both a BBA and an MBA from the University of Dhaka, specializing in Tourism and Hospitality Management. With a teaching tenure since 2021, Lina's expertise spans various courses in the field. Her research focal points encompass Community-based tourism development (CBT), examining the potential impacts of tourism in Bangladesh, gauging tourist perceptions and satisfaction, and exploring the role of smart technologies in advancing the tourism and hospitality industry. Committed to academic and professional growth, Lina is dedicated to contributing meaningful insights and knowledge to the field.

Dr. Priya Makhija is currently working as Associate Professor at the Center for Management Studies, Jain (Deemed-to-be University), has completed her M.Com, M.B.A, M.Phil, Ph.D., PGDHRM, and Executive Financial Data Analytics & has close to 16 years of academic work experience in the areas of Teaching, Research, Team building, Academic administration, faculty development & research enhancement. A keen researcher, her interest areas are Occupational Role Stress, Women's growth as Investors, Women's leadership in Higher Education, Enhancing the quality of higher education, and Employee Retention. She is responsible for teaching Quantitative Techniques I & II, Business Finance, Cost & Management Analysis at the undergraduate level & postgraduate levels. She is writing a book for M.Com Level at Bangalore university and has published over 28 research papers in journals and presented her research work at various national and international conferences. She is being awarded as Prof. Indira Parikh 50 Women in Education Leaders at the World Education Congress. She is being awarded as Distinguish Teacher award by MTC Education Global.

Rekha Mewafarosh is working as an Assistant Professor in Human resource management at IIFM, Bhopal. She has obtained her Ph.D. from the Institute of Commerce and Management, Jiwaji University, Gwalior. She has more than nine years of teaching and research experience and has published papers in reputed journals. She has also attended many FDP, national, and international conferences and seminars. She has also authored a book entitled Team Building and Leadership.

Mukul Bhatnagar is an accomplished Assistant Professor with over five years of experience in the field of academia and research. He can be reached at 7589063929 or 9888024343, and his email address is mukulbhatnagar@1993@gmail.com. Mukul is a highly regarded researcher with an impressive publication record. He has authored 12 indexed publications in well-known databases such as SCOPUS, Web of Science (WOS), and ABDC. Additionally, his work has been recognized by UGC-CARE, with three publications accredited by this prestigious body. Mukul's commitment to scholarly pursuits extends to four other publications, further establishing his expertise in his field. In recognition of his outstanding contributions to research, Mukul has received two Best Paper Awards, indicating his dedication to producing high-quality academic work. He has also ventured into the realm of journalism with a newspaper article to his name, showcasing his ability to communicate complex ideas to a wider audience. Mukul's innovation extends beyond publications, as he holds two patents that have been published. His commitment to continuous learning and professional development is underscored by his acquisition of two Google certifications and 13 Elsevier certifications, demonstrating his adaptability and pursuit of excellence. As a distinguished academic, Mukul has presented his research at various national and international conferences, with five national and 13 international paper presentations to his credit. Additionally, he has contributed his expertise as an author to three book chapters and has authored two books. Mukul's passion for education is evident through his participation in 16 Faculty Development Programs (FDPs), where he actively engages with the academic community to foster growth and knowledge-sharing. You can connect with Mukul Bhatnagar on LinkedIn () and explore his insights on YouTube (). His diverse and extensive background in research and education makes him a valuable asset to the academic community and beyond.

Nkholedzeni Sidney Netshakhuma is currently the Postdoctoral Research Fellowship with the University of Cape Town, Centre for African Studies effective from January 2023. His research interest includes Records Management, Archives management and Heritage management, and Political and liberation movements archives. He has published more than 60 articles and book chapters. He currently served as a Deputy Chairperson of the South Africa Higher Education Records and Archives Management Forum. He reviewed more than 60 research articles and book chapters. He obtained Ph.D. Information Science, Masters of Information Science, Post Diploma in Archival Studies, BTECH (Archival Studies at the University of South Africa (UNISA), BPHIL (Information Science at the University of Stellenbosch), BA (History and Political Studies at the University of Venda.

Itumeleng Khadambi completed Masters of Information Science at the University of South Africa. He worked as an Assistant Librarian and Head Librarian at Kutama Sinthumule Maximum Security. He curretnly worked at the South African National Parks since 2006 as knowledge Resource Officer and later Records Management Coordinator. He currently occupies the position of Senior Manager: Information and Records Management at SOuth Africna National Parks since December 2015. His research interest is on information governance, Records Management

Anju Rohilla is an Assistant Professor at the Department of Business Studies, Panipat Institute of Engineering and Technology, Panipat. She has 5 years of teaching experience. She incorporates the concept of "learning by doing" and "Experiential Learning" in her teaching-learning pedagogy. She has done a Ph.D. (Management) from Bhagat Phool Singh MahilaVishwavidyala, Khanpur Kalan, Sonipat titled

"Causes and Methodology of Banking Frauds: An Investigative Study of Indian Banking Sector". She graduated from Guru Jambeshwar University of Science and Technology in Hisar with a Master's in Management (Finance and Human Resource Management). Her focus has been on banking fraud. Her areas of interest include check fraud, cyber fraud, ATM fraud, banking system fraud, and fraud related to loans and advances. She has delivered ten research presentations at the national conference and published several research papers in national and international journals. She is skilled in using statistical tools such as SPSS, R square, AMOS, SEM, E-Views, and Jamovi.

Animesh Kumar Sharma is a Research Scholar at Mittal School of Business, Lovely Professional University, Phagwara, Punjab, India. His research interests are digital marketing, social media marketing, search engine marketing, remarketing, data analytics, artificial intelligence, machine learning, and the applications of technology in business.

Rahul Sharma is a highly accomplished professor of Marketing with over 14 years of experience in academia. He has a Ph.D. in Marketing and has published over 15 articles in high-quality journals in the field. Dr. Sharma's research interests include consumer behavior, business analytics, and digital marketing. In addition to his research, Dr. Rahul is also a highly sought-after resource person in various faculty development programs.

Rishi Prakash Shukla is a highly accomplished individual in the field of Artificial Intelligence (AI) and analytics. With 12 years of experience, he has made significant contributions to the field through his research and development work. He has 6 patents and has published 20 research papers, demonstrating his expertise and depth of knowledge in AI and analytics. Dr. Shukla has worked with institutions such as Symbiosis International University and has also contributed to projects at the Indian Institute of Management. He has a keen interest in new technologies, particularly in the area of metaverse. He is an IBM and SAS certified professional, further adding to his credentials in the field of AI and analytics. In addition to his work in AI and analytics, Dr. Shukla is also an author of 5 books on futuristic technologies. He is known for his friendly demeanor and love for travel, as well as his passion for social experimentation using technology. With his extensive experience, knowledge, and passion for technology, Dr. Rishi Prakash Shukla is a valuable asset to any organization.

Amrik Singh is working as Professor and Head of the Department in the School of Hotel Management and Tourism at Lovely Professional University, Punjab, India.

He obtained his Ph.D. degree in Hotel Management from Kurukshetra University, Kurukshetra. He started his academic career at Lovely Professional University, Punjab, India in the year 2007. He has published more than 40 research papers in UGC and peer-reviewed and Scopus/Web of Science) journals. He has published 12 patents and 01 patent has been granted in the inter-disciplinary domain. Dr. Amrik Singh participated and acted as a resource person in various national and international conferences, seminars, research workshops, and industry talks. His area of research interest is accommodation management, ergonomics, green practices, human resource management in hospitality, waste management, AR VR in hospitality, etc. He is currently guiding 8 Ph.D. scholars and 2 Ph.D. scholars have been awarded Ph.D.

Mohammad Badruddoza Talukder is an Associate Professor & Head of the Department, Department of Tourism and Hospitality Management, Daffodil Institute of Information Technology (at the National University), Dhaka, Bangladesh. He has been teaching various courses in the Department of Tourism and Hospitality at various universities in Bangladesh since 2008. His research areas include tourism management, hotel management, hospitality management, food & beverage management, and accommodation management, where he has published research papers in well-known journals in Bangladesh and abroad. Mr. Talukder is one of the executive members of the Tourism Educators Association of Bangladesh. He has led training and counseling for a wide range of hospitality organizations in Bangladesh. As an administrator, Mr. Talukder served as a debate advisor at the University, coordinator for courses and exams in the Department of Tourism and Hotel Management. He has experience as a manager in various business class hotels in Bangladesh. He is one of the certified trainers for the food and beverage service department of the SIEP project from Bangladesh. He just become an honorary facilator at Bangladesh Tourism Board's Bangabandhu international tourism and hospitality training institute.

Sanjay Taneja is currently an Associate Professor in Research at Graphic Era University, Dehradun, India. His significant thrust areas are Banking Regulations, Banking and Finance (Fin Tech, Green Finance), Risks, Insurance Management, Green Economics and Management of Innovation in Insurance. He holds a double master's degree (MBA &M.Com.) in management with a specialization in Finance and Marketing. He received his PG degrees in Management (Gold Medalist) from Chaudhary Devi University, Sirsa, India in 2012. He earned his Doctor of Philosophy (Sponsored By ICSSR) in Banking and Finance entitled "An Appraisal of financial performance of Indian Banking Sector: A Comparative study of Public, Private and Foreign banks in 2016 from Chaudhary Devi University, Sirsa, India. He received his Post Doctoral Degree from faculty of Social Sciences, Department of Banking and Insurance, Usak University, Turkey entitled on "Impact of the European Green

Deal on Carbon (CO2) Emission in Turkey" in 2023. He has published research papers in reputed SCOPUS/Web of Science/SCI/ABDC/UGC Care Journals. Prof. Taneja has more than fifty publications in total (Scopus/ABDC/Web of Science- 27)

Kanika Thapliyal is a Research Scholar at Graphic era deemed to be University. Ms Kanika Thapliyal is pursuing Ph.D. in Finance from the Department of Commerce, Graphic era deemed to be university . Her research interests cover green financing, green banking and sustainability. Ms Kanika Thapliyal has published 1 research paper in International journal of Green economics (under process), 2 book chapters which is under process.

Sonal Trivedi has more than 12 years of experience in academics. She has authored two national books, two Scopus indexed edited book and published 17 Scopus indexed papers. She has chaired 5 conferences and granted with 6 Patents. She has attended and presented papers in various international and national conference. She is also reviewer of various Scopus indexed journals.

Balraj Verma serves as an Assistant Professor at the esteemed Chitkara Business School-Doctoral Research Centre, affiliated with Chitkara University in Rajpura, Punjab. Holding a Ph.D. earned from Jaypee University of Information Technology (JUIT), Waknaghat, and a master's degree in Business Administration, he brings to the academic arena more than 16 years of rich experience in both academia and the corporate world. His qualifications extend to successfully passing the National Eligibility Test (NET) for teaching in the field of management, a testament to his dedication to education. Dr. Balraj Verma possesses a remarkable teaching portfolio, which includes courses such as Marketing Management, Strategic Management, Business Statistics, and Research Methodology. Furthermore, he is a strong advocate for rigorous research, as reflected in his extensive publication record. His research contributions encompass numerous papers published in ABDC listed and Scopus Index journals, as well as authorship and editorial work for books and book chapters, published by renowned major presses. Notably, he is not just an academic but also an active contributor to the academic community. He has played a pivotal role in organizing workshops and conferences, contributing significantly to the academic growth and development of his department and university.

Jia Yanan is a research scholar in the school of Hospitality, Tourism and Events, Faculty of Social Sciences and Leisure Management, Taylor's University, Malaysia.

Index

A

226-231, 233, 235-237, 241, 243, 245-248, 277, 288

P

performance indicators (KPIs) 17, 20, 22
productivity 3, 10, 16-18, 20, 22, 30, 35, 37-39, 41, 50-51, 72-73, 76-78, 84-85, 149, 151, 153, 200-201, 203-205, 234-235, 238, 251-252, 255-256, 264, 272, 287, 290-293
Psychological Well-Being 6, 36, 38, 40-43, 46-50, 77, 255, 266

R

records management 186-187
Records Retention Schedule 187, 194
Risk 6, 20, 27, 34, 37, 54, 56, 58-59, 61-63, 65-66, 69-70, 72, 74, 83, 112, 131, 140, 142-143, 146, 150-152, 155-156, 163, 165-167, 169, 172, 178, 228, 240-243, 245, 271, 275-278

S

smartphones 1-5, 30-31, 33, 71-73, 75-76, 84, 92, 95-96, 99, 109, 111-121, 124-125, 252-253, 255
Socioeconomic Implications 25

Startups 127, 129, 132, 138-142, 144, 228-233, 238, 240-244, 249, 270, 272
Structured Questionnaires 36, 42
Sustainable development 66-67, 70, 109, 126, 147, 166, 168, 172, 216, 218, 227, 245-246, 248, 269-270, 274-275, 277, 279, 281, 284-286

T

Technology and Phubbing 90, 125, 267
Technology Use 3, 36-37, 77, 89, 171, 207, 255, 259, 264, 266
Tourism Industry 91, 99, 106, 108-109

W

Waste Management 216, 224
Wealth Management 127, 130-131, 239
well-being 3-7, 11, 13, 16-17, 19-20, 22-23, 25, 30, 35-43, 46-50, 52, 71-78, 83-85, 87-89, 92-96, 98, 102, 104, 106, 111-112, 119, 122, 125, 153-155, 163, 171, 174, 198-199, 201, 203, 205, 244, 252, 255, 264, 266, 287-293
work-life balance 19, 82, 84, 204, 251, 287-289, 291-293

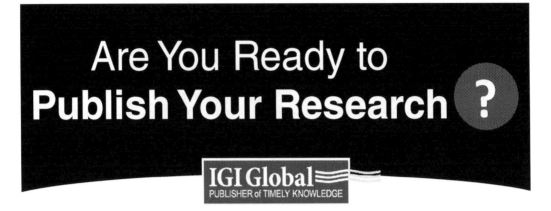